CLIMATE AND LITERATURE

In this volume, leading scholars examine the history of climate and literature. Essays analyse this history in terms of the contrasts between literary and climatological time, and between literal and literary atmosphere, before addressing textual representations of climate in seasons poetry, classical Greek literature, medieval Icelandic and Greenlandic sagas, and Shakespearean theatre. Beyond this, the effect of Enlightenment understandings of climate on literature are explored in Romantic poetry, North American settler literature, the novels of empire, Victorian and modernist fiction, science fiction, and Nordic *noir* or crime fiction. Finally, the volume addresses recent literary framings of climate in the Anthropocene, charting the rise of the climate change novel, the spectre of extinction in the contemporary cultural imagination, and the relationship between climate criticism and nuclear criticism.

Together, the essays in this volume outline the discursive dimensions of climate. Climate is as old as human civilisation, as old as all attempts to apprehend and describe patterns in the weather. Because climate is weather documented, it necessarily possesses an intimate relationship with language, and, through language, to literature. This volume challenges the idea that climate belongs to the realm of science and is separate from literature and the realm of the imagination.

ADELINE JOHNS-PUTRA is Reader in English Literature at the University of Surrey. She is the author of *The History of the Epic* (2006) and *Heroes and Housewives: Women's Epic Poetry and Domestic Ideology in the Romantic Age* (2001). Her edited books include *Process: Landscape and Text* (2010) and *Literature and Sustainability: Concept, Text, and Culture* (2017). She was Chair of the Association for the Study of Literature and Environment, UK and Ireland, from 2011 to 2015.

CAMBRIDGE CRITICAL CONCEPTS

Cambridge Critical Concepts focuses on the important ideas animating twentieth- and twenty-first-century literary studies. Each concept addressed in the series has had a profound impact on literary studies, as well as on other disciplines, and already has a substantial critical bibliography surrounding it. This series captures the dynamic critical energies transmitted across twentieth- and twenty-first-century literary landscapes: the concepts critics bring to reading, interpretation and criticism. By addressing the origins, development and application of these ideas, the books collate and clarify how these particular concepts have developed, while also featuring fresh insights and establishing new lines of enquiry.

Cambridge Critical Concepts shifts the focus from period- or genre-based literary studies of key terms to the history and development of the terms themselves. Broad and detailed contributions cumulatively identify and investigate the various historical and cultural catalysts that made these critical concepts emerge as established twenty-first-century landmarks in the discipline. The level will be suitable for advanced undergraduates, graduates and specialists, as well as for those teaching outside their own research areas, and will have cross-disciplinary relevance for subjects such as history and philosophy.

Published Titles

Law and Literature
Edited by KIERAN DOLIN University of Western Australia

Time and Literature
Edited by THOMAS M. ALLEN University of Ottawa

The Global South and Literature
Edited by RUSSELL WEST-PAVLOV University of Tübingen

Trauma and Literature
Edited by ROGER KURTZ The College at Brockport, State University of New York

Food and Literature
Edited by GITANJALI SHAHANI San Francisco State University

Animals, Animality, and Literature
Edited by BRUCE BOEHRER, MOLLY HAND and BRIAN MASSUMI Florida State University, University of Montreal

Climate and Literature
Edited by ADELINE JOHNS-PUTRA

Terrorism and Literature
Edited by PETER HERMAN San Diego State University

Forthcoming Titles

Orientalism and Literature
Edited by GEOFFREY NASH University of Sunderland

Technology and Literature
Edited by ADAM HAMMOND University of Toronto

Affect and Literature
Edited by ALEX HOUEN University of Cambridge

Decadence and Literature
Edited by JANE DESMARAIS and DAVID WEIR Goldsmith College and The Cooper Union for the Advancement of Science and Art

CLIMATE AND LITERATURE

EDITED BY

ADELINE JOHNS-PUTRA

University of Surrey

CAMBRIDGE
UNIVERSITY PRESS

CAMBRIDGE
UNIVERSITY PRESS

University Printing House, Cambridge CB2 8BSS, United Kingdom

One Liberty Plaza, 20th Floor, New York, NY 10006, USA

477 Williamstown Road, Port Melbourne, VIC 3207, Australia

314–321, 3rd Floor, Plot 3, Splendor Forum, Jasola District Centre,
New Delhi – 110025, India

79 Anson Road, #06–04/06, Singapore 079906

Cambridge University Press is part of the University of Cambridge.

It furthers the University's mission by disseminating knowledge in the pursuit of
education, learning, and research at the highest international levels of excellence.

www.cambridge.org
Information on this title: www.cambridge.org/9781108422529
DOI: 10.1017/9781108505321

First published 2019

Printed and bound in Great Britain by Clays Ltd, Elcograf S.p.A.

A catalogue record for this publication is available from the British Library.

ISBN 978-1-108-42252-9 Hardback

Contents

Illustrations

Contributors

CLAIRE COLEBROOK is Edwin Erle Sparks Professor of English, Philosophy and Women's and Gender Studies at Penn State University. She has written books and articles on contemporary European philosophy, literary history, gender studies, queer theory, visual culture, and feminist philosophy. Her most recent book is *Twilight of the Anthropocene Idols*, co-authored with Tom Cohen and J. Hillis Miller (2016).

DANIEL CORDLE is Associate Professor of English and American Literature at Nottingham Trent University. His publications include *Late Cold War Literature and Culture: the Nuclear 1980s* (2017) and *States of Suspense: the Nuclear Age, Postmodernism and United States Fiction and Prose* (2008). He also works more broadly on the relations between literature and science, with publications such as *Postmodern Postures: Literature, Science and the Two Cultures Debate* (1999).

LOWELL DUCKERT is Associate Professor of English at the University of Delaware, where he specialises in early modern literature, environmental criticism, and the new materialisms. He has published on various topics such as glaciers, polar bears, the colour maroon, rain, fleece, mining, and lagoons. He is author of *For All Waters: Finding Ourselves in Early Modern Wetscapes* (2017), co-editor (with Jeffrey Jerome Cohen) of *Elemental Ecocriticism: Thinking with Earth, Air, Water, and Fire* (2015) and *Veer Ecology: a Companion for Environmental Thinking* (2017), and co-editor (with Craig Dionne) of 'Shakespeare in the Anthropocene' (*Early Modern Culture* 13, 2018). He is currently researching two related book projects that aim to make critical interventions in contemporary cryo-politics: the first investigates the strange vitality of ice witnessed by sixteenth- and seventeenth-century writers, while the second follows the object of the snowball.

JAN GOLINSKI is Professor of History and Humanities at the University of New Hampshire. His books include *Science as Public Culture: Chemistry and Enlightenment in Britain, 1760–1820* (Cambridge University Press, 1992), *Making Natural Knowledge: Constructivism and the History of Science* (2005), *British Weather and the Climate of Enlightenment* (2007), and *The Experimental Self: Humphry Davy and the Making of a Man of Science* (2016). He has held distinguished fellowships at the Huntington Library and the Chemical Heritage Foundation, and currently serves as Vice-President of the History of Science Society. He is now investigating ideas about climate change in Europe and North America in the late eighteenth and early nineteenth centuries.

AXEL GOODBODY is Professor Emeritus of German and European Culture at the University of Bath, and Visiting Research Fellow at Bath Spa University's Centre for Environmental Humanities. His principal research interests are literary representations of nature and environment, and ecocritical theory. Current projects include *Climate Change Scepticism: a Transnational Ecocritical Analysis* (with Greg Garrard, George Handley, and Stephanie Posthumus), co-editing *Cli-Fi: a Companion* (with Adeline Johns-Putra), and co-editing a special number of *Resilience* on literary and historical stories of energy (with Bradon Smith).

DAVID HIGGINS is Associate Professor in English Literature at the University of Leeds. He is author of *Romantic Genius and the Literary Magazine* (2005), *Romantic Englishness* (2014), and *British Romanticism, Climate Change, and the Anthropocene* (2017). He has also published several pedagogical works, as well as the co-edited monograph, *Jean-Jacques Rousseau and British Romanticism* (with Russell Goulbourne, 2017). He is currently working on two book projects: a co-written history of British nature writing and an account of the relationship between environmentalism and philosophical pessimism.

JESSICA HOWELL is Associate Professor in the Department of English at Texas A&M University. She currently serves as Associate Director of the Glasscock Center for Humanities Research, where she also convenes the Health Humanities Laboratory. She was previously Wellcome Postdoctoral Research Fellow in the Centre for Humanities and Health, King's College London. She is author of *Exploring Victorian Travel Literature: Disease, Race and Climate* (2014) and *Malaria and Victorian Fictions of Empire* (Cambridge University Press, 2018).

ADELINE JOHNS-PUTRA is Reader in English Literature at the University of Surrey. She was Chair of the Association for the Study of Literature and Environment (UK and Ireland) from 2011 to 2015. Her books include *The History of the Epic* (2005), *Literature and Sustainability: Concept, Text and Culture*, edited with John Parham and Louise Squire (2017), and, most recently, *Climate Change and the Contemporary Novel* (Cambridge University Press, 2019). Her essays on climate change and literature have appeared in *English Studies, Modern Fiction Studies, ISLE: Interdisciplinary Studies in Literature and Environment*, and *Studies in the Novel*. She is currently editing *Cli-Fi: a Companion* (2019) with Axel Goodbody.

P. S. (PAUL) LANGESLAG studied English, Old Norse, and Medieval Studies in Groningen, Reykjavik, and Toronto. His first monograph is entitled *Seasons in the Literatures of the Medieval North* (2015), which interprets seasonal motifs in early English and Scandinavian literature. He is employed at Göttingen University as a lecturer and researcher in the fields of medieval English studies and digital humanities, and he writes on subjects ranging from Anglo-Saxon homiletics to Old Norse verbs.

DARYN LEHOUX is Professor of Philosophy and Classics at Queen's University, Kingston, Ontario. He is the author of *Creatures Born of Mud and Slime* (2017), *What Did the Romans Know?* (2012), and *Astronomy, Weather, and Calendars in the Ancient World* (Cambridge University Press, 2007). He is also the co-editor of *Lucretius: Poetry, Philosophy, Science* (with A. D. Morrison and Alison Sharrock, 2013).

ROBERT MARKLEY is W. D. and Sara E. Trowbridge Professor of English at the University of Illinois and editor of *The Eighteenth Century: Theory and Interpretation*. Author of more than eighty articles in eighteenth-century studies, science studies, and digital media, his books include *Two-Edg'd Weapons: Style and Ideology in the Comedies of Etherege, Wycherley, and Congreve* (1988), *Fallen Languages: Crises of Representation in Newtonian England* (1993), *Dying Planet: Mars in Science and the Imagination* (2005), *The Far East and the English Imagination, 1600–1730* (Cambridge University Press, 2006), *Writing China: Essays on the Amherst Embassy (1816) and Sino-British Cultural Relations* (edited with Peter Kitson, 2016), and a book in the Modern Masters of Science Fiction series, *Kim Stanley Robinson* (2019). His current book project examines the emergence of understandings of climatology between 1500 and 1800.

ANDREW NESTINGEN is Professor and Chair of the Department of Scandinavian Studies at the University of Washington in Seattle. His most recent books are *The Cinema of Aki Kaurismäki: Contrarian Stories* (2013) and *Scandinavian Crime Fiction* (co-edited with Paula Arvas, 2011), and other books include *Crime and Fantasy in Scandinavia: Fiction, Film, and Social Change* (2008), and *Transnational Cinema in a Global North: Nordic Cinema in Transition* (co-edited with Trevor Elkington, 2005). He has written articles on Aki Kaurismäki, Stieg Larsson, Leena Lehtolainen, Henning Mankell, Finnish cinema, Nordic cinema, and film authorship, among other topics. He is associate editor of the *Journal of Scandinavian Cinema* and review editor of *Scandinavian Studies*.

CHRIS PAK is a lecturer in Contemporary Writing and Digital Culture at Swansea University. He is the author of *Terraforming: Ecopolitical Transformations and Environmentalism in Science Fiction* (2016), and his research interests in science fiction combine insights from the environmental humanities, human–animal studies, and the digital humanities. He has previously worked on the Leverhulme-funded corpus linguistics project, '"People", "Products", "Pests" and "Pets": the Discursive Representation of Animals' (Lancaster University, 2013–16) and the Volkswagen Foundation-funded project, 'Modelling Between Digital and Humanities: Thinking in Practice' (King's Digital Lab, King's College London, 2017–18). He is currently sub-editor of the *Medical Humanities* blog (2016–ongoing).

JUSTINE PIZZO is Lecturer in English at the University of Southampton, where she teaches British literature from 1837 to 1939. Her work on climate and Victorian fiction has previously appeared in *PMLA* and *Victorian Literature and Culture*. She is currently working on a book that examines how aerial climates shape female characterisation in novels by Charlotte Brontë, Charles Dickens, Thomas Hardy, and other late nineteenth- and early twentieth-century writers.

TESS SOMERVELL is a British Academy Postdoctoral Fellow at the University of Leeds, working on a project titled 'Georgic Climates: Writing the Weather in Eighteenth-Century Poetry'. Previously, she was Research Assistant on the project 'British Romantic Writing and Environmental Catastrophe', also at Leeds, funded by the Arts and

Humanities Research Council. Her research interests include science and literature, ecocriticism, georgic and pastoral, and reception and influence.

JESSE OAK TAYLOR is Associate Professor of English at the University of Washington in Seattle. His publications include *Anthropocene Reading: Literary History in Geologic Times* (co-edited with Tobias Menely, 2017), *The Sky of Our Manufacture: the London Fog in British Fiction from Dickens to Woolf* (2016), which won the Association for the Study of Literature and Environment book award in ecocriticism and the Rudikoff Prize for a first book in Victorian Studies from the Northeast Victorian Studies Association, as well as *Empowerment on an Unstable Planet: From Seeds of Human Energy to a Scale of Global Change* (co-authored with Daniel C. Taylor and Carl E. Taylor, 2011).

MORGAN VANEK is Assistant Professor in the Department of English at the University of Calgary. She is currently at work at a monograph titled *The Politics of the Weather, 1700–1775*, and her publications include essays on scepticism, institutional secrecy, and the Hudson's Bay Company (in the *Journal for Eighteenth-Century Studies*); coldness of character and political sensibility in Frances Brooke's epistolary novels (in *Eighteenth-Century Fiction*); and scientific travel writing and the 'changeable' traveller (in *Literature Compass*). Her wider research and teaching interests include Restoration and eighteenth-century British literature, early Canadian literature, environmental literature, travel writing, and the history and philosophy of science.

Acknowledgements

The initial idea for this volume came from Ray Ryan at Cambridge University Press. I am grateful to Ray for seeing the importance of investigating climate as a concept in literary history and for being on hand for insightful advice throughout. I am also grateful to Edgar Mendez for his assistance through the project.

My deep thanks go to the contributors to this volume, not just for their chapters but for prompt and good-natured responses to all my queries, big and small. I would also like to acknowledge the support of Richard Klein, whose interest in comparing climate criticism with nuclear criticism – the field which he helped to inaugurate – informed the final chapter of this book.

My contributions to this volume were much improved by conversations with Hannes Bergthaller and Dana Phillips, and by the opportunity to present my ideas at a workshop entitled 'Climates of the Anthropocene' at National Chung-Hsing University in Taichung, Taiwan, organised by Hannes with the generous support of Eva Horn, and at a research seminar in the School of English at the University of Hong Kong. Finally, I thank Matthew Evans, whose support, in every way, made this volume possible.

ADELINE JOHNS-PUTRA

Introduction

Adeline Johns-Putra

Climate is not just weather but weather observed, measured, and recorded – a composite of meteorological events as they are correlated, compared, and contrasted over time and space. Climate is, as Paul Edwards puts it, 'the history of weather – the average state of the atmosphere over periods of years, decades, centuries, and more'.[1] Although such codification aims at accuracy and transparency – the production of data that throws up historical patterns that in turn aid forecasting – it is also, in some sense, an act of mediation. The discernment of structures, cycles, and paradigms emphasises order as normal and highlights disorder as remarkable. Pattern and predictability are what render this information useful. In the words of the climatologist F. Kenneth Hare, 'Climate is the ordinary man's expectation of weather . . . Climate is made up of the succession of weather events he has learned to expect, and to resign himself to.'[2]

Weather and/as Climate

If the patterns of climate emerge through records over time, statistically as well as narratively, then, one could say, climate emerges discursively – indeed, as Mike Hulme puts it, '*climate* is an idea invented in the human mind'.[3] The discourse of climate is not simply the kind of studiously 'objective' observation and measurement one tends to associate with climatological data; it encompasses the history, possibly as old as human civilisation, of attempts to apprehend and describe patterns in the weather. These attempts include, then, both ostensibly neutral observation and the embellished, affectively charged descriptions one might call literature – along with all the forms of description in between. Climate, as weather

---

[1] Paul N. Edwards, *A Vast Machine: Computer Models, Climate Data, and the Politics of Global Warming* (Cambridge, MA: MIT Press, 2010), p. xiv.
[2] F. Kenneth Hare, 'The Concept of Climate', *Geography*, 51 (1966), 99–100.
[3] Mike Hulme, *Weathered: Cultures of Climate* (London: Sage, 2017), p. 16, original emphasis.

documented, necessarily possesses an intimate relationship with language, and through language, to literature.

Early historical records of human activity, which in ancient societies would depend on or respond to weather, almost always involve some climatic observation. The Hindu Vedas, among the earliest sacred texts still in existence, contain discussions of weather cycles, some of which provided the basis for the *Rtusamhāra* ('The Garland of the Seasons') (fifth century CE), a chronicle of love through the seasons, written by the Sanskrit poet Kalidasa.[4] Ancient Chinese court records include details of, among other things, extreme meteorological events; they thus constitute a unique data bank for the emerging field of Chinese climate history.[5] One of the oldest chronological histories, *Chunqiu* ('The Spring and Autumn Annals'), covers a period from 722 to 481 BCE and comprises brief, month-by-month observations of such things as natural climatic disasters and celestial phenomena. The famous *Shi Ji* ('Records of the Grand Historian') (*c.* 94 BCE) by Sima Qian offers a comprehensive set of narratives of states and leaders, whose contexts include references to seasons and their weather.[6] Meanwhile, ancient Greek texts provide both phenological information and philosophical reflections on climate. In the first category, one might include the *parapegmata* or almanacs, with their records of seasonal changes in the weather, the night skies, day lengths, and so on, for primarily functional purposes such as agriculture and fishing. There also exist descriptions of climate, and the need for farmers to work in sympathy with it, in Hesiod's *Works and Days* (*c.* 700 BCE). In the second category, one encounters the Hippocratic *Airs, Waters, Places* of about the fifth century BCE, and Aristotle's *Meteorology* (or *Meteorologica*) written in the second century BCE, with their reflections on the significance of meteorological phenomena and, in both cases, the possible link between air, health, and national character.[7] In ancient Greco-Roman culture, in other words, there are attempts to record, understand, and predict weather

---

[4] Murali Sivaramakrishnan, 'Ecopoetics and the Literature of Ancient India', in John Parham and Louise Westling (eds.), *A Global History of Literature and Environment* (Cambridge University Press, 2017), pp. 68–9; Kalidasa, 'Rtusamhāram (The Gathering of the Seasons)', in *The Loom of Time*, trans. Chandra Rajan (New Delhi: Penguin, 1999), pp. 103–35.

[5] Ka-wai Fan, 'Climate Change and Chinese History: a Review of Trends, Topics, and Methods', *WIREs Climate Change*, 6 (2015), 225; J. Q. Fang, 'Establishment of a Data Bank from Records of Climatic Disasters and Anomalies in Ancient Chinese Documents', *International Journal of Climatology*, 12 (2006), 499–519; Zhu Kezhen, 'A Preliminary Study on the Climatic Fluctuation during the Last 5000 Years in China', *Scientia Sinica*, 16 (1973), 226–56.

[6] Zhu, 'A Preliminary Study'.

[7] David Bowker, 'Meteorology and the Ancient Greeks', *Weather*, 66.9 (2011), 249–51; James Rodger Fleming, *Historical Perspectives on Climate Change* (Oxford University Press, 1998), 11–12.

patterns. Alongside this, there occur attempts to discuss climatic conditions in different parts of the world: *klima*, after all, means inclination, and refers to the idea that climate depended on the angle of the sun and thus on latitude, on the basis of which Ptolemy, in the second century CE, posited the existence of fifteen climatic zones at different latitudinal bands around the globe.[8]

In even the earliest iterations, then, what one might think of as literature (that is, imaginative writing aimed at entertaining as well as informing) is the expression of a world in which weather, more than just the mere instantiation of divine or natural caprice, is climate inasmuch as it accedes to or diverges from stable, predictable patterns. It would be too simple, then, to suggest of pre- and early modern writing that climate is the proper subject of objective record and weather the domain of literature. From ancient literature onwards, we find recorded the effects of weather in both extraordinary and everyday terms. Certainly, from classical to Renaissance literature, dramatic weather events abound in literature, whether Homer's storms or Shakespeare's, but predictability and familiarity, too, have their affective dimensions; we see this in seasons poetry, through the ages and in various cultural traditions, where seasonal characteristics are linked to stock feelings, expressions, and subjects. In the literary – and, indeed, human – imagination, day-to-day climatic stability and unusual weather events are inextricably linked as two sides of the conceptualisation of climate as fundamentally stable (or at least as stable *in loco*, with geographical variations).

In the history of climate, the Enlightenment and what has been called its 'quantifying spirit' bring major developments. These are nothing less than the advent of climatological science, or what Theodore Feldman has described as the proper development of meteorology's two branches of 'weather observation' and 'climatology' (that is, the 'analysis of observations for weather patterns').[9] This formalisation of weather as climate through empirical, longitudinal recording and analysis aligns more clearly dramatic, one-off weather events with literary discourse, on the one hand, and observations of climate stability with scientific discourse, on the other.

Even so, the distinction between an affective response to climate and an objective description of it in early Enlightenment meteorology is not hard and fast. Eighteenth-century meteorology reiterates the classical

---

[8] Edwards, *A Vast Machine*, p. 29.
[9] Theodore Feldman, 'Late Enlightenment Meteorology', in Tore Frängsmyr, J. L. Heilbron, and Robin E. Rider (eds.), *The Quantifying Spirit in the Eighteenth Century* (Berkeley: University of California Press, 1990), pp. 145–6.

interest in the psychological and cultural significance of climate.
As Vladimir Janković describes it, meteorological study at this point
'was based on a conjunction of ideas drawn from several cognitive
provenances: Greco-Roman natural philosophy, Elizabethan and
Tudor paraphrase of that knowledge, and an interrelated set of beliefs
derived from astrology, magic, and weather folklore'.[10] That is, it oper-
ated within a framework of classical theories, including Aristotelian and
Hippocratic determinist notions about 'quality of air', 'health and
national character', supported by folk knowledge.[11] As James Fleming
writes, 'Enlightenment thinkers apprehended climate and its changes
primarily in a literary way. They compared the ancient writings to recent
weather conditions, linked the rise and fall of creative historical eras to
changes in climate, and promoted a brand of climatic determinism based
on geographic location and the quality of air.'[12] This is not to say,
however, that empirical observation did not occur. Janković elaborates
on how '*qualitative* and *descriptive*' observation dominated the popular
practice of weather diary-keeping in eighteenth-century England, itself
born of the seventeenth-century practice of maintaining regional geographical records, or chorography.[13] And yet, such record-keeping should
not be thought of as 'scientific' in the way of technical or statistical
discourse. By and large, it remained concerned with extraordinary, rather
than ordinary, weather and astronomical events (in the tradition of
Aristotle's *Meteorologica*, with its concern with meteors and other 'things
on high'), and was couched in 'ordinary rather than "technical"
language'.[14] Weather diary entries resembled 'personalized *narratives* of
extraordinary, striking, or rare phenomena'.[15] Meteorological philosophy
was primarily concerned with the influence of climate on individuals and
society, while meteorological observation focused on personal descriptions of dramatic climatic incidents. Both revolved around individual
experiences of weather.

The Climate of Enlightenment

A more profound shift to continuous and longitudinal weather observation
occurred towards the end of the eighteenth century. Feldman describes this
as a drastic turn in the 1770s towards '[o]rganized meteorology' in scientific

---

[10] Vladimir Janković, *Reading the Skies: a Cultural History of English Weather, 1650–1820* (Manchester University Press, 2000), p. 15.
[11] Fleming, *Historical Perspectives*, p. 11.   [12] Ibid., p. 12.
[13] Janković, *Reading the Skies*, pp. 34, 7–8.   [14] Ibid., p. 34.   [15] Ibid.

societies and networks across Europe.[16] As Janković explains, while the idea of a sudden 'transformation' is deceptively simple, one can nonetheless point to the gradual giving way of one empirical approach – the 'qualitative reportage of extraordinary weather events' – to another – 'the quantitative measurement of a "weather-continuum"'.[17] The meteoric tradition traceable to Aristotle, with its preoccupation with extraordinary weather, was replaced by an underlying impulse towards codifying orderly climatic patterns, emerging from a combination of natural theology with its understanding of 'an orderly system of laws' and the 'tradition of weather prognostication' with its desire for 'forecasting'.[18] Moreover, local, chorographical observation no longer existed in isolation, but took its place on 'a spatio-temporal grid – its nodes corresponding to the measurements made at remote observational posts'.[19] At first, comparative discussions of regional climates emphasised the Hippocratic notion that climates – particularly local atmosphere – determined cultural characteristics.[20] The immediate impetus behind such ideas was transatlantic colonisation, which, depending on political perspective, either confirmed notions about the relatively stable and thus civilising effects of European climates with regard to North America,[21] or supported American patriotic efforts to incorporate America's 'warmer, less variable, and healthier climate' into an 'integral component of a Republican ideal'.[22] As the nineteenth century progressed, however, the great 'climate debate' created the demand, at the instigation of Benjamin Franklin and Thomas Jefferson, among others, for climate data, and thence the expansion of climate observation networks in the USA, Europe, and Russia.[23] At the same time, the concept of isotherms, first developed by Alexander von Humboldt in 1827, would allow data about local climatic phenomena to be scaled up into larger – even global – images of climatic zones; in 1852, Humboldt's colleague Heinrich Wilhelm Dove published the first isothermal map of the entire planet.[24]

The shift from qualitative to quantitative, from local to comparative, was undergirded by an interest in climate as system: 'Scrutiny of local weather . . . mattered only to the extent to which atmospheric "unity" manifested itself in a locale . . . The culture of "country airs" lost out to the physics of planetary circulation.'[25] Meteorology moved away from an

---

[16] Feldman, 'Late Enlightenment Meteorology', p. 154.   [17] Janković, *Reading the Skies*, p. 36.
[18] Ibid., p. 130.   [19] Ibid., p. 35.   [20] Feldman, 'Late Enlightenment Meteorology', pp. 155–6.
[21] Jan Golinski, *British Weather and the Climate of Enlightenment* (University of Chicago Press, 2007), pp. 170–202.
[22] Fleming, *Historical Perspectives*, p. 32.   [23] Ibid., pp. 33–44.
[24] Edwards, *A Vast Machine*, p. 31.   [25] Janković, *Reading the Skies*, p. 11.

interest in the 'superficial correlations' between 'weather patterns, agriculture, and disease' towards an emphasis on 'interior forces that govern their
relations'.[26] The professionalisation of climate science and the understanding of climate as a physical system increased apace in the twentieth century.
The 'spatio-temporal grid' became, in Edwards's words, '*a climate knowledge infrastructure*', as 'separate systems' in different countries 'linked their
data reporting through loosely coordinated international networks'.
Moreover, as the complexity of the climate system became obvious, climatology came to be about climate modelling as opposed to the mere collection of climate data. This led to the 'long and painful process of
infrastructural inversion' in the 1970s, as climate scientists deconstructed
the world's disparate data collection methods in order to standardise them
and to achieve global comparability.[27]

Alongside this, in literature through the course of the nineteenth century and into the twentieth, several trends might be discerned. Imaginative
responses to striking climate phenomena are unavoidable in the context of
the 'Year without a Summer', which produced a concern with catastrophic
and apocalyptic imagery in European Romanticism. Through the century,
sophisticated evocations of climate determinism also occurred. One might
think of Emile Zola's meticulous – indeed, almost chorographic – detailing
of local milieu and its effect on individual and familial character in his
Rougon-Macquart novels or of Joseph Conrad's description of psychological declension in tropical climes in *Heart of Darkness*.[28] Such a concern
with place and climate looks ahead to twentieth-century genres as diverse
as Scandinavian crime fiction and Latin American fiction, particularly
magical realism.[29] At the same time, a very different preoccupation with
climate emerged at the end of the nineteenth century. In its overt engagement with science, science fiction appropriated science's growing knowledge of the workings of global climatological and ecological systems as
materials for both setting and plot, discernible, for example, in the Arctic
geo-engineering plan to adjust the tilt in the Earth's axis and thus its
climate in Jules Verne's *The Purchase of the North Pole* (*Sans dessus dessous*)

[26] Feldman, 'Late Eighteenth-Century Meteorology', p. 175.   [27] Edwards, *A Vast Machine*, p. xvi.
[28] See, for example, Jessica Tanner, 'The Climate of Naturalism: Zola's Atmospheres', *L'Esprit
Créateur*, 57 (2017), 20–33; Jessica Howell, *Exploring Victorian Travel Literature: Disease, Race and
Climate* (Edinburgh University Press, 2014), pp. 137–63.
[29] See, for example, George R. McMurray, 'The Role of Climate in Twentieth-Century Spanish
American Fiction', in Janet Pérez and Wendell Aycock (eds.), *Climate and Literature: Reflections of
Environment* (Lubbock: Texas Tech University Press, 1995), pp. 55–65; Gary S. Elbow, 'Creating an
Atmosphere: Depiction of Climate in the Works of Gabriel García Márquez', in Pérez and Aycock,
Climate and Literature, pp. 73–81.

of 1889, and in the global cooling on Mars that brings about the invasion of Earth in H. G. Wells's *The War of the Worlds* (1897).[30]

Climate science – particularly, climate modelling – in the twentieth century brings on the most revolutionary information of all. An understanding of the workings of planetary climate developed in tandem with an awareness of the growing problem of global warming. As Edwards explains, the 'climate knowledge infrastructure' culminated in the Intergovernmental Panel on Climate Change (IPCC) and a concentration of scientific investigations into the phenomenon of anthropogenic climate change towards the end of the century.[31] With this came the attendant possibility in the twenty-first century that its effects are significant enough to warrant the identification of a new geological epoch, the Anthropocene. In the age of climate change, the physical impacts of changes in global climate are recognisable not merely as a question of meteorological and ecological concern, but also – because these are dire in terms of loss and damage to human and non-human species – as having profound political and social effects. With these effects have come the need for a collective emotional, ethical, and psychological response, including literary engagements with climate and climate science. This has brought back into focus the affective dimensions of climate, highlighting just how tenuous the line is between the scientific and imaginative discourses of climate.

Climate, Time, and Space

To discuss the history of climate and literature, up to and including the Anthropocene, simply as an Enlightenment splitting off of scientific quantification from matters of affect, is to miss some of that history's finer points. To be sure, it is now a critical commonplace that scientific questions of climate occur at a very different spatio-temporal scale from the individual concerns of the literary. Climate criticism now abounds with observations on the scalar 'derangement' brought on by the unprecedented spatial and temporal dimensions of the climatic phenomena described by climatology.[32] Yet, it is much less often pointed out that the temporal

---

[30] Jules Verne, *The Purchase of the North Pole* (London: Sampson Low, 1890); H. G. Wells, *The War of the Worlds*, ed. David Y. Hughes and Harry M. Geduld (Bloomington: Indiana University Press, 1993).

[31] Edwards, *A Vast Machine*, pp. xvi–ii.

[32] See, for example, Timothy Clark, 'Derangements of Scale', in Tom Cohen and Henry Sussman (eds.), *Telemorphosis: Essays in Critical Climate Change*, vol. 1 (Ann Arbor: Open Humanities Press,

challenge of understanding climate – and climate change – is of a different order from any of the spatially oriented difficulties of comprehension; indeed, the discursive history of climate and time is distinct from that of climate and space.

Of course, we experience weather, corporeally and psychologically, in a way that is both immediate and individual, that is, in terms of time and space together. Also, climate is weather quantified over regular intervals and between different locales, that is, it is understood and expressed within the parameters of time and space together. Indeed, that very quantification of climate was enabled by pre-modern advances in the conceptualisation of time and space – namely, the ability to measure climate was made possible by the invention of what Nicholas Carr calls the 'intellectual technologies' of the clock and the map, respectively.[33] 'What the map did for space', notes Carr, 'the mechanical clock did for time'; both map and clock 'translate[d] a natural phenomenon into an artificial and intellectual conception of that phenomenon'.[34] Advances in cartographic and horological thought together enabled climate science, both 'global space' and 'universal time' eventually becoming crucial to modern climatology.[35]

As Enlightenment climate science progresses, literature evolves to record the spatial, even global, dimensions of climate, but struggles to apprehend its temporal dimensions. In the nineteenth century, as we have seen, both individual, corporeal experiences of weather and local observations of regional climates are joined by a notion of climate as a planetary phenomenon. In tandem with this, the formal characteristics of narrative fiction develop in that century into high realism – that is, they are refined into a particular method that invokes characters' psychological experiences while, at the same time, putting these into play with engaging settings and plots.[36] This dynamic between the two levels of engagement of affect and

2012), pp. 148–66; Amitav Ghosh, *The Great Derangement: Climate Change and the Unthinkable* (University of Chicago Press, 2016).

[33] Nicholas Carr, *The Shallows: How the Internet Is Changing the Way We Read, Think and Remember* (London: Atlantic, 2010), p. 44.

[34] Ibid., p. 41.

[35] Edwards, *A Vast Machine*, pp. 27–47. Even the ways in which climate translates itself into experience is in both dimensions at once. Mark Maslin opens his introduction to climate by invoking that mundane but necessary response to climate – what to wear; for Maslin, one's outfits will 'reflect the climate in which you live and how it changes throughout the year'; *Climate: a Very Short Introduction* (Oxford University Press, 2013), p. 1. Maslin's description recalls Hare's definition of climate as weather rendered predictable – specifically, it echoes Hare's assertion that, for the average person, a knowledge of climate means that 'there is a limit to the indignities that the weather can put upon him, and he can predict what clothes he will need for each month of the year'; Hare, 'The Concept of Climate', 99–100.

[36] Fredric Jameson, *The Antinomies of Realism* (London: Verso, 2015), p. 16.

story – what Fredric Jameson calls '*roman*' and '*récit*' – allows the novel to develop, in Jesse Oak Taylor's words, into a 'climate model'. For Taylor, the novel is capable of making the reader feel or perceive the effects of climate on both individual and geographical spaces: 'Reading novels ... involves the kind of suspended and associative thinking necessary for modelling the experience of climate as an aggregation of atmospheric effects.'[37] Taylor makes a case, furthermore, for the realist novel's capacity to enlarge the reader's experience to encompass the global, since any realist novel's 'storyworld' must potentially and hypothetically include the entire world, in order to retain its status as realism.[38] Certainly, it is on the same basis that the world-building of science fiction novels, which operate on realism's principles of internal coherence, are able to invoke planetary climatic systems. The conventions of literature, it seems, develop to capture the enlarged spaces of climate – from the individual to the regional to the global.

The formal study of climate science introduces the global to individual and local scales of experience, which literature – most obviously, the novel – accommodates. But literary convention is rather more stretched by climatic conceptions of time. Alongside individual and local timescales (that is, human lifetimes and historical epochs), climate science and, particularly, this century's concerns about climate change bring into purview not just individual and local but geological durations of time. It is, then, not the climatological expansion of the concept of time as universal time that is at stake here – universal time is a function of a global sensibility and thus a matter of rendering time as spatially simultaneous. What matters as climate science turns its gaze to climate systems and climate change is not the apprehension of time as universal, as a function of the apprehension of space as global, but the ability to expand time frames and durations. Concerns about the long-term effects of human activity on climate – and, in turn, the effects on human life of the climate thus changed – have reconfigured ideas of *longue durée* beyond that of historical grand narrative or individualised struggle, into supra-human views of the ecology and evolution of species, the human species amongst them.[39] To be sure, narrative literary form is not incapable of imagining time above and beyond the human. In Frank Kermode's estimation, narrative is predicated on an analogy between the prosaic sense of time as the day

---

[37] Jesse Oak Taylor, *The Sky of Our Manufacture: the London Fog in British Fiction from Dickens to Woolf* (Charlottesville: University of Virginia Press, 2016), p. 14.

[38] See Chapter 2 by Taylor in this volume.

[39] Dipesh Chakrabarty, 'The Climate of History: Four Theses', *Critical Inquiry*, 35.2 (2009), 197–222.

to day (or *chronos*) and the cosmological sense of it as human destiny (*kairos*).[40] Yet, kairotic time goes hand in hand with theological conceptions of the human, and hence its manifest destiny is human apocalypse, revelation, and renewal. The geological or evolutionary time of climate change, in contrast, demands a reckoning with non-human destiny, a reckoning that the still ubiquitous forms of literature, such as fiction and poetry, are only now beginning to perform.

Origins, Evolution, Application

This volume proceeds in three sections. The first part, 'Origins', explores some of the fundamental questions arising out of the discursive condition of the concept of climate. The first two chapters grapple with questions of time and space, respectively. In Chapter 1, Robert Markley considers the capacity of literature, particularly fiction, to depict not just experiential time but historical time, and, indeed, not just historical time but – with the advent of awareness of weather as climate – its incarnation as climatological time. In Chapter 2, Jesse Oak Taylor discusses fiction's intimate relationship with climate in spatial terms; Taylor shows how the novel's emotionally charged, literary atmosphere functions much like a meteorologically determined, literal atmosphere. It affects the psychologies and physiologies of individuals, and thus replays for the reader the experience of not just individual, experiential weather but geographical, regional climate. The chapters that follow explore some pre- and early modern literary texts that are both responses and contributions to the conceptualisation of climate. In Chapter 4 Daryl Lehoux discusses climatic concepts in classical Greek culture and literature, from Ptolemaic geographical divisions of the world into climatic bands of latitude (or *klimata*) to medical and anthropological considerations – such as those of Hippocrates – of climate determinism. Classical concepts of latitudinal *klimata* – and thus what zones might be habitable – extended well into the Middle Ages. P. S. Langeslag, in Chapter 5, contrasts the idea of climatic zones with two very different examples of medieval climatology: Icelandic and Greenlandic literature that details the effects of harsh sub-arctic climates on human activity and religious apocalyptic scenarios that warn of climatological degradation before the end of the world. Tess Somervell, in Chapter 3, chronicles seasons literature from the classical age to the

---

[40] Frank Kermode, *The Sense of an Ending: Studies in the Theory of Fiction* (1967; Oxford University Press, 2000), p. 47.

eighteenth century, showing how these contribute to the longstanding ideal of climate as cyclical and therefore predictable. However, the flipside of this, as Lowell Duckert's Chapter 6 shows, is a fascination with extreme weather events and thus with climate's intimate relationship with human activity, as evidenced by Shakespearean storms.

Part II, 'Evolution', pivots on the eighteenth century as a key moment in climate history – the formal codification and longitudinal observation of weather as the basis for an understanding of climate. Jan Golinski, in Chapter 7, demonstrates how empirical observation in the Enlightenment helped to establish the notion of climate as a stable object of study and set the stage for an understanding of global climate systems, themes taken up by subsequent chapters in this section. In Chapter 8, David Higgins explores how British Romantic writing was spurred, on the one hand, by Enlightenment climate science and, on the other, by the dramatic effects of the 'Year without a Summer'. Taking up Golinski's discussion of imperial notions of Britain's seasonally predictable climate as a moral and meteorological norm, Morgan Vanek, in Chapter 9, focuses on the establishment of national identities and literatures, via the construction of British climate as a temperate ideal and of colonial climates as deviant. As Jessica Howell's analysis in Chapter 10 then demonstrates, imperialistic climate discourse, girded by classical – specifically, Hippocratic – notions of climate determinism, allowed the white colonial body to emerge not as mere anomaly but as a signifier of a new kind of imperial dominance, one tested by the challenges of unfamiliar climes. The final chapters in the section return to questions of space in the novel, during and after the rise of realism. Justine Pizzo shows, in Chapter II, how the novel's capacity as climate model (in Taylor's terms) is highly gendered, exploring Victorian heroines' peculiar susceptibility to climatic influence as both a form of feminist resistance for female writers and a harbinger of modernism's anti-realist techniques. Meanwhile, Chris Pak's and Andrew Nestingen's chapters (Chapters 12 and 13) move discussions of climate and fiction into the twentieth and twenty-first centuries, exploring the interplay between climate, character, and plot in two prominent novelistic genres – science fiction and the Scandinavian crime novel.

The final part, 'Application', looks at climate's status in the literature of the Anthropocene, exploring, in particular, how contemporary concerns around climate and climate change interact with established literary norms, particular those around temporal setting and duration. In Chapter 14, I explore, with Axel Goodbody, the rise of the climate change novel, or 'cli-fi'. I follow this with Chapter 15, which considers the effect on literature of the need to read on the scale of climatological – rather than mere experiential or historical – time. Claire Colebrook's Chapter 16 asks that we look beyond our preoccupation with time and history as human, a preoccupation that includes the post-apocalyptic – and relentlessly anthropocentric – concerns of Anthropocene literary forms such as cli-fi. In Chapter 17, Daniel Cordle provides a reflection on the rise of twenty-first-century climate change criticism by exploring its connections to and, indeed, origins in twentieth-century nuclear criticism.

In their consideration of climate history, Fleming and Janković chronicle a historical bifurcation between climate as agency and climate as index. They argue that the rarefication of climate as index has been made possible only by modern climate science's 'instrumental, quantitative, and weather-biased understanding of the atmosphere'. They further argue for a reintroduction to climate discourse of the Greek word *klima* and its connotations of climatic agency, since the current state of climate anxiety requires just such a re-engagement with what climate '*does* rather than what it *is*'.[41] This volume, similarly, charts climate's progression from its ancient status as agency to its Enlightenment elevation into index, statistically derived and abstracted from experience, before considering climate change anxieties in the Anthropocene as a coming to grips with climate's materiality. What it also hopes to achieve, however, is an understanding of how the division between agency and index does not emerge from a simple distinction between scientific objectivity and literary affect; there is no clear demarcation between the quantitative and qualitative in the history of climate and literature. The chapters in this volume shed light on the complex, historical intertwining of the literary, the affective, the empirical, and the statistical discourses that comprise our understanding of climate thus far, in the hope of achieving a better understanding of climate in the age we call the Anthropocene.

---

[41] James Rodger Fleming and Vladimir Janković, 'Revisiting Klima', *Osiris*, 26 (2011), 1–2, original emphasis.

PART I

Origins

CHAPTER I

Literature, Climate, and Time: Between History and Story

Robert Markley

At the beginning of *The Great Derangement* (2016), Amitav Ghosh laments the lack of attention to the prospect of catastrophic climate change in 'serious fiction' and 'serious literary journals'. The 'mere mention' of abrupt climate change, he asserts, 'is often enough to relegate a novel or short story to the genre of science fiction ... as though in the literary imagination climate change were somehow akin to extraterrestrials or interplanetary travel'.[1] Ghosh's cordoning off of 'serious fiction' from science fiction suggests a larger cultural anxiety about the status of literature in a world where climate-enhanced disasters — like Hurricanes Harvey, Irma, and Maria in 2017 — can make CNN footage seem like the trailer for a dystopian film. For some novelists and many readers, it seems as though science fiction has overtaken literary realism as a vehicle for 'serious fiction'. In his Introduction to *Green Earth* (a one-volume version of his Science in the Capital trilogy), Kim Stanley Robinson suggests that 'if you want to write a novel about our world now, you'd better write science fiction, or you will be doing some kind of inadvertent nostalgia piece; you will lack depth, miss the point, and remain confused.'[2] In their different approaches to assessing the role of literature in an era of ongoing climate crises, Ghosh and Robinson explore the ways that climate fiction, or 'cli-fi', or Anthropocene fiction tries to distinguish itself from traditional ways of writing about humankind's relationship to the natural world. If, as Robinson suggests, 'our world now' seems to have outstripped the generic traditions of realism, the implications of climate change for literature past and present are recasting our conceptions of time and narrative, history and story.

---

[1] Amitav Ghosh, *The Great Derangement: Climate Change and the Unthinkable* (University of Chicago Press, 2016), p. 7.
[2] Kim Stanley Robinson, *Green Earth* (New York: Del Rey Books, 2015), p. xii.

Climate change has become such an urgent topic for Ghosh and others because it forces us to reassess the relationships among three different registers of time: experiential or embodied time, historical time, and climatological time.[3] If each of these registers resists hard and fast definition, it is the last that poses the most profound challenges to traditional ways of thinking about literature. Climatological time – a sense of non-anthropocentric, deep history accessible through, and mediated by, a range of complex technologies – complicates and disrupts the connections among personal identity, history, and narrative that (as Paul Ricœur argued) constitute the phenomenological and historical perceptions of time familiar to literary study.[4] In recent criticism, the Anthropocene – as a marker for industrial, fossil-fuelled modernity – has become the focus of efforts in the environmental humanities to confront new modes of imagining time, selfhood, and narrative.[5] But climatological time is not, or not simply, a posthumanist phenomenon that can be identified with the Anthropocene either as a stratigraphic marker of the human transformation of planetary geology or as a convenient shorthand for sociohistorical forces – notably the depredations of unrestrained capitalism and imperialism that have wreaked havoc on global climate. In their efforts to assign blame where blame is due for anthropogenic climate change, Andreas Malm and Jason Moore prefer the term the 'Capitalocene' and Donna Haraway the 'Plantationocene'.[6] But the very idea of climatological time has a complex genealogy, and to rethink anthropocentric knowledge

[3] See Dipesh Chakrabarty, 'The Climate of History: Four Theses', *Critical Inquiry*, 35.2 (2009), 197–222; Chakrabarty, 'Postcolonial Studies and the Challenge of Climate Change', *New Literary History*, 43 (2012), 1–18; Robert Markley, 'Time, History, and Sustainability', in Tom Cohen and Henry Sussman (eds.), *Telemorphosis: Essays in Critical Climate Change*, vol. 1 (Ann Arbor: Open Humanities Press, 2012), pp. 43–64; Srinivas Aravamudan, 'The Catachronism of Climate Change', *Diacritics*, 41 (2013), 6–30.

[4] Paul Ricœur, *Time and Narrative*, trans. Kathleen McLaughlin and David Pellauer, 3 vols. (University of Chicago Press, 1984–8).

[5] See Adam Trexler, *Anthropocene Fictions: the Novel in a Time of Climate Change* (Charlottesville: University of Virginia Press, 2015); Janet Fiskio, 'Apocalypse and Ecotopia: Narratives in Global Climate Change Discourse', *Race, Gender and Class*, 19 (2012), 12–36; Ian Baucom, '"Moving Centers": Climate Change, Critical Method, and the Historical Novel', *Modern Language Quarterly*, 76 (2015), 137–57; Kate Marshall, 'What Are the Novels of the Anthropocene? American Fiction in Geological Time', *American Literary History*, 27 (2015), 523–38.

[6] Andreas Malm, *Fossil Capital: the Rise of Steam Power and the Roots of Global Warming* (London: Verso, 2016); Donna Haraway, 'Anthropocene, Capitalocene, Plantationocene, Chthulucene: Making Kin', *Environmental Humanities*, 6 (2015), 159–65; Haraway, *Staying with the Trouble: Making Kin in the Chthulucene* (Durham., NC: Duke University Press, 2016). On debates about the Anthropocene, see Tobias Menely and Jesse Oak Taylor, Introduction, in Menely and Taylor (eds.), *Anthropocene Reading: Literary History in Geologic Times* (University Park: Pennsylvania State University Press, 2017), pp. 1–24.

systems – the project of 'reworlding' of the Earth and its biosystems that Haraway calls the 'Chthulucene' – is to go beyond instrumentalist conceptions of scientific climatology and beyond discussing anthropogenic themes in contemporary novels. To think about climate and literature is to explore the questions that Ghosh and Robinson pose about 'serious literature': the implications for fiction of living through the collision of experiential, historical, and climatological time.

Time and Narrative before 1900

Traditional understandings of serious fiction depend, to greater and lesser extents, on notions of subjective, experiential time, individual psychology, and character as the site of converging fields of neural impulses, bodily experiences, memories, the unconscious, belief systems and the internalisation of ideological values and assumptions that become indistinguishable from our own desires and fears.[7] 'Serious literature' typically assumes a backdrop of climatic stability against which the lives of characters and dramas of history unfold. The vagaries of the weather, in turn, often are treated phenomenologically, projecting on to the external world characters' inner turmoil: 'This tempest in my mind', says Lear in the storm, 'Doth from my senses take all feeling else.'[8] In other literary and non-fictional texts, storms herald the imminent catastrophism of eschatological history. The narratives of disaster, survival, and rebirth date back, in the Judeo-Christian tradition, to the tale of Noah's Ark, but invocations of divine punishment and grace typically acknowledge that climate change exceeds humankind's ability to comprehend or narrate it. In *The Storm* (1704), his compilation of eyewitness accounts of the extra-tropical cyclone that struck Britain in November 1703, Daniel Defoe struggles to find a language to describe the destruction of life and property: 'Horror and Confusion seiz'd upon all, whether on Shore or at Sea: No Pen can describe it, no Tongue can express it, no Thought conceive it.'[9] The inadequacy of language, in effect, implies that the storm has no narrative, only a typology

---

[7] See Nancy Armstrong, *Desire and Domestic Fiction: a Political History of the Novel* (Oxford University Press, 1987); Deidre Shauna Lynch, *The Economy of Character: Novels, Market Culture, and the Business of Inner Meaning* (University of Chicago Press, 1998).

[8] William Shakespeare, *King Lear*, 3.4.12–13, in *The Norton Shakespeare*, ed. Stephen Greenblatt, Walter Cohen, Jean E. Howard, and Katharine Eisaman Maus (New York: Norton, 1997), p. 2397.

[9] [Daniel Defoe] *The Storm: Or, a Collection of the Most Remarkable Casualties and Disasters Which Happen'd in the Late Dreadful Tempest Both by Sea and Land* (London: G. Sawbridge, 1704), p. 69. See Robert Markley, '"Casualties and Disasters": Defoe and the Interpretation of Climactic Instability', *Journal of Early Modern Cultural Studies*, 8 (2008), 102–24.

that reads disaster as a sign of God's displeasure. If Defoe voices a common
sentiment of his era that 'Nature plainly refers us beyond her Self, to the
Mighty Hand of Infinite Power, the Author of Nature, and Original of all
Causes' to account for the storm, he also displaces narrative authority on to
a divine 'Author' who exists beyond time and explanation.[10] As an instrument of God's 'Infinite Power', climatic disaster resists narrative form.

Defoe's gesture in linking the limitations of narrative to the 'Horror and
Confusion' of climatic instability is suggestive of the values and assumptions that traditionally have characterised humankind's relationship to the
natural world. For Western cultures throughout much of recorded history,
historical and climatological time were one and the same. Rather than
imagining a prehistory – or deep time – that antedated human activity,
philosophers and writers working within the five-thousand-year time
frame of biblical history envisioned a world that – since the sixth day of
creation – *always* has been inhabited, and therefore *always* had been shaped
and continually reshaped by human intervention. Pristine nature – that is,
the ideal climatic stability of an eternal spring – ended with the expulsion
from Eden. Variable climates were a consequence of the Fall because the
Earth itself suffered humankind's fate: 'cursed be the ground for thy sake',
says God in Genesis when he boots Adam and Eve out of the Garden into
the climatic instability of a postlapsarian world.[11] The idea of a pristine or
edenic nature consequently is a back formation, existing only as the
negation of the negative consequences of a climatologically unstable and
often hostile world. Throughout the histories of the seventeenth and
eighteenth centuries, humankind is enjoined not to return to a lost paradise but to work to improve hostile climates and make them fit for civilised
habitation.[12] The narrative of history – of moral redemption on Earth –
always has been anthropogenic.

In his *History of America* (1777), the Scots historian William Robertson
evokes the desolation and horror of the primeval landscapes of North and
South America as an incentive to drain swamps, plant fields, and manufacture more productive and healthier climates:

> The labour and operations of man not only improve and embellish the
> earth, but render it more wholesome, and friendly to life. When any region
> lies neglected and destitute of cultivation, the air stagnates in the woods,

---

[10] Defoe, *The Storm*, p. 2.
[11] Genesis 3:17, *The Bible*, intro. Robert Carroll and Stephen Prickett (Oxford University Press, 1997),
      Authorised King James Version.
[12] See Eric Gidal, '"O Happy Earth! Reality of Heaven!": Melancholy and Utopia in Romantic
      Climatology', *Journal of Early Modern Cultural Studies*, 8 (2008), 74–101.

putrid exhalations arise from the waters; the surface of the earth, loaded with rank vegetation, feels not the purifying influence of the sun; the malignity of the distempers natural to the climate increases, and new maladies no less noxious are engendered.[13]

Robertson describes, in effect, a feedback loop among civilisation, agriculture, climate, and health: clearing the land and planting fields not only eliminates stagnant air and 'putrid exhalations' but damps down 'noxious' illnesses and makes the land more productive and (as 'embellish' implies) more appealing. In this respect, 'nature' is a product of the anthropogenic 'improvement' of an environment that otherwise harbours only rotting vegetation and 'distempers' endemic to a postlapsarian world. John Williams in 1806 described humankind's relationship to the natural world in this way: 'To create worlds, to arrange the different parts, to organize the whole, furnish them with inhabitants of different descriptions, and to provide supplies for their various wants, is the glorious prerogative of the blessed Creator. To collect, modify, and adopt for necessary uses, is the privilege of his creature MAN.'[14] This ideology of 'necessary uses' underlies a progressivist view of anthropogenic climate change that persists well into the twentieth century: to 'modify' inhospitable lands for agriculture is to produce a more desirable climate for colonialist and profit-seeking 'MAN'.

But even as Williams was writing *The Climate of Great Britain* in the early nineteenth century, scientists were beginning to desacralise and disembody climate change by divorcing climatological time from historical time and banishing humankind from the centre of a divinely created universe. Two generations before Charles Darwin's *On the Origin of Species*, climatological time emerges as an ontological challenge to both biblical history and the ideology of agricultural improvement in three sets of scientific developments. In the course of two decades, the nebular hypothesis of planetary formation advanced by Pierre Simon de Laplace in *Exposition du système du monde* (1796), the 'discovery' of geological time by James Hutton in *Theory of the Earth* (1788), and the argument for species extinction by Georges Cuvier in *Recherches sur les ossemens fossiles de quadrupèdes* (1812) transformed conceptions of climate by decoupling history from experience, memory, myth, and biblical chronology.

<hr/>

[13] William Robertson, *The History of America*, 2 vols. (London: W. Strahan, 1777), vol. 1, p. 258.
[14] John Williams, *The Climate of Great Britain; or, Remarks on the Change It Has Undergone, Particularly within the Last Fifty Years* (London: C. and R. Baldwin, 1806), p. 1.

The nebular hypothesis anthropomorphised the life cycle of planets in terms of youth, maturity, old age, and heat-death, offering a model of terrestrial climate change as the consequence of irreversible, universal processes. The birth of planets in coalescing clouds of gas (Saturn and its rings) was succeeded by a brilliant youth as a gas giant (Jupiter), and followed by an adolescence in which dense clouds, water, and land masses formed (Venus). The Earth was a mature planet with a life-sustaining atmosphere and abundant water, but as its atmosphere slowly leaked into space (a common understanding of the implications of Newtonian mechanics), it was doomed to become a drier, dying planet (Mars), and eventually a dead, airless world (the moon). Laplace, in effect, removed Newton's voluntarist God from the mathematical principles that governed the structure of the solar system as well as its origins, evolution, and fate.[15] Hutton's vision of geological time with 'no vestige of a beginning, – no prospect of an end' presented a cyclical history of erosion and upheaval that continually reshaped the Earth.[16] This continual reshaping challenged the theological catastrophism, advanced in England by Thomas Burnet and William Whiston at the end of the seventeenth century, that ascribed geological evidence to a postlapsarian world disfigured from the perfect sphere it had been before humankind's expulsion from Eden.[17] Hutton's theories of geological history challenged the reliability of both experiential and theological notions of time, history, and nature. Describing evidence for upheavals and reshaping that lay far beyond biblical and pagan references to an antediluvian world, his re-theorised, geologically dynamic Earth itself became an *a-human* environment that resisted traditional modes of analysis and theological metanarratives. Cuvier's account of the extinction of fossilised species raised profound questions about the limits of Mosaic history and the ways in which past environments differed from present conditions.[18] The skeletal remains of giant sloths and mastodons that fascinated London, Paris, Philadelphia, and New York in 1800 suggested not only that nature had bred exotic species but that these prehistoric beasts had inhabited primeval ecologies no human ever had seen or

[15] See Ronald Numbers, *Creation by Natural Law: Laplace's Nebular Hypothesis in American Thought* (Seattle: University of Washington Press, 1977), pp. 3–16.
[16] James Hutton, *Theory of the Earth, with Proofs and Illustrations*, 2nd edn, 2 vols. (Edinburgh, 1795), vol. 1, p. 200.
[17] Stephen Jay Gould, *Time's Arrow, Time's Cycle: Myth and Metaphor in the Discovery of Geological Time* (Cambridge, MA: Harvard University Press, 1987), pp. 63–73.
[18] Martin J. S. Rudwick, *Bursting the Limits of Time: the Reconstruction of Geohistory in the Age of Revolution* (University of Chicago Press, 2005), pp. 349–415; Rudwick, *Worlds Before Adam: the Reconstruction of Geohistory in the Age of Reform* (University of Chicago Press, 2008), pp. 11–24.

described.[19] The emphasis throughout the nineteenth century on the savage violence of prehistoric carnivores indicates the extent to which it was difficult to imagine the climatic conditions that could provide forage for gigantic species of plant-eaters.

Even before Darwin published *On the Origin of Species*, then, scientific thought had begun to challenge the biblical monopoly on planetary history by offering radical visions of climatological time, the creation and reshaping of the Earth, and humankind's future. The popularity in the nineteenth century of end-of-the-world stories, beginning with Mary Shelley's *The Last Man* (1826), testifies to the ways in which the spectre of species extinction could be reimagined on a massive, planetary scale. These literary end-games reflected scientific views of planetary catastrophe. As Bruce Clarke has shown in examining the widespread effects, often misunderstood, of the second law of thermodynamics, the prospect of extinction haunts nineteenth-century efforts to chart, measure, and quantify both the natural world and the social regimes of economics and politics.[20] A world without the prospect of rebirth becomes, in the Victorian imagination, the abode of a civilisation without the hope of redemption or salvation. In this sense, the understanding of long-term change – of a climatological time that exists beyond human experience and understandings of temporality – gestures fatalistically towards embracing and resisting the deterministic universe imagined by Laplace. Yet it is difficult to imagine a time that transcends and beggars human experience within the generic strictures of nineteenth-century realism or 'serious fiction' without changing the narrative frames of reference, without suggesting that the impersonal and implacable forces of planetary and biological evolution exist beyond intention and comprehension.

In H. G. Wells's *The War of the Worlds* (1898), the Laplacean death grip of climatic desertification on Mars provokes the hyper-intelligent Martians to invade Earth, brushing aside human resistance and defying all efforts at communication or even, on the part of the shell-shocked Earthlings, interpretation. Wells's narrative unfolds with the relentless efficiency of a computer simulation, and the Martian invasion mimics the seemingly irresistible force of evolutionary laws. Once the initial postulates are programmed – the highly evolved life-forms on an older, dying planet invade Earth to secure new resources to survive – the narrative operates on

[19] See Ralph O'Connor, *The Earth on Show: Fossils and the Poetics of Popular Science, 1802–1856* (University of Chicago Press, 2007), pp. 31–70.
[20] Bruce Clarke, *Energy Forms: Allegory and Science in the Era of Classical Thermodynamics* (Ann Arbor: University of Michigan Press, 2001).

a self-perpetuating logic beyond human comprehension or control. Soon
after the relentless destruction begins, a curate goes mad, asking questions
that the narrator cannot answer: 'What do these things mean? . . . What are
these Martians?'[21] As the curate's faith shrivels to delusion, his questions
provoke the recognition that the only 'meaning' that can be derived from
the invasion is that intelligence exists merely to serve its own appetites: the
Martians' insatiable lust to consume human blood. The Martians have
perfected what nineteenth-century European colonial powers practise with
more malice but less efficiency: the technologies to overspread planets,
exhaust available resources, reshape what is left of the environment to their
own ends, and then seek new territories, new worlds, to invade. Wells's
alien invaders, in this regard, exist as sardonic displacements of Britain's
imperialistic appetites and ambitions, stripped of any ideological justifications. Although the Martians embody the ultimate ends of evolutionary
time, they remain subject to the climatological changes that have doomed
their planet. At the end of the novel, after the invaders have succumbed to
terrestrial disease, the narrator sees 'the busy multitudes in Fleet Street and
the Strand' as 'but the ghosts of the past, haunting the streets that I have
seen silent and wretched, going to and fro, phantasms in a dead city, the
mocking of life in a galvanised body'.[22] The emotional distance of these
'phantasms' from their own experience suggests that post-apocalyptic
London remains an 'unreal city', its 'ghosts' haunted by both their traumatic pasts and the grim futures programmed by the laws of evolution and
climate change. Rather than the social and environmental stability that
characterises much Victorian fiction, Wells's groundbreaking novel points
to the originary unreality of the phantasms of anthropogenic climatic
'improvement' and stability that underlie our systems of thought, belief,
self-identity.

Climate Change and Literature: To Dystopia and Beyond

Modern climatology emerged in the middle of the twentieth century with
the development of scientific understandings of the effects of greenhouse
gases and the resulting challenges to uniformitarian conceptions of climatic
variability.[23] New technologies for identifying and measuring climate

[21] H. G. Wells, *The War of the Worlds*, ed. David Y. Hughes and Harry M. Geduld (Bloomington: Indiana University Press, 1993), p. 103.
[22] Ibid., p. 193.
[23] Spencer Weart, *The Discovery of Global Warming*, 2nd edn (Cambridge, MA: Harvard University Press, 2008), pp. 8–22.

data – from satellite imagery to ice-core analysis – relocated observational and narrative authority from the individual scientist or naturalist to the scientific networks, alliances, and assemblages that collect, verify, interpret, and disseminate data; that then reaffirm or modify our understanding of the world; and that continually recalibrate the relationship between embodied experience and scientific data extracted from ice cores, tree rings, coral formations, and bog sediments.[24] If we ask ourselves why we believe in climate change, why the premises of Anthropocene fiction seem so credible, our answer (unless we have spent time studying ice cores in Greenland) involves some degree of trust in the institutions, procedures, and technologies of scientific testing and verification. In this respect, climatology might be described as an ongoing, collective effort to turn measurements, models, and scientific interpretations into coherent narratives, less absolute predictions than different science-fiction scenarios for possible planetary futures.

Yet if this displacement of narrative and observational authority in modern climatology shunts aside the experiential precepts of realist literature, the default assumptions about the time of climate change still centre on individuals' bodily experience and knowledge. The familiar rallying cries of the Green movement in the developed world, invoking 'the world our grandchildren will inherit' and urging us 'to save the Earth for future generations', reveal how indebted our ideas of climate are to the experience of embodied time – to individual experiences of wind, heat, cold, rain, drought, and the thousand climatic shocks that flesh is heir to. Climate, in this sense, is ontogenetic, evoking a succession of individual lifetimes – an unbroken sequence of embodied experiences that we have inherited from the past and project into the future. Literary texts can place characters in the tumult of catastrophic climate change, but these figures, to greater and lesser extents, mark the collision between unprecedented disasters and traditional perceptions of the natural world. Even as climate fiction often veers towards consensual visions of a dystopian future, it tacitly assumes that anthropogenic climate change can be mitigated by heroic actions or managerial expertise.

As I have suggested in a different context, narratives that imagine 'sustainability' as a socio-aesthetic and political response to climate change hedge on the fundamental question of what exactly they want to sustain: the *stability* of the planetary climatic system as a self-perpetuating,

---

[24] See Bruno Latour, *Facing Gaia: Eight Lectures on the New Climatic Regime*, trans. Catherine Porter (Cambridge: Polity Press, 2017).

Gaiaesque whole or the *productivity* of the natural world so that technologies of resource extraction can maintain and extend first-world standards of living.[25] In both cases, the vision of a 'sustainable future' that mitigates the 'Horror and Confusion' of climate change remains a function of anthropocentric time as a world to be managed, preserved, and willed to future generations; it is a vision of a preternaturally resilient ecology that exists outside of the dynamics of climatological time. The measure of several generations – of one or two extended human lifetimes – remains the narrative timescale of sustainability. The paradox is that the greater the hope for 'realistic' solutions to climate change in 'serious fiction', the closer they come to falling into an 'inadvertent nostalgia' that can be co-opted by the political hierarchies, centralized bureaucracies, technologies of economic calculation, the policing of resources and populations, and distributive political economies that are required to manage finite resources.

In mid-twentieth-century novels the consequences of catastrophic climate change stem from natural disasters. In J. G. Ballard's *The Drowned World* (1962), the global warming that melts the polar caps and submerges Europe under rising oceans is triggered by solar storms. But Anthropocene fiction, as Adam Trexler suggests, typically relocates the causes of climatic disaster from a hostile or indifferent natural world to greedy or indifferent human beings and corrupt or incompetent institutions.[26] In giving narrative form to the collision of experiential and climatological time, Anthropocene fiction confronts the narrative and ideational problem that science-fiction projections seem more believable, more credible, than imagining an indefinite extension of our day-to-day, present existence.[27] In this respect, narrative has become less premise than prediction, shifting from representing the past to simulating possible futures. In contrast to postmodern ideas of representation predicated on lack (the absence of the signified) or deferral (the gap between the signifier and the signified), simulation, Steven Shaviro argues, 'precedes its object: it doesn't imitate or stand in for a given thing, but provides a program for generating it. The simulacrum is the birth of the thing, rather than its death.'[28] In Shaviro's sense, climate fiction works by convincing its readers of the internal consistency of its simulations so that its treatments of time and history can serve as a means to analyse the ideological conditions of

[25] Markley, 'A Brief History of Chronological Time', *Danish Yearbook of Philosophy*, 44 (2009), 59–75.
[26] Trexler, *Anthropocene Fictions*, pp. 7–17.
[27] See Stephanie LeMenager, 'Climate Change and the Struggle for Genre', in Menely and Taylor, (eds.) *Anthropocene Reading*, pp. 220–38.
[28] Steven Shaviro, *Doom Patrols* (London: Serpent's Tail Press, 1997), p. 17.

existence that readers otherwise may take for granted. But in contrast to traditional science fiction – the domain of Ghosh's 'extraterrestrials' and 'interplanetary travel' – much of the best recent climate fiction explores the dystopias of indifference that overtake even the most sophisticated technological bulwarks against climatic apocalypse.

The unnamed narrator of Jim Shepard's short story, 'The Netherlands Lives with Water' (2009), is a hydrologist living in Rotterdam in the near future, some time after the 'collapse of the West Antarctic ice sheet' and the stalling of the Gulf Stream.[29] Facing 'the catastrophe for which the Dutch have been planning for fifty years' (147), he is part of a team that manages 'the jewel of [the country's] water defenses – the staggeringly massive water barriers at Maeslant and Dordrecht, and the rest of the Delta Works – ready to shut off the North Sea during the next cataclysmic storm' (149). This state-of-the-art defence is, in one sense, the culmination of a techno-climatological history of 'cooperative water management' (147) that is older than the state. The 'Delta Works' not only 'improve' and 'embellish' the Netherlands, they are essential for the nation's continued existence. The hero, however, lives through a radical break in the fabrics of historical and experiential time. The disastrous scenario of 'rising sea levels, peak river discharges, and extreme weather events' (149) turns the achievements of the Netherlands' water management system into a post-apocalyptic guessing game for whatever comes after the flood: 'For the last year and a half', the narrator tells us, 'we've been told to build into our designs for whatever we're working on features that restrict the damaging effects *after* an inevitable inundation. There won't be retreating back to the hinterlands, either, because, given the numbers we're facing, there won't be any hinterlands' (162). Although the hero recognises the apocalyptic implications of 'an inevitable inundation', he exists in a liminal state of dystopian detachment, an inertial persistence in performing his job day after day, as though, despite his knowledge, the future is destined to be a continuation of the climatological present. His failing marriage to Cato, a government public relations officer whose job entails downplaying the possibility of catastrophic flooding, reflects the disintegration of affective relations into the routinised resignation of pre-apocalyptic existence – a twenty-first-century version of Wells's London of 'phantasms'. She ultimately leaves with their son for the safety of Berlin just before the North Sea overwhelms

---

[29] Jim Shepard, 'The Netherlands Lives with Water', in John Joseph Adams (ed.), *Loosed upon the World: the Saga Anthology of Climate Fiction* (New York: Saga, 2015), p. 146 (originally published in *McSweeny's*, 32 (2009)). Hereafter cited parenthetically by page number.

the water barriers, while the hero's efforts to save his mother – her memory clouded by dementia – are dwarfed by the inexorable processes triggered by global warming. The hero's isolation – his ultimate inability to connect with those he loves – gestures towards the self-alienating effects of recognising climatic catastrophe but being unable to act.

In a telling scene just days before the final inundation of Rotterdam, the narrator watches a colleague's 'face during a recent simulation as one of his new configurations for a smart dike was overwhelmed in half the time he would have predicted' (162). He does not describe the expression on his co-worker's face, nor does he mention his own response to the foreboding 'simulation' that models the coming disaster. His silence reflects a larger crisis of inaction – a knowledge that distances the narrator from his family and colleagues and from investing in cultural narratives of hope or even survival. 'It had always been the Dutch assumption that we would resolve the problems facing us from a position of strength', he notes after the simulation. 'But we passed that station long ago. At this point, each of us understands privately that we're operating under the banner of lost control' (162). The modifier 'privately' gestures to the psychological toll on the individual of a centuries-long history of fossil fuel extraction, political waffling, and moral indifference. Climatic disaster seems, at once, undeniable and unimaginable.[30] The narrator does not evacuate Rotterdam when he learns his wife and son already are in Berlin, and he does not leave on the last helicopter with his colleagues as his building floods. He does not tell us anything about his moral paralysis or his seeming resignation to his fate. Instead, he recalls his mother's tales about the flood of 1953 that devastated the Netherlands, killing more than 1,800 people, and the Queen's speech after the disaster. For Shepard, who frequently turns to scenes of disaster in his fiction, the 'banner of lost control' serves emblematically as a lament for a narrative realism overwhelmed by global climate crises.

The dystopian tradition of Anthropocene fiction, represented by 'The Netherlands Lives with Water', often colours the end of civilisation with the fascinated moral outrage of Jacobean tragedy: readers in the developed world find themselves complicit in the unsustainable modes of transportation, communication, food production, and energy consumption that threaten their lifestyles, if not their very existence. In the strategic utopia of the Science in the Capital trilogy (2004–7),

---

[30] See David Collings, *Stolen Future, Broken Present: the Human Significance of Climate Change* (Ann Arbor, MI: Open Humanities Press, 2014).

later revised and condensed as *Green Earth*, Kim Stanley Robinson creates a near-future where scientific knowledge and technological advances ultimately contain the worst excesses of late capitalism in the struggle to engineer Earth into a world that is climatologically more stable, economically more equitable, and spiritually enriched.[31] If his trilogy reverse engineers the indifference and paralysis that often characterise dystopian climate fiction, some of his recent novels offer a different kind of thought experiment that reimagines history, time, and narrative outside the generic strictures of realism and the ideologies of modernity.

In *Shaman* (2013), Robinson immerses his readers in a history *before* history – before writing, agriculture, sophisticated technologies of calculation, and socioeconomic hierarchies. The novel is set during the ice age that enveloped much of the northern hemisphere between 30,000 and 40,000 years ago, and we encounter this ice age world through the eyes of the individuals and small tribal societies, struggling to survive in the harsh conditions of that era, who created the Chauvet cave paintings in southern France that date from that period.[32] In emphasising the complexity and sophistication of a prehistoric socio-climatological world, Robinson explores the narrative, sociocultural, and psychological possibilities of a steady-state culture that sees its environment as the natural state of existence. *Shaman*'s prehistoric world, in this respect, exists without the framing narratives of an apocalyptic environmental crisis and without the utopian striving that characterises the Science in the Capital trilogy.

Loon, the heir-apparent to the tribe's shaman, and the thirty or so other members of his pack live within a culture that survives by adapting, amid a host of challenges, to the seasonal rhythms of southern Europe in an era of mammoths, aurochs, and sabre-tooth tigers. In an ice world of late springs, short summers, and early snowfalls, the problems of getting,

---

[31] See Adeline Johns-Putra, 'Ecocriticism, Genre, and Climate Change: Reading the Utopian Vision of Kim Stanley Robinson's Science in the Capital Trilogy', *English Studies*, 91 (2010), 744–60; Gib Prettyman, 'Living Thought: Genes, Genres and Utopia in the Science in the Capital Trilogy', in William J. Burling (ed.), *Kim Stanley Robinson Maps the Unimaginable* (Jefferson, NC: MacFarland, 2009), pp. 181–203; Roger Luckhurst, 'The Politics of the Network: the Science in the Capital Trilogy', in Burling (ed.), *Kim Stanley Robinson Maps the Unimaginable*, pp. 170–80; Robert Markley, '"How to Go Forward": Catastrophe and Comedy in Kim Stanley Robinson's Science in the Capital Trilogy', *Configurations*, 20 (2012), 7–27; De Witt Douglas Kilgore, 'Making Huckleberries: Reforming Science and Whiteness in Science in the Capital', *Configurations*, 20 (2012), 89–108.

[32] The best introduction to the Chauvet caves remains Werner Herzog's documentary *Cave of Forgotten Dreams* (IFC Films, 2010), which he wrote and directed.

preparing, and storing food define the group's social structures. Eating organises culture. Schist, the tribe's chief,

> was always talking food ... He had dug their storage pits himself, and was always lining them with new things. He spoke with people from other packs to see what they knew. He and Thorn [the shaman] had worked out an accounting system ... using clean lengths of driftwood to notch marks for their pokes of animal fat, bags of nuts, dried salmon steaks, smoked caribou steaks; everything they gathered to eat in the cold months was stored and marked down. He knew how much every person in the pack would eat, based on the previous winter's markings and adjusted by everyone's summer health, by how much fat they had put on, and so on. He knew better than you how hungry you would be.[33]

Schist's methods of accounting, calculating, and modelling future needs suggest what is possible – even essential – for a culture with neither alphanumeric writing nor agriculture. The arts of prediction and probability, the notches on driftwood, mark a sophisticated knowledge of bioclimatology: 'he knew better than you how hungry you would be'. In an ice age environment, hunting, scavenging, and gathering are, at once, strategies, crafts, and modes of techno-scientific knowledge that structure the life-or-death calculus of food acquisition and storage. The novel is filled with scenes of hunting and trapping, and the pack's social organisation is structured by the craft knowledges and the divisions of labour centred on the problems of securing, preserving, storing, and rationing the food they need to accumulate before the onset of the 'hungry months' of late winter and early spring. 'Always talking food' is the bioclimatological offspring of scarcity.

History and time in *Shaman* emerge, then, in the patchwork strategies of individuals that must be passed down through generations. The temporal and geospatial coordinates that locate us within history and civilisation disappear into Robinson's imagining of pre-literate modes of memory and knowledge. In a key passage, Thorn recalls the pack's response to a climatological crisis – 'the ten years' winter' – that they barely survived. His song turns art into a life-or-death vehicle for fostering collective memory and social identity. As a record of climatological anomalies, such artful knowledge prepares the pack to recognise future crises by etching into its collective memories the strategies that might allow its members to survive:

---

[33] Kim Stanley Robinson, *Shaman* (New York: Orbit, 2013), p. 72. Hereafter cited parenthetically in the text.

> . . . if it were not for the great salt sea
> Everybody everywhere would have died and been dead . . .
> We ate what lived through ten years of winter,
> Meaning whelks and clams and mussels and sea snails,
> Meaning seaweed and sandcrabs and limpets and eels.
> We ate fish when we could catch them,
> We ate shit when we couldn't. (85–6)

Thorn's song challenges idealised notions of hunting and gathering – Stone Age peoples living in 'harmony' with or 'sustainably' in nature – by voicing the struggles and uncertainties that comprise pre-agricultural existence: 'We ate shit.' His history, as collective memory and art, defines a horizon of past knowledge and a mode of techno-scientific disaster preparedness: forget hunting or gathering, head to 'the great salt sea'. In deromanticising a pre-anthropogenic past, Robinson explores the experiential and psychic lives of the Chauvet cave-painters by reimagining their knowledge practices as art for survival's sake.

Shaman asks its readers to imagine living in an environment cut free – temporally and conceptually – from history. Loon understands time analogically, describing his experience of time as mineralogical rather than organic:

> The world would scrape [Loon] down just like he scraped this chunk of rock. It would go on until Thorn died, and then the pile of granules that was Loon would replace him, and do all the things Thorn had done, including scraping down some apprentice of his own; then he would die, and the apprentice would go on and do it to his apprentice, and on and on and on and on and on and on and on and on and on and on it would go, the earthblood and their own blood ground up together under the sun. (86)

For Loon, time is neither progressive nor cyclical: he does not complain about a history to come or an alternative that could be, but sees himself embedded in a shamanic succession without metaphysical contexts or consequences. Survival is a property of the group, not the individual. Late in the novel, the dying Thorn is seized by the fear that his shamanic knowledge will be lost; after he and Heather, the herbalist, die there will be no one left in the pack 'old enough to know everything you need to know' (419). This knowledge is, at once, experiential and extraordinarily fragile: a fabric of embodied memories and tales that can be preserved only through song and hands-on apprenticeships. 'There are no secrets, there is no mystery', Thorn tells Loon: 'You have to have enough food to get through winter and spring. That's what it all comes down to' (418–19). This is the craft knowledge of Haraway's Chthulucene: a kinship with the animals that the pack hunts, an impressive set of adaptation strategies for a near-glacial climate. Yet Thorn also dreams of a comprehensive, if world-bound, knowledge: 'I wanted to know everything', he tells his apprentice. 'I remembered every single word I ever heard, every single moment of my life, right up to a few years ago. I talked to every person in this whole part of the world, and remembered everything they said. What's going to become of all that?' (419). Loon's response suggests that at age fifteen or so he is indeed ready to become a shaman: 'We'll do what we can' (420). This quest for a knowledge of 'everything', even in a pre-literate world, provides an alternative to our contemporary culture obsessed by trying to account for, and profit from, whatever will happen next.

If Loon's tale generically seems a prehistoric *Bildungsroman*, his world is, at once, a utopia without any of the characters realising it and a long-term climatic disaster that none of them can imagine. Utopian survival strategies and a climate crisis without an end are the conditions of a natural world that 'goes on and on and on'. In this respect, *Shaman* poses fundamental questions about the relationships among time, narrative, and climate by reformatting narrative and historical time. Robinson, in effect, redefines 'serious fiction' by offering an alternative to a climatic world that is too much with us. By defamiliarising time and history, the novel asks its readers to imagine what is going to become of us when we must confront the near and long-term political, economic, humanitarian, and social crises provoked by climate change. If individual actions have only microscopic consequences for changing the climate or ameliorating planetary crisis, they remain essential to Thorn's question, 'What's going to become of all that?' In the novel, the narrative resolution, if not the direct response, to this question centres on Loon's three days and nights of painting in the Chauvet caves, contributing to the collective art of a now-vanished world. Thirty-five thousand years later, the ice age is gone, the artist who left his hand print on an entry wall is long dead, the animals he or she drew on rock mostly extinct. The Chauvet cave paintings seem an apt image for thinking about the role of literature in an age of unfolding climatic crisis: 'all that' takes the form of those narratives that strive to include multiple perspectives, that contribute to a collaborative art that stretches across generations. In climatological time, literature commits to collective memory the world as we once knew it.

CHAPTER 2

Atmosphere as Setting, or, 'Wuthering' the Anthropocene

Jesse Oak Taylor

On the second page of Emily Brontë's *Wuthering Heights* (1847), the narrator, Mr Lockwood, treats his reader to a quick lesson in cultural meteorology by way of describing Heathcliff's house and the setting of his tale: 'Wuthering', he explains, is:

> a significant provincial adjective, descriptive of the atmospheric tumult to which its station is exposed in stormy weather. Pure, bracing ventilation they must have up there, at all times, indeed; one may guess the power of the north wind, blowing over the edge, by the excessive slant of a few, stunted firs at the end of the house; and by the range of gaunt thorns all stretching their limbs one way, as if craving the arms of the sun.[1]

Since 'Wuthering Heights' refers not only to the dwelling so described, but also to the novel itself, this explanation does double duty, staging the intersection of literal and literary atmosphere in a manner that dramatises the longstanding entanglement between climate, atmosphere, and storytelling. In keeping with the goals of the present volume, my intent is not to offer a fully fledged interpretation of Brontë's novel, but rather to use it as an example around which to stage the multiple layers through which an atmospheric reading might proceed, highlighting the ultimate impossibility of distinguishing between either climate and atmosphere in their nominally literal (that is, meteorological) and historical senses through the mediating work of literary form.

Literal Atmosphere

First, the literal. What can we learn from taking Lockwood's description literally as an ostensibly accurate account of an actual place? Such

---

[1] Emily Brontë, *Wuthering Heights*, ed. Ian Jack (Oxford University Press, 2009), p. 2. Hereafter cited parenthetically.

investment in descriptive accuracy not only corresponds to the current move to literal, denotative, or 'surface' reading, but is also arguably ecocriticism's founding gesture, as when ecocritic John Elder and forest ecologist Glenn Adelson collaborate on a reading of Robert Frost's 'Spring Pools' to show how the poem both records and formalises a scientifically accurate account of the ecological phenomenon it describes.[2] In this case, such a reading would follow Lockwood in observing that the north wind is both strong and consistent enough to 'slant' the 'few stunted firs' and bend 'all the gaunt thorns' one way, and note that such effects are indeed an occasional feature of exposed ridgetop ecosystems. It might then proceed to note that the wind has also sculpted the local dialect, since 'a significant provincial adjective' exists to account for precisely such phenomena, whereas Lockwood, the urban neophyte, has to resort to a simile to produce the same result. He describes the wind-bent thorns 'stretching their limbs one way, as if craving the arms of the sun', thus ascribing the effects of wuthering to heliotropism instead, and substituting an effect only observable in such exposed environs with one that can be witnessed by watching houseplants turn towards the sun. Such a literal reading is by no means simplistic, quickly moving beyond recapitulating Lockwood's description to showcase the ways in which that description itself can index an ecosystem operating in ways that may or may not be fully apparent to the observer describing it. In so doing, it symptomatises the ways in which human culture, manifest in the distinctive 'provincial' word 'wuthering', is embedded within climatic conditions.

Even more expansively, one might turn from such a localised account to the study of botanical distribution and climatic conditions, noting that Alexander von Humboldt's *Essay on the Geography of Plants* (1807) introduced the idea of climate zones by mapping the distribution of flora up Mount Chimborazo in the Ecuadorian Andes. Humboldt uses elevation to map climatic conditions, extrapolating from the purely local distribution to the global, longitudinal distribution of climate zones between the equator and the poles.[3] Following similar logic, one can situate Brontë's literary account of 'wuthering' as the localised manifestation of a singular planetary phenomenon, a kind of synecdoche in which the 'tumult' of harsh conditions affects both the individual hardiness and adaptive characteristics of the species that inhabit it, whether plant, animal, or human,

[2] John Elder and Glenn Adelson, 'Robert Frost's Ecosystem of Meanings in "Spring Pools"', *ISLE: Interdisciplinary Studies in Literature and Environment*, 13.2 (2006), 1–17.
[3] Alexander von Humboldt and Aimé Bonpland, *Essay on the Geography of Plants*, ed. Stephen Jackson and trans. Sylvie Romanowski (University of Chicago Press, 2009).

offering an important precursor not only to evolutionary theory but also to Earth system science, the study of the Earth as a single interconnected system and thus the scale at which the Anthropocene becomes visible.

In this literal version, atmosphere operates as a key element of the novel's setting, first locally and then opening outward. Because *Wuthering Heights* takes place on the Yorkshire moors, Wuthering Heights can be situated high on a ridge where it is exposed to the 'atmospheric tumult' that in that particular region is known as 'wuthering'. Reading the novel in a manner that attends to these connections can, in turn, make that Yorkshire land-scape come to life for a reader far removed in time and space, as evidenced by the fact that generations of Brontë fans have journeyed to the landscape to experience firsthand a landscape first conjured for them in fiction. However, rather than an attempt to escape mediated quality of literary representation, such outward turns arguably extend that mediation to its fullest extent, conjuring an experience of the actual world as construed through, and made valuable by, literature. As Jonathan Bate asks, 'An artistic representation of a figure in a landscape cannot but be *mediated*. Is it possible, though, for a figure to stand in a natural landscape and relate to it in a manner that is *unmediated*?'[4] It is precisely because the answer is 'no' that ecological art matters. The Lake District came to be celebrated (and protected) as 'natural' precisely because it was also 'Wordsworth Country'; Yosemite was preserved not merely because it was 'wilderness' but because it was wilderness as *written* by John Muir. Such examples underscore the significant political potential of ecological aesthetics. There is an analogy, here, to what meteorologist John Thornes calls 'cultural climatology', in which he reads atmospheric history from cultural artefacts, such as the paintings of Constable or Monet, in order to escape (or, rather, complement) the simulated abstractions of meteorolo-gical modelling.[5] Gillen Wood, meanwhile, situates the composition of *Frankenstein* (1818) within the context of a climatic event, the eruption of Tambora in 1815 and the resultant 'Year without a Summer'.[6] In each instance, attending to the ways in which works of art or literature drama-tise, depict, or are historically coincident with meteorological phenomena not only showcases the operation of those phenomena themselves, but also

---

[4] Jonathan Bate, *The Song of the Earth* (London: Picador, 2000), p. 126, original emphasis.
[5] John E. Thornes, 'Cultural Climatology and the Representation of Sky, Atmosphere, Weather, and Climate in Selected Art Works of Constable, Monet, and Eliasson', *Geoforum*, 39 (2008), 570–80.
[6] Mary Shelley, *Frankenstein, or The Modern Prometheus*, ed. M. K. Joseph (Oxford University Press, 2008); Gillen D'Arcy Wood, *Tambora: the Eruption that Changed the World* (Princeton University Press, 2014).

highlights the way they impinge on human history. Literary depictions of atmospheric phenomena are productive not in spite of the fact that those descriptions are also historically and culturally situated, but rather because they are, and thus provide vantage points making visible the ongoing entanglement between human and climatic history. As we enter an age defined by anthropogenic climate change, the work of literature (at least when read through an ecocritical lens) shifts as well: it now seeks to *change* human/climate relations rather than simply recording or dramatising them. In this context, extending the aesthetic value of, and readerly attention to, atmospheric phenomena is no insignificant feat. And yet, literary atmosphere extends beyond the literal.

Literary Atmosphere

Wuthering Heights's atmospheric opening does not simply establish a feature of the place where the narrative will happen; it also establishes the conditions under which that narrative will occur. That is, it serves to establish the conditions of possibility for the narrative itself. This is a novel in which human adaptation to a harsh environment is not merely a facet of its plot, but integral to the mode of characterisation that the work itself deploys. In *Wuthering Heights*, all living beings, whether human, plant, or animal, are subject to being shaped by their environment, an environment that is not merely that of the Yorkshire moors, but also of the novel itself. The logic of its plot depends upon such situated shaping. Thus, the doubling between the literal and literary meanings of 'wuthering' as a localised conception of life modified by the harsh persistence of 'atmospheric tumult' carries throughout the novel. This is rendered most explicit later in the book when Heathcliff explains the vengeance he has planned for his abusive (and now dead) adoptive elder brother, Hindley, whose cruelty warped Heathcliff's own character. Having become guardian of Hindley's son, Hareton, Heathcliff asks 'we'll see if one tree won't grow as crooked as another, with the same wind to twist it!' (165). Heathcliff's planned cruelty and deprivation is not only intended to degrade (or, if you prefer, 'stunt') Hareton's development; it is also presented as an experiment ('we will see'), the conditions of which are suggested by the actual atmospheric phenomena operating in the place where that experiment is to take place: he could as easily have described his plan as 'wuthering' Hareton. However, such correlation occurs at the level of metaphor. Heathcliff is not describing what it is like to grow different species of tree at Wuthering Heights, but rather what it is like to develop as a character within *Wuthering Heights*. While that point may appear pain-fully obvious, it provides a way into understanding the shift from atmo-spheric phenomena as described *by* language in the novel, and atmosphere's operation as a property *of* literary language, which is to say the substance of the novel itself.

This process is more complicated than simply the transformation of an initially literal description into metaphor because that initial description was itself doing more than descriptive work. In addition to helping the reader picture 'Wuthering Heights', the place, it was offering the reader clues as to the kind of novel *Wuthering Heights* was going to be, and the kinds of events that might take place within it. In this sense, atmosphere is integral to the ways in which we inhabit literary worlds. As Erin James suggests, spatial and physical metaphors like 'transportation' or 'immer-sion' can 'describe the process of mental modeling and emotional inhabi-tation that underlie narrative comprehension' in ways that must be correlated to 'the deeply embodied nature of storyworld formation'.[7] Atmosphere is integral to both effects, in that it contributes not only to the sense in which the reader is surrounded by the storyworld, but also to the text's capacity to produce physical, embodied sensation. Hans Ulrich Gumbrecht describes this latter property of atmosphere through the German term *Stimmung*, which refers to both atmosphere and mood. 'Reading for *Stimmung*', Gumbrecht explains, 'means paying attention to the textual dimension of the forms that envelop us and our bodies as a physical reality – something that can catalyze inner feelings without matters of representation necessarily being involved.'[8] Though by no means an ecocritic, Gumbrecht, too, describes the 'atmospheres and moods that literary works absorb' as 'a form of "life"' and an 'environment with physical substance'.[9] Dividing the affective encounter with the text from 'representation' marks a turn from atmosphere as subject for descrip-tion and atmosphere as formal property of the work itself. As James argues, it also departs from a common ecocritical fixation on realism, since non-realist, experimental, and speculative fictions all transport their readers to alternative worlds, in ways that in no sense hinge on descriptive accuracy, and yet produce affects and experiences that open into ecological modes of being: 'ecocritics would do well to question how the process of losing

[7] Erin James, *The Storyworld Accord: Econarratology and Postcolonial Narratives* (Lincoln, NE: University of Nebraska Press, 2015), p. 33.
[8] Hans Ulrich Gumbrecht, *Atmosphere, Mood, Stimmung: on a Hidden Potential of Literature*, trans. Erik Butler (Stanford University Press, 2012), p. 5.
[9] Ibid., p. 20.

yourself in a book can be harnessed toward environmentalist ends'.[10] Atmosphere is essential to the way in which books work to produce such tangible, embodied, and yet highly subjective effects.

And yet, as a formal property, literary atmosphere is notoriously difficult to define. William Empson famously remarked that atmosphere was 'conveyed in some unknown way as a byproduct of meaning' and yet held that 'analysis cannot hope to do anything but ignore it' while 'criticism can only state that it is there'.[11] M. H. Abrams's *Glossary of Literary Terms* defines it as 'the emotional tone pervading a section or the whole of a literary work, which fosters in the reader expectations as to the course of events, whether happy or (more commonly) terrifying or disastrous', and gives examples ranging from the sentinels' nervous dialogue preceding the reappearance of the Ghost in *Hamlet,* the opening of Coleridge's *Christabel,* and Egdon Heath in Thomas Hardy's *The Return of the Native.*[12] Of these, only Hardy's heath corresponds directly to setting, and none refers to literal atmospheric phenomena (as might, say, 'a dark and stormy night'). In each case, the turn to what literary atmosphere *does* subsumes any account of what literary atmosphere *is.* Hardy's brooding heath and Shakespeare's nervous dialogue not only set the mood in which the audience will experience narrative events but also establish the conditions through which those events will be gauged as plausible or implausible. They thus delimit the conditions of possibility within the work by setting the conditions for what the reader can be expected to believe. *Hamlet* is a narrative in which a ghost appears; if the audience does not grant that ghost credence as an agent, then the narrative loses coherence. In that sense, it doesn't necessarily matter if you think the ghost is 'real' or a product of Hamlet's psychosis, as long as you accept that this is a play in which a ghost must be taken seriously. The entire first chapter of Hardy's *Return of the Native* describes the heath. There are no human characters. Hence, the opening chapter does not simply introduce a 'brooding' presence, it decentres the human from that most anthropocentric of genres, the novel. Hardy makes it absolutely clear that any event transpiring within the storyworld of

[10] James, *Storyworld Accord,* p. 34.

[11] William Empson, *Seven Types of Ambiguity* (New York: New Directions, 1966), p. 17.

[12] William Shakespeare, *Hamlet,* in Shakespeare, *The Norton Shakespeare,* ed. Stephen Greenblatt, Walter Cohen, Jean E. Howard, and Katharine Eisaman Maus (New York: Norton, 1997), pp. 1659–759; Samuel Taylor Coleridge, *Christabel,* in Coleridge, *The Major Works,* ed. H. J. Jackson (1985; Oxford University Press, 2008), pp. 68–86; Thomas Hardy, *The Return of the Native,* ed. Simon Gatrell, Nancy Barrineau, and Margaret R. Higonnet (Oxford University Press, 2008); M. H. Abrams and Geoffrey Galt Harpham, *A Glossary of Literary Terms,* 9th edn (Boston: Wadsworth, 2008), pp. 18–19.

The Return of the Native must be situated within the non-human world, including not only this particular environment but the timescales of geological and evolutionary change. Atmosphere, in other words, marks a crucial point of intersection between the world *described* by the work, and the functional formal properties of the work. In this sense, we might even say that atmosphere is an *effect* produced by a literary work rather than an objective property of the work, insofar as it only comes into existence through interaction. As Gumbrecht argues, 'concentrating on atmospheres and moods offers literary studies a possibility for reclaiming vitality and aesthetic immediacy that have, for the most part, gone missing'.[13] At the most fundamental level, this shift marks a turn from thinking about what a work *means* to asking what it *does*, how it produces effects upon (and affects within) the reader, and thus its agency in the world.

The Intersection of Literal and Literary Atmospheres

The intersection between literal and literary atmosphere is underscored by the coincident historical emergence of both concepts. As Jayne Elizabeth Lewis shows, the scientific articulation of air as a measurable entity in the experiments of Robert Boyle and Joseph Priestley is historically coterminous with the 'rise of the novel' and indeed the invention of fiction in its modern sense. As she explains, 'fiction was subtly theorized from within by writers well aware that its visual embodiment in books made it uniquely perceptible as a factitious object even as it is somehow experienced as all-encompassing', a condition it shares with atmosphere, an entity that 'cannot be stood outside of, so it can never be completely objectified, fixed, or, as a result, intellectually possessed'.[14] In Lewis's account, 'the rise of air as an object of uneasy knowledge . . . coincides with that of the ubiquitous print medium and with new ways of seeing "indirectly"', a point she suggests 'made it possible to see air as another such medium through the contiguous and not dissimilar one of writing'.[15] The point is thus not simply that literary atmosphere is composed of words, but rather that atmosphere and language share essential properties, troubling any notion of a straightforward divide between the literal and the figurative when speaking of atmosphere in its literary sense.

---

[13] Gumbrecht, *Atmosphere, Mood, Stimmung*, p. 12.
[14] Jayne Elizabeth Lewis, *Air's Appearance: Literary Atmosphere in British Fiction, 1660–1794* (University of Chicago Press, 2012), pp. 7, 6.
[15] Ibid., p. 25.

Experiments with air pumps and suffocating birds under glass bells vividly dramatised the necessity of air for life, thus opening a rather obvious literary correlate in realist fiction: like organisms, characters need a sustaining atmosphere in order to come to 'life'. Furthermore, as Siobhan Carroll argues, this articulation of the atmosphere as paradoxically empty and yet physical entity was not restricted to the indoor science of the laboratory, but also pertains to balloonists' experiments in human flight. These flights not only expanded the realm of technological possibility, they also remade the atmosphere as 'a new kind of space ... accessible to navigation' and 'therefore imagined in new ways' as a realm of fantasy akin to the long traditions of maritime literature.[16] They also made crucial aspects of Earth's atmosphere palpably visible. A balloonist collapsing for want of oxygen effectively took the place of those suffocating birds, illustrating the atmosphere's primary function: enclosing the Earth as a life-support system. They also made planetary unity visible in new ways, including the integration of weather patterns into a single interconnected system, and atmosphere's transcendence of national borders, even those apparently 'natural' ones demarcated by mountains or rivers.[17] Of the 1785 novel *The Aeronostic Spy*, Carroll explains, 'seen from an aeronotical perspective, national differences become less significant than the similarities between human beings from different parts of the world', such that the novel produces a form of atmospheric cosmopolitanism.[18] Attending to atmosphere is thus the beginning of acknowledging our own planetary internality, the fact that we live *in* Earth rather than on it.

In its first English usage, from 1638, atmosphere referred to the 'spheroidal gaseous envelope surrounding any of the heavenly bodies'.[19] Interestingly, the term was first used in relation not to Earth, but to the moon and only subsequently, in 1677, transferred to that 'subtile Body that immediately incompasses the Earth, and is filled with all manner of exhalations'.[20] Similarly, James Lovelock arrived at his famous 'Gaia Hypothesis' by first considering the prospect that extraterrestrial life would be discernible through the composition of a distant planet's atmosphere, and then turning to the implications of this idea for terrestrial life.[21]

---

[16] Siobhan Carroll, *An Empire of Air and Water: Uncolonizable Space in the British Imagination, 1750–1850* (Philadelphia: University of Pennsylvania Press, 2015), p. 12.
[17] Ibid., p. 130.   [18] Ibid., pp. 130–1.
[19] 'Atmosphere, n', def. 1a, *OED Online*, Oxford University Press, January 2018, oed.com/view/Entry/12552.
[20] R[obert] P[lot], 'The Natural History of Oxford-shire' (Oxford, 1677), 4; qtd in 'atmosphere, n', def. 1b, *OED Online*, Oxford University Press, January 2018, oed.com/view/Entry/12552.
[21] Tim Lenton, *Earth System Science: a Very Short Introduction* (Oxford University Press, 2016), p. 2.

In both cases, atmosphere delimits the internality of a distant body as perceived from outside. It is the substance through which we perceive what it would be like to be inside another world, and only then transfer that concept to our own. An exhalation implies that the exhaler is alive; it means that the heavenly body breathes. Atmosphere in this sense is neither internal nor external. The planet is recognisable as a separate object within, and yet never apart from, its 'gaseous envelope' 'filled with all manner of exhalations'. Viewing atmosphere as produced from within, rather than simply as a container, highlights the fact that it is both substance and space of interaction. These implications are made clear in later uses of the term to delimit the range of an object's influence, such as the range of a magnetic field. In Earth system science (ESS), the study of the planet as a single interconnected system, the atmosphere refers to the entirety of the gaseous layer that comprises Earth's border with outer space, filters and retains solar energy through the greenhouse effect, and provides the enabling conditions for all life. However, the notion of exhalation remains: the composition of the atmosphere is produced by the physical, chemical, and thermodynamic interaction of the biosphere, lithosphere, and hydrosphere. Life on Earth is enabled by the atmosphere that life on Earth creates, which is of course precisely the problem. We exist amidst others' exhalations, whether those others are human, animal, or machine.

Any act of reading occurs through a mixture of literary and literal atmosphere. Without oxygen, there can be no interpretation. However, this is true even in the absence of a living reader. There can be no music on the moon, because there is no atmosphere through which sound waves can travel. Pausing over such apparently obvious conditions of aesthetic experience can help us de-metaphorise the ubiquity of terms like climate and atmosphere within our understandings of culture. As Thomas Ford notes, the collapse between literal and literary atmosphere enacted by anthropogenic climate change is not an entirely novel phenomenon, but rather returns to the manner in which the term was first used in aesthetic or historical contexts, when the term's applicability to 'historical forms or processes' was 'not yet so clearly marked as metaphoric'.[22] On the contrary, when Romantic writers used words like 'climate' and 'atmosphere' to refer to 'an unarticulated totality of imaginative feeling', their use was largely literal and material', arising from the fact that 'they understood words to be

---

[22] Thomas H. Ford, 'Punctuating History circa 1800: the Air of *Jane Eyre*', in Tobias Menely and Jesse Oak Taylor (eds.), *Anthropocene Reading: Literary History in Geologic Times* (University Park: Pennsylvania State University Press, 2017), p. 86.

shaped bodies of air'.[23] The word that appeared on the page, in other words, retained a much closer approximation to the one spoken aloud, becoming a trace of authorial breath despite the fact that no direct causal connection could be posited between the two. Writing might not have literally reproduced the 'shaped body of air' to which it corresponded in speech, but was nonetheless designed expressly to recreate those shapes as exhalations from the body of the reader. This goes beyond the social practice of reading aloud common to pre- and early print literary cultures, because it highlights the persistence of orality within written literary form. As Ford demonstrates, the punctuation of Charlotte Brontë's *Jane Eyre* remains perched between the syntactic function it would come to serve in delimiting grammar and meaning and its residual of governing the respiration of an audible reader: 'There is an audibility to much eighteenth-century punctuation; when we read texts from that period, breathing at all the commas, a quiet respiratory patterning becomes perceptible. But punctuation lost this somatic and mimetic function throughout the nineteenth century, instead coming exclusively to mark abstract relationships of logic and grammar.'[24] In such 'silencing' of punctuation, we lose the bodily relation not only between reader and text but also between breath and thought retained in the double meaning of a word like 'inspiration', which means both to draw breath and to receive a powerful idea or motivation from outside oneself. Hence, Ford argues, the idea of a text as external inscription, or 'writing on the world', was never purely figurative. Rather, texts encode, and thus have the capacity to literally reproduce, the performative interaction between body, thought, and world in both author and reader. To read, in this sense, is to enact the body–respiration–word shaping action also performed by the author, even across great spans of time and space. This, in turn, brings us to the amorphousness and changeability of literary meaning.

Literary Atmosphere in the Anthropocene

Any work we read now is situated within the Anthropocene, regardless of where or when it was written. This is not to say that those important historical differences of original context cease to matter, but rather that the weight of subsequent history presses upon them, just as the weight of historical carbon emissions weighs upon us and defines the historical conditions of our existence. Like Walter Benjamin's ever-piling historical

---

[23] Ibid., p. 86.   [24] Ibid., p. 92.

catastrophe, the Anthropocene is an era in which history is, literally, accumulated in the atmosphere of the present, which in turn produces the conditions of future life.[25] Literary atmosphere registers, and enables us to think and talk about, setting in such counter-intuitive trans-historical terms, in part because it changes with historical conditions, affecting the mood in which we read. Understanding works of literature as *actors* in the Latourian sense both necessitates attention to their distinct material histories, and prohibits isolating them within the world of their initial composition. This property is further underlined in the context of the Anthropocene given that, as Ford puts it, 'writing must always be understood as writing on the world' insofar as any text – as also any event – is also 'so many kilograms of embodied CO_2'.[26] Charles Babbage's conception that 'the air itself is one vast library, on whose pages are forever written all that man has ever said or even whispered' is realised in the archives of polar ice through which scientists now read the material transcriptions of climates past.[27] In each of the above instances, atmosphere becomes a means of registering internality, whether the conditions of possibility within a given work, the shared 'sphere' of interpretation and experience that surrounds any given reader as she inhabits the storyworld of a given work, or the shared planetary sphere of Earth's atmosphere, in which all such events are ultimately enclosed. Comprising a sphere around both the book-as-object and the setting of the narrative it depicts, atmosphere also opens to the Earth system of which it is a part.

Atmosphere is the most obvious site at which the meaning-making system of a literary work corresponds to the Earth system. And yet the difficulty of interpreting that space of interconnection remains. Thus, in concluding this chapter, I want to return to my case study to illustrate how one might go about tracing (or at least acknowledging) a literary work's openness to the Earth system, and the benefits of doing so: an exercise I call Earth system poetics. What would it mean, then, to view *Wuthering Heights*'s 'atmospheric tumult' not simply as a manifestation of local climate as indicated by the 'provincial adjective' in the title, but also atmosphere as a singular, planetary entity thus situating it within the Earth system of which it is a part? What insights might such a reading offer into the ongoing systemic shift now known as the Anthropocene? Doing so means attending to the openness of the text itself, the way its

[25] Walter Benjamin, 'Theses on the Philosophy of History', in Hannah Arendt (ed.), *Illuminations*, trans. Harry Zohn (New York: Schocken, 1969), pp. 257–8.
[26] Ford, 'Punctuating History', p. 85.
[27] Charles Babbage, *The Ninth Bridgewater Treatise: a Fragment* (London: John Murray, 1837), p. 113.

imagined world extends beyond the specifically narrated events and locations included in its pages (that is, the expansiveness of its storyworld), the
circulation of the text itself as object, whether the ecological impact of its
production or the imaginative experiences it fosters in readers whose
associations with it Brontë couldn't have imagined, through the affor-
dances of its form, and particularly the radical openness of its world-
building, encoded in its title.

Taking an expansive view of the novel's storyworld begins with the
basic assumption that the setting described is part of a complete world,
the vast majority of which is never explicitly defined. Any divergence
between this implied fictive world and the actual world outside the text,
by contrast, would have to arise out of the novel. In the absence of
a specific description departing from the real world, that correspondence
between the two is to be assumed. At the same time, no specific relation
between the novel and entities that presumably exist within its fictive
world can be posited unless it connects to the described events or setting
in some way. For example, even though Prague is never mentioned in
Wuthering Heights, we can assume that it exists within the storyworld and
yet is hard to imagine having much to say about that fact, since the novel
does not establish that connection. This is why professional or 'serious'
readers generally refuse to acknowledge the expansiveness of the storyworld beyond narrated events: professors tend to snort or cringe when
students want to know what happens 'after' the end of a novel. Indulging
in such speculation verges towards the treatment of characters as 'real'
people that generations of narrative theorists have cautioned against.[28]
And yet, historicist readings are often premised on a similar move, as
when Elaine Freedgood traces the curtains in *Mary Barton* or mahogany
furniture in *Jane Eyre* into networks of production that can be assumed in
the fictive world because they existed in historical reality.[29] An atmospheric version of such a practice would acknowledge that the 'tumult'
actually extends around the globe and is partly archived in the polar ice,
and thus at least hypothetically legible as part of Babbage's atmospheric
'library', since the earth, air, and ocean are 'eternal witnesses' recording
'whatever motion communicated to any of their particles is communicated to all around it'.[30] Our view of the novel's world-building shifts, in

---

[28] Catherine Gallagher, 'The Rise of Fictionality', in Franco Moretti (ed.), *The Novel, Volume 1:
    History, Geography and Culture* (Princeton University Press, 2006), pp. 359–61.
[29] Elaine Freedgood, *The Ideas in Things: Fugitive Meaning in the Victorian Novel* (University of
    Chicago Press, 2006).
[30] Babbage, *Bridgewater Treatise*, p. 113.

other words, if we imagine the setting that is actually described as but a part of an expansive, interconnected totality.

Wuthering Heights is particularly explicit about invoking the openness of its fictive setting. Some of its most important locations are absences, such as the never-specified elsewhere into which Heathcliff disappears and from which he then returns transformed into a wealthy gentleman. Heathcliff's origins are made more explicit, but in ways that similarly gesture beyond the novel's ostensible setting in Yorkshire. Mr Earnshaw brings him home having found him as an apparent orphan on the streets of Liverpool, the centre of the British slave trade and thus a node from which the world of *Wuthering Heights* opens into that of *The Black Atlantic*.[31] This connection returns in an example that Babbage added to the second edition of *The Bridgewater Treatise*, in which he argued that the crimes of slavers throwing their living 'cargo' overboard to lighten the ship in a storm would be remembered 'when man and all his race shall have disappeared from the face of our planet', since 'every particle of the air still floating over the unpeopled earth . . . will record the cruel mandate of the tyrant'.[32] Dana Luciano has recently connected this hope for an atmospheric reckoning to climate scientists Simon Lewis and Mark Maslin's proposal that the Anthropocene be dated to 1610, when, they contend, a dip in CO_2 legible in ice-core data might be accounted for by the deaths of some fifty million Native Americans in the century following European conquest, with the near cessation of agriculture and resultant reforestation creating a carbon sink.[33] While this dating has been rejected as failing to meet stratigraphic criteria, Luciano notes that it nonetheless opens ground on which to

---

[31] Paul Gilroy, *The Black Atlantic: Modernity and Double Consciousness* (Cambridge, MA: Harvard University Press, 1995). The association between the two palpable absences that haunt the novel, Heathcliff's origins and the source of his wealth, produces a disturbing equation between them, insofar as the primary source for seemingly magical fortunes in the period was plantation slavery and the financial instruments surrounding it. See Ian Baucom, *Specters of the Atlantic: Finance Capital, Slavery, and the Philosophy of History* (Durham, NC: Duke University Press, 2005). While the novel does not confirm either that Heathcliff was the child of slaves or that he earned his fortune in a manner directly associated with the slave trade, both possibilities hover in the air around the narrative. See Maja-Lisa von Sneidern, '*Wuthering Heights* and the Liverpool Slave Trade', *ELH*, 62.1 (1995), 171–196.

[32] Babbage, *Bridgewater Treatise*, 2nd edn, qtd in Edward Hitchcock, *The Religion of Geology and Its Connected Sciences* (1857), p. 413, qtd in Dana Luciano, 'Romancing the Trace: Edward Hitchcock's Speculative Ichnology', in Menely and Taylor, (eds.), *Anthropocene Reading*, p. 113. I have detailed this trebly nested quoting because it underscores the diffusive quality whereby rippling words take on the very atmospheric quality of diffuse reference that Babbage is talking about, a point also echoed in the way a (presumably) spoken comment from Luciano's colleague ripples through both air and print.

[33] Simon L. Lewis and Mark A. Maslin, 'Defining the Anthropocene', *Nature*, 519 (March 2015), 171–80.

'speculate how this and other proto-environmental crisis factors, such as the toxicity of labor exploitation and racial violence' will become stratigraphically legible and 'begin to refine the kinds of material reading or sensing practices we use to detect these factors at present'.[34] In this context, she notes a colleague's response to Babbage's idea of an atmospheric archive: 'it feels right but it isn't true'.[35] One can't expect the air to detail the stories of past atrocities even if they remain materially present within it. And yet, in noting that the idea 'feels right', Luciano's colleague refers us back to the realm in which *literary* atmosphere operates: conditioning the mood or feeling of a work while also establishing the conditions of possibility within it – and, in this case, thus provoking precisely the written, representational testimony that it cannot inscribe on its own.

When it comes to the meaning-making encounter with a work of literature, for an occurrence to 'feel right' is for it to become possible, in the sense of being open to consideration in a state of suspended disbelief, like the ghost of a murdered father whose testimony will spark the subsequent action of the play. It is to be affected by the work, made to feel, and perhaps even be spurred to act in the world outside the text. In this regard, the question becomes less whether Emily Brontë imagined Heathcliff as African, or whether her original audience would have perceived him as black, but rather that the global history of imperial conquest and its alignment with the emergence of the Anthropocene coalesce around her novel, becoming part of the atmospheric tumult of history to which its events are subjected and to which they continue to speak. Atmospheric reading is thus a way of attending to the radical openness of literary texts, not merely to the ways in which they encode the climates of their inscription but also remain open, accruing new meanings, invoking new associations, and assembling new communities across time and space.

---

[34] Luciano, 'Romancing the Trace', p. 113.　　[35] Ibid., p. 112.

CHAPTER 3

The Seasons

Tess Somervell

European climates have been characterised as divisible into four seasons since at least the fifth century BCE, when Nonnus' Greek poem *Dionysiaca* identified four seasons instead of the older traditional three. The same four-part model may have emerged several centuries earlier in China.[1] The structure seems to reflect somewhat accurately the annual patterns of European weather, so the convention of four seasons of spring, summer, autumn, and winter has stuck. The seasons are one of the most prevalent means by which literary texts and other artworks engage with and represent climate, and have been consistently used as motif, metaphor, and structuring device. This chapter explores the implications of this seasonal perspective of climate, and particularly literary texts' use of the seasons as a domain for interrogating the interface between nature and culture.

Seasons are caused by the tilt in Earth's axis, which means that the sun's rays shine either more or less directly on each hemisphere as the planet completes its orbit. Seasons are also cultural constructs. They emerge, as Nick Groom puts it, as 'a rough compromise between nature and culture: between those things that happen independently of human engagement, such as the annual summer solstice, and those things that are dependent on that engagement – naming, recognizing, and celebrating the solstice as being somehow significant'.[2] There are two 'official' dating systems for the seasons: the mid-twentieth-century meteorological calendar, and the older astronomical calendar based on the solstices and equinoxes. However, for most people across history the seasons have been recorded with what Jan Golinski describes as 'a flexible attitude to temporal measurement, a way of handling time that was integrated with the seasonal routines of rural life

---

[1] See William Edward Soothill, *The Hall of Light: a Study of Early Chinese Kingship* (1951; Cambridge: James Clarke and Company, 2002), p. 58.
[2] Nick Groom, *The Seasons: an Elegy for the Passing of the Year* (London: Atlantic, 2013), p. 32.

and adaptable to the agricultural circumstances of particular locales'.[3] A season could be defined by trends in the weather, observed behaviours of animals or plants, human activities, or even human emotions and states of mind. These different features are both the effects and the occasions of seasons.

The various nuanced interactions between these different seasonal features form the material of seasons literature from antiquity to the present. This chapter uses examples from canonical and influential texts to draw out some of the varied ways in which literature has engaged with the seasons and utilised them as tools for interrogating the relationship between humans and their environment. It argues that, whether exploring the ethical and aesthetic implications of a cyclically changing climate (the subject of the first half of this chapter), or the emotional and psychological associations that have accumulated around particular seasons (the subject of the second half), seasons literature asks important questions about the human perspective of climate. Are individuals' perspectives shaped predominantly by the influence of the natural world, cultural custom, or their own feelings? Do we project ethical and aesthetic judgements on to the seasons, or do these values inhere in the seasons themselves? The richest literary engagements with the seasons not only ask these questions, but question whether we can make such distinctions between nature and culture at all.

The Cycle of the Seasons

As Chapter 1 of this volume has shown, there is already a temporal dimension to the concept of climate. The seasonal structure further supplements the various timescales of climate with a specifically cyclical (rather than linear) model of time. If climate is, in Mike Hulme's words, 'an idea that helps stabilise the human experience of weather and allows humans to live culturally with their weather', the seasons are a version of this idea that explicitly incorporates change into its version of stability.[4] The seasonal perspective is one of change-within-constancy. The implications of this perspective for our understanding of and attitude towards climate are revealed and explored in literature.

---

[3] Jan Golinski, *British Weather and the Climate of Enlightenment* (University of Chicago Press, 2007), p. 93.
[4] Mike Hulme, *Weathered: Cultures of Climate* (London: Sage, 2017), p. xv.

The most influential classical literary texts depict the changeableness of the seasons as a product and sign of human sin. In *Metamorphoses* I (*c.* 8 AD), Ovid describes a past Golden Age in which 'ver erat aeternum' ('Spring was everlasting').⁵ This is followed by the Silver Age, in which Jove, to make life harder for this Age's inferior race of men, 'shortened the bounds of the old-time spring, and through winter, summer, variable autumn, and brief spring completed the year in four seasons'.⁶ As a result, natural produce was no longer available all year round, and man had to work the earth in order to survive. The notion that the qualities of the climate might be attributable to the bad behaviour of humans might not look so strange in an era of man-made climate change. The idea that seasonal change is a punishment, however, might be harder to grasp in modern societies which frequently cultivate a nostalgia for seasonality, even as they develop technology and infrastructure to drastically limit its effects.

Later, this classical vision of eternal spring would be adopted into Christian accounts of prelapsarian nature. In Dante's *Purgatorio* (1472), Matelda explains that the classical poets who sang of the Golden Age perhaps dreamed of Eden: 'Here was man guiltless; here / Perpetual spring, and every fruit.'⁷ Milton's Eden is also one of 'Eternal Spring' and perpetual harvest: 'All *Autumn* pil'd, though *Spring* and *Autumn* here / Danc'd hand in hand.'⁸ Milton's American contemporary, Anne Bradstreet, presumably under the influence of the famous New England fall, argued for autumn as the season of Paradise, 'For then in Eden was not only seen, / Boughs full of leaves, or fruits unripe or green ... But trees with goodly fruits replenished'.⁹ But the trope of Paradise as a perpetual spring, only embellished with the happier qualities of autumn, was the more persistent. For Milton as for Ovid, the cycle in which each season is separated only comes about after a transition to a new and lesser Age. In *Paradise Lost* (1667) after the Fall the sun is instructed to move in order to bring in 'change / Of Seasons to each Clime; else had the Spring / Perpetual smiled on Earth' (X.677–9). Seasonal change represents imbalance, disorder, and

---

⁵ Ovid, *Metamorphoses, Volume I: Books 1–8*, trans. Frank Justus Miller and ed. G. P. Goold, Loeb Classical Library 42 (Cambridge, MA: Harvard University Press, 1916), pp. 9–10.
⁶ Ibid., p. 11.
⁷ Dante Alighieri, *The Divine Comedy*, trans. Henry Francis Cary (Ware, Hertfordshire: Wordsworth Editions, 2009), p. 272, XXVIII.147–8.
⁸ John Milton, *Paradise Lost*, ed. Barbara K. Lewalski (Oxford: Blackwell, 2009), p. 99, IV.268, p. 133, V.394–5. Hereafter cited parenthetically as line references.
⁹ Anne Bradstreet, 'The Four Seasons', in *The Works of Anne Bradstreet*, ed. Jeannine Hensley (Cambridge, MA: Belknap Press of Harvard University Press, 2010), p. 75.

uncomfortable extremes, and serves as a reminder of its cause, which was our sin.

However, there are multiple inconsistencies in Milton's account of the seasons, including references to seasons existing before the Fall.[10] The reason for these contradictions is Milton's conflicting sources. He, along with other Renaissance humanists, was influenced by the classical myths of the seasonless Golden Age, but in Genesis the seasons are part of God's design from the beginning. On the fourth day of creation, 'God said, Let there be lights in the firmament of the heaven to divide the day from the night; and let them be for signs, and for seasons, and for days, and years.'[11] (Milton paraphrases this in his account of the creation in Book VII.) The Hebrew word translated as 'seasons', *moadim*, might mean 'appointed times' or 'festivals' rather than the four seasons, but the Bible gives no account of the seasons being created at a later time. As a result, many early Christian texts interpreted the seasonal cycle as a part of God's benign creation.[12] Later, medieval seasons literature continued to celebrate the seasonal cycle, and is characterised, according to Rosemond Tuve, by a basic belief 'in a *good* Nature'.[13] The constancy of the seasons, Tuve writes, 'is in itself the refutation of that all-devouring Mutability of which the seasons were the sign and synonym'.[14] The orderly repetitiveness of the seasons troubled the claim that they represented the disorderliness or corruption of nature.

It is possible, therefore, to trace a vague narrative of portrayals of the seasonal cycle, from classical (negative), through early Christian and medieval (positive), Renaissance humanist (negative), and then a return in the Enlightenment to the positive portrayal. But this is too simplistic, because in every period there are examples of seasons literature – such as Virgil's *Georgics*, Chaucer's 'Franklin's Tale', and Milton's *Paradise Lost* – that mediate between the two perspectives: that of the reassuring constancy of the seasons, and that of their disturbing mutability. Whether they interpret it as something positive or negative, what is consistent is writers' use of the

[10] See S. Viswanathan, 'Milton and the Seasons' Difference', *Studies in English Literature, 1500–1900*, 13 (1973), 127–33.
[11] Genesis 1:14, *The Bible*, introd. Robert Carroll and Stephen Prickett (Oxford University Press, 1998), Authorised King James Version.
[12] See Clarence J. Glacken, *Traces on the Rhodian Shore: Nature and Culture in Western Thought from Ancient Times to the End of the Eighteenth Century* (Berkeley: University of California Press, 1967), pp. 177–9.
[13] Rosemond Tuve, *Seasons and Months: Studies in a Tradition of Middle English Poetry* (Cambridge: D. S. Brewer, 1933), p. 44.
[14] Ibid., p. 45.

seasonal cycle to represent and express broader cultural judgements of nature.

The combined variability *and* familiarity of the seasons has made them a useful tool for writers who draw comparisons and distinctions across places and times. The appeal of the four seasons model can be seen in its enduring use to describe climates which do not clearly follow such a cycle. Foreign climates were frequently described by Western writers in terms of static, perpetual seasons: not the eternally pleasant springs or autumns of Paradise, but interminably hot summers (in Africa and India) or cold winters. In the Arctic circle, for example, 'WINTER holds his unrejoicing Court' all year long.[15] In these instances, seasonal change is inferred as a marker not of human sin and nature's hostility, but of a moderated, fertile, and desirable climate. Alternatively, of course, Western colonialists have simply imported the four-season model and applied it to climates for which it is inappropriate, such as Australia.[16] Defining a foreign climate in terms of the European seasons might insist upon the foreign place's likeness to 'home', or it might define its difference in terms that are nevertheless familiar and Euro-centric.

As a tool for comparing different places, the seasonal cycle has its clear limitations as well as its utilities. Its effectiveness as a tool for comparing the same place across time, however, has made it a favourite structuring device for artists, who have used it to organise themes and narratives. The seasons invite the mental division of time into yearly rounds, not measured necessarily from January to December but from, say, the start of spring to the end of winter, and divided into four roughly equal parts. Many narratives have been structured in this way, from Roman mosaics to paintings such as Nicolas Poussin's *The Four Seasons* (1660–4), from poems like Pope's *Pastorals* (1709) to musical concerti like Vivaldi's *Four Seasons* (1725), from novels like Toni Morrison's *The Bluest Eye* (1970) to Hollywood movies like *La La Land* (2016) (despite the climate of Los Angeles appearing almost uniform across the film's four seasonal chapters).

Just as frequently, however, a season invites closer association with previous iterations of that same season than with the different seasons surrounding it. This perspective of seasonal time forges narratives that overleap much of the time that has actually passed. Examples of works of

---

[15] James Thomson, *The Seasons*, ed. James Sambrook (Oxford: Clarendon Press, 1981), p. 244, 'Winter', 895. Hereafter cited parenthetically as line references.

[16] Chris O'Brien, 'Rethinking Seasons: Changing Climate, Changing Time' in Tom Bristow and Thomas H. Ford (eds.), *A Cultural History of Climate Change* (Abingdon: Routledge, 2016), pp. 38–54.

literature that employ this perspective of seasonal time include *Sir Gawain and the Green Knight*, the action of which takes place over two Christmas periods, and William Wordsworth's poem 'The Two April Mornings', in which one spring day invites reminiscence of a similar one thirty years before.

There is, then, flexibility in the perception of time offered by the seasonal cycle. One seeming consistency is the seasons' association with a sense of the ongoing flow of time. This is the principle underlying Shakespeare's use of seasons imagery in his sonnets about ageing: 'For never-resting time leads summer on / To hideous winter'.[17] But the idea of the seasons also gives rise to concepts of abstracted individual seasons which, in their perpetual recurrence, come to appear timeless or eternal even though they sporadically manifest within that flow of time. The abstraction by which each season is understood as timeless must be distinguished from the 'eternal spring' of the Golden Age or the endless winters of the Arctic regions. One of the timeless qualities of each abstracted season is, paradoxically, its transitoriness. This tension is often registered in seasons literature.

Thus, the autumn in Keats's ode 'To Autumn' is characterised by both movement and stillness.[18] The 'Season of mists and mellow fruitfulness' in this poem is both the specific autumn of 1819 and an abstraction that outlasts this iteration of the season. Personified Autumn is depicted sitting, sleeping, 'steady', and 'patient', untroubled by passing time and history. 'Who hath not seen thee oft amid thy store?' the poet asks, invoking the season's presence and availability across years and generations; but that 'oft' inscribes the alternative temporal perspective of occasionality. 'Sometimes whoever seeks abroad may find thee': those some-times are the moments when autumn appears to human perception, in the form of the various signs in nature (fruits, animal behaviours, wind) and culture (ploughed furrows, oozing cider presses) by which we recognise the season. In the final line, gathering swallows prepare to migrate for winter.

Keats is building upon a longer tradition of seasons poetry, most overtly James Thomson's four-part poem *The Seasons* (1726–30). Thomson's poem offers the most sustained engagement with the implications of viewing nature and climate through the lens of the seasonal cycle. The seasons are, he writes,

---

[17] William Shakespeare, Sonnet 5, in *The Complete Works of William Shakespeare*, ed. Peter Alexander (2006; London: Collins, 2010), p. 1363. Hereafter cited parenthetically as line references.

[18] John Keats, 'To Autumn', in Keats, *The Major Works*, ed. Elizabeth Cook (1990; Oxford University Press, 2008), pp. 324–35.

A simple Train,
Yet so delightful mix'd, with such kind Art,
Such Beauty and Beneficence combin'd;
Shade, unperceiv'd, so softening into Shade;
And all so forming an harmonious Whole;
That, as they still succeed, they ravish still.   ('Hymn', 21–6)

The seasons form a 'Train', an ongoing movement through time, each one leading inexorably to the next. The continuousness of the train, however, results in an impression of stillness: 'as they still succeed, they ravish still'. Thomson's seasons are always in motion, 'coming', 'flowing', 'turning'. But even though each iteration of the season must come and go, it is nevertheless continuous with past and future iterations. In 'Winter', for example, it is emphatically the *same* season that presides over young Thomson wandering in the snow in his 'chearful Morn of Life' (7), the adult Thomson sitting reading in his study 'To chear the Gloom' (431), Sir Hugh Willoughby and 'his hapless Crew' freezing to death in 1554 (932), and every hypothetical swain who ever got lost on a cold night.

For Thomson, it is this combination of constancy and change that renders the 'Beauty and Beneficence' of the 'harmonious Whole' that is the seasonal cycle. This is despite the fact that Thomson, like Milton and Ovid, frames the seasons as a punishment for man's sin. Whereas 'great Spring, before, / Green'd all the Year' ('Spring', 320–1), after the Flood 'The Seasons since have … / Oppress'd a broken World' (317–18). By the Hymn at the end of the poem, however, this 'inward-eating Change' ('Spring', 333) has transformed into a glorious sign of 'the *varied* God' ('Hymn', 2), whose 'Skill' and 'Force' (21) are evidenced in his control, like a conductor, over the harmony of the 'simple Train'.

Used as an artistic structure, the seasonal cycle becomes something to be judged aesthetically (like a musical harmony) as well as morally. In this way, art influences as well as reflects a culture's perception of the seasonal cycle not only as good or bad, but as a pattern with aesthetic merits or demerits. Our narratives have been shaped by our seasonal climate, but they have also shaped our perspective of that climate. One might argue that Milton's nostalgia for an eternal spring is related to the cold climate of the so-called Little Ice Age in which he wrote, but it has as much to do with his education and reading. Thomson in turn constructed his 'delightful' seasonal cycle out of various sources including Milton, and then this rendering affected subsequent perspectives. 'The reader of the *Seasons*', as Samuel

Johnson puts it, 'wonders that he never saw before what Thomson shews him, and that he never yet has felt what Thomson impresses.'[19]

To Everything There Is a Season

The seasonal cycle has been freighted with cultural, moral, and aesthetic value since its earliest appearance in literature. But each individual season, elevated through abstraction to the status of eternal type (and often personified divinity), has also accumulated its own various associations.

'To every thing there is a season', states the Book of Ecclesiastes, 'and a time to every purpose under the heaven . . . a time to plant, and a time to pluck up that which is planted.'[20] The English word 'season', as well as the equivalents in many other European languages, derives from the Latin *sationem*, meaning the act of sowing seeds. Accordingly, in classical seasons literature and art the seasons are most often invoked in order to delineate different works of human agricultural labour. The archetypal examples are Hesiod's Greek *Works and Days* (*c.* 700 BCE) and its Latin counterpart, Virgil's *Georgics* (29 BCE). '[A]s mighty Zeus sends the autumn rain', writes Hesiod, 'So at that time be mindful and cut wood, a seasonable work.'[21]

But the seasons not only set the times to plant and reap. Ecclesiastes continues: 'A time to weep, and a time to laugh . . . A time to love, and a time to hate.'[22] Seasons are associated not only with particular activities, but with particular emotional or psychic states. Here the term 'affect' is useful, because it incorporates a wider range of states than are usually compassed under 'emotions' (e.g. arousal, reflectiveness, trauma), and because it invokes the bodily, prediscursive dimension to emotion that so much seasons literature insists upon. The modern affliction, 'seasonal affective disorder' (SAD), testifies to its aptness. These associations between seasons and affects have produced notions of seasonal determinism at least as old as theories of geographical climate determinism. Spring is the season in which to fall in love; summer is a season of leisure and perhaps licentiousness; autumn is the season of maturity, memory, and calm melancholy; winter is the season in which to retreat, fear, and lament, but also to be merry and cosy.

---

[19] Samuel Johnson, *The Lives of the Poets*, ed. John H. Middendorf, vol. XXIII of *The Yale Edition of the Works of Samuel Johnson*, gen. ed. Robert DeMaria, Jr. (New Haven, CT: Yale University Press, 2010), p. 1292.

[20] Ecclesiastes 3:1–2, *The Bible*.

[21] Hesiod, *Works and Days*, in *Theogony. Works and Days. Testimonia*, ed. and trans. Glenn W. Most, Loeb Classical Library 57 (Cambridge, MA: Harvard University Press, 2007), p. 121.

[22] Ecclesiastes 3:4–8, *The Bible*.

In Ecclesiastes, it is God who sets these seasons and their corresponding 'purposes'. In other discourses, it is less clear who, or what, makes the contract. The seasonal climate dictates the times to plant and harvest. But does the climate dictate the seasons to weep and laugh, or do humans? Often the most interesting usages of these seasonal mood motifs are those which interrogate them: texts that explore the processes by which seasons produce affects; characters who recognise that their moods might be out of sync with seasonal expectations; and instances when writers consider the possibility that culture as well as nature has shaped our emotional responses to, or expectations for, particular seasons.

The perceived correlation between seasons and affects has led understandably to associations between seasons and genres of literature. This effect can be seen emerging across various cultures in the medieval period: in northern Europe, for example, the dark nights of winter became associated with the ghost story;[23] in Japan, only mild spring and autumn were deemed fit subjects for high court poetry.[24] In France and Italy, and later England, the most notable case is that of spring, particularly the later spring months of April and May. Spring's aphrodisiacal effects made it the season of choice for romance and love lyric.

Medieval writers were keen to emphasise that this association between spring and love or lust was not only a literary convention, but had its basis in nature, to which humans were as susceptible as plants and animals. The *Roman de la Rose* (c. 1230), which, Tuve writes, 'crystallized . . . the phraseology in which the seasons were to appear for a long time to come, in many contexts and in many languages', opens with a dream of springtime:[25]

> I dreamed that I was filled with joy in May, the amorous month, when everything rejoices . . . The birds, silent while they were cold and the weather hard and bitter, become so gay in May, in the serene weather, that their hearts are filled with joy until they must sing or burst. It is then that the nightingale is constrained to sing and make his noise . . . and that young men must become gay and amorous in the sweet, lovely weather. He has a very hard heart who does not love in May, when he hears the birds on the branches, singing their heart-sweet songs. And so I dreamed one night that I was in that delicious season when everything is stirred by love . . .[26]

---

[23] P. S. Langeslag, *Seasons in the Literatures of the Medieval North* (Cambridge: D. S. Brewer, 2015).

[24] Haruo Shirane, *Japan and the Culture of the Four Seasons: Nature, Literature, and the Arts* (New York: Columbia University Press, 2012).

[25] Tuve, *Seasons and Months*, p. 111.

[26] Guillaume de Lorris and Jean de Meun, *The Romance of the Rose*, trans. Charles Dahlberg (1971; Hanover, NH: University Press of New England, 1986), pp. 31–2.

The passivity of both humans and birds is stressed. The bird 'must sing' (*chanter par force*) in response to spring, and young men are equally constrained to love. The affective response seems to be based at once in the body's biological reaction to the weather and the mind's aesthetic judgement; the 'heart' is a convenient catch-all organ for either type of response. The young man becomes amorous because he feels the 'sweet, lovely weather' *and* hears the birds' 'heart-sweet songs'. By conflating the aesthetic and bodily responses, Guillaume de Lorris passes over any question of competition or tension between nature and culture in the production of affect: art is nature, and vice versa, and a love poem is as natural a response to the season as birdsong. This kind of seasonal-deterministic thinking poses a potential challenge to anthropocentrism, emphasising as it does the entanglements between humans and non-human nature.

Some later writers who took up these traditional seasonal-affective-generic correlations expressed less confidence about their neatness. Spenser's *The Shepheardes Calender* (1579) appears, at first glance, to reiterate the same conventions. The poem's mysterious commentator, 'E.K.' (who may be Spenser himself), observes that the poet deliberately blurs the distinction between the characters' bodies and their surroundings. He describes the lines in 'Februarie' on 'the breme winter with hamfred browes, / Full of wrinckles and frostie furrowes' as 'A verye excellent and liuely description of Winter, so as may bee indifferently taken, eyther for old Age, or for Winter season'.[27] Good seasons literature, for E.K., is that which naturalises the correspondences between seasonal weather and human conditions. E.K.'s note, however, draws attention to Spenser's conscious aestheticisation of the seasons. The emphasis in the *Calender* on the craft of the poet – both Spenser and his various narrators – and the poet's role in interpreting and depicting the seasons, raises questions about the possible artificiality of such seasonal-affective correlations. In 'Januarye', for example, Colin Clout 'compareth his carefull case to the sadde season of the yeare, to the frostie ground, to the frosen trees, and to his owne winterbeaten flocke' ('Argvment'). 'Thou barrein ground', sings Colin, 'whome winters wrath hath wasted, / Art made a myrrhour, to behold my plight' (19–20). But precisely who or what has 'made' nature a mirror? Is it God, a responsive and empathetic Nature, Colin's own mind, or Spenser's imagination?

---

[27] Edmund Spenser, *The Shorter Poems*, ed. Richard A. McCabe (London: Penguin, 1999), pp. 42 (ll. 43–4), 48. Hereafter cited parenthetically as line references.

Later in the *Shepheardes Calender*, characters who find neat correlations between their feelings and the season are joined by those for whom the season is out of joint. The harmony between season and affect falters. 'Is not thilke the mery moneth of May', asks Palinode, 'When loue ladds masken in fresh aray? / How falles it then, we no merrier bene, / Ylike as others, girt in gawdy greene?' (1–4). The seasonal-affective correlation is invoked as received wisdom, but the influence of the season cannot necessarily overcome pre-existing emotional states. Alison A. Chapman has shown that the poem explores contemporary debates around the competing Julian and Gregorian calendars; it appears that the seasonal-affective cycle is another calendar that Spenser wants to hint is open to reform.[28]

Frequently, it is awareness of individuals' varying levels of susceptibility to seasonal determinism that leads to reflection on the nature of the correlation between season and affect. Even Lorris acknowledges that a 'very hard heart' may resist the influence of the season. The narrator of Shakespeare's sonnets finds that the moving cycle of seasons accords with his sense of time passing, but the individual seasons do not always match his emotions. 'How like a winter hath my absence been / From thee', he laments in Sonnet 97, 'What freezings have I felt, what dark days seen!' But this winter is a state of mind, not nature: 'And yet this time removed was summer's time'. The autumn which followed was 'big with rich increase . . . / Yet this abundant issue seemed to me / But hope of orphans, and unfathered fruit'.[29] His response to each season is shaped by his sorrow:

> For summer and his pleasures wait on thee,
> And, thou away, the very birds are mute:
> Or, if they sing, 'tis with so dull a cheer,
> That leaves look pale, dreading the winter's near.

Here the sonnet corrects its claim that the narrator's sorrow can prevent the very birds from singing. The natural signs of the seasons persist in spite of the observer's feelings. What is altered is their affective significance. The narrator is able to reinterpret the seasonal imagery, although he is aware that he is going against custom.

Both Spenser and Shakespeare accept that the seasonal-affective-generic conventions which they resist are the norm. In Spenser's 'Nouember',

[28] Alison A. Chapman, 'The Politics of Time in Edmund Spenser's English Calendar', *Studies in English Literature, 1500–1900*, 42 (2002), 1–24.
[29] Shakespeare, Sonnet 97, *The Complete Works of William Shakespeare*.

Thenot requests a love song and is scolded, 'now nis the time of merimake . . . / The mornefull Muse in myrth now list ne mask, / As shee was wont in youngth and sommer dayes' (9–20). Shakespeare's narrator laments in Sonnet 98 that 'nor the lays of birds, nor the sweet smell / Of different flowers . . . Could make me any summer's story tell'.[30] He knows what a 'summer's story' should ordinarily be. However, references to the Muse and to the particular genres associated with each season emphasise the artistry of seasons literature, which so often depicts itself as a spontaneous response to nature in which the poet is 'constrained to sing' like Lorris's nightingale. When the poet is out of tune with the seasons in the sonnets and *Shepheardes Calender*, it is not clear whether the fault lies in the individual whose perception has been distorted, or in the ubiquity and inflexibility of tradition.

For poets in the eighteenth century who wanted to be good empiricists, discovering and cultivating harmony between seasonal non-human nature and one's affective and aesthetic response became an ethical imperative. An improper response to birds and flowers like that in Shakespeare's sonnets signified the personal failure of allowing one's circumstances to cloud perception. In 'On Winter' (1748), Mary Leapor argues that weather's effects on human and non-human bodies gives natural rise to a season's aesthetic dimension. She describes the suffering of humans, animals, and trees, and asks whether poetry itself is appropriate to the season:

> Say gentle Muses, say, is this a Time
> To sport with Poesy and laugh in Rhyme;
> While the chill'd Blood, that hath forgot to glide,
> Steals through its Channels in a lazy Tide:
> And how can *Phœbus*, who the Muse refines,
> Smooth the dull Numbers when he seldom shines.[31]

Leapor's insistence upon natural realities is not a rejection of cultural seasonal associations, only a critique of improper ones. She advocates a particular aesthetic response to the season, albeit one that cannot, or should not, find expression in the refined and florid lines of Augustan poetry. Leapor's own response, framed as an honest empirical reaction to 'shiv'ring Nature', is of course shaped by social factors too: she is a labouring-class writer criticising literary culture's detachment from working people's realities.

---

[30] Shakespeare, Sonnet 98, *The Complete Works of William Shakespeare*.
[31] Mary Leapor, 'On Winter', *Poems upon Several Occasions* (London: J. Roberts, 1748), pp. 257–8.

Many Romantic-period writers would share Leapor's doubt about poetry's capacity to respond appropriately to nature or human suffering. Wordsworth's solution was not to disclaim poetry altogether, but to theorise a supposedly 'new' poetics that stayed closer to its 'natural' roots, and which would be 'the image of man *and* nature'.[32] Since so much Romantic writing is interested in exploring the 'dim sympathies' between the mind and the external world, the seasons remain a pertinent theme in this period.[33] Taking cues from those eighteenth-century poets they deemed to have been most successful as nature writers (notably Thomson, Gray, and Cowper), Romantic writers on the seasons aimed to produce a form of culture that did not necessarily corrupt the perception; as natural and instinctive as the birdsong in the *Roman de la Rose*, it could similarly lead its readers/listeners to a proper response to and appreciation of the season.

A quintessential example is the poetry of John Clare, whose *Shepherd's Calendar* (1827) reworks the self-conscious and often tense aestheticism of Spenser's calendar by blending the natural, cultural, and affective qualities of each month and season into one Thomsonian 'harmonious Whole'. Clare makes no distinction between each category of seasonal attribute. Within 'October', for example, the 'lone bards mellancholy way' appears alongside close natural observation ('the sear leaves on the blackning lea'), reference to humans' local traditions ('the peasants christmass keeping cheer'), and indeed aesthetic judgements ('Like to a map the landscape lies') and allusions to earlier literature.[34] The effect is that culture, both high and low, comes to look like nature, and nature like culture. The human 'nutters rustling in the yellow woods' are hardly distinguishable from the squirrels 'Picking the brown nuts from the yellow leams' a few lines later.[35] Both are seemingly instinctive creatures preparing for the change to winter, and they assume a kind of mutual solidarity which, again, resists anthropocentrism. Yet their activities are also romanticised by the poet's cultured perspective as 'secret toils oer winter dreams'.[36]

Romantic writers frequently idealised the interactions between nature, rural culture, and literature, harking back to the medieval romance

---

[32] William Wordsworth, 'Preface to *Lyrical Ballads*', in Wordsworth, *The Major Works*, ed. Stephen Gill (1984; Oxford University Press, 2008), p. 605, my emphasis.

[33] Samuel Taylor Coleridge, 'Frost at Midnight', in *The Major Works*, ed. H. J. Jackson (1985; Oxford University Press, 2008), p. 87.

[34] John Clare, *The Shepherd's Calendar*, ed. Eric Robinson, Geoffrey Summerfield, and David Powell, 2nd edn (Oxford University Press, 2014), pp. 111–15.

[35] Ibid., p. 112.   [36] Ibid.

tradition for which 'Romanticism' was named. But expressions of uncertainty over the proper or desirable balance of these different factors in our perception of the seasons did not cease in the Romantic period. In Jane Austen's *Persuasion* (1817), for example, Anne Elliot longs for 'the influence so sweet and so sad of the autumnal months in the country' which accord with her temperament.[37] But her enjoyment of the season, and, we might surmise, her interpretation of it as sweet and sad, is mediated by literature:

> Her pleasure in the walk must arise from the exercise and the day, from the view of the last smiles of the year upon the tawny leaves, and withered hedges, and from repeating to herself some few of the thousand poetical descriptions extant of autumn, that season of peculiar and inexhaustible influence on the mind of taste and tenderness, that season which had drawn from every poet, worthy of being read, some attempt at description, or some lines of feeling.[38]

Invoking 'poetical descriptions' in almost the same breath as 'tawny leaves' implies an equivalence between the natural and the cultural factors at work in seasonal determinism. But this is not Clare's seamless simultaneity of nature and culture; Austen does raise the question of which has 'drawn' the other. The season exerts its influence, but only upon the 'mind of taste', which has presumably been formed by education as well as by natural aptitude. Autumn draws out 'lines of feeling' from the poets, but those lines in turn shape – and not only reflect – the feelings of subsequent readers. There is an undertone of cynicism in the reference to 'the thousand poetical descriptions' which implies that our 'view' of the seasons has become trite. Austen mocks her own clichéd use of autumn as well as Anne's predictable tendency to identify with a season associated with fading beauty.

For Austen, like Spenser and Shakespeare, the aestheticisation of the seasons draws attention to the processes by which nature is 'made a mirror' of human affects, and the result is a faint trace of scepticism about the naturalness of the correlation. For other writers, like Lorris, Thomson, and Clare, the fact that we cannot find a clear root for seasonal-affective correlations in either nature or culture is not an indictment of man's thraldom to convention, but a reason to celebrate the interconnectedness of the universe. Attitudes towards the seasons and our relationship with them fluctuate with changes in other areas of culture and changes in the

---

[37] Jane Austen, *Persuasion*, ed. James Kinsley and Deirdre Shauna Lynch (Oxford University Press, 2004), p. 32.
[38] Ibid., p. 71.

climate itself. However, the continuities and trends in seasons literature across different periods and genres are as striking as the differences.

Today, many humans' lives are barely affected by seasonal temperature change or agricultural cycles. But seasons literature from earlier periods asks many questions that are pertinent to our relationship with the seasons and climate today. Does human behaviour determine climate as much as climate determines human behaviour? What are the cultural and personal circumstances that might make us more or less susceptible to different interpretations of our environment? Is culture, particularly art, necessarily removed from nature? Of all our conceptions and measurements of climate, the seasons invite these questions most overtly and insistently, because they have from their earliest theorisation been closely bound up with human thoughts, actions, and feelings.

CHAPTER 4

Climatic Agency in the Classical Age

Daryn Lehoux

From at least the fifth century BCE, most educated Greeks and Romans saw themselves as living on a spherical Earth. Two centuries later, estimates for its size put it at more or less the right order of magnitude (Eratosthenes having come up with a remarkably accurate value that would be debated, on and off, until after Columbus). And some time before Ptolemy in the second century CE, and possibly six or seven centuries before then,[1] astronomers and geographers had figured out that if one went far enough to the north or south, one would eventually encounter a zone that had twenty-four hours of daylight in the summer months and twenty-four hours of darkness in the winter. Greek speakers had settled from Crimea to North Africa, and from Gaul to Afghanistan (the latter briefly). They not only had a wide range of latitudes from which to observe the differences in the heavens that would suggest a spherical Earth, they also had a remarkably wide range of experiences with climate and its effects on plants and peoples. By Ptolemy's day at the height of the Roman empire, the world had been mapped from the Hebrides to Ethiopia, Morocco to Vietnam.[2]

It is in this context that we see two parallel streams of thinking about regional climates, one rooted in astronomy and geography, the other in medicine and anthropology. The astronomico-geographic approach begins with the idea that the spherical Earth can be divided up from north to south into *klimata*, bands of latitude that share similar qualities, other

---

[1] Diogenes Laertius tells us of a certain Bion, 'a follower of Democritus and a mathematician', οὗτος πρῶτος εἶπεν εἶναί τινας οἰκήσεις ἔνθα γίνεσθαι ἐξ μηνῶν τὴν νύκτα καὶ ἐξ τὴν ἡμέραν ('he was the first to say that there are certain regions in which the night is six months long and the day six [months]'), DL 4.58; *Lives of the Eminent Philosophers*, ed. Tiziano Dorandi (Cambridge University Press, 2013). All translations are the author's unless otherwise indicated.

[2] The accuracy of the farther parts of Asia drops off noticeably, but the rough shapes and relative sizes of the Malay and Indochinese peninsulas were certainly known. Trade (via intermediaries) with China, India, and even what is today Indonesia was flourishing.

60

things being equal.[3] But in medical and anthropological works, climates are treated according to a much wider range of factors and with much more specificity. Individual cities might be discussed with respect to their climates, the winds that strike them, the rivers that water them, their altitude, their vegetation, how unusual weather patterns affect them, and more. These factors were often of paramount importance in much ancient medical thinking – the local climate often was seen to have a strongly deterministic effect on human constitutions and health – as well as ancient conceptions of the differences among peoples and cultures. Part of what made Aethiopians look different from Romans, for example, was the burning-hot climate in which they lived. In what follows, I will treat the two streams separately before returning at the end of the chapter to the factors that unite them into a coherent view on climate and weather.

The Geographer's *Klimata*

Ancient geography had much to do with ancient astronomy. It was the vault of the sky that first was divided up into lines of latitude and longitude or that had tropics and poles, and it was only later that these features were projected down on to the Earth in order to talk about the characteristics of, and locations on, the smaller sphere inhabited by people. Aristotle is perhaps the earliest attestation we have for the division of the Earth into *klimata*, 'climates'.[4] In Book II of his *Meteorology*, Aristotle begins discussing the different characters of the various winds, as well as the origins of those winds. To head off a hypothetical reader's erroneous assumption that a south wind blowing over Greece might originate as far away as the Earth's South Pole, Aristotle shows how the sphere of the Earth is divisible into different zones, in bands from north to south, and that the comparable zones of each hemisphere have similar characteristics. The primary characteristic he uses for his divisions is the criterion of habitability: if we go far enough north we will eventually hit a region that is too cold for anyone to live in, so we draw a line of latitude at that point to mark off the uninhabitable *klima* that runs from there to the North Pole. Similarly, as we proceed south towards the equator, we will eventually reach a zone too hot to support habitation. Mark a latitude line at that point too. Thus far

---

[3] Here the phrase 'similar qualities' means different things to different authors, which we will return to clarify shortly.

[4] Literally 'inclinations' (to the sun): directly under the sun (the area between the tropics), at a more-or-less slight angle as one proceeds slowly north from there, and coming to a sharper angle as the traveller moves north and the noonday sun recedes farther and farther to the south.

we have two lines marking off three zones: an uninhabitable northern zone, a temperate zone that we call home, and an uninhabitable southern zone towards the equator. Aristotle then tells us that a similar habitable zone lying between extremes of cold and heat must exist, inverted, in the southern hemisphere and this zone must likewise have winds corresponding to our own in character, giving us a total of five *klimata*: the northern and southern habitable zones, the North and South Pole frigid zones, and the equatorial torrid zone. He does not in this passage discuss one further important matter, but the north–south symmetry seems to imply for him that there must also be people who live down there in the southern temperate zone, and in a difficult and surprising section of his *On the Heavens* (11.2), Aristotle explains that those people who occupy the southern hemisphere are, from a cosmological point of view, really living in the 'upper' hemisphere of the Earth, while we northerners occupy the lower. His reasons for this have to do with how he thinks of the significance and priority of up and down, right and left, and forward and backward as manifested in living things. Of these, he gives priority to up, right, and forward (versus down, left, and backward) and assumes that any motion that 'begins on the right' is superior to that from the left. If we now imagine lying on our backs with our heads towards the North Pole and looking up at the stars, we would see that the motion of the heavens 'begins' to our left, which is to say that the stars and planets begin their motion – their daily rising – in the east. If we now imagine our southern hemisphere counterparts, lying on their backs with their heads towards the South Pole, we see that the rising of the stars and sun is now 'from the right'. Therefore, the true 'up' of the cosmos must be the direction where their heads are pointing, which is to say that for the cosmos itself as a whole, *south is the true up*. One is hard pressed to find anyone in antiquity following Aristotle with this cosmic picture, but the idea that certain lines of latitude marked out different *klimata* in terms of habitability would, on the other hand, have very long traction in the geographical tradition.

Although Aristotle's five-zone system survived into the Middle Ages and beyond,[5] there was also an alternative, and finer-tuned, seven-zone system in common use as well, one that was applied only to the habitable zone. This seven-fold division of what had been, for Aristotle, just one zone is obviously much finer grained, and it was meant to more elaborately characterise the different climates that people actually lived in, which, after all, showed a great deal of variability north to south.

---

[5] See, for example, the discussion in Chapter 5 by P. S. Langeslag in this volume.

In Ptolemy's *Geography*, for instance, we see him trying to assess the reliability of reports from people claiming to have travelled significantly south of the equator, reports found in his predecessor, Marinus of Tyre. As part of his sceptical examination of Marinus, Ptolemy says that the people and animals one would find south of the equator should be similar to those north of the equator at similar latitudes. He says that skin colour to the south, for example, should be darker or lighter at the same latitudes as one finds north of the equator.[6] Rhinoceros should be found occupying symmetrical *klimata* north and south, and so on. Fundamental to his conception is that each *klima* should have broad characteristics determining what one can expect, more or less, from the people, animals, and plants that inhabit it. There will be variation, he knows, but he clearly has tacked at least a loose sense of environmental determinism on to his bands of latitude.

It is worth noting, though, that these *klimata* were not, when they were first developed, thought of as the primarily *geographical* markers that, in the course of time, they would eventually become. Instead, they developed from much earlier – in fact, Babylonian – astronomical considerations about the rising times of zodiacal signs.[7] As Babylonian astronomers had figured out, the farther north or south one stands, the slower or faster a given zodiacal sign will rise in the east (which was a significant variable in Babylonian astronomy-astrology). At the same time, the farther north one goes, the longer the days become in summer, and it was this – the length of the longest day rather than latitude directly – that Babylonian astronomers worked from to calculate expected rising times for zodiacal signs. Eventually, Greeks and Romans would see their *klimata* as geographical designations in the first instance, but their origin is always in this Babylonian longest-day scheme, and this leaves a clear mark on how the *klimata* are laid out in classical sources. Rather than working with some schematic latitude designation (a new *klima* every ten degrees, for example), they work with a schematic longest-day designation. When Ptolemy comes to tell us what lines of latitude one should mark on a map, he lays out as significant those that have longest-day differences of a quarter of an hour, and indeed, one invariably finds these same markers labelled explicitly, down the left-hand side of virtually any world map produced from Ptolemy's *Geography*. As he says in Book i:

---

[6] Ptolemy, *Geog.* 1.7–9.
[7] See Otto Neugebauer, *The History of Ancient Mathematical Astronomy* (New York: Springer-Verlag 1975), pp. 725–33.

τὸν μὲν πρῶτον ἀπ' αὐτοῦ τετάρτῳ μιᾶς ὥρας διαφέρειν ἀπέχοντα κατὰ
τὸν μεσημβρινόν, ὡς αἱ γραμμικαὶ δείξεις ἔγγιστα ὑποβάλλουσι, μοίρας δ°
δ'.
τὸν δὲ δεύτερον ἡμισείᾳ μιᾶς ὥρας διαφέρειν ἀπέχοντα ὁμοίως μοίρας η°
γ' ιβ'.
τὸν δὲ τρίτον ὥρᾳ ἡμισείᾳ καὶ τετάρτῳ μιᾶς ὥρας διαφέρειν ἀπέχοντα
μοίρας ιβ° L'.⁸

(The first parallel [to mark] differs from the longest day at the equator by
a quarter of an hour, which geometrical demonstrations fix at very nearly
4¼° from [the equator].
The second differs by a half hour, and [calculated] in the same way is at
8° 25'.⁹
The third differs by three-quarters of an hour, and is at 12½°.)

He continues from there by quarter-hour increments up to the latitude
where the longest day is sixteen hours and the shortest eight, the parallel
that runs, he tells us, through Thule at 63° north.¹⁰ We notice two features
of the list: one is that the latitude equivalents in degrees that correspond to
the (constant) quarter-hour length-of-day differences make for a rather
unpretty series: 4.25, 8.417, 12.5, 16.417, 20.25, 23.83, and so on. Second, as
Ptolemy tells us explicitly, even those values, messy as they may at first
look, are only approximate, calculated 'very nearly', ἔγγιστα.

So, time differences come first, both historically and conceptually, in the
divisions for marking Ptolemy's maps, and in the seven habitable zone
klimata that are built on the same system. In the most common version of
the seven-klima scheme, we change to each new klima at half-hour intervals
in day length (and so at every other latitude line in Ptolemy's scheme just
discussed). The first klima went through Meroe, with its longest day of 13
hours, the next through Syene (13½ hours), then Lower Egypt (14 hours),
Rhodes (14½ hours), the Hellespont (15 hours), Mid-Pontus (15½ hours),
and the northernmost went through Borysthenes in what is today Ukraine
(16 hours).

And it is not only latitude (zones and lines) that are determined by time
for Ptolemy. He also handles longitude in a similar way, dropping his
meridians at a spacing determined by twenty-minute differences in local
noon. Because the sun moves through seventy-two of these twenty-minute
intervals in a twenty-four-hour day, and because there are 360 degrees in

⁸ Ptolemy, Geog. 1.23.
⁹ Ptolemy uses so-called Egyptian fractions rather than minutes. The Greek literally says 8° plus 1/3 [of
  60 minutes (=20')] plus 1/12 [of 60 minutes (=5')].
¹⁰ Compare Ptolemy, Almagest 6.11.

a circle, each line of longitude will then be placed a nice round 5 degrees (= 360/72) apart. But, as Ptolemy makes clear, that value emerges from temporal considerations first. J. Lennart Berggren and Alexander Jones put it succinctly: 'it is fundamentally a net of time, not of degrees, that Ptolemy casts over the earth'.[11] Thus sky, stars, sun, and Earth; space and time – all come together in a complex, intertwined web that determines how we mark off where we are, and what peoples and places share our *klima* and the characteristics it determines.

Geography, Weather, and Calendars

The temporal schemes for geographical division just outlined are not, however, the only interactions between time and *klimata* in antiquity. The widespread pre-modern practice of astronomical weather prediction leveraged similar ideas about the world.

Until the introduction of the Julian reform of the Roman calendar in 46 BCE, ancient calendars were generally not fixed to the solar year with exactitude. As anyone familiar with a lunar calendar will know, the dates of festivals, new year's days, and so on tend to move around relative to the solstices and equinoxes (witness also the varying dates for Easter in the Christian tradition, which are calculated by means of an ancient lunar calendar scheme). Various lunar calendars handle this slippage differently, but Greek calendars tended to do something similar to what the Hebrew and Chinese calendars still do today, and that is to add a leap month every few years to fill in the difference between the (approximately) 354-day lunar year and the (approximately) 365¼-day solar year.[12]

For Greek farmers and sailors, it seems to have been felt at an early date that the slippage, relative to the seasons, that is inescapable in such lunar calendars made dates in those calendars too inexact to be used for determining when it was safe to plant the crops or to sail on the open sea. An alternative was needed, and we see that alternative being used pretty much as early as we see a Greek talking about farming and travel, in the pages of Hesiod's *Works and Days*:

[11] J. Lennart Berggren and Alexander Jones, *Ptolemy's Geography: an Annotated Translation of the Theoretical Chapters* (Princeton University Press, 2000), p. 11.

[12] On the variety and workings of Greek calendars, see Robert Hannah, *Greek and Roman Calendars: Constructions of Time in the Classical World* (London: Duckworth, 2005) and *Time in Antiquity* (New York: Routledge, 2009).

ἤματα πεντήκοντα μετὰ τροπὰς ἠελίοιο,
ἐς τέλος ἐλθόντος θέρεος καματώδεος ὥρης,
ὡραῖος πέλεται θνητοῖς πλόος ...
τῆμος δ᾽ εὐκρινέες τ᾽ αὖραι καὶ πόντος ἀπήμων.[13]

(Fifty days after the solstice, at the arrival of the season of weary heat, that is the time for mortals to sail ... Then are the winds orderly and the sea propitious.)

Since the lunar calendar date that would mark 'the fiftieth after the solstice' could vary by up to a month (just as the start of Hanukkah can fall anywhere from late November to late December today), ancient mariners and farmers chose to divide up the year for agricultural and seafaring purposes using (much more reliable) astronomical markers, rather than calendrical ones.

By the third century BCE (and possibly a couple of centuries earlier)[14] these markers came to be collected together into instruments called *parapegmata* (singular: *parapegma*), which were essentially inscriptions on stone of the significant astronomical events that marked the year, with holes drilled for a movable peg to show where in the year one was currently situated. The following example should give the basic idea:

- ἐν Ὑδροχόωι ὁ ἥλιος.
- [...] ἑῷος ἄρχεται δύνων καὶ Λύρα δύνει.
- •
- •
- Ὄρνις ἀκρόνυχος ἄρχεται δύνων.
- • • • • • • • • •
- Ἀνδρομέδα ἄρχεται ἑῷα ἐπιτέλλειν.[15]

(• The sun is in Aquarius.
- [A star] begins setting in the morning and Lyra sets.
- •
- •
- Cygnus begins to set acronychally.
- • • • • • • • • •
- Andromeda begins rising in the morning.)

The peg holes (•) were either marked with astronomical events or, as in the third and fifth lines here, inserted as null-content counters from the one astronomical event to the next, there being nine unremarkable days

[13] Hesiod, *Op.* 663–70.
[14] For the debate on this, see Daryn Lehoux, *Astronomy, Weather, and Calendars in the Ancient World: Parapegmata and Related Texts in Classical and Near-Eastern Societies* (Cambridge University Press, 2007).
[15] This example is from the so-called 'Miletus I' parapegma (C.ii in my catalogue in Lehoux, *Astronomy, Weather, and Calendars*).

between the setting of the constellation Cygnus and the rising of Andromeda, for example. And so, each day, someone went out to the wall on which this parapegma was inscribed (built into the theatre in the Asia Minor city of Miletus) and moved the peg one day forward. That this inscription was publicly accessible is important as it shows the wide interest this kind of time tracking commanded in the ancient city.

At an early date, ancient writers decided that it was desirable to incorporate this kind of material into more portable texts, and versions were adopted that could be written down on papyrus. Substitutes were needed for the peg holes, and various solutions were adopted, which ranged from writing out simple day-counts ('nine days later . . .'), to the use of zodiacal schemes, and eventually to the use of the Julian calendar itself. Where these texts begin to interact with conceptions of geography and *klimata* is when they make the connection with the Hesiodic material — with farming and seafaring — explicit, connecting astronomy, weather, and time into one system, as we see in the following excerpt from the first-century BCE author Geminus of Rhodes:

τὸν δὲ Λέοντα διαπορεύεται ὁ ἥλιος ἐν ἡμέραις λα´.
ἐν μὲν οὖν τῇ α´ ἡμέρᾳ Εὐκτήμονι Κύων μὲν ἐκφανής, πνῖγος δὲ ἐπιγίνεται· ἐπισημαίνει.
ἐν δὲ τῇ ε´ Εὐδόξῳ Ἀετὸς ἑῷος δύνει.
ἐν δὲ τῇ ι´ ἡμέρᾳ Εὐδόξῳ Στέφανος δύνει.
ἐν δὲ τῇ ιβ´ Καλλίππῳ Λέων μέσος ἀνατέλλων πνίγη μάλιστα ποιεῖ.
ἐν δὲ τῇ ιδ´ Εὐκτήμονι πνίγη μάλιστα γίνεται.
ἐν δὲ τῇ ιϛ´ ἡμέρᾳ Εὐδόξῳ ἐπισημαίνει.[16]

(The sun traverses Leo in thirty-one days.
On the first day: According to Euctemon Sirius is visible, stifling heat follows, there is a change in the weather.[17]
On the fifth: According to Eudoxus Aquila sets in the morning.
On the tenth day: According to Eudoxus Corona sets.
On the twelfth: According to Callippus the rising of the middle of Leo causes really stifling heat.
On the fourteenth: According to Euctemon there is really stifling heat.
On the sixteenth day: According to Eudoxus there is a change in the weather.)

---

[16] Geminus, *Isagog*.
[17] On this translation for the Greek intransitive and impersonal ἐπισημαίνει, see Lehoux, 'Impersonal and Intransitive ἐπισημαίνει', *Classical Philology*, 99 (2004), 78–85.

There are a number of features to unpack here. First is the use of the zodiacal division of time ('the sun traverses Leo ... ') as a workaround for the unreliability of the various lunar calendars in use. The second is the incorporation of weather predictions ('stifling heat ... there is a change in the weather'). One is hard pressed to know exactly how the ancients read these predictions, but one assumes that they are something like predictions for an ideal year, or else were seen as probabilities, perhaps. An interesting and rare phrasing at day twelve of the excerpt above involves the use of causal language, the rising of Leo *causes* stifling heat. In most parapegmata the associations between stellar phases and their weather phenomena are left unstated and it is interesting here to see a causal connection made explicitly. It may not be possible to extend the implication in this one line of Geminus to all stellar phases in all authors, however, and a note of caution is warranted. It may be that this is an outlier and that elsewhere the assumption was simple correlation rather than causation. But the fact that the connection – whatever it was – was thought to be a tight one can be seen in a passage from Ovid, where he inverts the order of signification, saying not that the star is a sign of weather to come, but that the weather we see tells us what is happening, unseen, behind the clouds: *institerint Nonae, missi tibi nubibus atris | signa dabunt imbres exoriente Lyra*[18] ('when the Nones [of January] approach, rains sent to you from dark clouds signal the rising of Lyra').[19]

Where we see this tradition of weather prediction join that of geography, which is to say of climates, is in Ptolemy's comprehensive expansion of this tradition in his little book called the *Phaseis* ('Phases'). There Ptolemy lays out a comprehensive list of astronomical signs, weather predictions, and the authorities attesting to the latter.[20] Even a cursory glance at Ptolemy's *Phaseis* will show how intimately it is connected to the geographical divisions we saw earlier:

Θώθ

α΄. ὡρῶν ιδ΄ ∟ ὁ ἐπὶ τῆς οὐρᾶς τοῦ Λέοντος ἐπιτέλλει. Ἱππάρχῳ ἐτησίαι παύονται. Εὐδόξῳ ὑετία, βρονταί, ἐτησίαι παύονται.

β΄. ὡρῶν ιδ΄ ὁ ἐπὶ τῆς οὐρᾶς τοῦ Λέοντος ἐπιτέλλει, καὶ Στάχυς κρύπτεται. Ἱππάρχῳ ἐπισημαίνει.

[18] Ovid, *Fasti* 1.315–16.
[19] On this inversion, see Otta Wenskus, *Astronomische Zeitangaben von Homer bis Theophrast* (Stuttgart: Franz Steiner, 1990).
[20] And note this is a different use of the authority of earlier astronomers from what we just saw in Geminus: there the authorities are cited for the stellar phases, whereas in Ptolemy they give us the weather.

γ΄. ὡρῶν ιγ΄ ∟΄ ὁ ἐπὶ τῆς οὐρᾶς τοῦ Λέοντος ἐπιτέλλει. ὡρῶν ιε΄ ὁ καλούμενος Αἴξ ἑσπέριος ἀνατέλλει. Αἰγυπτίοις ἐτησίαι παύονται. Εὐδόξῳ ἄνεμοι μεταπίπτοντες. Καίσαρι ἄνεμος, ὑετός, βρονταί. Ἱππάρχῳ ἀπηλιώτης πνεῖ.

δ΄. ὡρῶν ιε΄ ὁ ἔσχατος τοῦ Ποταμοῦ ἑῷος δύνει. Καλλίππῳ χειμαίνει καὶ ἐτησίαι παύονται.

ε΄. ὡρῶν ιγ΄ ∟΄ Στάχυς κρύπτεται. ὡρῶν ιε΄ ∟΄ ὁ λαμπρὸς τῆς Λύρας ἑῷος δύνει. Μητροδώρῳ δυσαερία. Κόνωνι ἐτησίαι λήγουσιν.

([Month of] Thoth

1. [For the latitude where the longest day is] 14½ hours: the star on the tail of Leo rises. According to Hipparchus the Etesian winds stop. According to Eudoxus it is rainy, thundery, the Etesian winds stop.

2. [Where the longest day is] 14 hours: the star on the tail of Leo rises, and Spica disappears. According to Hipparchus there is a change in the weather.

3. [Where the longest day is] 13½ hours: the star on the tail of Leo rises. 15 hours: the star called Capella rises in the evening. According to the Egyptians the Etesian winds stop. According to Eudoxus variable winds. According to Caesar wind, rain, thundery. According to Hipparchus the east wind blows.

4. 15 hours: the rearmost star of Eridanus sets in the morning. According to Callippus it is stormy and the Etesian winds stop.

5. 13½ hours: Spica disappears. 15½ hours: the bright star in Lyra sets in the morning. According to Metrodorus bad air. According to Conon the Etesian winds finish.)

Here we have come methodologically full circle: the maximum-length-of-day value that was originally astronomical, but then got co-opted by geographers, is once again astronomical, but now tracking the dates of visibility of stellar phases from various locations.[21]

And here we hit a puzzle that I am unable to answer: What is the geographical coverage for any one of those weather predictions? It looks at first glance as though they are meant to apply to the whole *klima* whose stellar phenomenon is listed, as in day 1's '14½ hours: the star on the tail of Leo rises. According to Hipparchus the Etesian winds stop.' It would make sense that the weather is attached to the zone, one would think, but then it's highly doubtful that anyone in antiquity would think of the Etesian winds stopping in stages, from north to south over consecutive days. To make matters worse, we actually find entries with Egyptian calendar dates tied to weather predictions directly, with no latitudes or stellar phases

---

[21] I note that, in the *Phaseis*, Ptolemy only gives us information for the middle five of the seven *klimata*, omitting the farthest north (maximum day 16 hours) and the farthest south (maximum day 13 hours).

intervening: 'Tybi 20: According to the Egyptians wintry air ... Tybi 29: According to Callippus and Euctemon rain falls. According to Democritus the middle of winter.' Clearly the weather predictions are meant to apply to the *dates* and not the phases somehow, but how? How broadly do they apply? How do we weigh conflicting ones?

One possibility is that the predictions were meant to be taken as representative of the weather in the area where the listed authority (Euctemon, Democritus) was working, but it is difficult to know for sure. Another possibility is that the weather was meant to apply broadly but that different readers might think different authorities were better or worse than others, in the same way we today each have our preferred source for weather forecasts. Personally, I tend to lean towards the first of these possibilities, largely because of the prominent Greek emphasis on the locality of climates, one town differing from another, sometimes greatly, even when located physically close by. Here the medical tradition offers some light.

Climates in Medicine

Ancient medicine was far from unanimous about the causes of health and disease. Nevertheless, one commonly recurring theme across many texts is the idea that the air we breathe affects our health and constitutions at a fundamental level (and this idea was one of the longest lived in the history of medicine). In cases of epidemic disease, we see physicians paying close attention to the weather in the preceding months as a way of understanding what may be going on in the bodies of their sick patients. In the case of travelling armies, we see outbreaks in camp blamed on the soldiers' unfamiliarity with local conditions.[22] And we are lucky enough to have what looks like an actual handbook for the itinerant physician in the Hippocratic text *Airs, Waters, Places*.

Airs, Waters, Places begins by explaining the paramount importance for the physician of understanding the effects of a city's local climate on the health of its citizens. From its opening sentence:

ἰητρικὴν ὅστις βούλεται ὀρθῶς ζητέειν, τάδε χρὴ ποιέειν· πρῶτον μὲν ἐνθυμέεσθαι τὰς ὥρας τοῦ ἔτεος, ὅ τι δύναται ἀπεργάζεσθαι ἑκάστη· οὐ γὰρ ἐοίκασιν οὐδέν, ἀλλὰ πολὺ διαφέρουσιν αὐταί τε ἑωυτέων καὶ ἐν τῇσι μεταβολῇσιν· ἔπειτα δὲ τὰ πνεύματα τὰ θερμά τε καὶ τὰ ψυχρά· μάλιστα μὲν τὰ κοινὰ πᾶσιν ἀνθρώποισιν, ἔπειτα δὲ καὶ τὰ ἐν ἑκάστῃ χώρῃ

---

[22] See, e.g., Herodian 6.6; Vivian Nutton, *Ancient Medicine* (New York: Routledge, 2004), pp. 25–6.

ἐπιχώρια ἐόντα. δεῖ δὲ καὶ τῶν ὑδάτων ἐνθυμέεσθαι τὰς δυνάμιας· ὥσπερ γὰρ ἐν τῷ στόματι διαφέρουσι καὶ ἐν τῷ σταθμῷ, οὕτω καὶ ἡ δύναμις διαφέρει πολὺ ἑκάστου.[23]

(Whoever wants to pursue medicine correctly must do the following: first consider the seasons of the year, what each of them brings about, for each is not like the others, but they differ greatly both from each other and in how they change. Next the winds, hot and cold, especially those that are common everywhere but then also the ones that are endemic to each place. It is necessary also to pay attention to the effects of waters. Just as these differ in taste and weight, so also does the effect of each differ greatly.)

The water that feeds a place is not normally considered part of that location's climate today, but, to the ancient way of looking at it, it was conceptually inseparable from that location's dominant weather patterns, for two reasons. One is just that it formed part of the same understanding of human, animal, and plant constitutions: the qualities of the local water affected what could grow in a place and how it developed in the same way as the dominant weather patterns did. The second reason is that the ferocity and frequency of the sun, as well as the qualities of the winds that blew over any given location, were seen as largely responsible for the qualities of the local water. Slow versus fast evaporation, freezing and thawing – all this changed the properties that the water otherwise might have had, and this directly affected the health and development of local populations. The hardness of the water, its temperature, turbidity, salinity, and general 'healthiness' were all, at least in part, bundled in with the qualities of the climate.

Airs paints a picture of the characteristics of the individual human body as being to a large extent a direct (if complex) function of the local climate, water included. Peoples under different climates, sometimes even quite close by, grew differently: strong or weak, infertile or prolific, sickly or healthy, their digestive tracts flabby or firm as their airs and waters and exposure to the sun and winds differed. Their statures and builds are affected, so much so that the author of *Airs* attributes broad racial differences to the fact that people live in different climates.[24] Dwellers on the river Phasis in the

---

[23] *Aër.* 1.1–2.

[24] I say 'the author of *Airs*' because we do not know who wrote any given book attributed to 'Hippocrates'. Authorship across the corpus is clearly very diverse both in date of writing and in opinion, such that we know there must have been many different authors for the sixty or so texts that have come down to us. *Airs, Waters, Places* was long thought to be one of the genuine works by Hippocrates himself (and the authenticity of other works was often judged by comparisons of style and content relative to it), but in more recent times scholars habitually eschew attribution of any Hippocratic work as fundamentally unknowable. On the authorship question, see Jacques Jouanna,

Caucasus mountains, for example, are very tall, heavy-set, and hard working. They have complexions 'as though they had jaundice'. All of this, says the author, is caused by their climate, where their stagnant waters are heated and putrefied by the sun, replenished by frequent rain, and where the north wind seldom reaches them, but a hot and stormy wind called the 'Kenchron' sometimes does. They have remarkably deep voices because of the heaviness of the air they breathe and the frequent fogs that blight them.

In general, the author of *Airs* tells us, one can attribute the characteristics of individual cities, of whole nations, and even whole regions, to their climates. 'Asians' (by which he may mean Persians, and in any case we will have to excuse his blatant racism in what follows) are 'less warlike and milder' than Europeans, 'less courageous', and 'weaker', and most of the reason for this is pinned on climate:

> αἱ ὧραι αἴτιαι μάλιστα, οὐ μεγάλας τὰς μεταβολὰς ποιεύμεναι, οὔτε ἐπὶ τὸ
> θερμὸν, οὔτε ἐπὶ τὸ ψυχρὸν, ἀλλὰ παραπλησίως. οὐ γὰρ γίγνονται
> ἐκπλήξιες τῆς γνώμης, οὔτε μετάστασις ἰσχυρὴ τοῦ σώματος, ἀφ' ὅτων
> εἰκὸς τὴν ὀργὴν ἀγριοῦσθαί . . . αἱ γὰρ μεταβολαί εἰσι τῶν πάντων, αἵ τε
> ἐγείρουσαι τὴν γνώμην τῶν ἀνθρώπων, καὶ οὐκ ἐῶσαι ἀτρεμίζειν.

> (The seasons [in Asia] are the greatest cause; they don't change much with respect to heat or cold, but instead happen with moderation. People's minds are not buffeted, nor is a strong alteration caused in their bodies by which their temperament might be made fiercer . . . For it is changes of the whole [atmosphere] that rouse the characters of peoples and prevent them from settling down.)

To be sure, there are other contributing factors to human constitutions (customs and laws figure as prominent, but secondary, causes in *Airs*), but as the author makes clear again and again, it is primarily the climate that determines the character. Not just races, but individual bodies come to be determined, to a large extent, by local climates, and are constantly and profoundly affected, moved, and changed by the weather in any given year. When we say today that a cold wind 'cuts us to the bone', we are being metaphorical. A Greek could mean it almost literally.

Heavens, Air, and People, Redux

The influential line of medical thinking that we have just surveyed now brings us around full circle. The importance of 'changes of season' for

Hippocrate (Paris: Fayard, 1992), and Elizabeth M. Craik, *The 'Hippocratic' Corpus: Content and Context* (New York: Routledge, 2015).

health and bodily constitutions is at this point quite clear. What may have been less obvious in that discussion is the tie-in to the astronomical material we outlined earlier. I mentioned above that physicians dealing with epidemic outbreaks looked to the preceding weather to help them understand the ailments affecting their patients. What I did not mention was how those physicians tracked the important changes of weather that were responsible for disease: they did it using the same phases of the fixed stars as the authors of the weather-predicting parapegmata had used. Witness the opening lines in the great set of Hippocratic case studies, the *Epidemics*, to take just one of many examples:

ἐν Θάσῳ, φθινοπώρου περὶ ἰσημερίην καὶ ὑπὸ πληϊάδα, ὕδατα πολλά, ξυνεχέα μαλθακῶς, ἐν νοτίοισι, χειμὼν νότιος, σμικρὰ πνεύματα βόρεια, αὐχμοί, τὸ ξύνολον ἔς γε χειμῶνα ὁκοῖον ἦρ γίγνεται. ἦρ δὲ νότιον, ψυχεινόν, σμικρὰ ὕσματα.[25]

(In Thasos, during the autumn around the equinox and until the [morning setting of] the Pleiades, there was much rain, continuing gently and under a south wind, north winds weak, droughts. On the whole the winter was spring-like; spring was southerly, fresh, little rain.)

The equinoxes and solstices, the annual risings and settings of the fixed stars – these are exactly the same phenomena used to track the seasons in the astrometeorological tradition (it is no coincidence that astrometeorological material is a commonplace in medical texts, and almanacs a common medical tool, right through to the Renaissance). What emerges from all of this is a rich picture of the climate, both hyper-locally and at the same time across broad bands of latitude, deeply affecting humans and other life here on the Earth, where that climate is caused or timed or somehow more loosely determined – but, in any case, tightly linked to – the motions in the heavens.

And it is not just the fixed stars that could have this important set of effects. We also see the planets acting in this way. It is hard to tell how widespread *planetary* astrological weather prediction was in antiquity, but it certainly had its practitioners, and it certainly had a wide spread in the centuries after antiquity, continuing through the Middle Ages, the Renaissance (Johannes Kepler was a prominent voice),[26] and even down to the present day in the form of the widely available *Annual Farmer's Almanac*.

---

[25] *Epid. I*, 1.
[26] On Kepler's astrometeorology (including its relationship with medicine), see Patrick J. Boner, 'Kepler's Early Astrological Calendars: Matter, Methodology and Multidisciplinarity', *Centaurus*, 50 (2008), 324–8.

It is important to note that not every source we have for ancient astrology goes out of its way to discuss what the actual mechanism of astrological causation is – how the stars physically shape affairs and destinies down here on Earth – but I would like to single out one such account, Ptolemy's, as being representative of at least one prominent view on the matter. Beyond the common astrological invocation of the ancient physical forces of sympathy and antipathy (the forces responsible for, among many other things, what we would now call magnetism or electrostatic attraction), we also see in astrology a widespread attribution of qualities like hot, cold, wet, and dry to the planets, sun, and moon. For Aristotle, the simple fact of the whirring motion of the heavens was what stirred up the fire, air, water, and earth down here below the moon, preventing all the matter from settling into stagnation. For Ptolemy, among other astrologers, we see a more complex account, where the hot/cold/wet/dry properties of the different planets bear down and cause changes in our atmosphere. For Ptolemy, it was these changes in the atmosphere that then caused changes and characteristics in people:

> τί δὴ οὖν κωλύει τὸν ἠκριβωκότα μὲν τάς τε πάντων τῶν ἀστέρων καὶ ἡλίου καὶ σελήνης κινήσεις, . . . ὡς δύνασθαι μὲν ἐφ᾽ ἑκάστου τῶν διδομένων καιρῶν ἐκ τῆς τότε τῶν φαινομένων σχέσεως τὰς τοῦ περιέχοντος ἰδιοτροπίας εἰπεῖν, οἷον ὅτι θερμότερον ἢ ὑγρότερον ἔσται, δύνασθαι δὲ καὶ καθ᾽ ἕνα ἕκαστον τῶν ἀνθρώπων τήν τε καθόλου ποιότητα τῆς ἰδιοσυγκρασίας ἀπὸ τοῦ κατὰ τὴν σύστασιν περιέχοντος συνιδεῖν. [27]

(What would prevent someone who had investigated carefully the motions of the stars and the sun and the moon . . . from being able to predict, at each of the given critical times, [and] from the arrangement of the phenomena, the particular characteristics of the atmosphere such as its becoming hotter or wetter, and from being able to know for each individual person the general quality of his particular temperament[28] from the composition of the atmosphere?)

He thus posits a two-tiered causal chain: planets move the atmosphere, and the atmosphere moves the fates and characters of humans. And so once

---

[27] Ptolemy, *Tetr.* 1.2.10.

[28] The noun ἰδιοσυγκρασία, which gives us the English *idiosyncrasy*, is in fact quite rare in Greek, turning up only in Ptolemy and his contemporary Galen (Hephaestion quotes it from Ptolemy, and it shows up once in a pseudo-Galenic text, the *Definitiones medicae*, but both contexts are clearly derivative). Galen equates it with the nature (φύσις) of the patient and adds that ὀνομάζουσι δέ, οἶμαι, τοῦτο πολλοὶ τῶν ἰατρῶν ἰδιοσυγκρασίαν, καὶ πάντες ἀκατάληπτον ὁμολογοῦσιν ὑπάρχειν, 'many doctors, I think, call this the *idiosyncrasy*, and all agree that it is incomprehensible' (*Meth. med.* 209ĸ).

again we move from the heavens to the climate to the individual in a seamless, interconnected causal chain: planets, airs, bodies all forming a single, intricate, and dynamic system.

Thus, we see that ancient conceptions of climate – or, better, *climates* – saw our atmosphere as one part of the larger dynamic system of the motions of the heavens. Human bodies both individual and collective were acted on, and to a large extent *determined*, by that atmosphere. Changes in the weather on a day-to-day or even hour-to-hour basis were monitored by physicians and predicted by astrologers in order to try and understand the subtle differences in the composition of different human bodies that could lead to sickness, madness, anger, or calm. City by city, small differences in orientation to the sun and winds could make the inhabitants of one place potentially very different from those of another. At the same time, though, general rules were sought to describe wider regions of the Earth, and to understand the characteristics of the flora and fauna of those *klimata*. But above all, it was the characteristics of their people – in health and in sickness for the physicians, and in their very essence, makeup, and fortunes for astrologers – that were the primary products of the atmosphere, the local climate, the weather on some given day. Add to this the more prosaic needs of farmers, armies, and sailors (crop maintenance, travel), and we see how tightly knit the very conception of weather was with that of the heavens, and the very broad significance of climate in the ancient imagination.

CHAPTER 5

Weathering the Storm: Adverse Climates in Medieval Literature

P. S. Langeslag

All life is conditional upon a precarious balance of climate variables. Astrophysicists capture the most basic requirements of life in the concept of the Goldilocks zone, an orbital range subjected to just enough stellar radiation to permit liquid water and thus water-based life. Once the first requirements are met, however, mammals are considerably pickier about the definition of a habitable zone than are many hardier organisms. It is the more remarkable that humans have learned to thrive in nearly every climate zone on Earth. Employing a range of technologies to take the edge off the struggle, a modest proportion of the human population today need not look to the skies to ascertain whether a change in precipitation or temperature will arrive in time to support their survival for another season. Many in the Global North have no pressing reason to take note of the climate they inhabit until it interferes with their commute.

There is, accordingly, much to be learned from experiments on the edge of the human habitable zone, where one cannot afford to disregard climate and season. Helped by technology and trade, this frontier has been pushed back over time so that human life is now possible even in the polar regions, but it was not always so. Starting from the world's warmer zones, human-kind gradually made its way ever further towards the poles, relying on such technologies as body insulation, animal husbandry, agriculture, and a succession of fuels.

In the Middle Ages, the fossil fuel revolution was not yet on the horizon, so that survival in the sub-arctic zone was not to be taken for granted. Accordingly, schematic world maps following the system described by Macrobius (c. 400 CE) discern five climate zones from pole to pole: a frigid zone at either extreme, thought too cold to sustain life; a torrid zone straddling the equator, impassable on account of its heat; and two temperate zones – Goldilocks zones – satisfying the necessary conditions of life in between these extremes (see Figures 5.1 and 5.2). According to this

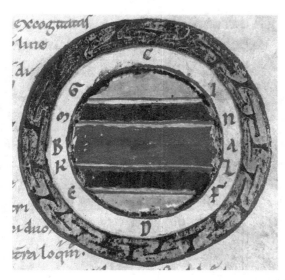

Figure 5.1 The five zones of the Earth. Detail from a continental manuscript of the mid-twelfth century containing Macrobius's *Commentarii in somnium Scipionis*. Royal Danish Library, NKS 218 4°, fol. 34ʳ·

worldview, then, only some 40 per cent of the world's latitude was habitable, and a mere 20 per cent was accessible, translating into even less in terms of effective surface area, as each degree of equatorial latitude covers more ground than a degree of moderate latitude. The equator, the Arctic, and the southern hemisphere were categorically beyond the human horizon.

One need not subscribe to Macrobian cosmology to recognise that it was no mean feat for Scandinavians to establish settlements in the remote and unforgiving environments of Iceland (*c.* 871) and southern Greenland (*c.* 985) using first-millennium technology. The study of these developments is made the more fascinating by the fact that Icelanders adopted quill-and-parchment technology some time after the spread of Christianity and spawned a lively written culture beginning in the twelfth century, so that early accounts and fictions of life in these parts may still be consulted. Even when it does not explore the geographic boundaries of the human habitable zone, however, medieval literature is a valuable storehouse of pre-modern responses to climate and the natural world. The written cultures of medieval Europe each had their own literary forms and emphases, but a great deal of material was also shared across the Latin sphere of influence. This is true of cosmological learning such as that of Macrobius, but also of religious

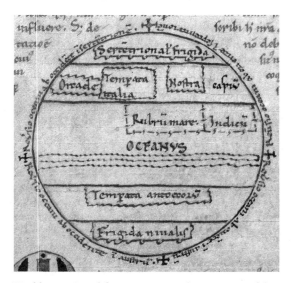

Figure 5.2 World map. Detail from a continental manuscript of the mid-twelfth century containing Macrobius's *Commentarii in somnium Scipionis*. Royal Danish Library, NKS 218 4°, 38ᵛ.

literature, which conveyed ideas about the climate of the Levant, but more especially of Eden, heaven, hell, and the end-time. To provide a sense of the range of climate themes in medieval literature, this chapter will introduce two literary motifs that form a sharp contrast in the degree to which they are rooted in local climatic concerns, translating into a corresponding difference in universal relevance. At one extreme, medieval Icelandic prose shows a keen understanding of the interface between climate, economy, and feuding in the unforgiving climate of the North Atlantic. The violence here depicted may not be conditioned by the sub-arctic climate, but it unquestionably responds to its effects. The overall dynamic is thus bound to this locale, and each conflict over food resources is informed by the author's first-hand knowledge of the annual production cycle and its climatically determined limitations. Against this tradition we may place the trope of the climatic extremes leading up to Judgement Day. Born and transmitted in an academic sphere, this motif depicts natural disasters beyond anyone's personal experience. It compensates for its lack of relatability with common-sense analogies demonstrating the decay over time of biological systems. The final strength of latter-day climatology, however, lies in its reliance on a universal imagination fuelled by the fear of damnation.

Climate Economics

The economic management of Norse settlements in the North Atlantic has invited a great deal of research, not least because the two Norse Greenlandic colonies established in the late tenth century were discontinued in imperfectly understood circumstances in the fourteenth and fifteenth centuries. Scholars have generally acknowledged a plurality of contributing factors, but emphases have shifted over the years. For some time, the leading narrative was that the settlers had shown themselves unwilling or unable to adapt to their new environment, clinging to a Norwegian model of pastoralism in a climate where the hunt for marine mammals held greater promise, particularly as the local climate cooled, beginning in the thirteenth century.[1] Added to this was the hypothesis that the Norse Greenlanders held some responsibility for the collapse of their newly settled ecosystems, eroding the land with irresponsible management, again born out of a cultural tradition better suited to mainland Scandinavia.[2]

As new evidence has come to light, scholars have begun to move away from this narrative, positing instead that the Greenland Norse practised responsible land management and demonstrated considerable flexibility adapting to the demands and opportunities of the Greenlandic environment and its changing climate. Their adaptation did nevertheless drive them to adopt a more monocultural subsistence economy, leaving them vulnerable to fluctuations in climate and seal migration patterns. Accordingly, the Norse Greenlanders' way of life may still have played

[1] The classical popular account of the Norse Greenlandic 'collapse' is Jared Diamond, *Collapse: How Societies Choose to Fail or Succeed* (London: Penguin, 2005), pp. 178–276. The climatic cooling in question corresponds to the onset of the so-called Little Ice Age, which in parts of the North Atlantic lasted into the nineteenth century. It should be pointed out, however, that the concepts of Little Ice Age and Medieval Warm Period (thought to have preceded it in the centuries around *c*. 1000) are misleading when used with global scope. The term Medieval Warm Period in particular is only minimally valid on a hemispheric level. Both remain useful with reference to Europe and the North Atlantic, with the caveat that temperatures varied both regionally and diachronically within each period. See Philip D. Jones and Michael E. Mann, 'Climate over Past Millennia', *Reviews of Geophysics*, 42nd ser., RG2002 (2004), 1–42; Michael E. Mann, Zhihua Zhang, Malcolm K. Hughes *et al.*, 'Proxy-Based Reconstructions of Hemispheric and Global Surface Temperature Variations over the Past Two Millennia', *PNAS*, 105.36 (2008), 13252–7; James W. Jordan, 'Arctic Climate and Landscape ca. AD 800–1400', in Herbert Maschner, Owen Mason, and Robert McGhee (eds.), *The Northern World, AD 900–1400* (Salt Lake City: University of Utah Press, 2009), pp. 7–29; Xuhui Dong, Helen Bennion, Richard W. Battarbee, and Carl D. Sayer, 'A Multiproxy Palaeolimnological Study of Climate and Nutrient Impacts on Esthwaite Water, England over the Past 1200 Years', *The Holocene*, 22 (2011), 107–18.

[2] Thomas Amorosi, Paul Buckland, Andrew Dugmore, John H. Ingimundarson, and Thomas H. McGovern, 'Raiding the Landscape: Human Impact in the Scandinavian North Atlantic', *Human Ecology*, 25 (1997), 491–518.

a role in their eventual disappearance, but their descent into unsustain-
ability was likely not as reckless and unsophisticated as earlier studies
suggest. The nature of the decline has also been reconsidered: it is now
thought of as a more or less voluntary and gradual decolonisation, not
a sudden cataclysm. Moreover, it is clear from the historical context that
climate and sustenance were not the only determinants in that decision.
There is today greater recognition of the role of trade: whether or not
Norse Greenland was originally settled with the walrus ivory trade in
mind,[3] it lost all contact with Europe once the market was flooded with
Russian and African ivory and the North Atlantic economy came to
specialise in dried fish, which was more profitably and securely sourced
from less remote waters.[4]

Through all these evolving insights, climate change has remained
a remarkable constant: whatever measures the Norse Greenlanders took
to secure their way of life, they eventually abandoned the project under
stress from a climate that grew increasingly hostile to pastoralism, agriculture, seafaring, and offshore hunting and fishery. The situation in Iceland
was nowhere near as dire, but it too pushed against the limits of traditional
pastoral-agricultural production. The most poignant demonstration of this
fact came in the eighteenth century, when the period's climatic low
combined with pestilence, volcanic eruptions, and erosion to reduce the
population to well below medieval levels.[5]

One thing that has become clear from research into Norse Atlantic
settlements is that adaptation to the local climate and ecosystem was key
to successful migration. When Norwegians set out to settle the North
Atlantic, pastoralism was already a central pillar of their livelihood, alongside fishery, the hunt, and the production mainly of the hardier crops
known to produce reliable returns at these latitudes. When they reached
Iceland, with its short growing season and lack of indigenous land mammals, some adjustment was necessary, and the literature shows great
sensitivity to the importance of grasping the climatic rules of a new habitat

[3] Karin M. Frei, Ashley N. Coutu, Konrad Smiarowski et al., 'Was it for Walrus? Viking Age
Settlement and Medieval Walrus Ivory Trade in Iceland and Greenland', World Archaeology, 74
(2015), 439–66.

[4] Andrew J. Dugmore, Thomas H. McGovern, Orri Vésteinsonn, Jette Arneborg, Richard Streeter,
and Christian Keller, 'Cultural Adaptation, Compounding Vulnerabilities and Conjunctures in
Norse Greenland', PNAS, 109.10 (2012), 3658–63; Eli Kintisch, 'The Lost Norse', Science, 354.6313
(2016), 696–701.

[5] Sigurdur Thorarinsson [Sigurður Þórarinsson], 'Population Changes in Iceland', Geographical
Review, 51.4 (1961), 519–33; Martin Bell and Michael J. C. Walker, Late Quaternary Environmental
Change: Physical and Human Perspectives, 2nd edn (Harlow: Prentice Hall, 2005), p. 179.

immediately upon arrival. After all, there would be no grain harvest in the first autumn, so one was dependent for one's survival on the livestock painstakingly transported across the North Atlantic and the luck of finding the place rich in fish, fowl, and sea mammals. These concerns are reflected in *Landnámabók* (*The Book of Settlements*),[6] a work extant in three main redactions from the thirteenth and fourteenth centuries and going back, it seems, to a lost twelfth-century written tradition that would in turn have drawn on oral history. It gives the following account of Flóki Vilgerðarson's settlement:

> Þeir Flóki sigldu vestr yfir Breiðafjǫrð ok tóku þar land, sem heitir Vatsfjǫrðr við Barðastrǫnd. Þá var fjǫrðrinn fullr af veiðiskap, ok gáðu þeir eigi fyrir veiðum at fá heyjanna, ok dó allt kvikfé þeira um vetrinn.
>
> (Flóki and his men sailed west across Breiðafjǫrðr and took land at the site that is called Vatsfjǫrðr, at Barðastrǫnd. The fjord was full of game at that time, and because of the game they did not bother gathering the hay, and all their livestock died that winter.)[7]

It should be added that Flóki does not seem much invested in the new land: rather than plant crops, he sails back to Norway the next year and has little good to say about Iceland. Those returning with him describe it more favourably, one companion inviting ridicule with his claim that 'every blade of straw in the land they had found had dripped with butter' (*Drjúpa smjǫr af hverju strái á landinu, því er þeir hǫfðu fundit*),[8] a strikingly pastoral image, and somewhat ironic in light of the narrator's assertion that they had not bothered to harvest fodder for their livestock. That claim is itself suspicious given the substantial sunk cost of bringing livestock to Iceland. More than anything, the assertion should be understood to reflect the saga author's own experience, or that of his sources, with the challenges of supporting livestock in Iceland.

The Icelandic climate was kinder to small mammals, such as sheep and goats, than to cattle, and Icelanders learned to adjust their livestock accordingly.[9] In addition, diversification of food production helped keep the threat of crop failure at bay. *Egils Saga*, a fictional prose narrative from the 1220s, describes how a settler during the reign of Harald Fairhair (872–930) establishes a network of farms, each specialising in the activities best suited to its particular setting, whether shepherding, salmon fishing,

---

[6] *Íslendingabók, Landnámabók*, ed. Jakob Benediktsson, Íslenzk fornrit 1 (Reykjavik: Hið íslenzka fornritafélag, 1986), pp. 29–397.

[7] Ibid., S Redaction, p. 38; all translations are my own.   [8] Ibid., S Redaction, p. 38.

[9] Dugmore *et al.*, 'Cultural Adaptation', p. 3659.

agriculture, or a combination of sea-fishing, the seal hunt, the collection of wild eggs, and the slaughter of beached whales.[10] To diversify was to make the most of the comparatively narrow margin of error offered by Iceland's short growing season, and *Egils Saga* emphasises the natural riches of Iceland at the time of its settlement, when the wildlife did not know to fear human hunters. The farming strategies described are surely representative, but animal husbandry always remained a central pillar of Icelandic subsistence, reflected in the fact that hay was and today remains the island's primary crop.[11] Accordingly, the economic bottleneck to which the literature keeps returning is the feeding of livestock, on pastures when available and else on hay stocks. In Old Icelandic prose, upsets in the delicate balance of resources rarely fail to lay bare the equally brittle equilibrium of social functioning, and the smallest disagreement is likely to escalate into violence.

Indeed, resource disputes are so frequently triggers of deadly feuds in the sagas of Icelanders that readers may feel tempted to centre the definition of the genre around that precise dynamic. Thus, the early fourteenth-century *Grettis Saga* tells how the beaching of a whale triggers a small battle over the prized meat, resulting in several deaths and a number of outlawries.[12] The thirteenth-century *Njáls Saga* describes how two women with a pre-existing rivalry escalate their differences in a row over a shared forest, ordering killings in each other's households.[13] In the aforementioned *Egils Saga*, disregard for a longstanding conventional boundary between two neighbouring pasturelands triggers a feud resulting in a series of deaths, including the ten-year-old sons of the two quarrelling farmers.[14] *Eyrbyggja Saga*, likewise from the earlier thirteenth century, puts hay at the root of a dispute between neighbours. A certain hay field is shared between two farmers, and when one of them brings home the full harvest but refuses to pay for the other's share, an enmity ensues that festers until it results in the death of the wronged farmer, but it also carries over into the next generation.[15]

---

[10] *Egils Saga*, ed. Bjarni Einarsson (London: Viking Society for Northern Research, University College London, 2003), p. 40.

[11] Gunnar Karlsson, *Iceland's 1100 Years: History of a Marginal Society* (Reykjavik: Mál og menning, 2000), pp. 45–6; Rannveig Sigurdardóttir, Bernard Scudder, Jónas Thórdarson, Lilja Alfredsdóttir, and Helga Gudmundsdottir, *The Economy of Iceland* (Reykjavik: Sedlabanki, 2007), p. 27.

[12] *Grettis saga Ásmundarsonar, Bandamanna saga, Odds þáttr Ófeigssonar*, ed. Guðni Jónsson, Íslenzk fornrit 7 (Reykjavik: Hið íslenzka fornritafélag, 1936), ch. 12.

[13] *Brennu-Njáls saga*, ed. Einar Ól. Sveinsson, Íslenzk fornrit 12 (Reykjavik: Hið íslenzka fornritafélag, 1954), chs. 36–42.

[14] *Egils Saga*, chs. 82–6.

[15] *Eyrbyggja saga*, ed. Einar Ól. Sveinsson and Matthías Þórðarson, Íslenzk fornrit 4 (Reykjavik: Hið íslenzka fornritafélag, 1935), chs. 31–3.

The integration of climate, resource management, and feud is brought out particularly clearly in *Hœnsa-Þóris Saga*.[16] This short thirteenth-century text describes a chain reaction of human weaknesses that spiral out of control when a single character refuses to show himself as pliable as his neighbours.

The saga tells of a wealthy farmer named Blund-Ketill in possession of thirty estates out on lease, in addition to his own farm. This particular alone draws the historicity of the saga's events into question, as mention of leaseholds is elsewhere in Icelandic sources so rare that it is hard to conceive of a single case of such large size.[17] The system does, however, serve the narrative, as will become clear. One summer, which may be identified with the help of other sources as the year 961,[18] is poor in terms of grass growth and too wet to yield sufficient hay to last the winter. Blund-Ketill announces a two-pronged solution: all his tenants are to pay their leases in hay, and Ketill determines how much of each farm's livestock is to be slaughtered in the autumn in order to avoid hardship. The order is not actively enforced, however, and so, as the six-month winter season advances into its latter half, tenants begin to approach Blund-Ketill for assistance, admitting that not as many heads of livestock have been slaughtered as had been ordered. Ketill gives the first tenant extra hay on condition of discretion, but the tenant again contravenes his command, so the arrangement is soon public knowledge across the district. Accordingly, two others come for aid the month after. By this time, Blund-Ketill himself has no hay to give away, so he has forty of his own horses slaughtered in order that their fodder may be given to his tenants instead. When two further tenants ask for aid in the third month, he is unwilling to slaughter more animals. Instead, he is forced to barter for hay elsewhere, which leaves him at the mercy of Hœnsa-Þórir, a notorious miser and the district's least sociable individual. When Þórir proves unwilling to part with his surplus of hay on any condition, Ketill takes it against the owner's wishes, leaving payment according to his own appraisal and declaring himself prepared to add however much an independent referee deems he owes in addition.[19] Hœnsa-Þórir in his stubbornness is dead set against any arrangement, and although he is universally despised, he succeeds in purchasing the support of a single individual, who is able to muster his own connections to be present at the summons of Blund-Ketill to the Assembly for prosecution.

---

[16] *Borgfirðinga sǫgur*, ed. Sigurður Nordal and Guðni Jónsson, Íslenzk fornrit 3 (Reykjavik: Hið íslenzka fornritafélag, 1916–18), pp. 1–47.

[17] Ibid., p. 5 n. 2.   [18] Ibid., p. xxi.   [19] Ibid., chs. 4–5.

It is at the summons that the dispute spirals out of control when one of Ketill's guests resorts to violence, which has the counterproductive effect of concentrating loyalties on Þórir's side and unleashing an all-out blood feud that claims dozens of lives over the course of the saga.

The particulars of the hay dispute in *Hœnsa-Þóris Saga* have a remarkable degree of detail in common with the phrasing of a law in the *Jónsbók* law code, commissioned by King Magnús VI Hákonarson of Norway (r. 1263–80) and put into force in Iceland in 1281. Iceland had been brought under the Norwegian crown during the transition of power from Hákon IV to his son Magnús, and Magnús made legal reform in all his territories an important part of his legacy. For Iceland, this began with the introduction of the *Járnsíða* law code over the period 1271–4, superseded by *Jónsbók* in 1281. Both were heavily based on Norwegian law. The land-lease section of Magnús's national law code[20] stipulates that anyone in need of grains or flour may force a purchase. The procedure is for the prospective buyer to put in a witnessed request at the king's commissioner, who is to appoint inspectors to locate surpluses. Where a surplus is found, the first order of business is to set aside sufficient grains for the sustenance of the owner and his dependants until the next harvest. The remainder is then to be sold at market price. Refusal to sell incurs penalties payable to the king, his commissioner, and the prospective buyer, but the grain or flour is still to be taken, now without payment. If the farmer physically obstructs the removal of his surpluses, he is outlawed.[21]

The passage does not occur in the earlier Icelandic *Járnsíða*, but it was copied into *Jónsbók* with minimal changes that nevertheless reflect the difference in climate and economic culture between Norway and Iceland.[22] Whereas the law-giver primarily had grains (*frækorn, sáðkorn*) and flour (*mjǫl*) in mind for his Norwegian setting, these terms are replaced by the word *hey* ('hay') in the Icelandic adaptation, in recognition of the fact that this is the island's most important crop. Provisions for the owner's needs are adjusted accordingly: since hay cannot itself sustain the farm's residents, it is instead to be set aside for the farm's horses, sheep, goats, and dairy cows, which in turn sustain the farm's human population.

Scholars have noted that parallels between the saga and the law codes, specifically *Jónsbók*'s stipulations for farmers unwilling to part with their hay,

---

[20] 'Landzleigu bolkr', in Rudolph Keyser and Peter Andreas Munch (eds.), *Norges gamle love indtil 1387* (Christiania, Oslo: Grøndahl, 1846–95), vol. II, pp. 104–49.

[21] Ibid., art. 14.

[22] *Jónsbók: Kong Magnus Hakonssons Lovbog for Island*, ed. Ólafur Halldórsson (Copenhagen: Møller, 1904), 'Landsleigubálkr', art. 12.

invite the reading of the saga as an apology for the introduction of Norwegian law to Iceland, which met with a great deal of resistance. However, several considerations speak against the law's chronological precedence over the saga. The most prominent argument is that the Sturlubók–Hauksbók redaction of *Landnámabók* relies on *Hœnsa-Þóris Saga*, and Sturlubók in turn pre-dates the introduction of *Jónsbók*.[23] Nordal and Guðni Jónsson therefore take the opposite view, that developments like those found in the saga may have informed the legislation.[24] However, we should not lose sight of the fact that the law was written for Norway in the first instance. Thus the laws and the saga should be understood to reflect the climatic challenges of sustenance farming in Norway and Iceland alike, and the hardship and social unrest that could result from a single poor harvest or protracted winter.

End-time Climatology

In learned medieval culture, climate and weather formed part of the macrocosm mirroring human concerns on a larger scale. Medieval treatises on time-reckoning, such as Byrhtferth of Ramsey's 1011 *Enchiridion*, relate the four seasons to the four winds and cardinal directions, but also to the four elements, ages of man, virtues, and letters in the sequences *ADAM* and *DEUS*.[25] The reasoning behind these connections is that all the world was thought to have been created for the benefit of humankind; accordingly, every part of it must be significant and contain information on God's plan for human salvation.

One node in the cosmic scheme of signification involves climate. This reading is widely found in medieval sermons and relies on an analogy between the ages of man (typically childhood, adolescence, youth, and old age) and the world's eras as identified with the aid of Scripture. This analogy is not as commonly adduced in the computistical treatises because the conventional number of world ages was six in the world as we know it, the number deriving from the days of Creation, plus an additional one or two in other states of existence (the Resurrection and, in Bede, a state of awaiting that Resurrection, coeval with the six historical ages).[26] The ages of man were

---

[23] Björn Magnússon Ólsen, 'Landnáma og Hœnsa-Þóris saga', *Aarbøger for nordisk oldkyndighed og historie*, 2nd ser., 20 (1905), 63–80.

[24] Nordal and Guðni Jónsson, Preface, *Borgfirðinga sǫgur*, pp. xxx–xxxi.

[25] Byrhtferth of Ramsey, *Byrhtferth's 'Enchiridion'*, ed. Peter S. Baker and Michael Lapidge, Early English Text Society, s.s. 15 (Oxford University Press, 1995), pp. 6–15, 198–203.

[26] *Opera didascalica II: De temporum ratione liber*, ed. Charles W. Jones, Corpus Christianorum Series Latina 123B: Bedae venerabilis opera 6 (Turnhout: Brepols, 1977), ch. 10; *Byrhtferth's 'Enchiridion'*, pp. 232–41; Peter Darby, *Bede and the End of Time* (Farnham: Ashgate, 2012), pp. 65–74.

not fully fixed either, but they were rarely more than four. Homilists, less concerned with numerology, were free to treat both sequences as numberless ranges and draw a simple analogy: just as human beings grow weak as they grow older, so also the world grows the worse for age.[27]

The most striking connection between climate and the ageing world may be found in the correspondences of the third-century bishop Cyprian of Carthage. Responding to Demetrianus, who held Christians responsible for the world's perceived degeneration, Cyprian writes:

> Qua in parte, qui ignarus diuinae cognitionis et ueritatis alienus es, illud primo in loco scire debes senuisse iam mundum, non illis uiribus stare quibus prius steterat nec uigore et robore ipso ualere quo ante praeualebat. Hoc etiam nobis tacentibus et nulla de scripturis sanctis praedicationibusque diuinis documenta promentibus mundus ipse iam loquitur et occasum sui rerum labentium probatione testatur. Non hieme nutriendis seminibus tanta imbrium copia est, non frugibus aestate torrendis solita flagrantia est, nec sic uerna de temperie sua laeta sunt nec adeo arboreis fetibus autumna fecunda sunt.

> (In this regard, you who are ignorant of divine understanding and a stranger to the truth ought first to know this, that the world has now grown old: it no longer stands in the strength in which it formerly stood, nor does it flourish with the vigour and strength in which it formerly excelled. This much indeed the world itself says already, and it testifies to its decline with the proof of its faltering condition, even if I remain silent and produce no documents from holy Scripture and religious sermons. There is not [now] such an abundance of showers for the seeds that want nutrition in winter; there is not the customary heat for the fruits that want drying in summer; the springs are not of so joyful a mixture, nor are the autumns so very rich in fruits of the tree.)[28]

Cyprian goes on to list reduced returns from mining, the lessened splendour of sun and moon, and the crippled physical strength and social efficacy of humankind. His point is clear: all this world is made of the same stuff, and it is failing from old age. This understanding of creation was fairly common; what is striking about Cyprian's version is that he associates the ageing of the world with a breaking down of the agricultural seasons not unlike that experienced eighteen centuries later, at the height of the Anthropocene.

---

[27] See also J. E. Cross, 'Aspects of Microcosm and Macrocosm in Old English Literature', in Stanley Greenfield (ed.), *Studies in Old English Literature in Honor of Arthur G. Brodeur* (Eugene: University of Oregon Books, 1963), pp. 1–22.

[28] *Ad Demetrianum* ch. 3, sections 1–2; see *Cyprien de Carthage: A Démétrien*, ed. and trans. Jean-Claude Fredouille, Sources Chrétiennes 467 (Paris: Cerf, 2003).

Anglo-Saxonists reading Cyprian's assessment are likely to be reminded at once of Wulfstan of York's famed *Sermo Lupi* (1014):[29]

> Leofan men, gecnawað þæt soð is: ðeos woruld is on ofste, 7 hit nealæcð þam ende, 7 þy hit is on worulde aa swa lencg swa wyrse, 7 swa hit sceal nyde for folces synnan ær Antecristes tocyme yfelian swyðe

> (Dearly beloved, know this to be true: this world is in haste, and it is drawing towards the end, and therefore it is in the world ever the longer the worse, and so because of the people's sin it must necessarily deteriorate greatly before the coming of the Antichrist.)[30]

When Wulfstan subsequently cites contemporary evidence for such decline, however, it becomes clear that he has not climate destabilisation but the degeneration of human morals in mind. Environmental degradation in his day did not, after all, assume the cataclysmic proportions found in the biblical Book of Revelation, so it would have made for less spectacular illustrations. All the same, Wulfstan thought of the two realms as intricately connected. He considered the Earth severely degraded as a result of human sin, as another homily attests: 'Leofan men, clæne wæs þeos eorðe on hyre frumsceafte, ac we hi habbað syððan afylede swyðe 7 mid urum synnum þearle besmitene' ('Dearly beloved, this earth was clean in its inception, but we have since greatly defiled and severely polluted it with our sins').[31] Environmental destruction is a result of sin, but it is also sent as a punishment of sin: 'And witodlice ealswa flod com hwilum ær for synnum, swa cymð eac for synnum fyr ofer mancynn, 7 ðærto hit nealæcð nu swyðe georne' ('And in truth, just as the flood once came on account of sins, so also fire will come over humankind on account of sins, and it is drawing very close to that now').[32]

It is accordingly in texts describing the lead-up to Judgement Day that the most dramatic climatic breakdowns are found. Such descriptions are ultimately inspired by biblical prophecy, particularly from the Book of Revelation. Though framed as divine intervention, an environmental cataclysm of the scale described in Revelation 8 must have biospheric disruption through climate change among its causes. Above all, verses 7 to 11 recall such mass extinction events as those marking the end of the Permian and Cretaceous periods, for which volcanic activity and meteorite

---

[29] Wulfstan, *The Homilies of Wulfstan*, ed. Dorothy Bethurum (Oxford: Clarendon Press, 1957), pp. 255–75.

[30] Wulfstan, *The Homilies of Wulfstan*, BH redaction, ll. 7–10.

[31] *Secundam Lucam*, in Wulfstan, *The Homilies of Wulfstan*, pp. 123–7 (ll. 27–9).   [32] Ibid., ll. 7–9.

impacts have been adduced, both causing extinction by way of atmospheric change.[33]

Apocalyptic material of this sort, rendered especially relevant in some circles by the understanding that the sixth age of the world was to end some time before the middle of the eleventh century,[34] spawned a rich medieval tradition of end-time descriptions. Lists of the signs before Judgement Day foretell a range of natural disasters, including flood and fire. These are frequent symptoms of historical climatic disruption, though drought-induced fires are rare in northern Europe. A variant of this tradition surfaces in the fragmentary Old High German poem *Muspilli*,[35] a composite Bavarian work from the ninth century. It identifies an end-time defeat of the prophet Elias at the hands of the Antichrist as the trigger event for environmental destruction, bringing drought along with a conflagration of land and sky alike (ll. 48–57).

Although the word *muspilli*, which gives the poem its modern title, has not been explained with certainty,[36] it occurs in similarly eschatological settings in two further Old Germanic texts. One of these, the Old Saxon verse gospel synthesis *Heliand*, incorporates it into Christ's parable of the tares, which ends with a reference to the hell-fire awaiting sinners.[37] In Old Norse myth, the term has been substantially reinterpreted to refer to a non-Christian mythological character and realm. Since its primary association in the thirteenth-century Icelandic *Prose Edda* is with fire, however, it is often assumed that something of the original apocalyptic setting stuck to the word in the transfer.

The Old Norse personal name *Muspellr* makes its first appearance in *Vǫluspá*,[38] a poem describing the world's origin and foretelling its violent

---

[33] Haijun Song and Paul B. Wignall, 'Two Pulses of Extinction during the Permian–Triassic Crisis', *Nature Geoscience*, 6 (2013), 52–6; Ying Cui and Lee R. Kump, 'Global Warming and the End-Permian Extinction Event: Proxy and Modeling Perspectives', *Earth-Science Reviews*, 149 (2014); Sierra V. Petersen, Andrea Dutton, and Kyger C. Lohmann, 'End-Cretaceous Extinction in Antarctica Linked to Both Deccan Volcanism and Meteorite Impact via Climate Change', *Nature Communications*, 7:12079 (2016).

[34] F. W. N. Hugenholtz, 'Les terreurs de l'an mil: Enkele hypothesen', in A. de Buck (ed.), *Varia historica: Aangeboden aan Professor Doctor A. W. Byvanck* (Assen: Van Gorcum, 1954), pp. 110–23; Richard Landes, Andrew Gow, and David C. Van Meter, eds., *The Apocalyptic Year 1000: Religious Expectation and Social Change, 950–1050* (Oxford University Press, 2003).

[35] *Althochdeutsches Lesebuch*, ed. Wilhelm Braune, 17th edn, rev. ed. Ernst A. Ebbinghaus (Tübingen: Niemeyer, 1994), pp. 86–9.

[36] Hans Jeske, 'Zur Etymologie des Wortes *muspilli*', *Zeitschrift für deutsches Altertum und deutsche Literatur*, 135.4 (2006), 425–34.

[37] *Heliand und Genesis*, ed. Otto Behaghel, 10th edn, rev. ed. Burkhard Taeger (Tübingen: Niemeyer, 1996), ll. 2538–620.

[38] *Die Lieder des Codex Regius nebst verwandten Denkmälern*, ed. Gustav Neckel, 5th edn, rev. ed. Hans Kuhn (Heidelberg: Winter, 1983), pp. 1–15.

end in a (probably self-consciously) non-Christian mythological framework. The character is not properly introduced, but his sons are associated with the giants who fight the gods in the end-time battle (stanza 51). It is only in Snorri Sturluson's 1220s interpretation of the material that any light is shed on the concept of *Muspell(r)*. Snorri presents his *Prose Edda*[39] as a handbook of mythology for use by poets, though a comparison of the work with its sources in eddic poetry makes clear that he has intervened in his material to increase its mythological systemacy. His creativity is apparent in the *muspilli* material. Snorri first conflates the person Muspellr with another character called Surtr, described in *Vǫluspá* as travelling to the end-time battle with fire, though from a different direction to the people of Muspellr (*Vǫluspá* stanza 52). He next transposes the name *Muspell* on to the region guarded by Surtr, thus turning it into a land of fire:

> Fyrst var þó sá heimr í suðrhálfu er Muspell heitir. Hann er ljóss ok heitir. Sú átt er logandi ok brennandi, er hann ok ófœrr þeim er þar eru útlendir ok eigi eigu þar óðul. Sá er Surtr nefndr er þar sitr á lands enda til landvarnar. Hann hefir loganda sverð, ok í enda veraldar mun hann fara ok herja ok sigra ǫll goðin ok brenna allan heim með eldi.

> (But first there was the land called Muspell in the south. It is bright and hot. That region blazes and burns, and it is impassable to those who are not its natives and do not have their home there. He who lives at the land's end as a guard is called Surtr. He has a blazing sword, and at the end of the world he will go raiding and he will overcome all the gods and burn all the world with fire.)[40]

In this form, the Old Norse *Muspell(r)* tradition evokes the world conflagration in the Old High German *Muspilli* and anticipates the hell-fire of the Old Saxon *Heliand*. It is therefore tempting to conclude Snorri had information beyond *Vǫluspá* that allowed him to keep the tradition's continental elements of *muspilli*, eschatology, and world conflagration together. However, the wider passage in the *Prose Edda* is one of Snorri's trademark systematisations. As a counterpart to the fiery land of Muspell in the south, Snorri posits a cold region called Niflheimr in the north, issuing ice and hoarfroast, as well as a temperate region called Ginnungagap in between. The three zones are instrumental in the development of life:

---

[39] Snorri Sturluson, *Edda*, ed. Anthony Faulkes, 4 vols. (London: Viking Society for Northern Research, University College London, 1988–99).
[40] *Gylfaginning*, ch. 4.

Svá sem kalt stóð af Niflheimi ok allir hlutir grimmir, svá var þat er vissi
námunda Muspelli heitt ok ljóst, en Ginnungagap var svá hlætt sem lopt
vindlaust. Ok þá er mœttisk hrímin ok blær hitans svá at bráðnaði ok draup,
ok af þeim kvikudropum kviknaði með krapti þess er til sendi hitann, ok
varð manns líkandi, ok var sá nefndr Ymir.

(Just as the cold and all grim things arose from Niflheimr, that [part of
Ginnungagap] which faced towards Muspell was hot and bright, but
Ginnungagap was as mild as windless air. And when the hoarfrost and the
flow of heat met, so that it melted and dripped, life arose from those life-
drops with the strength which the heat provided, and it took on the likeness
of a man, and he was called Ymir.)[41]

Snorri Sturluson was an educated man; it is no accident that his
mythological geography recalls the Macrobian climate zones. It should
therefore be read not as an accurate reflection of pre-Christian or para-
Christian beliefs, but as a creative synthesis of disparate materials
available to a thirteenth-century Icelandic scholar. Even *Vǫluspá*,
Snorri's chief source for the passage, shows signs of Christian influence,
for instance in its inclusion of a world conflagration and surrounding
events at the end of time (stanza 57). Whether cognate or disparate,
however, it is clear that flooding and runaway atmospheric warming are
prominent literary concerns in the apocalyptic literature of medieval
Europe.

Climatic concerns range from seasonal survival to long-term security. Where
the overriding societal challenge in today's Global North is to inspire de-
escalating environmental action, the returns of which may seem both distant
and abstract, pre-modern societies had few concerns more pressing than the
struggle for an annual harvest, particularly at the circumpolar limit of the
human domain. Even so, the longest-term climatic developments were
thought both urgent and close in time, even by the orthodox theologians
who pointed out that the precise moment of Christ's return could not be
known. The Day of Judgement could arrive at any time, and though one
could not prevent the climate cataclysm that was to precede it, one could
obtain personal protection through God's grace, whose fruits were believed to
take the form of penance and good works.

   If today's policy of climate mitigation is plagued by difficulties activating
some of its target audiences, there may be a lesson to be drawn from medieval
preaching. The strongest emphases of the homiletic corpus are the need for

[41] Ibid., ch. 5.

a change of heart; the personal consequences of ending up on the wrong side of history; and the closeness in time of those consequences, even if no reliable timeline may be given. Although the canonical Augustinian doctrine insisted that grace precedes good works, so one could not effect one's own salvation, preachers did not typically convey this level of detail to lay audiences, and good works received considerable attention in their sermons.

The medieval church was an authoritative channel by which to effect both political and grassroots change, and it pursued an aggressive awareness campaign around the issues it considered pressing. Though we cannot measure the efficacy of its messaging, a population familiar with immediate climatic pressures is likely to be comparatively receptive to activation in the service of long-term security. Indeed, the Western decline in religious membership since the Middle Ages may plausibly be linked to improvements in short-term security in such domains as food and health, including improved defences against annual climate fluctuation. Given this loss of a centralised moral authority on abstract issues, it is little wonder that today's advocates for climate action often seem like voices in the wilderness.

CHAPTER 6

The Climate of Shakespeare: Four (or More) Forecasts

Lowell Duckert

In early April 2017, tragedy struck the annual Shakespeare Association of America conference in Atlanta, Georgia: on its opening day, seven tornadoes, some of them ranked EF2 (111–135 mph) on the Enhanced Fujita Scale, touched down in the surrounding area, delaying, stranding, and scattering incoming Shakespeareans across the country. The turbulence birthed a witty Twitter hashtag, '#shakenado', an online space for would-be attendees to post their updated statuses and frustrated itineraries straightforwardly and – not surprisingly – in the playwright's own words, broadcasting who 'hath borne most', for example, because 'the rain it raineth every day'.[1] As co-leaders of the seminar 'Shakespeare in the Anthropocene', Craig Dionne and I received messages over the next few days from forlorn participants who were unable to arrive. The meteorological incident was inconvenient, of course – later providing me with a sleepless night on hold with the airline – but it also, given our seminar's theme, generated ample discussion in recognition of those who 'did not make it'. I find it fitting to begin a chapter about climate and Shakespeare with some logistical trouble; no mere coincidence, it compels me to think about the weather that surrounds and inhabits Shakespeare studies as well as environmental criticism: literary 'atmosphere',[2] that is, writers in and on the storm, missives from the mixed-up. Taking a page exactly three and a half centuries later from English natural philosopher Robert Hooke's 'A Method for Making a History of the Weather' (1667), what follows is an attempt to trace meteorological phenomena across ages

---

[1] Shakespeare, *King Lear*, 5.3.301 and 3.3.77. All quotations are from *The Norton Shakespeare*, ed. Stephen Greenblatt, Walter Cohen, Jean E. Howard, Katharine Eisaman Maus, Gordon McMullan, and Suzanne Gossett, 3rd edn (New York: Norton, 2016). Tweets from the conference are online: https://twitter.com/hashtag/shakenado?lang=en.

[2] For more about 'reading for atmosphere', see Jesse Oak Taylor, *The Sky of Our Manufacture: the London Fog in British Fiction from Dickens to Woolf* (Charlottesville: University of Virginia Press, 2016).

and through times-tornadoes, a series of enfolded tweets (or twists) from the (recent) past typed to the dactylic rhythm of 'meteor' twirling in ecopoetic footfall.

Timestorm

@casca Indeed, it is a strange-disposèd time. #shakenado

The climate scientists Simon L. Lewis and Mark A. Maslin identify the start of the Anthropocene (the 'Age of Man') with what they call the 'Orbis Spike' of 1610: a dip in global carbon dioxide coinciding with the commingling of peoples of Africa, Asia, Europe, and the Americas.[3] Staking that the 'age' (or epoch) of the Anthropocene was launched in Shakespeare's late career, however, does not make the weather totally timely (historical) or timeless (a perennial topic of conversation). Meteorology goes multitemporal, traversing past–present distinctions in its path. Michel Serres astutely remarks that the French phrase *le temps* refers to both 'weather' and 'time', a multivalence that resonates in the noun 'tempest': 'Meteorological weather, predictable and unpredictable, will no doubt some day be explainable by complicated notions of fluctuations, strange attractors . . . Someday we will perhaps understand that historical time is even more complicated.'[4] Time's straight arrow turns into a spiral; weather refuses to pass (into past); times storm. Shakespeare speaks to our predilection for predictions in the urgency of *now*;[5] at the same time, he exacerbates them. In the '*New Climate Regime*', as Bruno Latour puts it, 'the physical framework that the Moderns had taken for granted, the ground on which their history had always been played out, has become unstable. As if the décor had gotten up on stage to share the drama with the actors.'[6] Shakespeare's stage stayed open for dramatic re-decorating; consider, for instance, that the Thamesside theatre, under construction in 1599, was nearly washed away by a spring flood. Climatic confluences like these are not merely metaphors for 'weathering' life's travails: they are physical forces for thinking,

---

[3] For more on their stratigraphical point, see Steve Mentz, 'Enter Anthropocene, circa 1610', in Tobias Menely and Jesse Oak Taylor (eds.), *Anthropocene Reading: Literary History in Geologic Times* (University Park: Pennsylvania State University Press, 2017), pp. 43–58.

[4] Michel Serres and Bruno Latour, *Conversations on Science, Culture, and Time*, trans. Roxanne Lapidus (Ann Arbor: University of Michigan Press, 1995), p. 58.

[5] Cary DiPietro and Hugh Grady, eds., *Shakespeare and the Urgency of Now: Criticism and Theory in the 21st Century* (New York: Palgrave-Macmillan, 2013).

[6] Bruno Latour, *Facing Gaia: Eight Lectures on the New Climatic Regime*, trans. Catherine Porter (Cambridge: Polity Press, 2017), p. 3.

performing, and narrating how to weather *within* the tempests of our globe, wet/ter moments that mold plays and lives (and can too often take them). Recent work in material ecocriticism highlights just this co-constitutiveness of climate and culture, a co-occurrence discernible at the level of emotive embodiment and distributed across a range of 'meteorophysiological' effects.[7] The climate of Shakespeare cannot be compartmentalised: it is indicative of the historical climate in which he participated and which extends to today, one whose anthropogenic affronts affect time-beings unequally. Simple meteorological questions asked by the characters of *King Lear* (1605) – 'Art cold?' (3.2.68) or 'What is the cause of thunder?' (3.4.142) – crack into others of increasing complexity. What does it mean not just to think of Shakespeare writing *in* the Anthropocene, but to think about reading his and his contemporaries' works in anthropocenic times and complicated climates comprising 'strange attractors' who are 'strange[ly]-disposed'?

History's Climate

Storm still. #shakenado

Sixteenth- and seventeenth-century English writers bemoaned human-engineered environmental degradation – deforestation, air pollution, and war – but they also deliberated over ecosystemic catastrophes that occurred seemingly outside their influence – such as the debilitating spate of crop failures of 1594–8, the Bristol Channel floods of 1607, and the 1580 Dover Straits earthquake. In fact, early modern pamphleteers effectively popularised meteorological mishaps: while a theological or political cause was often pinpointed – be it God's disfavour with sinning Christians, a sign that the 'natural' social order had been upset, or an 'imperfect' admixture of warm-moist 'vapours' and hot-dry 'exhalations' taken from Aristotle's foundational *Meteorologica* (*c.* 340 BCE.) – these climatic events stressed, rather, the unpredictability and unknowability that underpinned early modern cultures' views on their weather and world. As Vladimir

---

[7] Rebecca Totaro, *Meteorology and Physiology in Early Modern Culture: Earthquakes, Human Identity, and Textual Representation* (New York: Routledge, 2018), p. 2. See also Gail Kern Paster's 'meteorology of passions' in *Humoring the Body: Emotions and the Shakespearean Stage* (University of Chicago Press, 2004), pp. 65–6; and Robert Markley's 'eco-cultural materialism' in 'Summer's Lease: Shakespeare in the Little Ice Age', in Thomas Hallock, Ivo Kamps, and Karen L. Raber (eds.), *Early Modern Ecostudies: From the Florentine Codex to Shakespeare* (New York: Palgrave-Macmillan, 2008), pp. 131–42. Serenella Iovino and Serpil Oppermann, eds., *Material Ecocriticism* (Bloomington: Indiana University Press, 2014) is an outstanding introduction.

Janković argues, '[t]he history of meteorology may ... be conceived as an effort to resolve ... uncertainty, or, better yet, as a series of recurring failures to do so'.[8] Early modern weather-watchers could only ride out the contentiousness of climate; they could respond to, but could not entirely calm, the tropospheric turmoil within which they found themselves and after which their writings chased.

Academic studies typically took one of two lines: theories of meteorological causation indebted to Aristotelian precepts on the one hand, weather-sign treatises replete with astrological prognostications on the other. William Fulke's *A Goodly Gallerye* (1563), for example, one of the most widely read treatises, would subscribe to the former, while the aptly named Adam Foulweather's *A Wonderfull, Strange and Miraculous Astrologicall Prognostication for This Yeere* (1591) would lean to the latter. (As meteors became empirically quantifiable, they carried over the language of prediction-based forecasting with them.) Despite the heavens' outpouring ambiguity, some (Fulke especially) could nevertheless adumbrate a cosmic order, a divine touch, in the meteoric mess. Regularity, to be sure, is still applied and is often reinforced: 'Even though daily weather is notoriously unpredictable', Craig Martin observes, 'the broad strokes of meteorology – climate and the passing of the seasons – are regular.'[9] But any methodological patterns – 'polytheistic', 'materialist', and 'Christian' paradigms, for example[10] – while helpful for identifying purposes, importantly remained flexible. Like the tumultuous ecosystems they were designed to represent, meteorological knowledge systems routinely refused codification because the meteors they described eluded their observers' edifying grasps.

If you turned here looking for an extended sixteenth- or seventeenth-century forecast in several pages, then I am afraid to disappoint. When it comes to any *meteōros* – in Greek, 'to be raised up', 'lofty' – it is disequilibrium all the way down. 'Climate change' by any other name would (and did) shudder as much; change has always been at the core of climate. A stable trend in both Shakespearean ecocriticism and historical climatology is, paradoxically, instability. As archaeologist Brian Fagan has demonstrated, the period of cooling in the northern hemisphere known as the

---

[8] Vladimir Janković, *Reading the Skies: a Cultural History of English Weather, 1650–1820* (Manchester University Press, 2000), p. 16.

[9] Craig Martin, *Renaissance Meteorology: Pomponazzi to Descartes* (Baltimore: Johns Hopkins University Press, 2011), p. 16. Any serious study should start here. See also S. K. Heninger, Jr., *A Handbook of Renaissance Meteorology* (New York: Greenwood Press, 1968).

[10] Totaro, *Meterology*, p. 16.

Little Ice Age (*c.* 1300–1850) was not an aberration in the Earth's existence –
so that a single eccentric winter will eventually give way to spring – but part
of the planet's disorderly, deeply historical, and ever-present dynamic
'flux', an 'endless zigzag': 'climate will have its sway', he says, because
'[h]umanity has been at the mercy of climate change for its entire
existence'.[11] Uniform in neither space nor time, we should be sceptical,
too, of the age's monolithic proclivity to centre western Europe as well as
the human in history: a 'little' world of man in a 'little' age. But the collapse
of macro- and micro- scales could just as well de-centre and re-define. Steve
Mentz hits on this dis-anthropocentric way of thinking directly in his
engagement with the 'new ecology', or the 'post-equilibrium shift' in *King
Lear*: 'neither receptive to nor reflective of human desires, this version of
the elements [strange weather] re-draws the boundaries between self and
world and puts the body–nature relationship in crisis'.[12] To phrase these
lines of disequilibria succinctly: '*Storm still*' (3.1.1). Colossal storms and
cryptic hot–cold fronts *still* storm as they always have, resoundingly, like
the play's seven startling announcements in stage direction. That storm is
unlikely to change even if the players have and will. The 'still' flexes its
temporal dimensions: Shakespeare's storms *still* storm in terms of interpretation; they stir up a world-storm, a 'weather-world',[13] which is never
physically *still*. Shakespeare weathers the intersection of pure theoretical
science and astrological prognostication, only to point out the precariousness of (any) patterns. The forecast calls for flux; his works wean us off
foolproof prediction. I am aware that I digress from what may be expected
of a study of Shakespearean ecology – to chart the dialectic between stable
backdrop and inclement weather – yet I cannot ignore the outlook from
the eyes of his storms. Prediction enclasps unpredictability; the storm we
ride is an endlessly spinning top – Feste's 'whirligig' (5.1.363) from *Twelfth
Night* (1600–1) – not a teetering seesaw promising eventual equanimity
(sustainability). The accustomed difference between climate and weather –
prevailing versus variable conditions – collapses once we recognise our
ephemeral whirl/ed.[14] The 'raised' only raise questions.

---

[11] Brian Fagan, *The Little Ice Age: How Climate Made History* (New York: Basic Books, 2000), pp. xv,
   xiii, xviii, xii.
[12] Steve Mentz, 'Strange Weather in King Lear', *Shakespeare*, 6 (2010), 140.
[13] See Tim Ingold, 'Landscape or Weather-World?', in *Being Alive: Essays on Movement, Knowledge,
   and Description* (New York: Routledge, 2011), pp. 126–35.
[14] See Jeffrey Jerome Cohen and Lowell Duckert, 'Introduction: Welcome to the Whirled', in Cohen
   and Duckert (eds.), *Veer Ecology: a Companion for Environmental Thinking* (Minneapolis: University
   of Minnesota Press, 2017), pp. 1–15.

Portents

*@cicero I believe prodigies are portentous things / Unto the climate
that they point upon. #shakenado*

'New ecology' is suddenly not that *new*. Chaotic climate is not just
'Shakespeare's' or 'in the Elizabethan age': his 'strange-disposèd'[15] time is
ours. Likewise, Latour's *'New Climate Regime'* – with its inter-agential
actors 'swelling'[16] our shaky, anthropocenic stage – is recognisable in
Renaissance decor. The G/g/lobe, site of the *'kakosmos'*, told *'geostor[ies]'* of
subject–object re-definition.[17] What these storied climates 'point upon'[18]
will be the subject of my brief foray, not to fight over whether the long-
dead bard and the daily weather should meet – the charge of anachronism
levelled against proponents of presentism[19] – but how, and on what terms,
the discussion should take place. I argue that the climate *in* Shakespeare's
plays, as well as the climate *in which* his works were composed, invite us to
critically re-examine the entangled relationships between climate and
culture in our current moment of global warming, of 'portentous' change
along a longer climatic continuum. The early modern weather is never
a mundane topic; indeed, I maintain that it is instructive still, for it can
usefully reframe onto-epistemological and politico-ethical questions
regarding the being, knowing, and doing of climate (more on those powers
of the 'above' below). It is easy to treat weather as a historical
background,[20] thrusting it back- or offstage, or, to cast climate reports
simply as hermeneutics, as unclouded lenses for interpreting early modern
emotional, spiritual, and discursive properties. (Allegory, even further
removed, risks neglecting material forces altogether.) I think less about
the adjudicating Jupiter of John Heywood's *The Playe of the Weather*
(*c.* 1533) – who, hearing '[a]ll maner people which haue ben offended',
decides whose 'weather mete to be a mended' – and more about weather *at
play*.[21] '[P]eople's physical encounters with weather in Shakespeare's

---

[15] Shakespeare, *Julius Caesar* (1599), 1.3.33.   [16] Shakespeare, *Henry V* (1599), 1.0.4.
[17] Latour, 'Agency at the time of the Anthropocene', *New Literary History*, 45 (2014), 3–4.
[18] Shakespeare, *Julius Caesar*, 1.3.32.
[19] See DiPietro and Grady, *Shakespeare and the Urgency of Now*; Robert N. Watson, 'Tell Inconvenient
  Truths, But Tell Them Slant', in Jennifer Munroe, Edward J. Geisweidt, and Lynne Bruckner
  (eds.), *Ecological Approaches to Early Modern English Texts: a Field Guide to Reading and Teaching*
  (Farnham: Ashgate, 2015), pp. 17–28; Ken Hiltner, 'Reading the Present in Our Environmental
  Past', in Munroe et al., *Ecological Approaches*, pp. 29–36.
[20] For an example of a strictly contextual approach, see Sidney Thomas, 'The Bad Weather in
  A Midsummer-Night's Dream', *Modern Language Notes*, 64:5 (1949), 319–22.
[21] John Heywood, *The Playe of the Weather* (London: Ihon Awdeley, 1573).

England were interpreted through an essentially imaginative construction of the idea of climate', Mike Hulme asserts, '[c]limate [being] an idea that allowed free passage between the physical and imaginative worlds of . . . Elizabethan audiences'.[22] Jennifer Mae Hamilton's practice of 'meteorological reading' in *King Lear* 'prompts the reader to consider how their interpretation of the weather is historically and ideologically inflected'.[23] By focusing on the passage between (-) the physical-imaginative, the material and the discursive, however, I both complement and complicate these critics' significant claims; drawing attention to matter–metaphor interchanges in and as art offers a way to 'read' meteors but also contemplates ethical – sensitive and responsible – ways of living well right now with the 'raised up'. My thinking throughout is less stratigraphic, that is, and more strategic: less concerned with identifying what is and is not anthropocenic according to discrete chronological points, and more involved in the mixed-up, non/human meteorological bodies of the high and low that Shakespeare trailed.

The 'forecasts' of my subtitle act as signposts for what lies ahead. A combination of the Old English prefix and preposition *fore-* (shortened from 'before') and the Old Norse transitive verb *kasta* – 'to throw', 'to project (anything)' – 'forecast' is a weather-word engendered, for its first pronouncers, in a local climate (v. 1413, n. 1535).[24] The prefix marks the anterior of time ('beforehand'), space/position ('in front of'), order/sequence ('in the front'), and rank (that which comes 'before'). The prepositional energy of *fore-* highlights movement, a lack of secure position, an untying of the fixity that 'forecasts' have come to signify. (It was not *supposed* to rain today.) I employ 'forecast' in its fullest conjectural sense, a projection of events before they (might) occur, an indication of (meteoric) happenings ascertained through failure as much as accuracy. Crucially, the fungible 'forecast' urges us to continue casting forth; we are not inheritors of an ineluctable doom pronounced before our time (victims of a prophetic eco-catastrophic vision) if we deliberately *cast* ourselves into the *fore-* ('before' of the present) to navigate, and then to narrate, the weather within and with which earlier forecasters found

[22] Mike Hulme, 'Climate', in Bruce R. Smith (ed.), *The Cambridge Guide to the Worlds of Shakespeare*, 2 vols. (Cambridge University Press, 2015), vol. 1, pp. 30–1.

[23] Jennifer Mae Hamilton, *This Contentious Storm: an Ecocritical and Performance History of* King Lear (London: Bloomsbury, 2017), p. 21.

[24] 'forecast, *v.*' def. 1a., *OED Online*, Oxford University Press, January 2018, oed.com/view/Entry/72980; 'forecast, *n.*', def. 2b., *OED Online*, Oxford University Press, January 2018, oed.com/view/Entry/72979. Accessed 12 March 2018.

themselves. The tales we tell from environmental history can bear upon the way we tell the precarity of today, 'speaking proverbs'[25] about who and what endures, why 'the poor worm doth die', as *Pericles* (1607–8) points out, for the telling of 'man's oppression' (1.1.103). In addition, the *fore*-interrogates the fixture of Shakespeare in the stratospheric firmament; the 'of' of my title is meant to be not possessive, however, but participatory: he and his works are 'of' the climate. If 'in our imaginative encounters with weather we are as one with Shakespeare', we are 'of' a mind made up of meteors, a *Lear*-like 'one' materially 'minded like the weather, most unquietly' (3.1.2).[26] The mantra that he was a universal poet – 'not of an age but for all time' – presents him as the perfect ecopoetic weatherman for all seasons, never wrong. But to associate Shakespeare with a controversial epoch of deep time justifiably tests, if I may extend Dipesh Chakrabarty's four theses on 'the climate of history', his 'appeal to our sense of human universals'.[27] In short, centring on the playwright who so often comes to the fore brings with it the added challenge of specifying persuasive reasons for doing so. I will cite three of his be/forecasts for us, in theatrics and for throws, from a few expected 'prodigies' to the more peripheral satellites of his meteoroidal canon. Roiling, not weatherproof, 'raised up' and put on a roll, the polysemous 'forecast' is meteorological force at work in the (early modern) meteorological imagination, stirring storm-story set forth in labile lines:

(1/3) distemperature #shakenado

Reflecting on the reality of swirling into an unforeseeable future, it should come as a surprise to find a critical interlocutor in a comedic source: *A Midsummer Night's Dream* (1594–6). If '[t]he course of true love never did run smooth' (1.1.134), neither does the climate. As the fairies Oberon and Titania quarrel over 'a lovely boy stolen from an Indian king' (2.1.22), the weather revolts, drowning the world in a fetid flood:

---

[25] Craig Dionne, *Posthuman Lear: Reading Shakespeare in the Anthropocene* (New York: Punctum Books, 2016), p. 18.

[26] Hulme, 'Climate', p. 34.

[27] Dipesh Chakrabarty, 'The Climate of History: Four Theses', *Critical Inquiry*, 35.2 (2009), 201. In response to Chakrabarty's broader 'geophysical force', Stacy Alaimo has rightly argued that 'we shift from the sense of humans as an abstract force that acts but is not acted on, to a trans-corporeal conception of the human . . . always material, always the stuff of the world', *Exposed: Environmental Politics and Pleasures in Posthuman Times* (Minneapolis: University of Minnesota Press, 2016), p. 155. I see 'meteorological force' as one such 'site for social justice and environmental practice'.

> Therefore the winds, piping to us in vain,
> As in revenge have sucked up from the sea
> Contagious fogs which, falling in the land,
> Hath every pelting river made so proud
> That they have overborne their continents.   (88–92)

Sickness swells with a dead tide of 'murrain flock' (97) so '[t]hat rheumatic diseases do abound' (105). The seasons stray as well:

> And thorough this distemperature we see
> The seasons alter . . .
> The spring, the summer,
> The childing autumn, angry winter, change
> Their wonted liveries, and the mazèd world
> By their increase now knows not which is which.   (106–114)

Who is to blame? According to Titania, the fault is theirs: 'And this same progeny of evils comes / From our debate, from our dissension; / We are their parents and original' (115–17). Her acknowledgement is a caution against human – or fairy – hubris, perhaps, made at the expense of 'a little changeling boy' (120) who has no say in the debacle. But there are other lessons here, for the speech troubles easy designations of causation: is the 'pelting' truly because of them? And if the seasons' timely change represents the most natural of progressions, what now is natural? As the temperature vacillates it casts confusion – 'hoary-headed frosts / Fall in the fresh lap of the crimson rose' (107–8) – and, in doing so, it throws temperament (in its etymological sense of 'correct mixture') into question. '[W]hich is which' is difficult to answer when all commingled bodies present are flowy, 'fatted' (97) and feted, sickly, saturated, distemperate. For Henry S. Turner, 'it is not merely the idea of "season" that is undone but the idea of individuation itself that threatens to dissolve into a tempest of force and constantly mutating elements'.[28] Although I wholeheartedly agree with his interpretation, I wish to linger longer on the 'merely'. The play's titular 'midsummer' draws attention to the *un*seasonable quality of the passage as well as its already noticeable disjunctions (such as Theseus's reference to '[t]he rite of May' (4.1.131)). I would like to rename this phenomenon of 'distemperature' the 'inseasonable' to underline the Latin prefix *in-* ('not') of season but also to defamiliarise the phrase of something 'in season'; in other words, the season

---

[28] Henry S. Turner, *Shakespeare's Double Helix* (London: Continuum, 2007), p. 40. See also Robert N. Watson, 'The Ecology of Self in *Midsummer Night's Dream*', in Lynne Bruckner and Dan Brayton (eds.), *Ecocritical Shakespeare* (Farnham: Ashgate, 2011), pp. 33–56.

already contains its unravelling with *in* it and thereby challenges the normality of 'right' time.²⁹ Time breaks out of quadcameral structure when weather acts 'out of season', unleashing the gale-force turbulence of *le temps*: time loses its time-honoured chronological ability to order human experience and notes vertiginous instabilities instead. When seasons do not 'end' or 'begin' as they should, one self-assuring phrase – 'it is the time of the *season*' – is replaced with a different climatic maxim: to everything there is an 'inseasonable' time. '[R]evenge' is what the 'mazèd' modern world 'now knows' too well, as the marked 'increase' in both number and frequency of storms in the Atlantic Ocean attests, unsettling whatever we know concerning the duration and ferocity of a 'season' which officially runs from 1 June to 30 November. (September 2017 was billed 'the busiest on record'.³⁰)

By destabilising ideas of time as well as order, the play's delugic forecast is a nightmare rather than a dream; it calls for more 'pelting', and it bombards a hypothesised starting-off point for the Anthropocene, agriculture: 'The plowman lost his sweat, and the green corn / Hath rotted ere his youth attained a beard' (94–5). At the same time, the play crucially does not provide a return to a lost order, the 'dream' of perfect unison and nature held in self-sustaining balance: it disorders order itself; it exposes, that is, the wish for (lost) harmony – total temperateness – *as* a dream. 'What fools these mortals be', to paraphrase Robin Goodfellow and Lysander, to ignore how 'quick bright things come to confusion' (3.2.115; 1.1.149). To think on recovery when facing hurricanes' unceasing arrivals – Irma (30 August) followed Harvey's path (17 August), while Maria (16 September) protracted the devastation upon Puerto Rico that Jose (5 September) had begun only a few weeks earlier – necessitates rethinking what practices and discourses we wish to recover when envisioning alternative ecological prospects, and it does so, importantly, through the past. Direction in Titania's talk is unclear – 'And the quaint mazes in the wanton green / For lack of tread are indistinguishable' (2.2.99–100) – meaning that paths must be made anew, or at least differently from the way they were before. Sustainability morphs into something like resilience; the dream and the nightmare are held in conjunction. As the play 'put[s] a girdle round about the earth' (2.1.175) – connecting local to global, the 'spicèd Indian air'

---

²⁹ Jeffrey Jerome Cohen similarly uses 'inhuman' to 'emphasize both difference ("in-" as negative prefix) and intimacy ("in-" as indicator of estranged interiority)' in *Stone: an Ecology of the Inhuman* (Minneapolis: University of Minnesota Press, 2015), p. 10.

³⁰ Philip Bump, 'This Has Been the Most Active Month for Hurricanes on Record', *Washington Post* (27 September 2017).

(2.1.124) to the Athenian sort – it draws attention to how areas and populations differ in their degree of vulnerability and receipt of aid. Susceptibility is geographically lopsided. That same 'Indian' boy is not simply a stand-in for the Global South allowed on to the stage of the (Grecian) Global North (and farther: England), he is a reminder to think on how climate change affects populations disproportionately. (Puerto Rican 'second-class citizens' vie with Houston 'Americans' over unevenly distributed resources.) Comparing the recent damages of 'distemperature' through which Texans waded to 'a great tempest of haile'[31] that fell on Kent in 1590 (which may have influenced Shakespeare's play) and *The Last Terrible Tempestious Windes and Weather* (1613) that battered the British Isles a generation after, might not convince modern-day misbelievers to *get woke* to climate change, but it at least urges us to 'expound this dream' (4.1. 202–3) of human and non-human atmospheric entanglement, one that 'hath no bottom' (210) to its cosmological complexity almost four hundred years later: not to exonerate humans' impact but to learn how to respond better to the fears and desires of those mortally striving to stay afloat; to examine, critique, and story tales of our participation in this turbulence; and to ask what collectives, what futures, we may build by dreaming them up.

(2/3) It will be rain tonight. #shakenado

Banquo turns forecaster before his death in *Macbeth* (1606–7), a weatherman who speaks in simple perfect (3.3.18). His casting about the rain – immediately punned upon by the first murderer: 'Let it come down!' (3.3.18) – circles back to the precipitation released in the play's first lines: the witchy 'hurly-burly' of 'thunder, lightning . . . rain' (1.1.2–3). There is no 'done' to it (1.1.3). Does Banquo believe he is about to die, remembering the 'weird women' (3.1.2) and their vatic prevarications, recalling his earlier prognosis that '[t]he earth hath bubbles as the water has' (1.3.80)? Or is his sky-gazing an attempt to start a conversation with Fleance, his aerial son, the one who flees the scene? Gwilym Jones argues that, whereas audiences would have expected a supernatural causation (witchcraft) behind the 'unruly' (2.3.48) events that took place during the 'rough night' (61) of Duncan's murder – 'the earth / Was feverous and did shake' (54–5), the play instead betrays a profound 'meteorological equivo-cation' in which the buckling earthquake – believed to be caused by

---

[31] *A Most True and Lamentable Report, of a Great Tempest of Haile* (London: J. Wolfe, 1590).

underground winds – blasts any claims of understandability.[32] 'Weather dominates *Macbeth*; and its origins, its effects and its meaning are always subject to the equivocal play of terror.'[33] Macbeth and James I linked turbulence to witches' spells – 'you untie the winds' (4.1.52), the former maintains – while on 29–30 March 1606, a truly terrifying tempest collapsed steeples and sunk ships in the North Sea.[34] Banquo's cursory observation about a coming rainfall adds to this epistemological terror since it voices the human desire to effectively, and safely, forecast within meteorological equivocality. The flux of 1606 is still fresh; like him, we keep an eye upon our ways homeward through the (highland) haze.

To Jones's point that staged storms are 'always in a flux in performance',[35] I suggest that what is being dramatised in the 'hurly-burly' performances of *Macbeth* is climate *as* flux. I think back on Banquo's thought of rain; yet for Jones, 'there is no inherent complexity in rain, nor is there any ferocity . . . Rain simply *resolves* itself', and, since it expresses a repetitive cycle, it is 'a crucial element of the replenishing sequence of order . . . Such is the equalizing nature of rain in early modern imagery'.[36] Other critics offer readings of early modern rain that contrast with these simple, sequential, and sustainable qualities; I, for one, have highlighted the 'it' within phrases like '[i]t will rain' as a marker of inorganic agency.[37] The 'strange' of 'strange weather' gets stranger, things *queerer*: 'the witches' spells', Christine Varnado states, 'blur any easy distinction between natural and unnatural forms of generation; they signal that this fragmented, dismembered, bubbling chaos *is how nature works*'.[38] A 'queer model of nature' appears in the play's non-anthropomorphic forms: bubbles and raindrops wrapped up in, and propelling, its 'uncanny animation'.[39] The 'hurly-burly', appropriately enough, is of unknown origin, a re-duplication ('hurly' comes from 'hurling') as well as a mishmash of animal ('burl' of wool) and plant ('burly', of stout figure, and thus related to the vegetal 'bowerly'). Banquo's forecast adumbrates

---

[32] Gwilym Jones, *Shakespeare's Storms* (Manchester University Press, 2015), p. 103.

[33] Ibid., p. 104.

[34] See 'The Hurricane of 1606' in Henry N. Paul, *The Royal Play of Macbeth: When, Why, and How It Was Written by Shakespeare* (New York: Macmillan, 1950), pp. 248–54.

[35] Jones, *Shakespeare's Storms*, p. 10. [36] Ibid., pp. 106–7.

[37] See 'Making (It) Rain' in Lowell Duckert, *For All Waters: Finding Ourselves in Early Modern Wetscapes* (Minneapolis: University of Minnesota Press, 2017), pp. 149–200. Charlotte Scott supernaturally associates the witches with an 'earthy rain' in *Shakespeare's Nature: From Cultivation to Culture* (Oxford University Press, 2014), pp. 137–8.

[38] Christine Varnado, 'Queer Nature, or the Weather in *Macbeth*', in Goran Stanivukovic (ed.), *Queer Shakespeare: Desire and Sexuality* (London: Bloomsbury, 2017), p. 192, original emphasis.

[39] Ibid., pp. 189, 195.

what I call a 'hurlicane', a jumble tumbled out of my own word-cauldron. Like the notes of addition and relation designated in the hyphenation and rhyming (respectively) of 'hurly-burly', '[i]t' will not stop raining; '[i]t will' continue to multiply, coming down by being brought up. The 'hurlicane' is the throwing up and down of meteoric things, and when the witches convene – '*dancing in a circle*' (1.3.33) – of spinning multi-directionality and non-normative reproduction. Even an uninvited third assassin must join the murder party before rainfall, the first killer's query '[b]ut who did bid thee join with us?' (3.3.1) echoing Banquo's opening question to the witches: '[w]hat are these?' (1.3.40).

Timothy Morton describes dark ecology's thought-process as '[e]*cognosis*, a riddle ... like a knowing that knows itself ... a *weird* knowing'.[40] Acclimating ourselves to the effervescence of the Scottish heath does not make it any less weird. Because the play conditions both its characters and audiences to know that 'nothing is but what is not' (1.3.144), a ho-hum prediction like Banquo's ironically suggests the *opposite*: in other words, Shakespeare states the obvious in a climate in which nothing is obvious, where everything is obviating, extra-ordinary, and defined by 'what [it] is not', in order to make a *weird* meteorological point. (As weather is wont to do.) So, let '[i]t' come to mean several strange things: (1) the homophonic pun of raining down blows; (2) raindrops' stabbing pricks – to the amount of 'twenty trenched gashes on [Banquo's] head' (3.4.28) – an allusion to weather's real violence; and (3) the supposed cause of Scotland's disorders, Macbeth's *reign*. The rain he foretells, once allied with the 'hurly-burly' of unidentifiable origin and interminable prolongation, truly is '[t]he least a death to nature' (3.4.29), at least a 'nature' that separates the (rightly) ruled from its cacophonous ('unruly') counterpart. We certainly are vexed (or is it hexed?) when we try to engage in 'a long-standing tradition of vexed interpretations of the weather'.[41] Banquo's forecast sets off a linguistic chain of meteorological effects, a self-fulfilling prophecy, perhaps, but one that changes in and by the interpretation of another. (An 'imperfect mixture' indeed.) If 'climate' is that which orders (as seasonal and geographic normality) while 'weather' weirds (wreaking supernatural abnormality), then *Macbeth*'s rain really is queer: any question concerning the normal-normative cannot be asked of the order-restoring state,

---

[40] Timothy Morton, *Dark Ecology: for a Logic of Future Coexistence* (New York: Columbia University Press, 2016), p. 5, original emphasis.

[41] Hamilton, *This Contentious Storm*, p. 30.

the ecological sovereign and scientifically sanctioned God-king who oversees the realm of the orderly skies; it will be forever pondered from inside meteorological precipitousness, un-'done' ambiguity.

(3/3) do climate #shakenado

How does one 'do' climate? For hot-headed King Leontes of Sicilia, 'climate' refers to the classical division of the Earth's surface – from the Greek *klima* ('slope, zone') and *klinein* ('to slope') – a zone between lines of latitude. He thought he had done away with his infant daughter by banishing her to one of these regions 'quite out / Of our dominions', leaving Perdita 'to [her] own protection / And favour of the climate' (*Winter's Tale*, 2.3.175–8). Kindness ('favour') does not reside in his clime; indeed, the climates of this seasonal play, *The Winter's Tale* (1611), are hostile. The sea coast upon which she is placed, '[t]he deserts of Bohemia' (3.3.2), is uncomfortable: 'The skies look grimly / And threaten present blusters', a Mariner tells Antigonus (3–4). While the latter is infamously devoured by a bear, the former is shipwrecked, drowned with his mates; all their fates are narrated by a clown to a shepherd: 'I have seen two such sights, by sea and by land. / But I am not to say it is a sea, for it is now the sky' (79–80). The rustic recounts the climatic violence along the coast, but his report also removes the noun 'climate' from its neat delineations. Sea-becoming-sky announces a meteorological inversion in which meteors ('sky') come up from below ('sea'); the below now becomes the up (and vice versa). The 'climate' of latitudinal lines, that is, starts to slope. *Klima*'s fixity takes a curve. There is no difference between 'climate' (*klima*) and 'weather' (which comes from Old English *weder*, related to 'wind') if both designate instability. '[B]etwixt' them, to quote the wise clown, 'you cannot thrust a bodkin's point' (81). Despite this confession, Leontes disbelieves any news of climatic salubriousness outside of unsavory Sicilia; in the '[f]ertile ... isle' of Delphos, for example, where '[t]he climate's delicate, the air most sweet' (3.1.1–2), the oracle's pronouncement of Hermione's faultlessness instantly turns into 'falsehood' (3.2.138). If there 'is not truth at all i' the oracle' (137), then Cleomenes and Dion's description of the isle's weather serves to reaffirm the cold demeanour of the court, whose king '[c]harge[s] too coldly' and who will face the statue '[a]s ... it coldly stands' in the end (1.2.30; 5.3.36).

The most chilling forecast the play propounds is not just a hostile (to human) idea of 'climate' – a stormy sort of sloping – but the inhospitality that may take place within any clime. Shakespeare was not the first to use

'climate' in its traditional nounal guise, but this play – which includes three
of the word's nine total appearances in his work – marks the first recorded
use of the verbal form in English.[42] The intransitive sense of 'residing' in
a particular region comes, coincidently, from a wiser (of 'sixteen winters'
(5.3.50)) Leontes who welcomes Florizel and Perdita (as yet unknown to
him) to his shores: 'The blessèd gods / Purge all infection from our air
whilst you / Do climate here' (5.1.167–9). Julia Reinhard Lupton writes
eloquently of risk in the play: 'In the drama of hospitality, actors traditionally excluded from the scene of politics ... wander into the space of
publicity by virtue of their participation in the social drama of hospitality,
inevitably dragging with them the needs of life and the objects of utility,
convenience, and desire that support them.'[43] The king's speech is an
invitation, an attempt, even, to change his current climate. As an auxiliary,
or helping, verb, 'do' turns the 'to slope' of climate into an ethical
imperative, a doing (something) for others. Consider the help requested
by ecological refugees of increasingly susceptible regions (like 'Hurricane
Alley') and by populaces left to fend for themselves against sea-level rise
(such as Small Island Developing States (SIDS)). Coldness is what precipitated one play's questions of un/accommodation, *King Lear*'s, 'to feel
what wretches feel' (3.4.35) when they sense a storm on skin: one king's
gesture reveals how sympathy shifts soppy, solipsistic perspectives. And so
can Leontes's compassionate *Tale*: care can come from re-encountering
scenes of regal re-orientation such as his. What matters of concern, and
(with) whom, do we 'take up' (3.3.105) with the 'raised up'? Shakespeare's
tautologous forecast for us is more of 'climate', but it also brings with it the
wonders of hospitality and the possibilities of the 'warm' – intimate – 'life'
(5.3.35). If there is such a thing as meteorological justice, the 'do' of climate
is it.

(4/?) It is the quality o'th' climate. #shakenado

Early modern meteorology teaches us how to raise objections with objects
'raised up' in order to live with their un/predictable results, trains us to map
obscurities rather than revelations, and forecasts world-puzzles – weird
words like 'inseasonable', 'hurricane', and '*klinein*' – unsolvable by either
proto/scientific reason (teleological certainty) or divine determination

---

[42] 'climate, *v.1*', *OED Online*, Oxford University Press, January 2018, oed.com/view/Entry/34320.
Accessed 12 March 2018.
[43] Julia Reinhard Lupton, *Thinking with Shakespeare: Essays on Politics and Life* (University of Chicago
Press, 2011), p. 164.

(theological design). The hashtag (#) has always been a punctuational symbol of fore-casting in this piece, that which typographically comes before and that which tags words thereafter. One more from me, then: to wonder whether examining the storms that inhabit playtexts – and that will certainly continue to dis- and interrupt the Shakespearean conference season – may influence the 'quality o'th'' professional climate;[44] that is, to meditate upon early modern meteors' capacities to affect our critical practices and to imagine how they might develop different (and necessary) means to weather the #shakenado together.[45] I wish to raise a constellation of questions in conclusion: how do we (if we do) narrate this flux to ourselves, students, colleagues, and general audiences? What is there to 'do' when what to expect from 'climate' is more climate (sloping), from 'weather' more weather (wind)? (There 'will be rain'.) Is it enough – if only for appeasement purposes – to point out that Shakespeare's works survive four hundred years later, that there is one 'darling bu[d]' (3) left on the 'temperate' (2) branch of Sonnet 18 (1609), swaying against amplifying degrees of 'distemperature'? To say that early moderns were more connected, up to cosmos if not down to earth, resembles a nostalgic wish to restore a foregone, forever-elusive climatic past. But by being deliberately anachronistic in my 'method' of 'making', I have tried to suggest that it is through the tempests of Shakespeare's lifetime that we arrive at anti-apocalyptic thinking and investments in (the) future. 'Wise passivity',[46] or just putting up with the weather, is not something I am advocating. (Or, conversely, better mastery: that includes techno-scientific kinds closely related to the anthropocentricity that sponsors it and that furthers anthropogenic harms.) To do either would be to show how climate stultifies, loses its movement by being bound to authority, discipline, region, period. The reports may repeat but they also afford new opportunities to apprehend 'climate' as a verb, a doing in and of practice. If my 'forecast' from the '#shakenado' is hopeful, it should be: just as long as the climate of Shakespeare actualises – not merely augurs – meteoric 'casts' with and for others, various and variable communities who, weathering their 'whirligig' environments, believe that rifeness *is*, but that it is not *all*.

[44] Shakespeare, *The Tempest* (1611), 2.1.192.
[45] One example is Craig Dionne and Lowell Duckert, eds., 'Shakespeare in the Anthropocene', special issue of *Early Modern Culture*, 13 (2018).
[46] Tom MacFaul, *Shakespeare and the Natural World* (Cambridge University Press, 2015), p. 11.

PART II

Evolution

CHAPTER 7

Weather and Climate in the Age of Enlightenment

Jan Golinski

Weather is the perennial setting for all human activities. In the British Isles, it has provided the substance of numerous proverbs, featured in countless conversations, and formed the scenic background for a thousand years of literary narrative.[1] We are tempted to believe the weather has always been with us in just the form we are accustomed to think of it today. But that is not so. In certain important respects, the modern concept of weather emerged during the cultural transformation known as the Enlightenment. It was in the eighteenth century that people in Britain and elsewhere began to conceive of weather as a constant – and not merely occasional – presence in human lives. Atmospheric conditions began to be recorded, reported, and measured on a daily basis, so that the weather became a quotidian entity, present at all times and not just when it impacted human activities in a particularly dramatic way. The new notion of weather also gave rise to a new understanding of climate, defined in terms of the long-term averages of atmospheric variables. It is in relation to this normalised concept of climate that we now conceive of the possibility of climatic change. Beliefs that the climate is changing are premised on the assumption that it has heretofore been stable, an assumption grounded on the systematic compilation of weather statistics that began to gather steam during the eighteenth century. Paradoxically, however, the idea that the climate was changing was also articulated in the same period. As they sought more information about weather patterns, enlightened observers also contemplated the possibility that human activities might be altering the climate. In these respects,

---

[1] This chapter draws heavily on Jan Golinski, *British Weather and the Climate of Enlightenment* (University of Chicago Press, 2007). See also: Alexandra Harris, *Weatherland: Writers and Artists under English Skies* (London: Thames and Hudson, 2015); Vladimir Janković, *Reading the Skies: a Cultural History of the English Weather, 1650–1820* (Manchester University Press, 2000); Lucian Boia, *The Weather in the Imagination* (London: Reaktion Books, 2005); Tom Fort, *Under the Weather: Us and the Elements* (London: Century, 2006).

ideas about the constancy and alteration of the atmospheric environment
assumed the form familiar to us today.

In this chapter, we trace the emergence in the eighteenth century of
concepts of weather and climate that are familiar features of modernity.
We shall see how weather came to be studied through the enterprise of
regular recording, its anomalies de-emphasised as belief in miraculous
divine intervention gave way to faith in the lawlike regularity of general
providence. This enterprise provided the foundation for a new consciousness of climate, celebrated by British commentators as a providential
blessing to the nation. British people took pride in their stable and
moderate climate, regarding its steady temperature and precipitation as
underpinning the nation's health and prosperity. We shall also see that sites
of overseas settlement, such as the British colonies in North America,
presented a stark contrast with the normalised climate of the homeland.
In these sites, indications that climatic extremes were lessening as settlement advanced were eagerly seized upon. The creole population was keen
to believe that they were bringing their seasons into alignment with the
European temperate ideal as they cultivated the American landscape. Thus,
the notion of climatic alteration entered eighteenth-century learned discourse against the background of a newly stabilised concept of climate and
in the context of exchanges between metropolitan centre and colonial
periphery.

Providence and the Temperate Ideal

The word 'weather' is as old as the English language itself, with roots in
Old Germanic and even more ancient words referring to storms and winds.
From Anglo-Saxon times, the word was used to refer to conditions of the
air, including precipitation, gales, remarkable heat or cold, or even temperate calm. In all its forms, weather was something that happened, an event
that occurred; the usage encompassed the possibility not just that the
weather might change but that it might *end*, ceasing to impinge on
human activity and thus becoming unworthy of further notice.
The *Oxford English Dictionary* quotes examples of this use of the term in
singular and plural forms. Chaucer's *Troilus & Criseyde* (c. 1374) has: 'This
were a weder for to slepen inne.' And the anonymous *Le Morte Arthure*
(c. 1450) offers: 'Wederes had they feyre and good.' The notion of weather
as an event or series of events was embedded in both popular speech and
the science of meteorology descending from Aristotle, Seneca, Ptolemy,
and other ancient authorities. The classical science was directed at the

study of meteors, understood as atmospheric phenomena that rose from the Earth to inhabit the turbulent sphere below the orbit of the moon. These phenomena included thunder and lightning, rain, snow, and hail, and such other entities as auroras, comets, and shooting stars that we would not associate with weather at all. All shared the characteristic of transience typical of the sublunary sphere; they occurred for a certain amount of time but did not participate in the permanence of the celestial domain.[2]

In the seventeenth century, many writers recorded extreme or unusual weather events, labelling them as 'wonders', 'prodigies', and 'marvels', and often interpreting them as portents sent by God to warn or punish humankind. The sixteenth-century *Goodly Gallerye* (1563) by William Fulke, republished in 1670, proclaimed that 'the first and efficient cause' of all atmospheric phenomena 'is God the worker of all wonders'.[3] Fulke classed violent thunderstorms, large hailstones, whirlwinds, auroras, and strange cloud formations, along with comets and shooting stars, as meteors, all located in the middle heavens between Earth and moon. Comets, thunderstorms, earthquakes, and auroras continued to be interpreted as omens in connection with the political events of the time. Even the fortuitous 'Protestant wind', which guided the fleet of William III across the Channel to dethrone the Catholic king James II, was celebrated as a divine intervention in the affairs of the British nation. An anonymous author of a work published in 1692 declared that, 'The sudden and unaccountable changes which are sometimes observ'd in the Air and other Elements ... [are] set in the fair and spacious Theatre of Heaven as the fittest place to represent those Divine shews to the view of all.'[4] The idea that extraordinary weather events were dramatic spectacles, orchestrated by a divine impresario, still found support at the end of the seventeenth century.

Remarkable weather events were also recorded at this time as attributes of particular locations, rather in the way that naturalists would collect peculiar specimens or curiosities of their place of residence. Meteors featured regularly alongside topography and wildlife in local natural histories and works of descriptive chorography. The Oxford chemistry

---

[2] Aristotle, *Meteorologica*, trans. H. D. P. Lee (Cambridge, MA: Harvard University Press, 1987); Liba Taub, *Ancient Meteorology* (London: Routledge, 2003).

[3] W[illiam] F[ulke], *Meteors: Or a Plain Description of All Kinds of Meteors* (London: William Leake, 1670), p. 7. On wonders in general, see William E. Burns, *The Age of Wonders: Prodigies, Politics and Providence in England, 1657–1727* (Manchester University Press, 2002). See also the discussion of sixteenth-century attitudes to meteors in Chapter 6 of this volume by Lowell Duckert.

[4] *A Practical Discourse on the Late Earthquakes* (London: J. Dunton, 1692), p. 15.

lecturer Robert Plot included aerial phenomena in his natural histories of
Oxfordshire (1677) and Staffordshire (1686), as did the naturalist and
antiquarian Charles Leigh in his work on Lancashire (1700).
The Cumberland clergyman Thomas Robinson also recorded thunderstorms and other meteors as features of local chorography. Robinson was
convinced that weather phenomena were caused by vapours released from
'Internal Heat and Fermentation' beneath the surface of the earth.[5]
Observing from the top of Cross Fell near Penrith, he believed he could
discern these vapours circulating between earth and sky. As Ralph Bohun,
a fellow of New College Oxford, wrote in 1671: 'The Earth is the first
Mother of Meteors; and contains the Principles of them all in her Fruitful
Womb.'[6] Because meteorological phenomena were believed to originate
under the earth, it seemed appropriate to include them in topographical
works.

In the decades around the turn of the eighteenth century, however, an
alternative conception of the weather was beginning to make its appearance. Those who were sympathetic to new trends in natural philosophy
argued that atmospheric events reflected the uniformity of a world governed by regular laws. They saw nature as the domain of God's steady
providential care rather than of occasional miraculous interventions.
Protestant intellectuals believed that miracles had ceased at an earlier
point in history, and they were becoming less likely to ascribe extraordinary
or preternatural events to either divine or demonic interference. Learned
opinion preferred to emphasise God's general providence, manifested in
the uniform laws governing natural processes. The astronomer and mathematician Edmond Halley studied the motions of comets using Isaac
Newton's theory of gravitation, treating them as celestial rather than
atmospheric phenomena. Halley issued predictions of comets' appearances
to lessen the popular apprehension surrounding them. He predicted
eclipses for the same purpose, and took the lead in mapping the patterns
of winds across the oceans, attempting to tame even those notoriously
capricious powers of the air.[7] In the 1690s, theorists of the Earth, including
Thomas Burnet and William Whiston, argued that one could give
a naturalistic explanation even of the biblical flood, while recognising

---

[5] Thomas Robinson, *New Observations on the Natural History of this World of Matter* (London: John
  Newton, 1696), p. 181. On the chorographic tradition of weather observation, see Janković, *Reading
  the Skies*, pp. 78–81.
[6] Ralph Bohun, *A Discourse concerning the Origine and Properties of Wind* (Oxford: W. Hall, 1671),
  p. 26.
[7] Alan Cook, *Edmond Halley: Charting the Heavens and the Seas* (Oxford University Press, 1998).

that it nonetheless served God's purposes. The point was that God had acted through the normal forces of nature, even while bringing about an event that was unique in the Earth's history.

In 1703, an extreme and catastrophic episode brought these different ways of interpreting weather events into conflict. In the night of 26–27 November of that year, southern England and the Low Countries were struck by what came to be known as the Great Storm, when hurricane-force winds uprooted trees, toppled buildings, and sank ships at sea. More than a hundred people died on land, as chimneys collapsed and roofs were torn off houses, and thousands of mariners perished when their ships were submerged or driven aground. As the Worcestershire gentleman Thomas Appletree wrote in his journal, it was 'a most dreadful night for violence of [wind] & rage of it most tremendous & inexpressible . . . as if [the] whole mass of air were putt into a ferment of convulsions & haunted with Furies, or Exasperated by Aeriall demons'.[8] Many observers agreed that the event was the result of divine intervention. Daniel Defoe, who edited a compilation of graphic narratives under the title *The Storm* (1704), declared that the tempest was 'the dreadfulest and most universal Judgment that ever Almighty Power thought fit to bring upon this Part of the World'. Defoe denied that such an extraordinary occurrence proceeded from natural causes, claiming that the great wind had 'blown out the Candle of Reason' of those philosophers who judged it part of the normal course of nature.[9] Other writers agreed. An anonymous pamphleteer, who believed the storm was a punishment for the depravities of the London theatre, insisted, 'when Natural Agents act in a strange, unnatural manner . . . this is from the Lord'.[10]

Natural philosophers did not dispute that God was ultimately responsible for the storm, but they ascribed it to general providence acting through natural causes and normalised it by reference to weather records compiled on a regular basis. Thus, William Derham, vicar of Upminster in Essex, who had published a journal of the weather for every day from 1697 to 1702, stoically continued recording barometer readings and rainfall measurements throughout the hurricane. He reported 'some particulars

[8] [Thomas Appletree], 1703 Weather Diary, Lancing College Archives, Lancing, West Sussex, p. 422. On this document, see also Jan Golinski, '"Exquisite Atmography": Theories of the World and Experiences of the Weather in a Diary of 1703', *British Journal for the History of Science*, 34 (2001), 149–71.
[9] [Daniel Defoe], *The Storm, or a Collection of the Most Remarkable Casualties and Disasters Which Happen'd in the Late Dreadful Tempest* (London: G. Sawbridge, 1704), sig. A8R, p. 2. See also Defoe, *The Storm*, ed. Richard Hamblyn (London: Penguin, 2003).
[10] *The Terrible Stormy Wind and Tempest* (London: W. Freeman, 1705), p. 10.

of a more Philosophical consideration' regarding the event in a letter to the *Philosophical Transactions* of the Royal Society of London. Derham related the November episode to the weather earlier in the year, noting that the damp and mild season had built up 'nitro-sulphureous or other hetero-geneous matter [in the air], which when mix'd together might make a sort of Explosion'. He mentioned that Halley would also be offering a naturalistic explanation, since he had 'undertaken the Province of the late Tempest'.[11] A similar report was sent to the Royal Society by the Dutch microscopist and cloth merchant Anton van Leeuwenhoek. Watching his barometer closely in Delft, van Leeuwenhoek noted that the mercury had never been so low in the tube as when the wind was strongest. When the mercury began to rise, however, he remarked to those with him 'that the Storm would not last long; and so it happened'.[12] It seemed that those who observed the storm as part of a programme of regular observations could attain a degree of philosophical detachment from the terrors it inflicted on the population at large.

A few years later, another writer responded similarly to a heavy thunder-storm striking Richmond in Surrey in 1711. Although the event occurred on Whit Sunday, the anonymous author insisted that 'there is nothing in all this which supposes or implies any immediate Interposition of God'.[13] John Pointer, chaplain of Merton College, Oxford, laid out the naturalistic position more systematically in his *Rational Account of the Weather* (1723). Drawing on the work of Derham, Halley, and others, Pointer proposed that 'Natural Causes do Naturally (that is, according to the settled Order and Nature of things) produce Natural Effects.' He explained the theolo-gical principle that God's extraordinary providences should not be invoked too readily, but rather his ordinary providence – as shown in the design of the natural world – should be respected. What could possibly be gained, Pointer asked, by playing to the fears of the people he called 'the Vulgar'?[14] Elite opinion was moving away from a fascination with wonders and marvels, which were increasingly relegated to the realm of popular errors and superstitions. The counterpart to this shift was a heightened regard for the uniformity of nature, viewed as a manifestation of God's general

---

[11] William Derham, 'A Letter ... Containing his Observations concerning the Late Storm', *Philosophical Transactions of the Royal Society*, 24.289 (1704–5), 1531–2.

[12] Anton van Leeuwenhoek, 'Part of a Letter ... Giving his Observations on the Late Storm', *Philosophical Transactions of the Royal Society*, 24.289 (1704–5), 1535–7.

[13] *A True and Particular Account of a Storm of Thunder and Lightning* (London: John Morphew, 1711), pp. 15–16.

[14] John Pointer, *A Rational Account of the Weather* (Oxford: S. Wilmot, 1723), pp. vii, 196.

providence. The author who reported the 1711 Richmond thunderstorm denied that God was immediately active on that occasion but reminded readers that it was appropriate to praise the deity for the temperateness of the British climate, which prevented this kind of event occurring very often. Ultimately, even the 1703 Great Storm was remembered not for the damage it caused or even the casualties, but for the fact that it was such a singular and extreme departure from the English weather's normal equanimity.

Notwithstanding the Great Storm, the image of the British climate as even and temperate became part of an emerging national consciousness in the decades that followed. This was in no small part due to regular recording of the weather in daily journals, an activity promoted by some of the leading lights of the Royal Society in the 1660s. Robert Hooke, Robert Boyle, and John Locke were among those who took up the practice. Derham's meticulous record was offered to the public in the *Philosophical Transactions*, as was part of Richard Townley's from Lancashire and Robert Plot's from Oxford. The first few decades of the eighteenth century saw the publication of journals from Surrey, Cornwall, Devon, Somerset, Northamptonshire, Edinburgh, Dublin, and several overseas locations. In the middle of the century, the *Philosophical Transactions* was joined by the *Gentleman's Magazine*, which published an annual weather diary contributed by (among others) Thomas Barker in Rutland and Gilbert White in Hampshire. Many medical practitioners also kept such journals as they struggled to understand how atmospheric conditions affected the health of their patients. And some books were published that consisted entirely of weather records, such as Benjamin Hutchinson's *Calendar of the Weather for the Year 1781* (1782).

Maintenance of a regular weather record required a high degree of self-discipline. Conditions had to be noted and instruments read at set times, normally at least once a day. Hooke's 'Method for Making a History of the Weather', published in Thomas Sprat's *History of the Royal Society* (1667), instructed readers to tabulate their daily observations under eight categories: winds, temperature, humidity, pressure, clouds, prevailing illnesses, incidents of thunder and lightning, and tides. Observers would be required to calibrate and maintain a thermometer, barometer, hygrometer, and wind gauge. They would have to be of steady temperament, regular habits, and fixed residence, or as Hooke put it, 'some one, that is always conversant in or neer the same place'.[15] Two later weather diarists who fulfilled this

---

[15] Robert Hooke, 'Method for Making a History of the Weather', in Thomas Sprat, *The History of the Royal Society of London* (London: J. Martyn, 1667), 175.

requirement were the Irish Quaker physician John Rutty (1698–1775), and the English landowner Thomas Barker (1722–1809). Rutty kept his weather journal in Dublin from 1725 to 1766, while simultaneously monitoring his own spiritual development, as recorded in his posthumously published *Spiritual Diary* (1776). His rigid temperance, asceticism, and intense vigilance over his own behaviour kept him fixed on a task that demanded constant self-discipline. Rutty believed that his record would demonstrate the divine design of the natural world, and thereby defeat the 'blasphemy' of those who complained when the weather was bad. He gave thanks to God for the habits of industriousness and regularity that enabled him to complete the work.[16]

Thomas Barker, squire of Lyndon Hall in Rutland, lived a life of even greater immobility; he was born and died in the same house and rarely spent any time away from it in the course of his eighty-seven years. He recorded his first weather observation at the age of eleven, began a systematic journal when he was fourteen, and kept it up for nearly sixty years. From the 1770s to the 1790s, his journal was abstracted in the *Philosophical Transactions*, and the record is still referred to by historical climatologists today. Twice a day, month after month, year after year, Barker read his thermometer and barometer, at times measured to the minute by his clock. He collected rainfall in his rain gauge and recorded unusual meteorological and astronomical events when they occurred. Barker was described by an acquaintance as 'naturally prone [to] extreme Abstractedness & Speculativeness'.[17] A telling instance occurred at the time of his marriage, which he registered only as the cause of an interruption in his weather journal. On previous visits to the home of his friend, the naturalist Gilbert White, he had recorded 'at Selbourne'; on the occasion when he married White's sister Anne, the note read 'at Selbourne, etc.'.[18] Barker's asceticism was also remarked upon: an almost lifelong vegetarian, he was said to be still thin and athletic into his sixties. He showed an extraordinary degree of patience in his work, sustaining a routine of strenuous regimen and abstraction from the social world around him. In these respects, he modelled the emerging modern construct of scientific objectivity, in which emotions and demands of the body were suppressed as a condition of reliable observation.[19]

---

[16] John Rutty, *A Chronological History of the Weather and Seasons and of the Prevailing Diseases in Dublin* (London: Robinson and Roberts, 1770); Rutty, *A Spiritual Diary and Soliloquies*, 2 vols. (London: James Phillips, 1776).

[17] John Kington, ed., *The Weather Journals of a Rutland Squire: Thomas Barker of Lyndon Hall* (Oakham: Rutland Record Society, 1988), p. 10.

[18] Ibid.

[19] On this topic, see Lorraine Daston and Peter Galison, *Objectivity* (New York: Zone Books, 2007).

Barker's case may have been extreme, but regular habits and a fixed domicile were requirements for the role of weather diarist, and strict self-discipline – even a degree of asceticism – was often noted among their characteristic features. By these means, they trained their bodies to serve the purposes of repeated observation and precise measurement. Several diarists demonstrated their rigid self-control by keeping up their records to within a few days of their deaths. In a later period, such observations were delegated to employees trained to behave in a mechanical manner, or were made by self-registering machines themselves. Weather observation became mechanised or industrialised. But, in the eighteenth century, records were kept by self-motivated individuals – doctors, clergymen, or landed gentlemen – whose efforts were voluntary and coordinated only through the institutions of the early modern public sphere. The enterprise had to rely on individuals who invested their sense of identity in the project.

The efforts of the weather diarists contributed to an emerging picture of the British climate, in which the hand of God's general providence was discerned in the prevailing moderate conditions. Rutty wrote that his forty-year study disclosed 'the footsteps of divine Wisdom and Goodness, presiding over these seemingly irregular operations' of the weather in Dublin. He believed his journal would correct the 'too frequent, not to say wicked exclamations we hear against the inclemency of the Climate, our changeable, and particularly our moist and windy weather'.[20] Damp and windy the British Isles might be, but rain made the land fertile and the wind was harvested to support maritime power and commercial shipping. Rutty was not the only writer to urge his fellow-nationals to stop complaining and be grateful for the British climate. The historian and topographical writer John Campbell summed up the emerging consensus in his *Political Survey of Britain* (1774): 'The climate, though we sometimes hear it censured, as being subject to frequent and considerable Alterations, is, upon the whole, both temperate and wholesome; ... [although] less steady and serene than in some other Countries of Europe, it is not so sultry in one Season, or so rigorous in another.'[21] Even the character of the British people, it was argued, was shaped by their climate; changeable weather was said to make them more active and independent-minded than those who lived in more placid regions.

[20] Rutty, *An Essay towards a Natural History of the County of Dublin*, 2 vols. (Dublin: W. Sleater, 1772), vol. II, pp. 275, 280–1.
[21] John Campbell, *A Political Survey of Britain*, 2 vols. (London: Richardson and Urquhart, 1774), vol. I, p. 47.

Medical writers generally concurred with this picture, even though they had a professional interest in how the British climate made people unhealthy. Many doctors undertook research on weather and diseases in the eighteenth century, often drawing inspiration from the classic works of Hippocrates on the environmental causes of illness.[22] As systematic weather recording was harnessed to this programme of inquiry, some conclusions about health and the British climate emerged. It was commonly believed that unseasonable weather or extreme changes in conditions brought on episodes of sickness in the population at large. The London physician John Fothergill noted that increased mortality generally followed 'some very sensible change in the temperature of the air'. He nonetheless insisted that foreigners were wrong to think the air had 'something in it extremely pernicious'. Rather, the British people had 'abundant cause to be satisfied' with their climate, since it was more moderate than that of any other country.[23] William Falconer, an Edinburgh-trained physician who wrote extensively about climate and national characters, claimed that the diurnal mutability of the British weather stimulated the mental alertness of the people, while its general temperateness subdued the passions and thereby fostered good judgement. Charles Bisset, another Edinburgh-trained physician who practised in Yorkshire, reflected the general view in his *Essay on the Medical Constitution of Great Britain* (1762). He noted that 'the frequent changes of weather peculiar to Great Britain' could give rise to diseases, but the prevailing moisture and moderate cold strengthened the bodily fibres, so that the natives 'in general, are bigger bodied, broader chested, and more robust, than those of most other countries'. Bisset reassured the British people that their climate was basically a healthy one, and that 'epidemic diseases of great malignity are much greater strangers in this island, than in most countries on the continent'.[24]

Improving the American Climate

Such ideas were framed by comparisons between Britain and other nations. In France, Jean-Baptiste Du Bos and the Baron de Montesquieu invoked

[22] Andrea Rusnock, 'Hippocrates, Bacon, and Medical Meteorology at the Royal Society, 1700–1750', in David Cantor (ed.), *Reinventing Hippocrates* (Aldershot: Ashgate, 2002), pp. 136–53.
[23] John Fothergill, *The Works of John Fothergill*, ed. J. C. Lettsom (London: Charles Dilly, 1784), pp. 89, 96.
[24] William Falconer, *Remarks on the Influence of Climate . . . [on] Mankind* (London: C. Dilly, 1781), p. 50; [Charles Bisset], *An Essay on the Medical Constitution of Great Britain* (London: A. Millar and D. Wilson, 1762), pp. 6, 11.

climate to explain differences of character between peoples, trying in this way to account for physical and cultural variability within the limits of a supposedly common human nature. Some British writers, including Falconer and John Arbuthnot, claimed for their own nation the benefits associated in antiquity with a temperate climate, such as enterprising and intellectually creative inhabitants. They also agreed that emotional volatility and political passivity were characteristic of the residents of warmer zones. Although other authors, including the historian and philosopher David Hume, doubted that climate could account for the differences between European nations, they did not completely discount the possibility that the physical environment could have an influence at the earliest stages of social development.[25]

Proceeding alongside this general discourse on climate and historical progress, medical research also explored international comparisons, especially with overseas locations where the British ventured on military service or as colonists. Bisset served as a military surgeon in the West Indies and North America in the 1740s, and he wrote about the health risks for British settlers on the Caribbean islands. Warm temperatures, he said, would rarefy the blood of migrants, but also promote perspiration, which was good. The real danger arose from air that was humid as well as hot. Then the fibres of the body would become dangerously 'relaxed', leading to fevers and diarrhoea. William Hillary, a Yorkshire physician who relocated to Barbados in the early 1750s, agreed about the dangers of heat and humidity. Hillary made regular measurements of the temperature and atmospheric pressure on the island, resuming a weather journal he had previously kept for more than a decade in England. On Barbados, he recommended that European settlers abandon their native styles of clothing and adopt looser garments that would allow freer perspiration. Thereby, they could hope to become acclimated to a climate much less healthy than the providentially blessed one of their homeland.[26]

New ideas about climate and its effects on human life emerged especially from the Americas, where Europeans had been settled for more than a century by this point. From the beginning, the encounter with the natural environment of the New World – its animals, plants, and peoples – had

[25] For a classic survey of this subject, see Clarence J. Glacken, *Traces on the Rhodian Shore: Nature and Culture in Western Thought from Ancient Times to the End of the Eighteenth Century* (Berkeley: University of California Press, 1967).

[26] Charles Bisset, *Medical Essays and Observations* (Newcastle-upon-Tyne: I. Thompson, 1766), pp. 11–20; William Hillary, *Observations on the Changes of the Air and the Concomitant Epidemic Diseases in the Island of Barbados*, 2nd edn (London: L. Hawes et al., 1766), pp. ix–xi.

forced Europeans to reconsider what they thought they knew about climates. In late antiquity, Ptolemy's *Geography* had asserted that a zone of latitude would have common conditions, and hence give rise to common types of animals and plants, throughout the world. The experience of actual settlement in the New World jolted this classical doctrine out of place. Winters in the northern regions turned out to be much more severe than latitude alone had led colonists to expect. Attempts to transplant Old World crops along latitudinal parallels failed. European grains did not flourish in the expected places in North America. Citrus fruits could not in fact be grown in Maryland and Virginia, although those colonies shared the latitude of Seville. Settlers in the Americas were obliged to broaden their conception of what a climate was and the physical features of the environment that could give rise to it. They studied the weather in the places they occupied, recording its extremes and its norms, and pondering its implications for the viability of crops and the health of humans and livestock. They also invoked the character of soils and waters, and the disposition of landmasses and mountain ranges, to try to explain why American climates differed from what Europeans had originally expected.[27]

Recording the weather on a systematic basis began in the North American colonies in the second decade of the eighteenth century, with observers in Massachusetts compiling journals in the 1710s and 1720s. Isaac Greenwood, a Harvard professor of natural philosophy, used a barometer shipped from London in 1727 to make measurements of atmospheric pressure, and the instrument was used for the same purpose by his successor, John Winthrop, in the 1740s. John Lining, a physician from Lanarkshire who settled in Charleston, South Carolina in the 1730s, took regular measurements of temperature, pressure, rainfall, and humidity as he tried to determine how the climate was affecting the health of the colonial population.[28] By the 1750s, similar projects were underway in Connecticut, Maryland, Pennsylvania, and Quebec. At the same time, the subject of the American climate was featuring in a transatlantic debate that drew European philosophers and historians into dialogue with American creoles and colonists. John Mitchell, a Virginia-born colonial agent and Edinburgh-educated physician, wrote in his 1767 work,

---

[27] Karen Ordahl Kupperman, 'The Puzzle of the American Climate in the Early Colonial Period', *American Historical Review*, 87 (1982), 1262–89; Sam White, 'Unpuzzling American Climate: New World Experience and the Foundations of a New Science', *Isis*, 106 (2015), 544–66.

[28] Jan Golinski, 'American Climate and the Civilization of Nature', in James Delbourgo and Nicholas Dew (eds.), *Science and Empire in the Atlantic World* (New York: Routledge, 2008), pp. 153–74.

The Present State of Great Britain and North America, that the American climate, 'if it were duly known, would perhaps appear to be the most singular thing in nature'. Mitchell insisted that the equivalent of the European temperate zone could not be found in North America. Drawing on his own fifteen-year record of the weather in Virginia, he declared that, 'It is only from the 41st to the 36th degree of latitude, or from the town of New-York to the middle of North Carolina, that we meet with a tolerable good soil and climate in all that Continent, on this side of the mountains.'[29] Confined to the coastal strip by the Appalachian range, the settler population was subject to unhealthy heat and humidity in summer, and in winter was blasted by Arctic winds blowing as far south as the Carolinas.

Mitchell's bleak picture of the climate of his native land was picked up by other British authors. The Scottish historian William Robertson, whose *History of America* appeared ten years later, agreed that, in the western hemisphere as a whole, 'cold predominates'.[30] Because of the northward extension of the continental landmass, he declared, frigid winds swept from the Arctic to a remarkable distance. Robertson saw this as a reflection of America's primitiveness, the absence of civilising influences on its topography that might have moderated its climatic extremes. He shared with other European writers – including the great French naturalist Georges-Louis Leclerc, the Comte de Buffon – the conviction that centuries of cultivation had improved the climate of their own continent. In America, on the other hand, the first explorers had confronted a scene in which 'the air stagnates in the woods, putrid exhalations arise from the waters; the surface of the earth, loaded with rank vegetation, feels not the purifying influence of the sun; [and] the malignity of the distempers natural to the climate increases'.[31] Robertson asserted – quite wrongly – that Native Americans had taken no steps to cultivate the landscape or improve their unhealthy environment.

Faced with this dismal image of the original state of nature in America, with its frightening implications for their prospects on the new continent, it is not surprising that colonial writers sought comfort in the notion that the climate was improving. They discerned welcome signs that the weather was trending towards the temperate ideal of the Old World as forests were cleared and swamps drained. The prospect was first discussed in scientific

[29] John Mitchell, *The Present State of Great Britain and North America ... Impartially Considered* (London: T. Becket and P. A. de Hondt, 1767), pp. xiii, 134.
[30] William Robertson, *The History of America*, 2 vols. (London: W. Strahan, 1777), vol. 1, p. 252.
[31] Ibid., p. 258.

circles in a paper delivered by Hugh Williamson to the American Philosophical Society in Philadelphia in 1770. Williamson, a doctor who had recently returned from medical studies at Edinburgh and Utrecht, acknowledged his debt to European discussions of climate change. He cited an earlier publication by Daines Barrington, in which the English antiquarian and naturalist considered how centuries of cultivation had moderated the extremes of weather in Germany, Poland, and Italy. Williamson held out the prospect of similar changes in America as the landscape was cleared of trees and agriculture extended into the former wilderness. Summer heats would moderate and winter frosts ease, and the diseases associated with each season would consequently decline, according to Williamson, 'when the virtuous industry of posterity shall have culti-vated the interior part of this country'.[32] The suggestion was noted by Europeans, including the Edinburgh-educated physician Alexander Wilson, who wrote in 1780: 'The more quickly [American land] is deprived of its woody covering, the more rapid will its improvements be in every thing that hath distinguished the European nations in equal latitudes.'[33]

The idea that the American climate was being civilised as the landscape was cultivated flourished in the years after the United States gained its independence. Thomas Jefferson reported in his *Notes on the State of Virginia* (1787) that 'both heats and colds are become much more moderate within the memory even of the middle aged'.[34] The Philadelphia physician William Currie claimed in 1792 that, 'When in the course of time, this continent becomes populated, cleared, cultivated, improved ... the bleak winds will become more mild, and the Winters less cold.'[35] Similar assertions about the rapidity of climatic change and its positive benefits for the new republic were made by Samuel Williams in Vermont and David Ramsay in South Carolina. The notion served to reassure the white population that they would not share the fate of the native peoples, whose decline had been tied by European writers to the debilitating effects of the American climate. Buffon and Robertson had asserted that populations of natives had dimin-ished because they shared the general feebleness of all New World creatures,

---

[32] Hugh Williamson, 'An Attempt to Account for the Change of Climate Which Has Been Observed in the Middle Colonies in North-America', *Transactions of the American Philosophical Society*, 1 (1769–71), 277.

[33] Alexander Wilson, *Some Observations Relative to the Influence of Climate on Vegetable and Animal Bodies* (London: T. Cadell, 1780), p. 276.

[34] Thomas Jefferson, *Notes on the State of Virginia* [1787], in Jefferson, *The Portable Thomas Jefferson*, ed. Merrill D. Peterson (New York: Viking Press, 1975), p. 119.

[35] William Currie, *An Historical Account of the Climates and Diseases of the United States of America* (Philadelphia: T. Dobson, 1792), p. 86.

a symptom of the hostile climatic conditions in which they lived. Jefferson and other American writers defended the natives against this imputation by praising their vigour and social instincts.[36] They also sought comfort in the idea that the climate was being civilised. Whatever the enervating effects of New World air on the natives, Americans of European descent were reassured that they would benefit from its improvement.

American observers who tried to establish the reality and magnitude of climate change were motivated to record the weather systematically. Jefferson himself began to keep a meteorological journal shortly after the Declaration of Independence, and later called for the establishment of a national network of weather observers to determine how much the climate was really changing.[37] Other investigators, including the historian Samuel Williams and the physician Benjamin Rush, tried to subject the claims of climatic alteration to the test of measurement and long-term weather recording. They thereby strengthened the identification of climate with long-term averages of atmospheric conditions, although the original notion of human-caused change had emerged from a richer and more complex cluster of ideas. As commentators remarked at the time, the idea was common among the settler population in North America before it emerged as a topic of learned debate or experimental inquiry.[38] People identified climate as a marker of a certain stage of historical development; hence they thought it would improve as America caught up with civilised Europe. Because they associated it with features of the landscape in which they lived, they believed it could be ameliorated by cutting forests and draining mephitic swamps. They also associated it with properties of their own bodies, including individual constitutions and racial characteristics. Thus, they sought to distinguish themselves from the native populations by remaking the American climate into a suitable abode for a healthy and civilised nation.

In these ways, the idea of anthropogenic climate change in the eighteenth century reflected the complexities of the notion of climate itself. Especially in the context of the European encounter with the Americas, climate had become a capacious term to encompass many aspects of the physical environment in their bearing on human life. It embraced terrain as

[36] On this debate, see: Antonello Gerbi, *The Dispute of the New World: the History of a Polemic*, trans. Jeremy Moyle (University of Pittsburgh Press, 1973).
[37] Alan Bewell, 'Jefferson's Thermometer: Colonial Biogeographical Constructions of the Climate of America', in Noah Heringman (ed.), *Romantic Science: the Literary Forms of Natural History* (Albany: State University of New York Press, 2003), pp. 111–38.
[38] See, for example, the remarks of the Swedish traveller Pehr Kalm, who visited North America around 1750, in *Peter Kalm's Travels in North America*, ed. Adolph B. Benson, 2 vols. (New York: Wilson-Erikson, 1937), vol. I, pp. 271, 275–7; vol. II, pp. 509, 513.

well as atmosphere, soils and waters as well as airs. It was believed to permeate the human body, disturbing or suppressing the passions, and bringing on or alleviating diseases. It was also thought to shape the character of different human populations, from primitive tribes to the most refined nations. Climate retained all of these connotations, even while investigators were trying to define it by regular and long-term weather recording. The British weather diarists tried to smooth out anomalies and fluctuations, bringing to light the benevolence of God's general providence in the overall moderation of the national atmosphere. They thereby hoped to normalise climate, as the weather itself had been normalised by reducing it to quotidian regularity.

In America, on the other hand, the settler population tended to believe they were altering their climate to bring it into line with European norms of temperance and equanimity. They continued to invoke notions that tied climatic conditions to human characteristics, including those that differentiated creoles from native peoples, and they saw climatic moderation as suited to the developed civilisation they were building on the continent. These associations continued to inform people's thinking about climate throughout the eighteenth century. In fact, they sustained the idea that humans were altering their climate to an observable degree – at least in certain localities – well into the following century. Settlers in many places in the American Midwest and West were convinced, as the saying had it, that 'rain follows the plow'.[39] At the same time, expert climatologists were using statistical normalisation to cast doubt on the idea that the climate was changing on a historical timescale. It proved impossible to establish conclusively that such anthropogenic alteration was occurring. By the middle decades of the nineteenth century, climatologists had established to their own satisfaction that there was no evidence of secular change. To some extent, this was because they defined climate as a statistical mean over a long period of time, implying permanent stability. It was only towards the end of the nineteenth century that scientists restored the notion of dramatic changes on a planetary scale, as the sequence and timing of the ice ages was established by geologists.[40] Smaller-scale changes within the compass of

---

[39] Conevery Bolton Valenčius, *The Health of the Country: How American Settlers Understood Themselves and their Land* (New York: Basic Books, 2002), p. 215.

[40] James Rodger Fleming, 'Global Environmental Change and the History of Science', in Mary Jo Nye (ed.), *The Cambridge History of Science, Volume v: The Modern Physical and Mathematical Sciences* (Cambridge University Press, 2002), pp. 634–50; Gregory Cushman, 'Humboldtian Science, Creole Meteorology, and the Discovery of Human-Caused Climate Change in South America', *Osiris*, 26 (2011), 16–44.

historical time were only restored to scientific respectability during the twentieth century, allowing climate to again feature as part of human history.

The ideas about weather and climate that prevail in the early twenty-first century preserve vestiges of eighteenth-century thinking on these topics, overlaid with the legacies of later developments. Methods of numerical weather forecasting and computer climate-modelling, as they developed in the decades after the Second World War, are descendants of the 'quantifying spirit' of the Enlightenment.[41] Both emerged from the ambition to record precise measurements of atmospheric variables, the same ambition that motivated the first weather diarists reading their thermometers and barometers. William Derham, Thomas Barker, and their peers hoped thereby to display the reach of God's general providence and encompass the weather within the realm of natural law. They worked against a background of popular beliefs about climate and weather, some of which they dismissed as superstition, some of which they sought to appropriate as scientific knowledge. And, of course, vernacular notions continue to this day to diverge in some respects from the knowledge of experts. People still have their ideas about what causes the weather and how it affects their health. They still talk about shifts in the character of the seasons, recognising climatic change in a way that may or may not coincide with the findings of experts.[42] The social distribution of beliefs is different today, but the overall gulf between lay and expert understandings can be traced back to the eighteenth century. The beginnings of a field of expert knowledge about weather and climate that distinguished itself from popular beliefs can be traced to that era. In this respect, as in many others, the eighteenth century witnessed the birth of modernity.

[41] Paul N. Edwards, *A Vast Machine: Computer Models, Climate Data, and the Politics of Global Warming* (Cambridge, MA: MIT Press, 2010); Kristine C. Harper, *Weather by the Numbers: the Genesis of Modern Meteorology* (Cambridge, MA: MIT Press, 2008); Theodore S. Feldman, 'Late Enlightenment Meteorology', in Tore Frängsmyr, J. L. Heilbron, and Robin Rider (eds.), *The Quantifying Spirit in the Eighteenth Century* (Berkeley: University of California Press, 1990), pp. 143–79.

[42] William B. Meyer, *Americans and their Weather* (Oxford University Press, 2000); Stephen Daniels and Georgina Endfield, 'Narratives of Climate Change: Introduction', *Journal of Historical Geography*, 35 (2009), 215–22; Sarah Strauss and Benjamin S. Orlove (eds.), *Weather, Climate, Culture* (Oxford: Berg, 2003).

CHAPTER 8

British Romanticism and the Global Climate
David Higgins

The development of meteorological science during the eighteenth century made possible for the first time reasonably accurate comparisons between the climates of different parts of the world. These comparisons were mobilised to support typologies of racial and cultural difference. As scholars such as Jan Golinski have shown, eighteenth-century and Romantic writers were often concerned with the relationship between climate and civilisation.[1] The supposedly inferior climates of some countries and regions were used to argue for the value of their 'improvement' through colonisation. Ideas about climate, therefore, were highly political and connected to the interests of nation-states and powerful organisations such as the East India Company. However, the early nineteenth century also saw the emergence of a nascent idea of climate as a dynamic *global* system. The relatively systematic measuring of weather for the first time allowed for not only comparison between different regions, but also the mapping of climate 'across national boundaries'.[2] (A key stage in this process was Alexander von Humboldt's invention of the isotherm in 1817.[3]) While meteorology was opening up new ways of understanding global space, rapid developments in geoscience were revolutionising ideas about the Earth's history. For influential figures such as the Comte de Buffon and Georges Cuvier, the planet was not a stable environment, but subject to sudden geological and climatic disruptions over a much deeper chronology than had hitherto been imagined. Romantic visions of global climate change were inevitably inflected by providential and apocalyptic religious discourses, but also included a more scientific and secular element

---

[1] Jan Golinski, *British Weather and the Climate of Enlightenment* (University of Chicago Press, 2007), pp. 179–202.

[2] Mike Hulme, *Weathered: Cultures of Climate* (London: Sage, 2017), p. 20.

[3] Andrea Wulf, *The Invention of Nature: Alexander von Humboldt's New World* (London: John Murray, 2015), pp. 177–9.

that opened up the possibility of an end to the human species without any sort of eschatological recompense.

The origins of modern climate science have often been identified in the 1830s, with the work of Jean Louis Rodolphe Agassiz to develop an Ice Age theory.[4] But there were earlier scientific speculations about the global climate. In 'Les époques de la nature' (1778) and other later works, Buffon described how the planet had undergone a process of gradual cooling since its creation and imagined an icy future in which it would be rendered uninhabitable.[5] However, he also suggested that global cooling might be at least temporarily delayed, or even reversed, by human cultivation of the earth: 'the draining, clearing, and peopling a country will give it a warmth which will continue for some thousand years'.[6] Buffon's global cooling theory had some literary influence, as I will suggest below, but was not generally accepted by natural philosophers. For example, Joseph Fourier's groundbreaking essay 'On the Temperatures of the Terrestrial Sphere and Interplanetary Space' (1827) argued that future changes to the interior heat of the planet would have no effect on its surface temperature, which he believed was dependent on solar energy and the general temperature of interplanetary space.[7] It was, however, generally accepted that human activities could 'improve' the climate at a regional level and some thinkers even envisaged anthropogenic climate change on a planetary scale. In the *Botanic Garden* (1792), for example, Erasmus Darwin argued that the European nations should unite in a project to tow icebergs to the tropics, thereby producing a more balanced and comfortable global climate for everyone.[8] Utopian discourse on global climate change in the Romantic period reaches its apex in the poetry of Percy Bysshe Shelley. In *Queen Mab* (1813) and *Prometheus Unbound* (1820), a climatic shift into an eternal spring or summer signifies the world's socio-political liberation and the perfectibility of humanity.[9]

---

[4] Mike Hulme, *Why We Disagree about Climate Change* (Cambridge University Press, 2009), p. 41.

[5] Martin J. S. Rudwick, *Bursting the Limits of Time: the Reconstruction of Geohistory in the Age of Revolution* (University of Chicago Press, 2005), pp. 142–9.

[6] [Georges-Louis Leclerc] Comte de Buffon, *Natural History, General and Particular*, trans. William Smellie, 3rd edn, 9 vols. (London: A. Strahan and T. Cadell, 1791), vol. ix, p. 396.

[7] Jean-Baptiste Joseph Fourier, 'On the Temperatures of the Terrestrial Space and Interplanetary Space', trans. R. T. Pierrehumbert (2004), https://geosci.uchicago.edu/~rtp1/papers/Fourier1827Trans.pdf. For a fine discussion of the essay, see Jerome Whitington, 'The Terrestrial Envelope: Joseph Fourier's Geological Speculation', in Tom Bristow and Thomas H. Ford (eds.), *A Cultural History of Climate Change* (London: Routledge, 2016), pp. 55–71.

[8] For a more detailed account of Darwin's plan, see Siobhan Carroll, 'Crusades against Frost: *Frankenstein*, Polar Ice, and Climate Change in 1818', *European Romantic Review*, 24 (2013), 213–15.

[9] Percy Bysshe Shelley, *Queen Mab* and *Prometheus Unbound*, in *Shelley's Poetry and Prose*, ed. Donald H. Reiman and Neil Fraistat, 2nd edn (New York: Norton, 2002), pp. 15–71, 202–86; see also

This chapter, however, addresses more troubled Romantic visions of the global climate. I focus on textual responses to two periods of short-term climate disruption caused by the volcanic eruptions of Laki in 1783 and Tambora in 1815.[10] My case studies reflect not only on how Romantic period writers responded to particular meteorological conditions, but also on how they began to imagine climate as an interconnected system in which changes in one region of the world could affect other regions. These texts entangle scientific, political, and religious discourses around weather and climate. In particular, they combine empirical observation of localised phenomena with apocalyptic forebodings that invoke the Bible and *Paradise Lost* (1667). I offer my analysis as part of the ongoing critical project of constructing a genealogy for thinking about climate in the Anthropocene. While the present-day environmental crisis may well require new ways of thinking, understanding the Anthropocene as a kind of epistemological breach risks dehistoricising climate change and presenting it as the inevitable result of human 'progress', rather than as the result of a wide range of contingent factors.[11] A better understanding of the complex interactions of climate and culture in the past may contribute to a better understanding of our current predicament and to the remarkable persistence of apocalyptic rhetoric around climate change within an ostensibly secular context.

The Laki Eruption of 1783

In June 1783 a system of volcanic fissures around Mount Laki in Iceland began an eruption that would last for eight months. 'The largest-known lava-flow eruption of the last millennium', it produced something like 15 km³ of lava, and an estimated 122 megatons of sulphur dioxide, as well as large amounts of other gases.[12] The lava did not directly affect populated areas, but led to famine and fluoride poisoning that is thought to have killed around ten thousand people; that is, about 20 per cent of Iceland's

Eric Gidal, '"O Happy Earth! Reality of Heaven!": Melancholy and Utopia in Romantic Climatology', *Journal for Early Modern Cultural Studies*, 8 (2008), 74–101.

[10] For a more comprehensive account of the Tambora eruption and British Romanticism, see David Higgins, *British Romanticism, Climate Change, and the Anthropocene: Writing Tambora* (London: Palgrave-Macmillan, 2017).

[11] For the Anthropocene as breach, see Timothy Clark, *Ecocriticism on the Edge: the Anthropocene as a Threshold Concept* (London: Bloomsbury, 2015). The literature around history and the Anthropocene is too vast to cite here, but for an interesting recent discussion of Romanticism, historicism, and the Anthropocene, see Devin Griffiths, 'Romantic Planet: Science and Literature within the Anthropocene', *Literature Compass*, 14 (2017).

[12] For an overview of the eruption and its effects, see Clive Oppenheimer, *Eruptions that Shook the World* (Cambridge University Press, 2011), pp. 269–94.

population at the time. The resulting toxic smog spread throughout Europe in the summer of 1783, causing respiratory problems and thousands of deaths. (For example, William Cowper noted that 'such multitudes are indisposed by fevers in this country, that the farmers have with difficulty gather'd in their harvest, the laborers having been almost every day carried out of the field incapable of work, and many die'.[13]) That summer was unusually hot and was also marked by other strange phenomena, such as a major earthquake in Italy (killing around thirty thousand people) and meteor sightings, followed by a severely cold winter that the eruption probably caused.[14] It is hardly surprising that some people looked for religious explanations, fearing that the Day of Judgement was at hand. However, natural philosophers suggested other causes, and several made the connection between the haze and volcanic activity. Benjamin Franklin, for example, postulated that the haze might be caused by 'the vast quantity of smoke, long continuing to issue during the summer from Hecla in Iceland, and that other volcano that arose out of the sea near that island, which smoke might be spread by various winds over the northern part of the world'.[15] In an example of the nascent scientific interest in climate as a complex global system, Franklin also suggested that the haze might have diminished the warming power of the sun's rays and thus led to the severe winter of 1783–4.

The Laki haze was described by several British writers of the period, although none of them knew of its cause. Writing to Lady Ossory in July, Horace Walpole remarks on the 'constant mist that gives no dew, but might as well be smoke':

> I wish modern philosophers had not disturbed all our ideas! two hundred good years ago celestial and terrestrial affairs hung together, and if a country was out of order, it was comfortable to think that planets ordered or sympathized with its ails. A sun shorn of his beams, and a moon that only serves to make darkness visible, are mighty homogeneal to a distracted state.[16]

---

[13] William Cowper, letter to William Unwin 7 September 1783, in *The Letters and Prose Writings of William Cowper*, ed. James King and Charles Ryskamp, 5 vols. (Oxford: Clarendon Press, 1979–86), vol. 11 p. 157.

[14] Laki may also have contributed to the very hot summer in Europe in 1783, although its effects on the global climate are still debated: see Alexandra Witze and Jeff Kanipe, *Island on Fire: the Extraordinary Story of a Forgotten Volcano that Changed the World* (London: Profile, 2014), pp. 125–45.

[15] Benjamin Franklin, 'Meteorological Imaginations and Conjectures', qtd. in Witze and Kanipe, *Island on Fire*, p. 127.

[16] Horace Walpole, letter to Lady Ossory, 15 July 1783, in *Horace Walpole's Correspondence with the Countess of Upper Ossory*, ed. W. S. Lewis, Joseph W. Reed, and Edwine M. Martz (Oxford University Press, 1965), pp. 404–5.

Walpole contrasts a scientific materialist understanding of the operations of non-human nature as separate from human life with
a religious or magical discourse that connects 'celestial and terrestrial
affairs'. His prose reflects the attraction of that latter mode of thinking by conflating the personal, political, and the climatological.
The 'distracted state' refers both to the feelings of the observing
subject, who seeks a kind of ironic reassurance in strange meteorological phenomena, and to the disordered body politic that such phenomena parallel. In describing the sun and the moon, he alludes to
two famous passages from Book 1 of *Paradise Lost*. Eighteenth-century
writers often reached for Milton when they wanted to invoke the
sublime, but it is worth paying attention to the specifics of Walpole's
allusions. Early on, Milton describes how the 'dungeon horrible' in
which Satan and his 'horrid crew' are imprisoned is lit by 'darkness
visible' produced by the flames of a 'great furnace'.[17] Walpole's use of
Milton's paradoxical expression suggests a hellish disruption to
a normally conducive season. (It is possible that the haze's sulphurous
smell may also have evoked hell.) Later in Book 1, Satan's partial
ruination and the occlusion of his inner light is compared to that of
a sun covered by mist or eclipsed by the moon:

> as when the sun new-ris'n
> Looks through the horizontal misty Air
> Shorn of his beams, or from behind the moon
> In dim eclipse disastrous twilight sheds
> On half the nations, and with fear of change
> Perplexes monarchs.[18]

Alastair Fowler writes that the eclipse 'presages doom for creation in
general and the sun king Charles in particular'.[19] The aptness of Milton's
lines in 1783 is reflected in Walpole's implication that the nation is 'out of
order': a widespread view after Britain's defeat in the American
Revolutionary War. However, his witty reference to the modern discon-
nection between the 'celestial' and 'terrestrial' allows him to invoke
Milton's apocalyptic discourse without fully endorsing it.

Gilbert White, pottering around in his Selborne garden, made the same
allusion to Milton in his *Naturalist's Journal* for 24 June 1783: 'The sun,

[17] John Milton, *Paradise Lost*, ed. Alastair Fowler, 2nd edn (London: Longman, 1998), pp. 62–4, 1.
51–63.
[18] Ibid., p. 97, 1. 594–9.   [19] Ibid., p. 97.

"shorn of his beams" appears thro' the haze like the full moon.'[20] He developed further the idea of the relationship between climate and apoc-alypse in the penultimate letter (to Daines Barrington) of *The Natural History of Selborne* (1789):

> The summer of the year 1783 was an amazing and portentous one, and full of horrible phaenomena; for besides the alarming meteors and tremendous thunder-storms that affrighted and distressed the different countries of this kingdom, the peculiar haze, or smokey fog, that prevailed for many weeks in this island, and in every part of Europe, and even beyond its limits, was a most extraordinary appearance, unlike anything known within the mem-ory of man ... The sun, at noon, looked as blank as a clouded moon, and shed a rust-coloured ferruginous light on the ground, and floors of rooms; but was particularly lurid and blood-coloured at rising and setting ... The country people began to look with superstitious awe at the red, louring aspect of the sun; and indeed there was reason for the most enlightened person to be apprehensive; for, all the while, Calabria and part of the isle of Sicily, were torn and convulsed by earthquakes; and about that juncture a volcano sprung out of the sea on the coast of Norway.[21]

For a book associated with a strong sense of place, it is notable that *Selborne* ends by evoking 'horrible phaenomena' that spread beyond local and national boundaries.[22] White leaves it open as to whether the earth-quakes and new volcano are connected to the 'peculiar haze', but cer-tainly implies that there is something ominous, perhaps even apocalyptic, in their coincidence. As Stuart Peterfreund has argued, despite White's emphasis on empirical observation in natural history, he was also working within a tradition of natural theology. Peterfreund identifies a significant tension between Selborne as 'the type of an unchanging earthly Paradise' and a sense of 'temporal change' in the apocalyptic language used to describe meteorological phenomena.[23] He finds echoes of the passage above in the Book of Revelation.[24] However, its most direct allusion is actually to the Gospel of Matthew: 'When it is evening, ye say, It will be fair weather: for the sky is red. And in the morning, It will be foul weather

---

[20] Gilbert White, *The Journals of Gilbert White: 1774–1783*, ed. Francesca Greenoak, vol. 11 of *The Journals of Gilbert White*, gen. ed. Richard Mabey (London: Century, 1988), p. 465.

[21] Gilbert White, *The Natural History of Selborne*, ed. Richard Mabey (London: Penguin, 1987), p. 265.

[22] For local and global in White, see Tobias Menely, 'Traveling in Place: Gilbert White's Cosmopolitan Parochialism', *Eighteenth-Century Life*, 28 (2004), 46–65.

[23] Stuart Peterfreund, '"Great Frosts and ... Some Very Hot Summers": Strange Weather, the Last Letters, and the Last Days in Gilbert White's *The Natural History of Selborne*', in Noah Heringman (ed.), *Romantic Science: the Literary Forms of Natural History* (Albany: State University of New York Press, 2003), p. 93.

[24] Ibid., p. 99.

to day: for the sky is red and lowring. O ye hypocrites, ye can discern the face of the sky; but can ye not discern the signs of the times?'[25] Here Jesus is addressing the Pharisees and the Sadducees, who have asked him to give them a sign from heaven to prove that he is the Son of God. Whereas for Walpole, modernity had sundered the relationship between weather ('the face of the sky') and history ('the signs of the times'), White suggests that the two may remain connected. He goes on to quote 'Milton's noble simile of the sun' (the six lines from *Paradise Lost* addressed above) as 'particularly applicable' owing to its connection between 'strange and unusual phaenomena' and 'a superstitious kind of dread'. The line between ignorant superstition and enlightened apprehension is fuzzy, for both involve a 'fear of change' and a kind of perplexity that affects everyone, from 'monarchs' to the 'enlightened person' to 'country people'.[26] *The Natural History of Selborne*, so often associated with a vision of England as a kind of static Eden, ends by invoking environmental and political crisis.

A week after White evoked Milton in his *Naturalist's Journal*, William Cowper, a hundred miles away in Olney, made the same reference in a letter to his friend John Newton: 'We never see the Sun but shorn of his beams ... he sets with the face of a red hot salamander.'[27] As a fervent Evangelical Christian, Cowper was more willing than Walpole or White to interpret the Laki haze in relation to an imminent Day of Judgement. However, his views on this issue were not straightforward. In a slightly earlier letter to Newton, he noted that 'I am and always have been a great Observer of natural appearances, but I think not a superstitious one ... what the God of the Scriptures has seen fit to conceal, he will not, as the God of Nature, publish.'[28] Like White, Cowper seeks to distinguish between enlightened and superstitious responses to unusual meteorological phenomena but, as in *Selborne*, the distinction is fuzzy. The poet notes that the strange appearance of the sun means that:

> Some fear to go to bed, expecting an Earthquake, some ... assert with great confidence that the day of Judgment is at hand. This is probable, and I beleive it myself, but for other reasons. ... Signs in the heavens are

---

[25] Matthew 16:2–3, *The Bible*, introd. Robert Carroll and Stephen Prickett (Oxford University Press, 1998), Authorised King James Version.

[26] White, *Natural History*, p. 265.

[27] Letter to John Newton, 29 June 1783, in Cowper, *Letters*, vol. 11, p. 148. For an excellent discussion of Cowper and Laki, see Tobias Menely, '"The Present Obfuscation": Cowper's *Task* and the Time of Climate Change', *PMLA*, 127 (2012), 477–92.

[28] Letter to John Newton, 13 June 1783, in Cowper, *Letters*, vol. 11, p. 143.

predicted characters of the last times, and in the course of the last 15 years I have been a witness of many.[29]

Having sundered the face of the sky and the signs of the times by distinguishing between the 'God of Nature' and the 'God of the Scriptures', Cowper seems keen to put them back together again. In a passage from *The Task* (1785) – probably the most famous literary emergence of Laki – the connection is made very firmly:

> Is it a time to wrangle, when the props
> And pillars of our planet seem to fail,
> And Nature with a dim and sickly eye
> To wait the close of all?[30]

Cowper may be half-recalling the 'dim eclipse' of Milton's passage here. But, in a surprising reversal, the Laki mist is significant not only because of the perplexity it produces in human observers, but also because 'Nature' is itself experiencing the slow death of its own perceptions. The failing 'eye' may primarily be a metaphor for the dimming of the sun, but also suggests a more general planetary collapse: as Cowper states in a footnote, the haze is widespread across 'Europe and Asia'.

It is worth paying attention to the specific context of this passage in Book II of *The Task*, which he described as 'dealing pretty largely in the *signs* of the *times*'.[31] The book starts with a horrified diatribe against war and oppression – 'the natural bond / Of brotherhood is severed' (ll. 9–10) – and particularly against the practice of slavery ('human nature's broadest, foulest blot' (ll. 22)). If the English climate is peculiarly liberating – for 'Slaves cannot breathe in England; if their lungs / Receive our air, that moment they are free' (ll. 40–1) – then the nation's participation in the slave trade cannot be justified. Freedom, Cowper suggests, should 'circulate through ev'ry vein' (ll. 44) of the British empire, for global fellow-feeling is required now more than ever at a time of environmental crisis, when the 'world' seems 'To toll the death-bell of its own decease / And by the voice of all its elements / To preach the gen'ral doom' (ll. 50–2). As well as the Laki haze, he also alludes to the 'late calamities at Jamaica' (a hurricane and a tidal wave), the unusual 'meteors' observed in Britain in August 1783, and (like White) the earthquakes in Sicily and Calabria.

---

[29] Letter to John Newton, 29 June 1783, in Cowper, *Letters*, vol. II, pp. 148–9.
[30] Cowper, *The Task*, in Cowper, *The Poems of William Cowper*, ed. John D. Baird and Charles Ryskamp, 3 vols. (Oxford: Clarendon Press, 1980–95), vol. II, p. 140, ll. 62–5. Hereafter cited parenthetically by line number.
[31] Letter to John Newton, 11 December 1784, in Cowper, *Letters*, vol. II, p. 309.

The preacherly voice of *The Task*, in contrast to the more sceptical and modest persona of Cowper's letters, understands these phenomena as revealing God's anger at humanity's sins. That 'England' has so far not been badly affected is certainly not a reflection of its purity, for Cowper warns that that there are 'none than we more guilty' (ll. 154) and that 'we' need to heed the signs of God's displeasure. In addition to his opposition to the slave trade, Cowper was also concerned by the British empire's oppressive presence in India, and interpreted the loss of the American colonies as another sign of divine displeasure with the nation's despotic and luxurious excesses.[32] And yet if the sins of Britain and other nations are contributing to the collapse of the global climate, *The Task* finds solace in a more localised vision of the 'fickle' but nonetheless lovable English 'clime', 'deform'd / With dripping rains, or wither'd by a frost' (ll. 210–11). As so often in Cowper's work, England is imagined as a localised 'nook' (ll. 207) in which he can retreat from his wider fears, even if it is threatened by corruption. His understanding of climate is more obviously moralistic, theological, and apocalyptic than that of Walpole and White. But, like them, he understands the Laki haze in the context of national and global crisis. Milton offered a powerful model for all three writers as a way of reflecting on the entanglements of climate and human activity, rather than their separation.

The Tambora Eruption of 1815

In the evening of 5 April 1815, the inhabitants of Java heard a number of explosions that continued intermittently until the following day. At first, they were 'almost universally attributed to distant cannon', but in fact this was the opening salvo in the eruption of Mount Tambora on the isle of Sumbawa, hundreds of miles to the east.[33] A hazy atmosphere and slight fall of ash followed over several days. At about 7 p.m. on 10 April, the mountain blew up. According to an eyewitness account, 'three distinct columns of flame burst forth near the top ... In a short time the whole Mountain ... appeared like a body of liquid fire extending itself in every direction.'[34] The explosions could be heard more than 2,000 km from the

---

[32] For nation and empire in Cowper, see David Higgins, *Romantic Englishness: Local, National, and Global Selves, 1780–1850* (Basingstoke: Palgrave-Macmillan, 2014), pp. 17–44.

[33] [Charles Assey], 'Narrative of the Effects of the Eruption from the Tomboro Mountain, in the Island of Sumbawa, on the 11th and 12th of April 1815', *Transactions of the Batavian Society, of Arts and Sciences*, 8 (1816), 3–4.

[34] Ibid., p. 23.

eruption. As a result of the huge amounts of volcanic material emitted, 'many places within a 600-kilometre radius remained pitch black for a day or two' and the ash fall affected a much larger area.[35] This was one of the very largest documented eruptions of the Holocene epoch and it had devastating consequences for local populations. It wiped out the kingdom of Tambora, and the ash destroyed agriculture and contaminated drinking water across Sumbawa and nearby islands. The exact death toll from the explosions, pyroclastic currents, tsunami, and local famine and disease is impossible to know, but plausible estimates put it at between 60,000 and 120,000 people across Sumbawa, Bali, and possibly other parts of the archipelago such as Lombok and eastern Java.[36] The huge amount of sulphur released into the atmosphere formed a sulphuric acid aerosol, leading to a global cooling of 1–2°C (strongest in the northern hemisphere) and severe climatic disruption in the period from 1816 to 1818.[37] In particular, 1816 became known in Europe and North America as the 'Year without a Summer' owing to unseasonably cold and wet weather.[38] Following the groundbreaking work of John D. Post, scholars have identified Tambora as a key factor in the harvest failures and food scarcities across the globe in the late 1810s, and perhaps even the typhus and cholera epidemics of the period.[39] The history of the eruption shows on a global scale the catastrophic consequences of a powerful natural hazard in combination with large numbers of people made vulnerable by their poverty.

Tambora's impact on British Romanticism is principally apparent in the works of Byron and the Shelleys written or conceived during the literary *annus mirabilis* of 1816, but it also appears in other texts of the period.[40] Owing to the short interregnum from 1811 to 1816 during which Britain was in control of Java, the principal source for eyewitness accounts of the eruption and its aftermath is an English-language document collected together under the auspices of Sir Stamford Raffles, the island's governor during this period. Scholars have tended to treat this text as

---

[35] Oppenheimer, *Eruptions*, pp. 302–3.   [36] Ibid., p. 311.

[37] J. Kandlbauer, P. O. Hopcroft, P. J. Valdes, and R. S. J. Sparks, 'Climate and Carbon Cycle Responses to the 1815 Tambora Volcanic Eruption', *Journal of Geophysical Research: Atmospheres*, 118 (2013), 12497–507.

[38] For the weather conditions in Britain in 1816, see Lucy Veale and Georgina H. Endfield, 'Situating 1816, the "Year without Summer", in the UK', *Geographical Journal*, 182 (2016), 318–30.

[39] John D. Post, *The Last Great Subsistence Crisis in the Western World* (Baltimore: Johns Hopkins University Press, 1977); also Gillen D'Arcy Wood, *Tambora: the Eruption that Changed the World* (Princeton University Press, 2014).

[40] For Byron, the Shelleys, and Tambora, see Higgins, *British Romanticism and Climate Change*, pp. 55–108, and Wood, *Tambora*, pp. 45–71.

a straightforward source of information about the eruption and its effects. However, it is in fact a heteroglossic and collaborative production that emerges from a particular historical moment. It is dated 28 September 1815, and so we might reasonably assume that it was composed during that month. During 1814 and 1815, the Raffles administration existed in an unstable geopolitical context. Java had been returned to the Dutch by the Anglo-Dutch Treaty of August 1814. A year later, news arrived on Java of Napoleon's escape and resurgence, which potentially voided the treaty and excited Raffles with the possibility of a longer British presence in Java. And yet in September he received the devastating news that he was likely to be dismissed from office. The sense of political crisis is apparent in the narrative's description of the weather on Java following the initial explosions: 'From the 6th, the sun became observed: it had every where the appearance of being enveloped in fog, the weather was sultry and the atmosphere close and still; the sun seemed shorn of its rays, and the general stillness and pressure of the atmosphere foreboded an Earthquake.'[41] This account alludes, rather gracefully, to the passage in Book 1 of *Paradise Lost* also referenced by Walpole, Cowper, and White. It connects the mist-covered sun (and the potential 'Earthquake') to a catastrophic overturning of the normal state of things – as indeed it was – and, more specifically, it connects meteorological phenomena to political ones. The invocation of the Miltonic sublime might seem to emphasise the status of the document as a product of elite Western culture. But it also connects the imperialistic metanarrative to the more localised indigenous accounts that the document also reports, and that read sudden environmental change as signalling some change in the political realm.

Many of the eyewitness reports collected in Raffles's document registered the peculiar intensity of the 'unusually thick darkness' caused by the ash fall. The captain of an East India Company cruiser reported that by noon on 12 April, 'complete darkness covered the face of the day', noting that he had never seen 'any thing equal to it in the darkest night – it was impossible to see your hand when held up close to your eyes'. This 'darkness visible' was also emphasised by Raffles when he introduced a reprinted version of the narrative in his *History of Java* (1817): 'the sky was overcast at noon-day with clouds of ashes, the sun was envelloped in an atmosphere, whose "palpable" density he was unable to penetrate'.[42]

---

[41] [Assey], 'Narrative of the Effects', p. 4.
[42] Thomas Stamford Raffles, *The History of Java*, 2 vols. (1817; Oxford University Press, 1965), vol. 1, pp. 25–6.

By putting 'palpable' in quotation marks, Raffles signifies that it is an allusion. There are two relevant passages in *Paradise Lost*. An account in Book XII of the ten plagues of Egypt includes the following lines: 'Darkness must overshadow all his bounds, / Palpable darkness, and blot out three days' (XII. 187–8). Raffles's account of the eruption tends to avoid providential readings of environmental catastrophe, but the apocalyptic connotations of the ash fall are registered here. A more complex connection can be found to the scene in Book 11 in which the devils in Pandaemonium are debating the best course of action. Beelzebub, Satan's mouthpiece, suggests taking vengeance on God by corrupting the world that he has created:

> But first whom shall we send
> In search of this new world, whom shall we find
> Sufficient? Who shall tempt with wandering feet
> The dark unbottomed infinite abyss
> And through the palpable obscure find out
> His uncouth way, or spread his airy flight
> Upborne with indefatigable wings
> Over the vast abrupt, ere he arrive
> The happy isle. (11. 402–10)

'The happy Isle' is Earth, the 'new world' created by God for his favoured creatures. Penetrating the dark abyss – 'the palpable obscure' – between Pandaemonium and Earth will lead Satan into Eden. Raffles's *History of Java* is in part an attempt to argue for a permanent British colonial settlement there. The reader has to see through the dark veil of Tambora – an epistemological as well as a sensory phenomenon – if they are to arrive at an understanding of the colonial potential of the 'happy Isle' as a fertile paradise. The volcano threatens the abyssal and destructive, but it can also be transcended and controlled by a 'sufficient' and 'indefatigable' colonialist such as Raffles.

The reach of the Tambora eruption was truly global. Despite its widespread cooling effects, it actually led to warming in the Arctic and a temporary decrease in sea ice.[43] Writing to Andrew Bell in February 1818, Robert Southey notes that no 'public matters' interest him as much as 'the revolution about the North pole, & the breaking up of the ice'. He suggests that it is likely that 'earthquakes & volcanos have caused the disruption of the ice, – the combustibles which used to explode in Iceland have probably broken out nearer the pole'. As with many writers

---

[43] Wood, *Tambora*, pp. 45–71.

in the period, Southey's understanding of climate was more geomorphic than atmospheric. He concludes that 'these speculations interest me as much as a continental war, or a Spafields mob, & a great deal more than the preparations for a Westmorland election'.[44] Southey's distinction between the political and climatological realms breaks down when viewed in the light of modern scholarship on Tambora's effects. Spa Fields was the site of a large reformist meeting in December 1816, which ended in disorder, and contributed to the passing of the Seditious Meetings Act and the suspension of Habeas Corpus in 1817. There is no doubt that the climate disruption caused by Tambora was a significant factor in the so-called 'distresses' that affected many of the poorer inhabitants of Britain in the late 1810s and led to intense political debate and public unrest.[45]

The decrease in the Arctic ice was widely reported in the press, but a key influence on Southey's excitement was his fellow contributor to the conservative *Quarterly Review*, Sir John Barrow (who was also second secretary to the Admiralty). From 1816, Barrow successfully used his journalistic platform to promote the value of Arctic exploration. A particularly important article, published in February 1818, addressed the possibilities opened up by the recent ice-melt, and in particular the potential warming of the British climate, access to Greenland, and the discovery of the Northwest Passage. As Adeline Johns-Putra has shown, Barrow's article was a significant influence on Eleanor Anne Porden's poem *The Arctic Expeditions* (1818).[46] Porden emphasises how 'Science' will inspire heroic Britons to penetrate the new spaces opened up by the melting ice and to rediscover the 'long lost country' of Greenland, which in future will experience 'milder summers'.[47] Furthermore, the British climate will also be improved: 'our happier clime / Again shall hail returning Summer's prime; / Its ruddy grapes shall lavish Autumn bring'.[48] Like Barrow, Porden predicts the improvement in the national climate as a return ('again') to a warmer period, as found in 'the descriptions of our elder poets'.[49] The opening up of the Arctic offers a kind of apocalypse: an

[44] Robert Southey, letter to Andrew Bell, 17 February 1818, in Southey, *The Collected Letters of Robert Southey: a Romantic Circles Electronic Edition: Part Five: 1816–1818*, ed. Tim Fulford, Ian Packer, and Lynda Pratt, *Romantic Circles*, www.rc.umd.edu/editions/southey_letters/Part_Five/HTML/letter EEd.26.3083.html#back14.

[45] For the Regency crisis, see Post, *The Last Great Subsistence Crisis*, and R. J. White, *Waterloo to Peterloo* (Harmondsworth: Penguin, 1957).

[46] Adeline Johns-Putra, 'Historicizing the Networks of Ecology and Culture: Eleanor Anne Porden and Nineteenth-Century Climate Change', *ISLE: Interdisciplinary Studies in Literature and Environment*, 22 (2015), 27–46.

[47] [Eleanor Anne] Porden, *The Arctic Expeditions: a Poem* (London: John Murray, 1818), pp. 12–13.

[48] Ibid., p. 13.   [49] Ibid., p. 13.

'unveiling' of a glorious future that reprises a glorious past. Cowper had found solace in the idea of a 'fickle' but lovable national climate that offered a kind of bulwark against imperial corruption and chaos. In contrast, Barrow and Porden understand global climate change as an opportunity for imperial self-aggrandisement and, like Robert Walton and Victor Frankenstein, emphasise the power of human beings to conquer recalcitrant elemental forces.

I conclude this chapter with the contrary vision of Byron's 'Darkness' (1816): an account of the total collapse of the global climate system, which offers the most radical of all the textual responses to Tambora. The poem's prophetic narrator allows us to experience 'darkness visible' by describing a future Earth unlit by the sun's rays:

> The bright sun was extinguish'd, and the stars
> Did wander darkling in the eternal space,
> Rayless, and pathless, and the icy earth
> Swung blind and blackening in the moonless air.[50]

As the words 'rayless', 'pathless', and 'moonless' suggest, the poem is defined by absence, loss, and confusion. The image of the Earth swinging blindly through the air suggests a movement that deviates from its normal orbital trajectory. The usual order of the universe has collapsed; the darkening of the sun is mirrored by the other stars which now wander without a clear path. The Enlightenment's sundering of climate and history, as identified by Walpole, is treated with brutal irony by Byron. The poem presents a celestial and climatic system on which human beings are entirely dependent, but which is entirely careless of human life. The resulting poem is dizzyingly nihilistic and atheistic, presenting religion as irrelevant and existence as a feeble joke:

> The crowd was famish'd by degrees; but two
> Of an enormous city did survive,
> And they were enemies; they met beside
> The dying embers of an altar-place
> Where had been heap'd a mass of holy things
> For an unholy usage; they rak'd up,
> And shivering scraped with their cold skeleton hands
> The feeble ashes, and their feeble breath
> Blew for a little life, and made a flame
> Which was a mockery.[51]

---

[50] [George Gordon] Lord Byron, 'Darkness', in Byron, *The Complete Poetical Works*, ed. Jerome J. McGann, 7 vols. (Oxford: Clarendon Press, 1980–93), vol. IV, p. 40, ll. 2–5.

[51] Ibid., vol. IV, p. 42, ll. 55–64.

It is tempting to read this as a moment of self-reflexivity. After all, Byron's poem 'heaps' together religious allusions for irreligious purposes and offers a 'mockery' of human aspirations to control the environment.[52] Like his contemporaries, Byron did not know of the relationship between Tambora and the global climate. The poem's influences are diverse, from the wet and stormy weather of 1816, to various apocalyptic passages in the Bible, to the European sun-spot panic of the same year. Byron's understanding of the catastrophist geoscience of Cuvier and Buffon was also significant. The latter's global cooling theory was explicitly referenced by Percy Bysshe Shelley when responding to glacial augmentation in the vale of Chamonix in July 1816, and had a notable impact on two of the most significant Romantic texts of the period: 'Mont Blanc' (1817) and *Frankenstein* (1818).[53] The problem in Byron's poem is the cooling of the sun rather than of the Earth, but the endpoint is the same: an uninhabitable planet. The end of the poem reveals darkness to be much more than an absence of light: rather, 'she' is a powerful – indeed, a 'palpable' – agent.

The question of agency is fundamental to current debates around climate change. One key criticism of the concept of the Anthropocene is that it implies a species-wide responsibility for global warming, rather than focusing on those countries that have benefited the most from the carbon-fuelled capitalism that emerged in Britain at the end of the eighteenth century. Another criticism is that it exaggerates human agency and downplays that of non-human creatures and forces. Understood simply as a stratigraphic marker, of course, the term does neither of these things and, indeed, the scientific literature around the Anthropocene is often more nuanced than humanities scholars like to suggest.[54] Perhaps the real problem is not the concept itself, but the complexity of our political-environmental crisis. The Romantics found in Milton a useful way of thinking about climate and culture because, whatever scientific advances had occurred since the late seventeenth century, his understanding of the intertwining of 'celestial and terrestrial affairs' still resonated. Similarly, and despite the significant changes wrought by two centuries of fossil capitalism, Romantic writing offers a valuable genealogy for present-day

---

[52] Catherine Redford gives a useful account of the poem's biblical allusions, although I disagree with her conclusions: '"No Love Was Left": the Failure of Christianity in Byron's "Darkness"', Byron Journal, 43 (2015), 131–40.

[53] Percy Bysshe Shelley, 'Mont Blanc', in *Shelley's Poetry and Prose*, pp. 96–101; Mary Shelley, *Frankenstein, or The Modern Prometheus*, ed. M. K. Joseph (Oxford University Press, 2008).

[54] For a useful discussion, see Ian Angus, *Facing the Anthropocene: Fossil Capitalism and the Crisis of the Earth System* (New York: Monthly Review Press, 2016), especially pp. 224–32.

thinking about the global climate in the Anthropocene. The utopian schemes of contemporary geo-engineers have their analogues in the Romantic period, as do the bleakest prognostications of modern-day doomsayers. Despite remarkable advances in climate science and mathematical modelling, predicting how the global climate will behave still involves a large degree of speculation. And apocalyptic thinking remains resilient, even in apparently secular contexts. Perhaps the reality is that the climate can change more quickly than some of the ways in which climate change is framed.

CHAPTER 9

The Literary Politics of Transatlantic Climates

Morgan Vanek

Among scholars of environmental history, one story about climate's role in the literary construction of national identity is familiar. Informed by classical theories of climate defined by latitude, this story goes, early modern travellers looked to local climatic features both to explain the differences of culture and character they encountered abroad and to affirm the superiority of the conditions for prosperity and health they identified with home. Over the course of the eighteenth century, observations about the contrast between climates became an increasingly prominent feature of writing about cultural and political difference – and for transatlantic travellers in particular, the wide gap between the conditions in temperate Europe and the extremes of North America helped to both explain and sharpen the national identifies emerging on each shore. Britons, embracing temperance as a national characteristic, insisted that the culture this climate helped to cultivate also positioned their 'island race' as the rational masters of civil society (both at home and abroad), while Americans, more invested in the strength of character demonstrated by mastering the climate, emphasised instead the work required to improve their much more severe conditions, and the liberty they secured through these improvements.[1] For some environmental historians, however, the analytic frame of the nation has always been an awkward fit with research on matters of climate. After all, as Richard White observes, 'there is much about the natural environment that is not particularly national', and although environmental issues – for instance, the fate of plants and animals designated as natural resources – are often shaped by national policy,

[1] Alan Bewell, 'Jefferson's Thermometer: Colonial Biogeographical Constructions of the Climate of America', in Noah Heringman (ed.), *Romantic Science: the Literary Forms of Natural History* (Albany: State University of New York Press, 2003), p. 113; Jan Golinski, *British Weather and the Climate of Enlightenment* (University of Chicago Press, 2007), p. 156; James Rodger Fleming, *Historical Perspectives on Climate Change* (New York: Oxford University Press, 1998), p. 32. For more, see Chapter 7 by Jan Golinski in this volume.

Andrew Graybill notes further that the effects of these policies often come most sharply into focus through comparative studies of borderland environments.[2] In response, scholars like White and Ian Tyrrell have advocated for more transnational approaches to environmental history, noting that these approaches are especially well suited to work on the 'pre-national period' of North America and Europe.[3] Inspired by this transnational turn, this chapter aims to re-examine that familiar story of how early modern climatic encounters in North America helped to define national identities on each side of the Atlantic, and to demonstrate how these transatlantic exchanges about the meaning of climatic difference in fact helped to redefine climate itself.

To this end, this chapter traces two interrelated stories: one through the challenges that early modern travellers' encounters with North American extremes offered to classical theories of climate, and the other through the political opportunities that writers both for and against the expansion of European activity in North America found in revising this theory of climate. In the first of these stories, it's an encounter with unexpected difference that inspires change, as early modern travellers must admit that classical climate theory simply could not predict or explain the years of miserable winters, failed transplantation efforts, and 'hopes ... frozen to death' they found in North America.[4] In the second of these stories, however, it's the slow change in the meaning of climate in the wake of these unsettling reports that inspires new forms of differentiation – between the settlers and species slow to thrive in North America and the people, plants, and animals indigenous to the region, first of all, and also between the methods of agriculture identified as responsible for these changing rates of survival. Taken together, these two stories demonstrate how, in order to establish the survival of settlers' bodies and European plant and animal species as meaningful evidence of climatic improvement,

[2] Richard White, 'The Nationalization of Nature', *Journal of American History* 86.3 (1999), 983; Andrew R. Graybill, 'Boundless Nature: Borders and the Environment in North America and Beyond', in Andrew C. Isenberg (ed.), *The Oxford Handbook of Environmental History* (Oxford University Press, 2014), pp. 578–94; for more, see Alfred Crosby, *Ecological Imperialism: the Biological Expansion of Europe, 900–1900*, 2nd edn (Cambridge University Press, 2004).
[3] White, 'The Nationalization of Nature', 983; see also Ian Tyrrell, *True Gardens of the Gods: Californian–Australian Environmental Reform, 1860–1930* (Berkeley: University of California Press, 1999).
[4] Ferdinando Gorges, 'A Brief Narration of the Originall Undertakings of the Advancement of Plantations into the Parts of America', in James Phinney Baxter (ed.), *Sir Ferdinando Gorges and His Province of Maine*, 20 vols (Boston: Prince Society, 1890), vol. XIX, pp. 16–17. For more on Gorges's remarks, see Sam White, *A Cold Welcome: the Little Ice Age and Europe's Encounter with North America* (Cambridge, MA: Harvard University Press, 2016), pp. 132–53.

early modern advocates for American settlement effectively narrowed the definition of climate, both strengthening its association with improvable environmental conditions (like productivity) and loosening its association with more unpredictable measures (like temperature). Ultimately, this approach opened a gap between the narrative of climatic improvement that became common in reports on North America and the consistently severe conditions on the ground – and though recent climatological reconstructions have helped contemporary scholars to confirm just how wide this gap could be, this distance between report and reality was no less obvious, and no less legible as evidence of political and economic interest, to early modern observers. From satire to scepticism to sentimental critique of imperial negligence, this gap inspired a range of responses from seventeenth- and eighteenth-century writers, all attentive to both the change in the meaning of climate that made this condition appear more available to governance, and to the turns by which imperial claims in North America now seemed to be justified by change in an increasingly narrow set of environmental conditions. Motivated, then, by Anya Zilberstein's recent work on the efforts of British imperial agents to maintain these claims by managing the reputation of the climate in the territory they sought to govern,[5] this chapter proposes that early modern advocates for American settlement were similarly invested, to similar ends, in managing the meaning of climate itself, and argues that close study of the slow change in the concept of climate facilitated by these transatlantic exchanges can both expose and unsettle presumptions, still operating in responses to the present climate crisis, about what constitutes meaningful evidence of climatic change.

A Cold Welcome

For the seventeenth-century travellers who launched the first of these stories, of course, the suggestion that transatlantic travel might produce a change of climate would have been predictable, as most would have presumed that climate could change only with location.[6] Prior to the seventeenth century, the classical view of *klimata* imagined the inhabited world divided into a series of parallel bands that encircled the

---

[5] Anya Zilberstein, *A Temperate Empire: Making Climate Change in Early America* (Oxford University Press, 2016), especially pp. 91–117.
[6] Karen Ordahl Kupperman, 'The Puzzle of the American Climate in the Early Colonial Period', *American Historical Review*, 87 (1982), 1262–89; Zilberstein, *A Temperate Empire*, pp. 17–88; and Chapter 7 by Golinski in this volume.

Earth.[7] According to this model, climate could vary widely between bands at different latitudes, but the prevailing conditions that distinguished the temperate, torrid, and frigid zones were imagined to be consistent throughout each band. As a result, Karen Kupperman explains, English writers 'confidently believed that they could extrapolate from the familiar climates of Europe to predict the climate of North America', thus expecting Newfoundland, 'which is south of London, ... to have a moderate climate, and Virginia ... to be like southern Spain'.[8] This theory fuelled both fantasies and fears. For many Britons, the possibility that North America might produce the wine, silk, olive oil, sugar, and spices otherwise found only in Spain, Portugal, and France was exciting; for others, this dream of an abundant New World also represented an important proof of God's benevolence.[9] For some, however, these predictions were fraught with danger, as this sense that climate was stable within these zones defined by latitude was grounded in a related theory of climatic determinism, or an abiding faith in climate's power to shape both character and culture throughout each zone.[10] From this perspective, as Thomas Morton explains in 1637, 'This Torrida Zone is good for Grasshoppers', and the 'Zone Temperata for the Ant and Bee', but those who travel between zones risk wandering too far from what is best suited to their type.[11] As Morton's metaphor suggests, however, even those early modern writers worried about overwhelming climatic influence held an optimistic view of the North American climate itself – and as a prevailing mood of writing about early efforts to transplant

---

[7] See Chapter 4 by Daryn Lehoux and Chapter 5 by P. S. Langeslag in this volume.

[8] Kupperman, 'The Puzzle', 1262. For more on these classical theories of determinism, see Clarence J. Glacken, *Traces on the Rhodian Shore: Nature and Culture in Western Thought from Ancient Times to the End of the Eighteenth Century* (Berkeley: University of California Press, 1967), pp. 80–115. For more on how these ideas shaped writing about America's climate in particular, see Zilberstein, *A Temperate Empire*, pp. 26–8; Kupperman, 'The Puzzle', 1262–5; Susan Scott Parrish, *American Curiosity: Cultures of Natural History in the Colonial British Atlantic World* (Chapel Hill, NC: University of North Carolina Press, 2006), pp. 103–4; Brant Vogel, 'The Letter from Dublin: Climate Change, Colonialism, and the Royal Society in the Seventeenth Century', *Osiris*, 26 (2011), 111–28.

[9] Linda Williams, 'The Anthropocene and the Long Seventeenth Century', in Tom Bristow and Thomas H. Ford (eds.), *A Cultural History of Climate Change* (London: Routledge, 2016), pp. 87–107.

[10] Parrish, *American Curiosity*, especially pp. 77–102.

[11] Thomas Morton, *New English Canaan, or New Canaan containing an abstract of New England, composed in three bookes...* (Amsterdam: Jacob Frederick Stan, 1637), p. 14; see also Kupperman, 'The Puzzle', 1266, and 'Fears of Hot Climates in the Anglo-American Colonial Experience', *William and Mary Quarterly*, 41 (1984), 213–40.

potentially lucrative plant species to North America, this optimism
proved durable enough to rebuff even concrete evidence of risk.
Forced to admit, for instance, that the sugar cane he carried would
not grow in Virginia, Thomas Hariot maintains that this experiment
failed only because the cane was 'not so well preserved' in transit 'as
was requisite', and because the 'time of year ... for their setting ...
[was] past ... when we arrived'; nonetheless, he insists, 'seeing that
[cane] grow[s] in the same climate, in the South part of Spaine and in
Barbary, our hope in reason may yet continue'.[12]

As reports like Hariot's continued to mount, however, some of this
optimism turned into curiosity about how part of the torrid zone could
possibly be so cold – and in the search for an explanation, both the
epistemological challenge that this gap between expectations and experience had created and the pressure to maintain some hope for North
America's growing potential become clear. One common response, as
Kupperman has observed, was to emphasise the speed with which conditions in North America appeared to change, in part because this narrative
held out some hope that the severity of these conditions could change
quickly, too.[13] It was this hope, for instance, that seemed to inspire
physician John Lining, writing in 1740, to continue to insist that the
North American climate is jarring to the system not because it is so
much warmer or cooler than expected, but because 'the Excursions from
Heat to Cold, in the different Seasons, are very great, and the
Transitions ... surprisingly sudden'.[14] As early as 1612, however, the bad
reputation of the North American climate had started to stick, particularly
after reports on the failure of the Virginia colonies at Jamestown and
Sagadahoc (now Maine) so prominently decried the 'extreame unseasonable and frosty Winter', and John Smith, remarking on the country in
which these plantations were 'begunne and ended in one year', declared it
'a cold, barren, mountainous, rocky Desart'.[15] Confronted with this

[12] Thomas Hariot, *A Briefe and True Report of the New Found Land of Virginia* ... (London, 1588), pp. 11–12.
[13] Kupperman, 'The Puzzle', 1271–2.
[14] John Lining, 'Extracts of Two Letters from Dr John Lining, Physician at Charles-Town in South Carolina, to James Jurin, MDFRS', *Philosophical Transactions of the Royal Society*, 42.462–471 (1742), 491–509; for more on Lining, see Parrish, *American Curiosity*, p. 84.
[15] William Strachey, qtd. in Charles Edward Banks, 'New Documents Relating to the Popham Expedition, 1607', *Proceedings of the American Antiquarian Society*, 39 (1929), 312; for more on Strachey, see Kupperman, 'The Puzzle', 1272. John Smith, *The Generall History of Virginia, New England, and the Summer Isles with the Names of the Adventurers, Planters, and Governours from their First Beginning* (London: Michael Sparkes, 1624), p. 204.

creeping sense that prospects in America might not improve quickly, some early modern writers instead adopted a long view of both the causes of this climatic puzzle and the likely horizon for change. According to Edmond Halley, for instance, writing for the Royal Society, 'the extream Cold felt in the North North-West of America, about Hudson's Bay' could be explained best by 'the casual Choc of a Comet' that had only recently 'occasion[ed] the Sea to recede from those Parts'; it was as a result of this impact, he proposed, that 'those Parts' were so strangely cold, because they had 'once been much more Northerly', and still remained under 'immense Quantities of Ice *yet* unthaw'd ... which chill the Air'.[16] Here, Halley's 'yet' reveals his optimism about the climate's potential to improve in the distant future, but it also presents a challenge to the classical theory of *klimata*. To begin with, Halley's effort to attribute the prevailing conditions in North America to the presence of ice, water, and mountains takes for granted that climate is not determined solely by latitude – and if this was true, then the field of explanations for the present climate and predictions for the future opened wide. Untethered from a theory that insisted its characteristics must be consistent throughout a band around the world, climate could be reimagined as a condition it was possible to change – and though Halley here identifies thawing ice as the best evidence of this changeability, other travellers would more cannily observe that if this new theory of climate happened to take, as proof of improvement, some condition that was *already* changing for the better in America, the investment potential of the colonies there would surely warm up, too.

Inventing Improvement

This process is usefully illustrated by the change in the significance of failed or faltering efforts to transplant European plants, animals, and people to North America. Initially, writing about these transplantation efforts treated climate as a determining factor, following the classical model in presuming both that climate acts on all things equally and that the failure of some transplantation experiments therefore anticipates the failure of others. Over time, however, and as a result of a concerted effort to revise the characterisation of the indigenous species and peoples positioned at the end of these degeneration narratives, advocates for American settlement

---

[16] Edmond Halley, 'Some Considerations About the Cause of the Universal Deluge, Laid before the Royal Society, on the 12th of December 1694', *Philosophical Transactions of the Royal Society*, 33.383 (1724), 122–3, original emphasis; for more on Halley, see Fleming, *Historical Perspectives*, pp. 23–4.

increasingly identified climate as a variable condition with variable effects, often framing evidence of environmental conditions that seemed to be improving – like crop yields – as evidence of climatic change already underway. By the end of this process, stories of those early failures to thrive had been reimagined as evidence that some species and settlers were simply better suited to the present condition of the climate than others – and so, in the hands of late eighteenth-century observers with an interest in American settlement, proof that European settlers could grow European crops became proof that the climate was changing, becoming more accommo-dating to the European bodies responsible for this improvement.

At one end of this process, as James Rodger Fleming and Jan Golinski have demonstrated, was a popular and tenacious narrative about the universally enervating effects of American air. Emerging with seven-teenth-century travellers' laments for 'hopes ... frozen to death' and reinvigorated by the fascination with the small size and seeming weakness of North American plants, animals, and people that European naturalists would maintain well into the eighteenth century, these narratives pre-sume that any movement between climatic zones will necessarily bring about a change in the subject transported, and identify climate as 'the means by which natural forces would fit the organisms to their new environments'.[17] Because this tradition of writing about transplantation tends to presume both that a process of gradual adjustment is inevitable and that this adjustment will take place from the outside in, however, writing about acclimation also frequently presumes a continuity in the kind of adjustment the environment will produce across species. After all, as Cotton Mather declares in 1696, if 'It is affirmed that many sorts of Inferior Creatures, when Transplanted from Europe to America, do Degenerate by the Transplantation', it should be no surprise that 'this Remark must be made upon the People, too'.[18] Here, in addition to illustrating the sense that change in transplanted subjects is inevitable, Mather implicitly affirms a classical view of climate, suggesting first that there is something about America that will facilitate the degeneration he describes, and that this environmental condition will act in the same way upon both 'inferior Creatures' and 'people'. In other words, Mather presumes the outcome of early transplantation efforts will foreshadow

---

[17] Golinski, *British Weather*, pp. 188–9, 200–1; Fleming, *Historical Perspectives*, p. 24. For more on medical writing about acclimation, see Chapter 7 by Golinski in this volume.

[18] Cotton Mather, *Things for a Distress'd People to Think upon Offered in the Sermon to the General Assembly of the Province of the Massachusetts Bay* (Boston: Duncan Campbel, 1696), 14. For more on Mather, see Parrish, *American Curiosity*, p. 91.

the outcome of future settlements – and, as Susan Scott Parrish has demonstrated, the same logic was widely used to identify changes in early travellers as evidence of the change that more recent travellers should anticipate in themselves, and to position the characteristics of the plants, animals, and people indigenous to North America at the end of these narratives of decline. In her journal of a trip to New York in 1704, for instance, Sarah Kemble Knight recalls an encounter with a fellow settler quite transformed, 'an Indian-like Animal', riding 'a creature very much like himself, in mien and Feature'; in her doorway, he 'makes an Awkerd [*sic*] Scratch with his Indian shoo . . . [and] fell to suckling [his tobacco] like a calf'.[19] In this case, as Parrish observes, Knight associates both creolisation and atavism with degeneracy, such that the settler has become more 'Animal' by becoming more 'Indian-like'. However, Knight also imagines herself separated from her fellow settler only by a threshold – a spatial reminder, perhaps, of both the role exposure to the North American elements has so far played in his transformation, and the fact that she is differentiated from this settler, and from the 'Indian' and the 'Animal' he approaches, only by the time she has spent exposed to the same climate.

On one hand, some of this writing about climatic influence illustrates what Roxann Wheeler calls the 'elasticity of race' in Enlightenment thought, as stories like Knight's inspire concern only insofar as they resist categorical differences between recent settlers and those the climate has already transformed.[20] On the other hand, the presumption at the heart of these stories – that the adjustment by which climate fits all things to its temper is necessarily degenerative – clearly serves a number of imperial objectives. In addition to affirming European claims to cultural superiority, for instance, a narrative of decline that aligns weakness with 'Indianisation' also helped to obscure the devastating effects of the strange germs, new weapons, and forced labour practices responsible for the indigenous genocide unfolding since the Columbian Exchange, as it recast the consequences of invasion as a constitutional weakness, and repositioned the European colonist as subject to, rather than the agent of, this

---

[19] Sarah Kemble Knight, *The Journal of Madam Knight*, ed. George Parker Winship (Boston: Small, Maynard and Company, 1920), pp. 25–6. For more on Knight, see Parrish, *American Curiosity*, p. 92.

[20] Roxann Wheeler, *The Complexion of Race: Categories of Difference in Eighteenth-Century British Culture* (Philadelphia: University of Pennsylvania Press, 2000), p. 39. For more, see Joyce E. Chaplin, 'Nature Philosophy and an Early Racial Idiom in North America: Comparing English and Indian Bodies', *William and Mary Quarterly*, 54 (1997), 229–52; Dror Wahrman, *The Making of the Modern Self: Identity and Culture in Eighteenth-Century England* (New Haven, CT: Yale University Press, 2004), pp. 83–126.

destructive environmental change.[21] However, even as the popularity of this degeneration theory helped, in Mary Louise Pratt's terms, to 'narrate the anti-conquest', the view of climate that naturalised these effects posed a challenge to those still invested in the potential of the North American colonies.[22] Within the context of the persistent failure of transplanted crops, settlements 'begunne and ended in one year', and the devastation of indigenous communities post-contact, the explanatory power of a narrative that presumed these failures necessarily foreshadowed the failures of future settlements pulled strongly against claims that the prospects in North America might improve over time – and so, in an attempt to imagine an alternative future for the colonies, some advocates for North American settlement mounted a challenge to the theory of climate that insisted this decline was inevitable.

These rebuttals took many forms, ranging from stories celebrating settlers' efforts to cultivate North American crops to fervent defences of the strength settlers observed in their indigenous allies. Most famous, of course, is Thomas Jefferson's years-long endeavour to counter the Comte de Buffon's claims about the 'diminish[ing]' influence of a 'niggardly sky' by sending him the seven-foot body of a North American moose, but all of these campaigns pose a similar challenge to the theory of climate that underpins Buffon's argument.[23] Unlike the continental naturalists who identify the small size of some North American species as an inevitable effect of the air, the authors of these counterpoints insist that the sheer size and number of other plants, animals, and people in North America prove that these degenerative effects could not be universal – and if climate did not act on all things equally, they argue further, then the success of future settlements might not be fated by the failure of early transplantation efforts. Alongside writing like Buffon's, this suggestion appears radical, a whole new way of conceiving of climate as a changeable condition – but,

---

[21] Parrish, *American Curiosity*, pp. 90–102; Golinski, *British Weather*, pp. 192–3; Louis Warren, 'Owning Nature: Towards an Environmental History of Private Property', in Andrew C. Isenberg (ed.), *Oxford Handbook of Environmental History* (Oxford University Press, 2014), pp. 406–7. For more on the Columbian Exchange, see Williams, 'Anthropocene', 99–103; Crosby, *Ecological Imperialism*, pp. 132–44.

[22] Mary Louise Pratt, *Imperial Eyes: Travel Writing and Transculturation*, 2nd edn (New York: Routledge, 2008), pp. 37–66.

[23] [Georges-Louis LeClerc] Comte de Buffon, *Natural History, General and Particular*, trans. William Smellie, 2nd edn (London: W. Strahan and T. Cadell, 1785), vol. v, p. 129. For more on these rebuttals, see Fleming, *Historical Perspectives*, pp. 24–7; Golinski, *British Weather*, pp. 192–3; Glacken, *Rhodian Shore*, pp. 655–705; Lee Alan Dugatkin, *Mr Jefferson and the Giant Moose: Natural History in Early America* (University of Chicago Press, 2009), pp. 10–30.

in fact, campaigns like Jefferson's merely amplified a tradition that had, from the seventeenth century forward, consistently dismissed claims that early 'hopes ... frozen to death' foreshadowed future disaster, insisting instead that the contrast between these early disappointments and the relatively greater success of more recent efforts proved that a change in the climate was not only possible, but already underway. In 1672, for instance, cartographer Richard Blome insisted that Virginia's 'Clime of late [has been] very agreeable to the English, since the clearing of Woods, so that now few dyeth of the Countreys disease, called the Seasoning'; in 1676, likewise, the portion of *Speed's Theatre of the Empire of Great Britain* that treats Virginia described 'a temperature ... agreeable to English constitutions (especially since ... the cutting down of the Woods)', and reiterates that 'the seasoning was formerly more violent and dangerous here to the English at their first landing'.[24] In each of these examples, the writer identifies clearing the woods as the mechanism of climatic change, but ultimately identifies a change in the rate of 'seasoning' casualties – that is, the number of people who died within their first year – as proof that the clearing has worked. Typical of mid-seventeenth-century climate writing, both claims are grounded in a view of climate as agency, a force acting on the species and settlers under it – but by recasting a positive change in the size, strength, or number of the species and settlers at a particular latitude as evidence of a positive change in the climate itself, texts like these made it possible for European observers to imagine that if settlers could continue to improve these characteristics of the species and settlers in question, they would have changed the climate, too.[25]

For writers like Blome, that is, any evidence of new or improved forms of life in North America could become evidence that the climate was changing for the better – and so throughout the early eighteenth century, stories of increasing crop yields joined these narratives about the changing rate of 'seasoning' as popular evidence of this improvement.[26] Of course, as Zilberstein cautions, many of these stories contained more wishful thinking than truth, as 'tensions between local and distant elites about how to mobilize climate knowledge in the service of colonial settlement and economic expansion' often contorted

---

[24] Richard Blome, *A Description of the Island of Jamaica with the Other Isles and Territories in America, to Which the English are Related* (London: T. Milbourn, 1672), pp. 141–2; John Speed, *An Epitome of Mr John Speed's Theatre of the Empire of Great Britain and His Prospect of the Most Famous Parts of the World* (London: Thomas Basset, 1676), 209. There is some speculation that Blome may be the source of the details in the epitome of Speed's Theatre that he printed, and that Blome borrowed his own statements about Virginia from Speed. For more, see Vogel, 'The Letter from Dublin', 118–19.

[25] James Rodger Fleming and Vladimir Janković, 'Revisiting Klima', *Osiris*, 26 (2011), 1–15.

[26] Zilberstein, *A Temperate Empire*, pp. 91–117; Golinski, *British Weather*, pp. 198–200.

reports on just how much adjustment would be necessary for imported plants and foreign settlements to thrive in northern climates.[27] 'Particularly in areas that bordered Catholic New France', for instance, Zilberstein finds that 'British officials . . . manipulated perceptions of regional climate in attempts to increase the Protestant settler population . . . by introducing frost-tolerant silkworms and wine grapes'; elsewhere, likewise, optimistic ministers of Nova Scotia and New Brunswick championed winter's providence to sceptical parishioners, insisting that 'Long Experience has taught us that by Means of a large Coat of Snow upon the Earth . . . our Fields are less torn to Pieces by Rains: are left softer, lighter, and as it were, enrich'd with a coat of Dung.'[28] These claims are hyperbolic, but the fact that so many of these campaigns emphasise the success of particular crops nonetheless reveals an important shift in thinking about the changeability of the climate. In each case, these detailed descriptions of what the land can support stand in for descriptions of the other forces acting on that land, both tightening the connection between the condition of the climate and productivity in the popular imagination, and displacing those early travellers' tales of permanently 'frozen . . . hopes' with new stories focused on effects that could be changed for the better.

At the same time that these stories about surprising survival and unexpected yields both insisted the North America climate was improving and redefined what constituted relevant evidence of this improvement, furthermore, another change in climatic thought was taking place; taken together, these theories further refined the characteristics of the subject best suited to North America, more closely aligning these characteristics with the European settler. Broadly, this additional revision to the classical theory of climatic determinism was motivated by British natural philosophers and political theorists who hoped to better account for the problem of social progress, or the challenge that two centuries of travellers' observations of religious, social, and political diversity had offered to the argument that climate (or latitude) alone could be responsible for all cultural difference.[29] For David Hume, for instance, it seemed impossible to 'attribut[e] the differences of manners, in Wapping and St James's, to a difference of air or climate', and equally difficult to explain how peoples who live under entirely different climates could come to seem so similar.[30] Inspired,

---

[27] Zilberstein, *A Temperate Empire*, pp. 11–12.

[28] Ibid., pp. 12, 114, as well as 109–17 for more on snow as the 'poor man's Dung'.

[29] Golinski, *British Weather*, pp. 173–4; Glacken, *Rhodian Shore*, pp. 551–622.

[30] David Hume, 'Of National Characters', in Hume, *Essays: Moral, Political Literary*, ed. Eugene F. Miller (Indianapolis: Liberty Classics, 1987), vol. 1, p. 220. See also Eric Gidal, 'Civic Melancholy: English Gloom and French Enlightenment', *Eighteenth-Century Studies*, 37 (2003), 31–4.

then, by this broad sense that laws, customs, and morals must play a role in mitigating the influence of climate in at least some parts of the world, writers of the Scottish Enlightenment – including Adam Smith, John Millar, Adam Ferguson, and Henry Home, Lord Kames – developed a four-stage theory of civilisation to explain this variation, placing societies of different times and places in different stages according to their modes of subsistence (respectively, hunting, pasturage, agriculture, and commerce). Implicit, however, in this teleological view of civilisation was also a spectrum of susceptibility to environmental influence: on one pole, the subjects of 'primitive' civilisations were presumed to be especially susceptible to environmental influence, while on the other, the superiority of more 'advanced' civilisations was marked by their ability to resist – and then direct – the influence of their environments.[31]

Immensely popular through the second half of the eighteenth century, this stadial theory had significant implications for writing about the risks of travel between climatic zones. Most importantly, it helped to turn climate into a differentiating force, as it recast evidence previously used to support a narrative of inevitable decline as proof, instead, of differences between those susceptible and those impervious to degenerative influences. This is why, by century's end, Hudson's Bay Company Adventurer Samuel Hearne can describe his Chipewyan guides' inclination to 'eat their victuals quite raw' in the same terms that Sarah Kemble Knight once used to register her dismay at the deterioration of an 'Indian-like' fellow settler, but without raising any concern about his own possible decline. Unlike himself, Hearne observes, the Chipweyans have been habituated to eating meat raw by 'early custom and frequent necessity . . . in this inhospitable part of the globe', and now 'frequently do it by choice' – and it is this choice, for Hearne, that marks the difference between those who master the climate and those who are mastered by it.[32] This stadial theory had a similar effect on the presumed end of positive narratives of acclimation. For those who subscribed to this four-stage theory of civilization, to have fully acclimated was not just to have become inured to local environmental risks, as in the old pattern of writing about transplantation, but rather to

[31] Golinski, *British Weather*, pp. 178–80; Fleming, *Historical Perspectives*, pp. 11–19; Kevin Hutchings, 'Writing Commerce and Cultural Progress in Samuel Hearne's *A Journey . . . to the Northern Ocean*', *ARIEL: a Review of International English Literature*, 28 (1997), 53–4.

[32] Samuel Hearne, *A Journey from Prince of Wales's Fort in Hudson's Bay to the Northern Ocean 1769, 1770, 1771, 1772*, ed. Richard Glover (Toronto: Macmillan, 1958), p. 203; for more on this passage, see Hutchings, 'Writing Commerce', 67.

have taken control of those local conditions to direct their influence to ends that better suit the acclimating subject.[33] Turning to Hearne, again, the change in his response to the climate north of Prince of Wales' Fort over the course of his four-year expedition reflects just such a narrative of mastery: throughout his first two journals, Hearne complains often about the effects of the cold (or jarring thaw) on his spirit and his company's progress, but by his third journal, he has shifted his focus to the weather's influence on animal migration, now framing his observations as instructions to help future Company agents trap animals at the moment their fur will be most valuable.[34] By the end of the eighteenth century, then, these two new strains of thought – one about the relationship between climate and civilisation, one about the end and outcome of acclimation – had significantly changed the context in which interested observers could interpret stories of European crops, settlers, and enterprise flourishing in North America. In addition to reversing those longstanding narratives about how the climate would weaken all it touched, this new emphasis on distinguishing differences invited those invested in North America's growing potential to speculate instead about how the climate could be changed to better suit the needs of the traveller – and to identify travellers from zones already temperate as uniquely well prepared to facilitate this change.

Sceptics and Politics

For English writers enthusiastic about the expansion of imperial activity in North America, these changes served a number of political ends. According to Fleming, for instance, many of the Enlightenment thinkers who identified the flourishing of familiar crops as evidence that European agriculture had made North America more suitable for European settlement further speculated that the same change had made the climate 'less suitable' for indigenous cultures, reframing both European land claims and indigenous deaths caused by contact as natural consequences of climatic change.[35] At the same time, Golinski elaborates, this stadial theory of susceptibility to environmental influence helped these Enlightenment thinkers to rewrite the history of settlement in North America. In particular, he notes, this

---

[33] Golinski, *British Weather*, p. 180; for more on the appropriation of local knowledge, see Zilberstein, *A Temperate Empire*, pp. 53–88.

[34] Compare Hearne's mood at the end of his second journey (23 February 1770 to 11 August 1770) to his mood at the end of his third journey (19–25 August 1771); Hearne, *A Journey*, pp. 37, 127.

[35] Fleming, *Historical Perspectives*, p. 18.

theory encouraged European settlers to imagine that the North American 'wilderness had remained unimproved until [their] arrival', and so to reframe the fatal 'trials by frost' that foiled early settlements and transplantation efforts as merely the consequences of indigenous neglect.[36] In each case, however, the force of these arguments comes from the shift in interpretative context facilitated by this new theory of climate, or the way this new commitment to representing climate change through crop yields made it possible to reinterpret early travellers' accounts of brutal cold as merely the baseline for a process of slow change, excluding counter-evidence (of persistent cold, say) not directly related to productivity. In addition to turning stories of European vulnerability into stories of European superiority, then, this new theory turned the challenge that travellers' encounters with North American extremes once posed to classical *klimata* into a permanent condition, a formalised gap between persistent conditions (like the cold) and the vision of an improvable climate circulating in promoters' reports – and as this gap, and the interests it protected, became more obvious than the conditions on the ground, the same change in thinking about climate that helped to naturalise the European presence in America also helped to politicise, or denaturalise, writing about climate in general.

For historians of early American settlement, this gap has long been obvious in the archive, clear in the space between the optimism about the 'healthfulness of the climate' in early promotional narratives and the anxiety about degeneration that so often turned up in private correspondence.[37] More recently, however, reconstructions based on historical climatological data have cast new light on the environmental consequences of this approach to treating changes in productivity as evidence of climate change, confirming that, in addition to obscuring both the sophistication and scale of indigenous agricultural practices and the local knowledge of climatic indicators appropriated by European agents of empire (as in Hearne's journal, above), this new theory of climate also obscured the worst effects of the very agricultural practices – clearing forests, planting monocultures, and eradicating wild competition with livestock – that supported those European narratives of climatic improvement grounded in the productivity of the land.[38] Likewise, these climatological reconstructions have confirmed just how little change, either day-to-

---

[36] Golinski, *British Weather*, p. 197; Zilberstein, *A Temperate Empire*, p. 8. See also Chapter 7 by Golinski in this volume.
[37] Parrish, *American Curiosity*, p. 89.   [38] Warren, 'Owning Nature', pp. 408–9.

day or year-over-year, early American weather-watchers would have witnessed to support those declarations that the climate was improving as
a result of European agriculture.[39] Following the cues this data has provided
back into the early modern texts that explicitly address the matter of the
North American climate, however, new archives emerge – and as it turns
out, neither this gap between report and reality nor the political interests it
serves have become obvious only in hindsight.

Inundated by stories of improvement but surrounded by evidence to the
contrary, many early modern writers explicitly identified this emphasis on
the success of certain species or settler communities as propagandistic, and
implicitly rejected the connection between these communities' success and
climatic improvement. As early as 1682, in fact, both these propagandistic
claims and their distance from the truth were such familiar features of
reports from North America that John Dryden, writing on the union of
two rival theatre companies, could take up this pattern of writing about
climate as a metaphor for factionalism itself. To open his prologue to the
first performance by the united King's and Duke's Houses, Dryden
observes that, 'Since faction ebbs, and rogues grow out of fashion, /
Their penny-scribes take care to inform the nation / How well men thrive
in this or that plantation', and then outlines the conditions rumoured to
support each project: From one faction, Britons hear of 'How
Pennsylvania's air agrees with Quakers', yet from another, that
'Carolina's [air agrees] with Associators', while each insists their project is
'e'en too good for madmen and for traitors'.[40] Here, the tenor of the
metaphor is the feud between the theatre companies (who had, before the
union, treated 'this theatre [as] our new plantation', a struggle for territory), but the vehicle illustrates all that Dryden could presume his readers
would already know about the competing schemes to improve the
American colonies -- and, as a shorthand for transparently false and interested claims, writing about the quality of the air seems to have been
a recognisable mark. Following the logic of Dryden's joke, both the
suggestion that the air is different in different colonies and the suggestion
that the air in any one colony might be better suited to any one type of
person become ridiculous upon repetition, and especially so in light of the
reports – decades-old even in 1682 – that large swaths of North America
might be no more than 'a cold, barren, mountainous, rocky Desart'.[41]

[39] Zilberstein, *A Temperate Empire*, p. 3; Fleming, *Historical Perspectives*, p. 27.
[40] John Dryden, *Prologue to the King and Queen at the Opening of Their Theatre, Spoken by Mr Batterton* (London: Jacob Tonson, 1683), ll. 1–6.
[41] Smith, *The Generall History of Virginia*, p. 204.

Similarly, as the joke's punch-line about the theatre as contested territory makes clear, Dryden presumes his listeners would hear, in these effusions about the healthfulness and variability of the air, not meaningful descriptions of atmospheric conditions, but rather promises intended to support each faction's claim to the 'plantation', or empty words intended to draw free settlers into territory they would not otherwise visit.

What Dryden's joke demonstrates, then, is that even in the seventeenth century, the wide gap between promoters' claims about an improvable climate and the persistent (if private) reports on the brutal cold had created an interpretative context in which writing about climate seemed as likely to reveal factional allegiances as to report prevailing conditions. Under these circumstances, this joke suggests, any description of the climate in America appeared fraught, presumed partisan and open to suspicion – and looking outwards from the metaphorical context of Dryden's prologue to the wider sphere of eighteenth-century writing about the environments of the expanding British empire, it appears that the assumptions animating this joke also shaped the role climate would play in genres as diverse as political pamphlets on monopoly rights and sentimental captivity narratives. In 1749, for instance, critics of the Hudson's Bay Company would ground a Charter challenge in doubt about the Company's reports on the frigid conditions in Rupert's Land, insisting that the 'prodigious Accounts of the Effects of Cold' returned by Company representatives simply must be 'calculated only ... to prevent people from going there to settle, and encroach[ing] upon the Company's monopoly'.[42] As in Dryden's prologue, these complaints presume a wide and well-known gap between the reports on and the reality of the conditions in North America – and although it is the pessimism of these reports, rather than their optimism, that attracted suspicion in this case, the debate nonetheless illustrates the prominent place that questions of economic interest had come to occupy in conversation about climate in North America.

As the politicisation of reports on climatic change appears to become a transparent condition of debate about all kinds of imperial activity in North America, furthermore, writing about dramatic encounters with the climate itself became legible as political commentary about how these activities were being governed, and by whom. It is to this end, for instance, that Susannah Johnson's 1792 narrative of her experience among the Abenaki First Nation devotes pages to complaints about the pain of travel,

[42] John Campbell, ed. *Navigantium Atque Itinerantium Bibliotheca. Or, A Complete Collection of Voyages and Travels* (London, [1744–]1748), p. 292.

on foot and without shoes, through 'darkness, then thunder, and lightning, and rain', promising that the experience of sleeping 'on the cold earth, without a cover ... may be imagined, but not described'.[43] Unlike a standard degeneration narrative, however, which might have framed these complaints as evidence of a climate incompatible with Johnson's constitution, Johnson's grievances are interspersed with a series of bureaucratic letters between her husband and agents of the British and French forces that refuse to help him ransom his family. As a result of her husband's delay, Johnson finds herself 'friendless and alone', exposed first to the cold, then to the terror of starvation and smallpox – and so, as these letters denying her husband support begin to appear as much an environmental condition as the cold, the whole narrative of her exposure becomes an indictment of the European forces that have left her family so unprotected. Reiterating but reversing the terms of Dryden's joke, Johnson's anecdote thus suggests that, by 1792, the association between writing about climate and political interests had become so entrenched that Johnson could here present a complaint about prolonged exposure to North America's extremes as a critique of political interests left unprotected – and presume that her readers would appreciate the argument, implicit in this critique, that the inability of these European forces to mitigate climatic risk suggests a weak claim to the territory in question.

What Johnson's critique makes visible, in other words, is not just how closely this new theory of climate had tied imperial interests to the strength and safety of European bodies under North American air, but how transparent, for better or for worse, that relationship was to observers throughout the eighteenth century – and to this end, what makes Johnson's critique possible is the whole arc of the change in thinking about climate this chapter has traced. Some parts of this story have been familiar: it is not novel, for instance, to observe that theories of improvement, and the use of increased yields as evidence of the superiority of European agricultural practices in particular, have a prominent place in eighteenth-century British imperial rhetoric. Scholars of eighteenth-century political theory and property rights have long traced Enlightenment ideas about ownership to John Locke's agrarian capitalism, and more recently, theorists interested in the relationship between state sovereignty, private property, and environmental justice have returned to eighteenth-century theories of

[43] Susannah Willard Johnson, *A Narrative of the Captivity of Mrs Johnson. Containing an Account of Her Sufferings, During Four Years with the Indians and the French* (Walpole, NH: David Carlisle, 1796), pp. 46, 89.

improvement to explore how the power of the modern state is still grounded in the state's ability to make environmental resources available to capital.[44] By widening this sphere of inquiry, however, to include the slow shift in thinking about the meaning of climate that helped to give these improvement narratives some of their political weight, this chapter has aimed first to illuminate the role that this change in the meaning of climate has played in naturalising British claims to territory in North America, and to unsettle the theory of climate that still underpins contemporary efforts to respond to catastrophic climatic change. Following Zilberstein's recent study of British efforts to manipulate the reputation of North America's climate, this chapter has set out a number of the ways in which advocates for American settlement also attempted to change the significance of unsettling encounters with the North American climate by changing the meaning of climate itself.[45] To this end, the long conversation this chapter has traced adds nuance to our current history of the relationship between writing about acclimation and writing about improvement, clarifying how and why concerns about the slow or limited success of early transplantation efforts gave way to triumphant tales of early American settlers fitting a formerly intemperate climate to their needs. At a moment when the climate crisis we have inherited from the Enlightenment has motivated a wide range of new experiments in the fields of geo-engineering, genomics, and even terraforming, this story – of how the meaning of climate changed, and how that change turned worries about the rate of travellers' acclimation into narratives of improvement – speaks to present as well as past concerns. As we return to debate about the relative merits of modifying both environments and species to adapt to environmental change, for instance, and to debate about who owns and governs the environments that these interventions will create, this story reminds us that the ideas about what constitutes climatic change still operating in these debates already bear the imprint of the imperial project that shaped them.[46] Most importantly, however, by looking back to the early modern sceptics most attentive to how this narrow theory of climate – and still narrower

---

[44] Vogel, 'The Letter from Dublin', 127. For more, see Warren, 'Owning Nature', 398–424; White, 'Nationalization', 976–86; Richard Grove, *Green Imperialism: Colonial Expansion, Tropical Island Edens, and the Origins of Environmentalism, 1600–1860* (Cambridge University Press, 1995); Christian Parenti, 'Environment-Making in the Capitalocene: Political Ecology of the State', in Jason W. Moore (ed.), *Anthropocene or Capitalocene? Nature, History, and the Crisis of Capitalism* (Oakland, CA: PM Press, 2016), pp. 166–84.

[45] Zilberstein, *A Temperate Empire*, pp. 91–117.

[46] Graybill, 'Boundless Nature', 668–7; Sophia Roosth, *Synthetic: How Life Got Made* (University of Chicago Press, 2017), pp. 81–98.

sense of what constitutes meaningful evidence of its change – was constructed in order to maintain specific and transparent political and economic interests, this chapter has aimed to open the possibility that this theory of climate could be changed again. As we become more aware of the ways in which a definition of climate that centres its effects on productivity continues to hamper analysis of present challenges and future risks,[47] the history of this change in the meaning of climate further reminds us that these terms are contingent – and can be stretched, just as they have been narrowed, to register all of those other aspects of environmental change for which the present sense of climate has, for so long, struggled to account.

---

[47] Jason W. Moore, *Capitalism in the Web of Life: Ecology and the Accumulation of Capital* (London: Verso, 2015), pp. 1–32.

CHAPTER 10

Climate and Race in the Age of Empire

Jessica Howell

Victorian explorer Sir Richard Francis Burton prefaces his travelogue *Wanderings in West Africa* (1863) by stating that the book will address 'the subject of West African mortality'.[1] Having lived and worked as Consul to Fernando Po, Burton believes that 'the land might be rendered not more unhealthy than the East or West Indies' (xiv) for white subjects. He asserts that West Africa's current 'fearful mortality' is caused 'principally [by] the bad positions of the settlements' (xiv) – an error he seeks to remedy by suggesting better placement and design. Burton displays confidence that settlements can be made healthy for colonists, in spite of the fact that he had suffered greatly from earlier exposures to unfamiliar African disease environments. For example, when he returned from his previous trip to Lake Tanganyika, his fiancée, Isabel, described him as resembling 'a mere skeleton . . . his yellow-brown skin hanging in bags, his eyes protruding, and his lips drawn away from his teeth'.[2] During his travels, he told her, he had suffered from twenty-one attacks of fever, 'in addition to being partly paralyzed for some months and partly blind for others'.[3]

In *Wanderings*, Burton draws upon the Hippocratic 'air, water and places' tradition of medical geography when he suggests that moving or reconfiguring settlements can decrease the death toll suffered by colonists.[4] If the white body is not exposed to noxious vapours from rot and putrefaction, as associated with the low-lying tropical landscape, or to exhaustion from tropical heat, Burton believes that it can survive and thrive. Further, pro-imperial appropriations of this ancient tradition of climatic

---

[1] Richard F. Burton, *Wanderings in West Africa* (New York: Dover, 1991), p. xiv. Hereafter cited parenthetically in the text.

[2] Qtd. in Mary Lovell, *A Rage to Live: a Biography of Richard and Isabel Burton* (New York: Norton, 2000), p. 305.

[3] Ibid., p. 305.

[4] For more on the Hippocratic tradition, see Chapter 5 by Daryn Lehoux in this volume.

determinism would suggest that northern races are fated to expand their influence and control over vast swaths of the Earth, owing to their more vigorous and martial natures.

However, as indicated by the disparity between Burton's ostensible belief in climatic control and his actual experience of illness in Africa, nineteenth-century discourses of colonial medical geography and topography were often deeply ambivalent and contradictory. For example, pro-imperial authors had to grapple with the contradiction between the belief that national and racial types developed certain physical characteristics in the context of their own climates and the apparently inevitable conclusion that other climates were thus unsuitable for the white body. This unsuitability would seem to obviate long-term tropical settlement, except at the risk of immediate death or long-term racial degeneration.

In spite of the promises made by the growing field of tropical medicine that it would identify and eliminate threats to colonists' health abroad, thus opening tropical environments to white settlement, illness from cholera, malaria, dysentery, plague, and yellow fever haunted both indigenous and white populations throughout the nineteenth and into the twentieth century. Popular protective measures in the first half of the nineteenth century included sanitary improvements to colonial cities and the seasonal migration of colonists to hill stations, meant to separate them from the most dangerous disease environments. Then, in the later nineteenth and early twentieth century, growing knowledge regarding bacteriology and parasitology was pressed into the service of expansionism, oftentimes alongside pre-existing measures of medical climatism. In spite of this, in places like India, Africa, and the Caribbean, debilitating diseases persisted.

However, many writers did not react by using pro-imperial discourses of climatic control. Some used the imaginative potential provided by the structures of fiction, for example, to grapple with concepts of chronic disease, bodily transformation, adaptation, and degeneration in the tropics. This chapter outlines the ways in which historical traditions of climatic medicine influenced nineteenth- and early twentieth-century colonial discourses. It will then examine three authors' engagements with and reaction to these discourses, in both fictional and non-fictional literatures of empire.

Though the chapter begins with Burton's methods of narrating medical geography, it also examines in detail alternative engagements with climate and the body offered by fiction. For example, pro-imperial authors such as Rudyard Kipling rewrite the spectre of racial degeneration by using the language of 'seasoning' and adaptation. In novels such as *Kim* (1901), Kipling suggests that shifting physical and racial markers are not a threat to British identity, but instead represent a new mode of colonial dominance. Subjects like Kim can appear racially hybrid but meanwhile maintain an unassailable white 'character'. In contrast, Joseph Conrad's *Heart of Darkness* (1899) embodies the breakdown of mental and physical order in the colonial context. The feverish quality of Conrad's prose immerses his readers in the inevitable illness and decline of white bodies, which he associates with the project of imperial domination.

Climate and Race

Before modern parasitology and bacteriology, the move to a new disease environment was most often articulated in terms of movement to an unfamiliar climate, which opened individuals to the risk of new diseases. Nineteenth- and early twentieth-century British colonial discourse built on the Hippocratic tradition of analysing the spatial and seasonal causes of disease. By investigating a location's elevation, temperature, and the quality of its air and water, the Hippocratic treatises theorised that one could predict both the most common diseases as well as the physical characteristics of the inhabitants. The body was not separate but inextricably linked to its environment, through the vitiating or invigorating quality of local climates.

The groundwork for the connection between the medicine of climate and racial anthropology was established within the Hippocratic corpus itself. For example, *On Airs, Waters, and Places* states that the inhabitants of Asia and Europe 'differ from one another' in 'all respects' owing to 'the temperature of the seasons'.[5] In Asia, for example, 'the country is milder, and the dispositions of the inhabitants are also more gentle and affectionate'.[6] In contrast, inhabitants of northern climates display 'Manly courage, endurance of suffering, laborious enterprise, and high spirit'.[7] The assertion that 'you will find the forms and dispositions of mankind to correspond with the nature of the country' is used in this treatise to imply that certain races are predisposed to political domination over others.[8] As a result of the regularity and gentleness of the climate, the book states, the 'Asiatic race is feeble'.[9] This allows certain political systems to dominate: 'monarchy prevails in the greater part of Asia', where 'men are

---

[5] Hippocrates, *On Airs, Waters and Places* (London: Wyman and Sons, 1881), pp. 57–8.
[6] Ibid., pp. 57–8.   [7] Ibid., p. 61.   [8] Ibid., p. 103.   [9] Ibid., p. 71.

not their own masters, but are the slaves of others'.[10] In contrast, the inhabitants of Europe are deemed 'more courageous': they are 'more war-like than the Asiatics' owing to their 'laborious exertions and pains'.[11] The analogy between moral superiority and climatic temperament later offered nineteenth-century British colonialism a medical vocabulary to justify its expansion. However, this was just the latest iteration of a discourse by which 'medical elements' were transposed 'onto a political model', which dates back to Plato, Thucydides, and the ancient Greeks.[12]

Hippocratic medicine claimed that disease is not 'mythical or divine in origin', instead establishing a system of 'rational medicine' based on the observation and documentation of climatic elements.[13] Such a system also held appeal for later Enlightenment scientists seeking to craft a natural history of human-as-species. Eighteenth-century French naturalist Georges-Louis Leclerc, the Comte de Buffon, was a monogenist who believed that climate had changed one human race into many according to region.[14] Buffon's *Natural History of Man, the Globe, and of Quadrupeds* (1749) begins with an extended description of different portions of the globe, superimposing climatic 'zones' on to racial and national differences. For example, he states of 'the Negroes of Senegal and Nubia' that 'the portion of the globe which Nature has allotted to this race of men' extends 'parallel to the equator' about 'nine hundred leagues in breadth . . . beyond the latitude of eighteen or twenty, there are no longer any Negroes'.[15] Climate demarcates not only geographic zones but characterological mar-kers: 'The Negroes in general are a remarkably innocent and inoffensive people.'[16]

Buffon's work also focuses on the physiological change of races over time under certain climatic influences. He states, 'climate, food, manners and customs' are some of the factors that 'produce not only a difference in sentiment', but also in the 'external form of a different people'.[17] He correlates the degenerative effects of place on human physiology with cultural degeneration as well. The heat of Egypt, for example, creates 'inherent' temperamental 'defects' in the Egyptians, including 'idleness and cowardice'.[18] Both physical and moral degeneration have allowed them to lose 'everything noble they once possessed'.[19] Buffon's rhetoric of

[10] Ibid., p. 71.   [11] Ibid., p. 97.
[12] Jacques Jouanna, *Greek Medicine from Hippocrates to Galen* (Boston: Brill, 2012), pp. 21, 36.
[13] Ibid., p. 81.
[14] Georges-Louis Leclerc, Comte de Buffon, *Natural History of Man, the Globe, and of Quadrupeds* (New York: Leavitt and Allen, 1857), vols. 1–11, p. 135.
[15] Ibid., p. 127.   [16] Ibid., p. 129.   [17] Ibid., p. 118.   [18] Ibid., p. 125.   [19] Ibid., p. 126.

cultural degeneration would be adopted by colonial discourses of the later centuries, which worked to establish the responsibility of 'greater' nations such as Britain either to salvage failing civilisations or to cultivate those who had yet to aspire to certain markers of economic development.

As Jan Golinski observes, during the eighteenth century, climate discourse became assimilated into ideas of national identity in new ways, with British subjects concluding that 'the damp and chilly air was invigorating, "incessant changes" of weather were mentally stimulating, [and] changeableness of atmospheric conditions on the island was ... a positive influence on the spirit of the people'.[20] The climate was then correlated with 'the country's bustling commercial life and its population's health'.[21] Not surprisingly, nationalist discourses of British weather depicted other locations as less salubrious, so that 'our' weather was even more sharply distinguished from 'their' weather. British writers decided they 'would rather not have tropical sunshine or heat, which brought with them lassitude, immorality, and disease'.[22] The Enlightenment period also saw the deployment of tools of weather documentation, in the form of 'medico-meteorological journals', within foreign lands earmarked for colonial settlement.[23] These maps worked to identify aspects of the environment that needed improvement.

Baron de Montesquieu also read climatic influences as influencing different societies' development.[24] His theory that temperature directly affected 'nerve fibres', which in turn 'shaped the characters of different nations', allowed him to argue that 'where climate tended to weaken the moral strength of the population', legislators should 'act forcefully to counter its effects'.[25] Such ideas helped justify the deployment of nineteenth-century colonial public health interventions and laws, whereby controlling health habits in tropical climates became the medical and moral responsibility of government. Further, if climate determined levels of civilisation, then the wrong climate could encourage immoderate or immoral behaviours in those who relocated there. These concerns manifest in nineteenth-century debates about the suitability of African and Indian climates for the white constitution, particularly in terms of whether colonial settlers could maintain the decorum and responsibility demanded of their position, or whether they would 'go native' and become like the less-civilised subjects amongst whom they lived.

---

[20] Jan Golinski, *British Weather and the Climate of Enlightenment* (University of Chicago Press, 2007), 2. See also Chapter 7 by Golinski in this volume.
[21] Golinski, *British Weather*, p. 4. [22] Ibid., p. 4. [23] Ibid., p. 149. [24] Ibid., p. 175.
[25] Ibid., p. 176.

By the early nineteenth century, human differences were identified not only with the effect of location and climate upon the body but also with inherent racial difference. With the rising popularity of polygenism, theorists began to ascribe racial characteristics to different human species. In order to compensate for the seeming limitations placed on colonial settlement by concepts of racial immutability, nineteenth-century colonial medicine became focused on articulating the concept of 'seasoning' or acclimation. The term 'seasoning', developed to describe the preservation of food with salt, the tanning of hides, or the tempering of wood and metals, indicates a process that makes materials stronger and longer lasting.[26] In the nineteenth century, the term was also used to describe the process of human bodies becoming hardened or inured to disease in a new environment.[27] The 'seasoning fever' acquired by whites travelling abroad was thought to be a necessary part of an adjustment to colonial environments. Theories of 'seasoning fever' evolved throughout the nineteenth century: in 1828, W. F. Chambers asserted that a subject who survived seasoning fever would be not only 'perfectly recovered' but also 'defended' against further attacks, while famous colonial doctor James Johnson asserted in 1848 that initial illness 'will not prevent' future sickness 'from marsh exhalations' but that later episodes of fever would 'assume' the '[less severe] periodic type'.[28]

Imperialists who invoked the concept of seasoning were navigating a double edge of tropical illness, calling themselves 'demi-Orientals', in Burton's case, or 'savages', in Kipling's, in order to argue that suffering from tropical disease made them insiders; at the same time, they clung to the idea that they could reassume their colonial identities without the taint of tropical degeneration.[29] However, even if they survived repeated bouts of seasoning fever, the health of European colonists would likely be seriously compromised. Medical and social theorists worried that, by

[26] 'seasoning, n.' def. 1c and def. 1i, *OED Online*, Oxford University Press, January 2018, oed.com/view/Entry/174362, provides illustrative examples from 1859 to 1897, respectively. Accessed 12 March 2018.
[27] 'seasoning, n.' def. 1d and def. 1e, *OED Online*, Oxford University Press, January 2018, oed.com/view/Entry/174362, shows this to be in common usage during the nineteenth century; for example, 'This was merely the seasoning which people who passed from one country to another must expect', in Thomas Babington Macaulay, *The History of England from the Accession of James II*, vol. v, 1st edn (London: Longman, Brown, Green and Longmans, 1861), xxxix, p. 229. Accessed 12 March 2018.
[28] W. F. Chambers, *The London Medical Gazette: Or, Journal of Practical Medicine*, 2 (1828), 64; James Johnson, *The British and Foreign Medico-Chirurgical Review, or, Quarterly Journal of Practical Medicine and Surgery*, 51 (1848), 191.
[29] See Richard F. Burton's *Goa and the Blue Mountains* (London: Richard Bentley, 1851) for more on his self-perception as a 'demi-Oriental'.

'acclimatising' to a new disease environment, the body of the explorer or colonist might be changed permanently.[30] Even in the Enlightenment, the study of climate had shown 'how much was determined by natural forces' that 'would not submit to the power of reason'.[31] Arguably, this inherent resistance of climate to systems of rationality and control contributed to the deep contradictions at the heart of colonial medicine.

The ambivalence at the heart of medical climatism is clearly evident when considering interventions in the colonial context. The field of tropical medicine developed during the nineteenth century in order to understand and control for foreign disease environments (the Liverpool School of Tropical Medicine was founded in 1898, and the London School of Hygiene and Tropical Medicine was founded in 1899). During the nineteenth century, British colonial forces were urgently motivated to identify healthy and unhealthy zones in India. This project was 'not so much medical' as 'moral, political and aesthetic', built upon the representation of Britain and India as at 'different stages on a linear course of civilization'.[32] However, while medical topography was one of the 'largest scientific enterprises in British India during the first half of the nineteenth century', medical historian Mark Harrison observes that many 'expressions of European superiority' often 'masked a sense of insecurity'.[33]

Harrison identifies the drive to medical and climatic separatism as receiving two major spurs: the First Burma War of 1824–6 and the so-called Indian Mutiny of 1857. The 'growing ... conviction that each "race" was uniquely fitted to a particular environment' during the nineteenth century led to a topographical and moral separatism that privileged hill stations for white colonists.[34] However, there was substantial doubt about the benefit of such hill stations, especially since the effects of light and heat were sometimes exacerbated by higher elevations. A 'sense of vulnerability' grew through the century, manifesting as fears about degeneration.[35] This fear often stimulated race hostility and prejudice, where British colonists cited the 'soporific'

---

[30] For more on the effects of the 'tropics' on white bodies, see Mark Harrison, *Climates and Constitutions: Health, Race, Environment and British Imperialism in India, 1600–1850* (Oxford University Press, 1999), pp. 1–24.

[31] Golinski, *British Weather*, p. xiii.

[32] Mark Harrison, 'Differences of Degree: Representations of India in British Medical Topography, 1820–c.1870', in Nicolaas A. Rupke (ed.), *Medical Geography in Historical Perspective*, vol. xx of *Medical History* (London: Wellcome Trust Centre for the History of Medicine, 2000), pp. 52–3.

[33] Ibid., pp. 53–4.

[34] For more on the racial separatism perpetuated by colonial hill stations, see Dane Kennedy, *Island of White: Settler Society and Culture in Kenya and Southern Rhodesia, 1890–1939* (Durham, NC: Duke University Press, 1987).

[35] Harrison, 'Differences of Degree', p. 61.

effects of India's climate as justification for British rule and blamed the 'insanitary' habits of Indians for epidemic disease.[36] However, as Harrison stresses, one should keep in mind that the colonial practice of medical topography was 'a project born of crisis', as much as a tool of dominance.[37] Discourses of medical climatism in the colonial context therefore manifest 'feelings of vulnerability and superiority' as 'two sides of the same imperial coin'.[38]

Climate in Nineteenth-Century Literatures of Empire

Burton deploys medical climatism in his work in a manner that manifests this sense of both vulnerability and superiority. A polygenicist, pro-imperial writer, linguist and amateur racial anthropologist, Burton travelled to Mecca and East and West Africa during the heyday of English exploration. His two-volume work *Wanderings in West Africa* (1863) is notable for the ways in which he correlates different kinds of climatic 'zones' – both elevation and latitude – with physical and moral racial characteristics. His deeply contradictory rhetoric attempts to map racial hierarchies on to the landscape. According to Burton, local Africans' 'Fate' (175) (to be ruled) is determined by their local environment, while Anglo-British subjects can be socially and geographically mobile, owing to their intellectual capacity to identify and inhabit the most salubrious places of West Africa.

Burton travelled by steamboat from England to Fernando Po in 1861. After having commented upon the comparatively healthy, 'Mediterranean'-like climates of Madeira and Tenerife, when approaching Bathurst, Gambia, he writes that he and his shipmates 'had reason to believe that we had quitted the parallels, north of which . . . health and comfort have made their homes' (128). As he approaches the last island, Cape Verde, before he reaches the west coast of Africa, he claims 'we are now on the threshold of tropical luxuriance' (133). The change in latitude is marked by dramatic weather patterns, including a storm that reminds Burton of a tornado. Burton says, 'The ears are deafened by the rush and roar of a mighty wind' (130). He observes that stormy winds in this location are so common that 'the trees are twisted sideways like natural vanes as it were' (130). The extreme wind forms a kind of meteorological as well as symbolic passage from the fresh breeze of the islands to the sickening air of the coast. As Burton comes closer to the

[36] Ibid., p. 66.   [37] Ibid., p. 65.   [38] Ibid.

West African mainland and the Gambia river, the 'sun burst through the sick yellow swamp-reek and the dew clouds with a sickly African heat' (143).

As when he observes the twisted trees, while approaching Bathurst, Burton 'reads' the climate's negative effects upon the plant and animal life, as well as upon the architecture. He observes 'mud' and 'mildew' and equates them with the area's predisposition for 'miasma and malaria' (145). After observing that the site of the settlement is 'execrable', Burton enumerates even more diseases to which the town is susceptible: 'the chances are that all the Bathurstians are dying of dysentery and yellow fever' (146). Burton's very prose embodies the impulse to move past the sickly location: after detailing the dangers of specific locations, he says 'matters of climate are becoming too serious to make us linger long about such places or subjects' (160). That is to say, the danger to one's health comes not only from time spent in 'bad air', but also from time spent lingering on the mere thought of unhealthy climates.

Instead, Burton contrasts the 'fatal coast' (147) with possible settlement positions further inland and at higher elevation, crafting a medico-climatological map that allows white subjects to survive 'lower' latitudes by compensating with 'higher' living quarters. He examines the location of Cape House, at the top of a cliff where it is exposed to healthful breezes. When considering such situations, he expresses confidence that hygienic science will provide remedies to white fatality in West Africa: 'the antiquated horror of Western Africa, which methinks is really but little worse than Western India, will soon pass away from the memory of the British public' (165–6). Upon taking an extended ride further inland with his hosts, Burton depicts a bucolic scene, contrasting it with the unhealthy lands he has passed through: 'The country, on either hand ... appeared positively beautiful, after the foul swamps of St Mary's island' (174). He observes 'a velvety green expanse of grass, sloping inland, and in one part a glade of baobab and other trees, where gorgeous birds sit and sing' (174). In order to encourage his readers to support moving colonial settlements, he mocks the opposite perspective: 'and yet there are men who would prefer the fever haunts of Bathurst' (175).

Burton also uses climatological mapping to equate spatial zones with race hierarchies. He holds 'as a tenet of faith', the 'doctrine of ethnic centres, and their comparative gradation' (175). Though ostensibly a theory of ethnology, Burton uses diction more often associated with religion (faith, doctrine) to show his commitment to white superiority. He continues, 'I believe the European to be the brain, the Asiatic the heart, the American and African the arms, the Australian the feet, of the man-figure'

(175). In addition to the moralistic connotations of the different body parts – whereby intellectualism is associated with the brain, emotion with the heart, brute strength with the arms – this doctrine also stresses the elevation of the head over other parts. That is to say, Burton's subscription to this doctrine creates a corporeal 'map' of his climatic determinism, where the zones of climate are superimposed on a racialised human body.

This conceptual overlap is even more evident as Burton transitions to the physiological analyses of racial anthropology. Using hyper-specific, pseudoscientific language, he continues by describing the 'aboriginal and typical African' as 'prognathous, and dolichol-kephalic, with retreating forehead, more scalp than face; calfless, cucumber-skinned, lark-heeled, with large and flat feet; his smell is rank, his hair crisp and curly, and his pile like peppercorns. His intellect weak, morale deficient, amiability strong, temperament enduring, destructiveness highly developed, and sensibility to pain comparatively blunt' (177–8). The shortness of phrases, combined with a surfeit of words used to describe inanimate objects such as 'cucumber', 'crisp', and 'peppercorns', strips the African subject of human qualities and endows the passage with racist authoritarianism. Burton concludes the passage by saying it is not surprising that the 'Caucasian man' has concluded that Africans are cursed to be 'servants of servants' (178).

However, as observed at the outset of this section, Burton's aggressive supremacy is paired with a sense of innate physical vulnerability.[39] He is nervous to linger, either physically or mentally, upon the dangers of the 'fatal coast'. For physical protection, he suggests that visitors procure a 'means of ready escape' (147). For protection against the lurking and insidious doubts inspired by the landscape, he refocuses his narrative on the healthful potential of higher settlements and on the innate superiority of white races. Finally, rather than 'wandering', as implied by the book's title, Burton structures his travel narrative in such a way that he quickly passes through, and passes beyond, the areas of greatest danger.

Joseph Conrad's novella *Heart of Darkness* (1899) also focuses on travel by steamboat in colonial Africa. However, Conrad's fiction emphasises internal imbalances within the white body as caused by tropical heat. There is no effective escape to higher elevation from the malignant quality of the light. As I have remarked elsewhere, critics frequently employ climatic

---

[39] For more on illness narration in Burton's travel writing, see Jessica Howell, *Exploring Victorian Travel Literature: Disease, Race and Climate* (Edinburgh University Press, 2014).

imagery in analysing Conrad's style, citing the 'vapour' and 'atmospherics' of his work.[40] In *Conrad in the Nineteenth Century*, Ian Watt links the persistent imagery of 'mist or haze' in Conrad's work to his impressionistic writing style.[41] However, tropical mist and miasma also were associated with disease, even by late Victorian travellers.[42] Therefore, the presence of climatic forces such as thick and stifling mist in *Heart of Darkness* is not only a stylistic strategy but indicates individuals' perception of danger, inspiring them to become more watchful for signs of illness in their own bodies. Conrad implies that this self-protection is doomed to failure and that, for the majority of white subjects, illness is inevitable.

In *Heart of Darkness*, Charlie Marlow narrates his journey up the Congo river to save Kurtz. Whereas Burton avoids lingering on the language of miasma and illness in Africa, the structure of Conrad's fiction – the repeated interruptions to Marlow's forward momentum, the repetition throughout of key climatic images, and the interiority of characters' observations – allows the author to plunge his readers into the lived experience of nebulous, omnipresent tropical disease. For example, Marlow portrays the land's excessive fecundity, as the steamboat winds 'in and out of rivers, streams of death in life, whose banks were rotting into mud, whose waters, thickened into slime, invaded the contorted mangroves that seemed to writhe at us'.[43] An excess of fecundity often leads to rot, and theorists of climate tell us that rot, filth, and putrefaction give off disease-causing stench. Usually a source of life, this river of death instead consists of rotting vegetative and animal matter. Trees appear to 'writhe' in the poisonous slime invading the mangroves. The still and fetid rivers lend to Marlow's African journey a sense of unreality, as 'a sense of vague and oppressive wonder' steals over him (17).

The colonial ideal that Burton presents, of white functionaries being able to survive in Africa, is treated by Conrad with disgust. The man with the most persistent good health, the Manager, is described as having 'no

---

[40] E. M. Forster, 'The Pride of Mr Conrad', qtd. in Ian Watt, *Conrad in the Nineteenth Century* (Berkeley: University of California Press, 1981), p. 169; Paul Zweig, *The Adventurer: the Fate of Adventure in the Western World*, qtd. in Andrea White, *Joseph Conrad and the Adventure Tradition: Constructing and Deconstructing the Imperial Subject* (Cambridge University Press, 1993), p. 172.

[41] Watt, *Conrad in the Nineteenth Century*, p. 169.

[42] 'Miasma' is defined by the Oxford English Dictionary as 'Noxious vapour rising from putrescent organic matter, marshland, etc., which pollutes the atmosphere; a cloud of such vapour' and it was thought for centuries to be the cause of malaria; 'miasma, *n*.' *OED Online*, Oxford University Press, January 2018, oed.com/view/Entry/117825. Accessed 13 March 2018.

[43] Joseph Conrad, *Heart of Darkness*, ed. Robert Kimbrough, 3rd edn (New York: Norton, 1988), p. 17. Hereafter cited parenthetically in the text.

learning, and no intelligence' but simply earning his position 'because he
was never ill' (25). The men who conquer Africa are there by default, as
their only skill is staying alive. The Manager's uncle observes, 'You stand
the climate – you outlast them all' (34). Conrad's book implies that the
type of man who is suited to serve in Africa is useless, even harmful, to both
'the natives' and his country.

India-born British novelist Rudyard Kipling was well educated in medical matters, and well versed in colonial medical triumphalism.[44] One
might assume, therefore, that he would employ in fiction medical and
scientific knowledge in a manner that creates a clear racial hierarchy, as did
Burton. Certainly, in his early writings, Kipling employs the well-
established medical discourse of sanitation as a method to manage the
'natives', using miasmatic descriptions to support racial separatism. For
example, in his essay 'The City of Dreadful Night', first published in 1885
and again in 1891, the narrator demonises Indians for producing a disease-
causing stench. Even the strongholds of colonial civilizsation, such as
European men's clubs, are inundated by miasma, called the 'Great
Calcutta Stink'.[45] He complains about the practice of placing Indians on
the Municipal Health Board. How, he asks, are Indian men meant to help
solve Calcutta's sanitary problems when they are 'of the breed born in and
raised off of this surfeited muck heap'?[46] The aesthetic of aversion is based
on an urban geography where the narrator feels compelled to live closely
with unhygienic locals, whose bodies are associated with the 'filth' of the
environment where they were 'born and raised'.

However, his own sickness from malaria offered Kipling a different
model for writing about disease in India, one based on cyclical and spatial
imagery. A clue to how malaria influenced his later fiction can be found in
his 1885 article, 'De Profundis (A Study in a Sick Room)'. Kipling
uses second-person narration to plunge his readers into this lived experience of malarial fever. The narrator introduces his episode of malaria by
saying that fever 'has you bound hand and foot for the night'. He stresses,
'You . . . are alone in that strange phantasmal world that lies open to us all
in time of sickness.'[47] Of note is the use of atmospheric and spatial imagery

---

[44] W. K. Beatty, 'Some Medical Aspects of Rudyard Kipling', *The Practitioner*, 215.1288 (1975), 532–4.
[45] Rudyard Kipling, *The City of Dreadful Night and Other Places* (Allahabad: A. H. Wheeler and
Company, 1891), p. 5.
[46] Ibid., p. 6.
[47] Kipling, 'De Profundis (A Study in a Sick Room)', *Civil and Military Gazette* (7 August 1885), rpt. in
Kipling's India: Uncollected Sketches, 1884–1888, ed. Thomas Pinney (New York: Schocken, 1986),
p. 120.

to describe the sufferer's experience of illness as he teeters on the edge of consciousness, 'preparatory to a final glissade down a rolling bank of black cloud and thick darkness, and out into the regions beyond'.[48] The cyclical nature of malarial fever and chills gives the impression of an 'advancing and receding tide'.[49] The symptoms of disease in this passage establish malaria as a disease of 'place': a disease that whites cannot successfully resist but may adapt to, in order to make colonial settlement possible.

In his later fiction, Kipling revisits the sensations of cyclical and chronic illness in order to establish a different model for colonial domination. His 1901 novel *Kim* depicts a British orphan in India who serves both as a Tibetan lama's disciple and as a spy for the British Raj. As he travels through India, Kim both treats those who are ill and also repeatedly falls sick himself. Kim practises his nascent colonial authority through administering cures to others, but he is also able to 'pass' as Indian by having a body changed by illness. Rather than focusing on Kim curing malaria, the novel instead provides a model of adaptation to the disease. Because Kim has suffered endemic disease, he has been changed by the Indian environment. Therefore, not only can he respond to the symptoms he observes more accurately, but he also has the makings of a 'seasoned' colonist.

Both Kim's travels and the novel's development wander, crossing and re-crossing geographic and cultural borders. The non-linear plot structure shows an alternative, circuitous model of colonial mapping, which allows for inevitable setbacks, such as probable disease recurrence. Rather than supporting a discourse of scientific dominance and cure, Kim's illness offers an alternative model for imperialism based on an adaptable colonial identity. The novel suggests that indigenisation through disease and adaptation to colonial climates can be a rite of passage for the British subject in India, through which a more resistant hybrid constitution is created.

Climatic Determinism: Twentieth-Century and Contemporary Legacies

Medical climatism was not only deployed by white British writers, but also adapted as a tool for subversion by writers of colour. The writing of nineteenth-century West African doctor and writer Africanus Horton, for example, demonstrates that climatism can also be used for anti-colonial ends, by establishing the writer's authority regarding the disease environments of his or her native land.[50] Climatic or environmental

---

[48] Ibid., p. 121.   [49] Ibid., p. 121.   [50] Howell, *Exploring Victorian Travel Literature*, pp. 83–108.

determinism has enabled nationalist writers to argue for the 'renaturalisa-tion' of people 'into their appropriate climates'.[51] This deployment of climate continues into the twentieth century. For example, twentieth-century Indian nationalist Radhakamal Mukerjee wrote more than forty books between 1916 and 1968, within which he documented and discussed 'Asiatic physiology'.[52] This economist, sociologist, and human ecologist reappropriated what Alison Bashford calls 'the physiological knowledge produced from the tropical medicine tradition, and the canon of environ-mental determinism' for anti-colonial ends.[53] The 'politicized connection between people and land' allows Mukerjee to assert a 'twentieth-century physiology of belonging' on behalf of Indian subjects – a 'right to claim' their native lands.[54]

However, the biopolitical complications inherent in the 'airs, waters, and places' tradition are evident in two ways within Mukerjee's redeploy-ment of this rhetoric. First, his work relies heavily on the theories of Andrew Balfour, one-time director of the London School of Hygiene and Tropical Medicine and author, in 1923, of a treatise on white men in the tropics.[55] Mukerjee therefore uses epistemological frames of medical knowledge developed specifically within a long historical legacy of white racial entitlement. Second, his treatises make the case for Indian indepen-dence and the end to British rule, but fail to acknowledge any 'necessary claim' of certain groups of 'indigenous people to land'.[56]

Finally, while it may be tempting to observe the continuities between historical concepts of climate and the body with contempor-ary 'holistic' ideas of the interrelationship between human and envir-onmental health, this would divorce the study of climatic determinism and medical topography from its colonial legacies. Indeed, as Bashford and Sarah W. Tracy observe, 'A self-conscious twenty-first-century "reincarnation" of tropical medicine is interestingly situated between the historical legacies of colonialism, reborn as international health in an age of globalization, and the legacy of medical climatology, reborn as climate-affected health in the age of the Anthropocene.'[57] They conclude, 'the medical history of climate and humans has been benign,

[51] Alison Bashford, 'Anticolonial Climates: Physiology, Ecology, and Global Population, 1920s–1950s', Bulletin of the History of Medicine, 86.4 (2012), 598.
[52] For examples of Mukerjee's work, see Radhakamal Mukerjee, The Political Economy of Population (London: Longmans, Green, 1942) and Migrant Asia: a Problem in World Population (Rome: I. Failli, 1936).
[53] Bashford, 'Anticolonial Climates', 598.   [54] Ibid., 602.   [55] Ibid., 602.   [56] Ibid., 605.
[57] Alison Bashford and Sarah W. Tracy, 'Introduction: Modern Airs, Waters, and Places', Bulletin of the History of Medicine, 86.4 (2012), 502.

progressive, and dangerous in equal measure'.[58] One must consider the legacies of both colonialism and medical climatology when analysing contemporary deployments of climatic medicine. For example, in what ways are current concerns about climate change also always concerns about 'tropical' diseases breaking out of their climatic 'zones', zones that were first conceptualised as a discursive tool of colonialism?

In addition to the fields of global health and climate sciences, David N. Livingstone notes a resurgence of environmental determinism in the study of human evolution. He observes that a 'new environmentalism' has become a 'staple of human evolutionary accounts', citing a recent *Science* article by a palaeoanthropologist that concludes 'climate-driven environmental changes during the past 7 million years were responsible for hominin speciation, enlarged cranial capacity, behavioral adaptability, cultural innovations, and intercontinental immigration events'.[59] Livingstone worries that such scientific authors, convinced 'that climatic pulsations governed humanity's evolutionary story', are perhaps unknowingly using the language of evolution in a way that hearkens back to the colonialist belief in the suitability of different climatic 'zones' for different races. As he points out, the slippery slope between climatic determinism and racist hierarchies was one of the main tenets of twentieth-century eugenics.[60] He suggests that we not let evolutionary justifications for human emplacement dominate debates about the climate-driven emergencies of our time, including 'forced migration, international conflict, and crises over food and water security'.[61] There are signs that the field of human geography is incorporating this awareness as well. For example, the most recent edition of the *Dictionary of Human Geography* (2009) acknowledges within the definition of 'medical geography' the ideological function of disease mapping. The authors suggest that contemporary medical geographies should avoid perpetuating the 'colonial origins of geography', focusing less on 'causal relations between easy-to-define environments' and more on 'a mosaic of "health inequalities"' across 'diverse, multiple and fluid bodies and places'.[62]

---

[58] Ibid., 513.

[59] David N. Livingstone, 'Changing Climate, Human Evolution, and the Revival of Environmental Determinism', *Bulletin of the History of Medicine*, 86 (2012), 566–7. Livingstone is glossing the work of paleoanthropologist Anna K. Behrensmeyer.

[60] Ibid., 574.   [61] Ibid., 594.

[62] Derek Gregory, Ron Johnston, Geraldine Pratt, Michael J. Watts, and Sarah Whatmore, *The Dictionary of Human Geography*, 5th edn (Malden, MA: Wiley-Blackwell, 2009), p. 2.

In order to avoid these possible neo-colonial abuses of climatic determinism, literary and cultural critics in the fields of literature and medicine,
post-colonial and ecocritical studies should also use an awareness of the
long biopolitics of climate when considering the relationship between
the human body and environment.[63] Instead, one must read carefully for
the impact upon narrative structures of historical concepts of climate and
the body, many of which were crystallised in the colonial context. This
impact can be seen in both the content and form of literary works. For
example, travel writers often invoke racialised bodies as a way to engage
both political and biological risk, whether depicting 'native' bodies at
home in foreboding tropical heat or vulnerable white bodies attempting
to adjust to the foreign climate. Further, the lived experience of specific
diseases also influences the forms of literatures of empire, whether in terms
of their impressionistic prose or the ways in which their plots engage with
the temporal and spatial mapping of colonial geographies. Finally, rather
than stabilising climatic racism as a historical belief system meant to
control and dominate foreign spaces and places, one can cultivate a more
nuanced viewpoint of the various iterations of these discourses. As has been
shown, nineteenth-century writers used discourses of climate to call into
question the limits between body and the environment, to articulate
anxieties about colonial hubris, and to explore the kinaesthetic relationship
between the travelling body and the process of reading itself.

[63] For more on malaria narratives and the legacies of colonial medicine, see Jessica Howell, *Malaria
and Victorian Fictions of Empire* (Cambridge University Press, 2018).

CHAPTER 11

Ethereal Women: Climate and Gender from Realism to the Modernist Novel

Justine Pizzo

In her April 1919 essay 'Modern Novels' – revised and retitled 'Modern Fiction' for inclusion in *The Common Reader* (1925) – Virginia Woolf claims that the 'ordinary course of life' is composed of 'myriad impressions – trivial, fantastic, evanescent, or engraved with the sharpness of steel'. Generations of scholars have found this statement helpful in theorising both the 'pattern that ... each sight or incident scores upon the consciousness' and the syntactically fluid interior monologues that authors such as James Joyce, and Woolf herself, use to express this pattern in early twentieth-century fiction.[1] Despite recent movements away from notions of break or rupture as fitting the twentieth-century novel's often recursive engagement with earlier literary forms, many critical histories continue to oppose modernism's focus on the internal and experiential with realism's interest in the external and empirical. Students of the modernist novel are still familiar with the resulting, linear narrative that contrasts the personal and impressionistic interiority of stream of consciousness with the earlier panoramic insight of the omniscient storyteller or authoritative blending of first- and third-person perspectives in free indirect discourse, for example. And although scholars such as Robert Macfarlane persuasively maintain that modernism is not 'a movement preoccupied with newness, but instead one obsessed with return', it is hard not to continue to find truth in Woolf's wry notion that the modern novelist can no longer carry on with the 'appalling narrative business of the realist: getting on from lunch to dinner'.[2]

However, as I argue in the present chapter on Charlotte Brontë's *Villette* (1853), Dorothy Richardson's novel sequence *Pilgrimage* (1915–38), and

[1] Virginia Woolf, 'Modern Novels', in *The Essays of Virginia Woolf*, ed. Andrew McNeillie, new edn, 6 vols. (London: Hogarth Press, 1995), vol. III, pp. 33–4.
[2] Robert Macfarlane, *Original Copy* (Oxford University Press, 2007), 12; Woolf, *A Writer's Diary* (New York: Harcourt Brace Jovanovich, 1973), p. 138.

selections of non-fiction writing by Woolf published between 1919 and 1925, the close association between female subjectivity and climate in the Victorian novel inaugurates the fluid consciousness we traditionally associate with modernist, rather than realist, fiction. Elsewhere, I have written about how the embodied subjectivity and circumscribed consciousness we traditionally associate with characters in the Victorian novel prove surprisingly ethereal.[3] In Charlotte Brontë's *Jane Eyre* (1847) and Charles Dickens's *Bleak House* (1853), for example, the female protagonists and fictional authors Jane Eyre and Esther Summerson possess an empowered, yet volatile, connection to climate. Atmospheric events crucially authorise their respective narratives, giving rise to Jane's ability to prophesy future events (such as the destruction of Thornfield Hall) and Esther's occasional knowledge of faraway sights and sounds ('the unseen buildings of the city' and 'distant voices in the town').[4] The rising wind that precedes Jane's prophetic dream of Thornfield's ruin and the cloud-streaked London sky that facilitates Esther's expanded perception respectively transform these female characters' – and first-person narrators' – atmospheric sensitivity into an expansive diegetic insight and implied form of authorial power.

Both these novels leverage contemporary biomedical perceptions of women's sensitivity to climatic events, which remained a widely accepted cause of hysteria from the 1840s through to the turn of the century. However, the common assertion that the moon controlled female periodicity as well as so-called atmospheric tides also granted women an empowered connection to the weather which becomes, as we see throughout Dickens's and Brontë's work, a means of exploring the narrative possibilities – and gendered authority – of female character and its influence on realist form. Indeed, the movement away from a temporally situated and spatially delimited first-person perspective and towards the wide-ranging insights we traditionally associate with narrative omniscience in nineteenth-century fiction is not an isolated occurrence. In realist novels throughout the period, women's bodies and minds periodically – and significantly – become co-extensive with air. Critics often read the infamously fog-filled scene in Thomas Hardy's *Tess of the D'Urbervilles* as an ominous obscuration of the sexual violence that transforms Tess from

[3] Justine Pizzo, 'Charlotte Brontë's Weather Wisdom: Atmospheric Exceptionalism in *Jane Eyre*', *PMLA*, 131 (2016), 84–100; Pizzo, 'Esther's Ether: Atmospheric Character in Charles Dickens's *Bleak House*', *Victorian Literature and Culture*, 42 (2014), 81–98.
[4] Charlotte Brontë, *Jane Eyre*, ed. Margaret Smith (Oxford University Press, 2008), pp. 280–2; Charles Dickens, *Bleak House*, ed. George Ford and Sylvère Monod (New York: Norton, 1977), p. 380.

'The Maiden' in the novel's first book to 'Maiden No More' in 'Phase
the Second'. Yet close attention to the scene reveals the ways in which the
'beautiful feminine tissue' of Tess's sleeping body – alternately 'invisible',
'moonlit', and 'nebulous' – condenses and expands like the 'webs of
vapour' that form 'veils between the trees' in Cranborne Chase.[5] Rather
than obfuscating the character Tess, this atmospheric attenuation of her
body and semi-conscious state ushers in a diffuse sentience that the novel
continues to associate with climate: it was 'a typical summer evening
in June', Hardy's narrator later asserts: 'the atmosphere being in such
delicate equilibrium and so transmissive that inanimate objects seemed
endowed with two or three senses, if not five'.[6]

This tendency to transfer the sentience we traditionally associate
with bodily materialism on to the physical, highly feminine, properties
of ether troubles the critical commonplace that nineteenth-century
realism privileges what Pam Morris succinctly describes as an 'accuracy
of detail and correspondence to external reality'.[7] Yet the move away
from the archetypal persona and towards the ordinary 'individualised
character, located in a carefully specified place and time' that sums one
long-running strand of critical discourse on realism from György
Lukács to Erich Auerbach and Ian Watt continues to inform many
recent accounts of realist fiction.[8] In his study of character in nineteenth-century fiction, Alex Woloch marshals the discrete physical
embodiment and defined narrative space occupied by individual characters as a means of explaining 'social realism's dual focus on psychological depth and social expansiveness'.[9] In sharp contrast to the
atmospheric expansion of female embodiment and psychology in the
novels discussed above, Woloch's description of 'character space' (or
'the encounter between an individual human personality and
a determined space and position within the narrative') and 'character
system' ('the arrangement of multiple and differentiated character-
spaces') emphasises the degree to which major and minor characters'
consistent embodiment and discrete location in narrative time and
space remain defining features of the realist novel.[10]

[5] Thomas Hardy, *Tess of the D'Urbervilles*, ed. Simon Gatrell and Juliet Grindle (Oxford University Press, 2005), pp. 81–2.
[6] Ibid., p. 138.   [7] Pam Morris, *Realism* (London: Routledge, 2003), pp. 77, 79.   [8] Ibid., p. 77.
[9] Alex Woloch, *The One vs. the Many: Minor Characters and the Space of the Protagonist in the Novel* (Princeton University Press, 2003), p. 31.
[10] Ibid., p. 14.

Yet, if Morris helpfully emphasises the importance of women writers including 'Austen, the three Brontës, Gaskell and Eliot' in defining these key features of realism, the present chapter argues for the importance of gender and climate in rethinking them. As I demonstrate below, nineteenth-century science establishes a reciprocity between atmospheric materiality and embodiment that allows narrative to move subjectivity outside the self – shaping the form as well as the function of female character in the Victorian novel. Accordingly, Woolf's rejection of the 'materialism' embraced by her male contemporaries H. G. Wells, John Galsworthy, and Arnold Bennett is not a critique of those novels or novelists we associate with the realist tradition – for Thomas Hardy 'we reserve our unconditional gratitude' she admits – but rather, as Lyn Pykett asserts, a critique of masculinism associated with 'old ... ways of looking'.[11] In Woolf's words, 'It is because [the materialists] are concerned not with the spirit but with the body that they have disappointed us.'[12] This implicit assertion that the diegetic focus on the body privileges materialism over and above the spiritualism that Victorian fiction and climate science placed in conversation with it leads Woolf to a distinctly non-masculinist concept of climate. The atmosphere becomes, in other words, a feminine space where spirit and matter meet.

This ethereal femininity allows fictional female authors from *Villette*'s Lucy Snowe to *Pilgrimage*'s Miriam Henderson – along with the real-life author Virginia Woolf – to leverage the aerial climate as a mode of artistic production: one that outstrips the antiquated, unimaginative, and materialist views their respective narratives gender male. As the following discussion makes clear, Woolf's enduring definition of modernist form is not only an extension of her engagement with women's writing and Victorian climate science, but also a movement towards the ethereal femininity embraced in such influential realist novels as those discussed above. Her movement towards this ethereal femininity has been overshadowed by her apparent rejection of realism as a prosaic narrative form. Yet, as I demonstrate in the first section of this chapter, Woolf's engagement with the work of Victorian physicist John Tyndall – in particular his study of the atmospheric transmission of light, heat, and sound – allows us to better understand how nineteenth-century conceptions of climate shape her theory of modern writing and women's contribution to it; the

---

[11] Virginia Woolf, 'Modern Fiction', in *The Essays of Virginia Woolf*, vol. IV, p. 158; Lyn Pykett, *Engendering Fictions: the English Novel in the Early Twentieth Century* (London: Edward Arnold, 1995), p. 95.

[12] Woolf, 'Modern Fiction', p. 158.

analogy Tyndall makes between the movement of molecules in air and the study of human consciousness, I will ultimately show, catalyses Woolf's definition of the modern novel.

Moreover, the close association between climate and consciousness in Woolf's influential essays on Brontë's and Richardson's fiction tacitly acknowledges these female authors' innovative uses of climate to capture 'spirit' and circumvent a 'materialist' fixation on external appearances and events. In 'Modern Novels' she inquires: 'Is it not possible that . . . if one were free and could set down what one chose, there would be no plot, little probability, and a vague general confusion? Is it not perhaps the chief task of the novelist to convey this incessantly varying spirit with . . . as little admixture of the alien and external as possible?'[13] Brontë similarly diminishes the importance of plot in *Villette*: 'I do not think the interest culminates anywhere to the degree you would wish', she writes to her editor; 'What climax there is does not come on till near the conclusion and even then I doubt whether the regular novel-reader will consider the . . . colours dashed on to the canvas with the proper amount of daring'[14] *Villette*'s conclusion, a cataclysmic ocean storm presumed to leave Lucy's lover, M. Paul, dead, is just one of the scenes that substitutes the protagonist's subjective responses to climate in place of temporally and geographically specific events. 'Three times in the course of my life', she explains early in her story, 'events had taught me that these strange accents in the storm – this restless, hopeless cry – denote a coming state of the atmosphere unpropitious to life.'[15] Yet the focus here, as at key moments throughout the novel, is not on the alien or external (the details of lost life), but rather on the spiritual relationship Lucy has to a series of atmospheric accents audible only to her.

This focus on ethereality over and above objective event predicts May Sinclair's pioneering application of William James's psychological term 'stream of consciousness' to literary technique. In her review of the first three 'chapter-volumes' of *Pilgrimage*, Sinclair remarks: 'In this series there is no drama, no situation, no set scene. Nothing happens. It is just life going on and on. In identifying herself with this life, which is Miriam's stream of consciousness, Miss Richardson produces her effect of . . . getting

---

[13] Woolf, 'Modern Novels', p. 33.
[14] Brontë, 'Charlotte Brontë to W. S. Williams', in Muriel Spark (ed.), *The Brontë Letters* (London: Peter Nevill, 1954), p. 189.
[15] Brontë, *Villette*, ed. Margaret Smith and Herbert Rosengarten (Oxford University Press, 2000), p. 37. Others have noticed the substitution of storm for event in this novel; see, for example, Penny Boumelha, *Charlotte Brontë* (New York: Harvester Wheatsheaf, 1990), pp. 106–7.

closer to reality.'[16] For Sinclair – as for Brontë and Woolf – 'reality' connotes not realist convention but rather the seemingly unmediated representation of thought or perception over and above external action. Thus, when Lucy buries her personal letters in the *allée défendue* outside Madame Beck's *pensionnat*, she focuses not on her ill-fated attraction to Dr John Graham but rather on 'some quality . . . . In this air, or this mist, [that] was – electrical, perhaps – [and] acted in strange sort upon me'.[17] Similarly, as Woolf drolly remarks of Richardson's protagonist: 'A man might fall dead at her feet (it is not likely), and Miriam might feel that a violet-coloured ray of light was an important element in her consciousness of the tragedy.'[18] As the second section of this chapter maintains, the formal inauguration of 'stream of consciousness' in *Pilgrimage* builds on Brontë's use of ethereal femininity to produce a central consciousness that rejects the 'regular novel reader's' demand for incident. Through their engagements with climate, Lucy and Miriam blur the boundary between 'matter' and 'spirit' that Woolf found so troubling – and so difficult to prise apart from nineteenth-century realism.

Victorian Climate Science and Woolf's Physics of Form

In August 1874 John Tyndall delivered his influential address to the British Association for the Advancement of Science gathered in Belfast. Considered one of the Victorian period's most important and controversial arguments for the objectivity of science in opposition to what Tyndall saw as the subjective beliefs of theology, the Belfast Address focuses on the fraught relationship between spirit and matter. In one of its more controversial passages, Tyndall maintains that what his audience familiarly perceives as 'spirit' is nothing more than molecules moving in the brain. He acknowledges the difficulty of comprehending this fact by appealing to the empiricism of atmospheric science:

> Given the nature of a disturbance in . . . air, or ether, and from the physical properties of the medium . . . we can infer how its particles will be affected . . . But when we endeavour to pass by a similar process from the physics of the brain to the phenomena of consciousness, we meet a problem which transcends any conceivable expansion of the powers we now possess.[19]

---

[16] May Sinclair, 'The Novels of Dorothy Richardson', *The Egoist*, 4 (1918), 58.
[17] Brontë, *Villette*, p. 296.
[18] Woolf, 'Romance and the Heart', *The Nation and the Athenaeum*, 33 (1923), 229.
[19] John Tyndall, *Address Delivered before the British Association Assembled at Belfast with Additions* (London: Longmans, Green and Company, 1874), p. xxix.

This analogy between climate and consciousness draws on Tyndall's famous public demonstrations which made visible, as if by magic, the seemingly immaterial qualities – and colours – of air and 'ether': the phantasmal element he defines, in keeping with Victorian scientific belief, as the 'almost infinitely attenuated and elastic medium, which fills all space'.[20] Elsewhere, Tyndall describes the experiments that vividly revealed these physical properties. In an 1869 lecture at the Royal Institution, he demonstrated what we now know as the 'Tyndall effect' by mounting an electric light at one end of a glass tube filled with aqueous vapour into which 'We have now to pour a beam of light; which most of you know to be a train of minute waves, excited in and propagated through ... the ether.' As the impression of 'pure azure' in the tube makes clear, the 'infinitesimal size' of the particles scatters the shortest light waves.[21]

Five years on, Tyndall's Belfast Address implicitly recalls this famous demonstration by comparing the molecules of the brain with those of ether. The aesthetic and poetic value of the sky's 'pure azure' thus enables him to advance his argument about the material origins of human thought and feeling: a way of exhorting his audience to consider how the molecular cause of something as intangible as the colour of the sky might inform a similar explanation of the human soul. And although Tyndall acknowledged the conceptual challenges these views entailed, he refused to admit this made them any less true: 'By an intellectual necessity, I cross the boundary of experimental evidence, and discern [creative power] in that Matter which we, in our ignorance of its latent powers ... have hitherto covered with opprobrium.'[22] Put another way, Tyndall's apparatus replicates and renders visible the molecular physics of the sky, but in attempting to pass from laboratory experiment to the 'phenomena of consciousness' he encounters a practical impasse – namely, the inability to see inside the human sensorium.

For the mid-Victorians the physics of the brain were conceived primarily through analogy and Tyndall was not the first philosopher to theorise the movement of invisible particles of matter by observing the aerial climate.[23] As his fellow physicist James Clerk Maxwell notes, Tyndall's experiments share much with classical physics: 'When Lucretius wishes to form

[20] Tyndall, *Fragments of Science for Unscientific People* (New York: D. Appleton and Company, 1971), p. 241.

[21] Ibid., pp. 241, 259.   [22] Tyndall, *Address*, p. 55.

[23] Late Victorian mental science would attempt to bridge the gap between analogy and transparency through controversial techniques including vivisection. See Anne Stiles, 'Introduction', in Stiles (ed.), *Neurology and Literature, 1860–1920* (Basingstoke: Palgrave-Macmillan, 2007), pp. 2–3.

a mental representation of the motion of atoms ... he tells us to look at a sunbeam shining through a darkened room (the same instrument of research by which Dr Tyndall makes visible to us the dust we breathe,) and to observe the motes which chase each other in all directions through it.' More than just a study of the air quality in London, Tyndall's demonstrations imply the 'far more complicated motion of the invisible atoms which knock the motes about'.[24] And, as the Belfast Address makes clear, Tyndall held these invisible motions responsible for both conscious thought and artistic endeavour:

> The world embraces not only a Newton, but a Shakespeare ... not only a Darwin, but a Carlyle ... And if unsatisfied with them all, the human mind ... will still turn to the Mystery from which it has emerged ... then, casting aside all the restrictions of Materialism, I would affirm this to be a field for the noblest exercise of what ... may be called the creative faculties of man.

This concluding appeal to future thinkers to uphold scientific and secular inquiries into the origins of consciousness even after 'you and I, like streaks of morning cloud, shall have melted into the infinite azure of the past' echoes Tyndall's firm alliance of the creative and intellectual faculties, on the one hand (Shakespeare and Newton), with climate and spirit, on the other (the infinite azure of the past).[25]

For Woolf, early twentieth-century questions about authorship collapse into a similarly powerful atmospheric metaphor. In the quotation that opens this chapter, she describes the 'myriad impressions' that comprise 'consciousness'. It is worth considering the passage from 'Modern Novels' at greater length:

> The mind, exposed to the ordinary course of life, receives upon its surface a myriad impressions [sic] – trivial, fantastic, evanescent, or engraved with the sharpness of steel. From all sides they come, an incessant shower of innumerable atoms, composing in their sum what we might venture to call life itself; and to figure further as the semi-transparent envelope, or luminous halo, surrounding us from the beginning of consciousness to the end. Is it not perhaps the chief task of the novelist to convey this incessantly varying spirit with whatever stress or sudden deviation it may display, and as little admixture of the alien and external as possible?[26]

---

[24] James Clerk Maxwell, 'Molecules', in Noel George Coley and Vance M. D. Hall (eds.), *Darwin to Einstein: Primary Sources on Science and Belief* (New York: Longman, 1980), p. 96.
[25] Tyndall, *Address*, p. 65.   [26] Woolf, 'Modern Novels', p. 33.

Here, Woolf seems to have found an escape from the 'materialism' of her male contemporaries. In place of a gendered and particularised character body 'dressed down to the last button', we find an ethereality unbounded by either the external or the social.[27] She expands upon this definition of a luminous and diffuse consciousness in 'Modern Fiction': 'Life is not a series of gig lamps symmetrically arranged; life is a luminous halo'; similarly 'incessantly varying spirit' becomes 'this varying, this unknown and *uncircumscribed* spirit'.[28] Emphatically and progressively, then, Woolf asserts that the modern novelist should focus not on the bodily envelope but rather on the luminous ether that surrounds it: 'This, the essential thing, whether we call it life or spirit, truth or reality ... refuses to be contained any longer in such ill-fitting vestments as we provide.'[29] This distinction between early twentieth-century realism and the nineteenth-century innovations that precede it allows Woolf to associate herself with a modern, feminine way of seeing, thinking, and writing that provides an alternative to Tyndall's Shakespeare and Carlyle: 'so much of the enormous labour of proving the solidity, the likeness to life of the story', she complains of the male materialists, 'is labour misplaced to the extent of obscuring and blotting out the light of the conception'.[30]

For Woolf, then, the work of the modern author – and implicitly the female author – is to represent an ethereal rather than embodied materiality, and in doing so, to capture the experience of consciousness itself. More than that, the 'ordinary course of life' Woolf tasks the modern author with capturing in the passage above is nearly a direct quotation of Tyndall's description of consciousness in the Belfast Address:

> By myriad blows (to use a Lucretian phrase) the image and superscription of the external world are stamped as states of consciousness upon the organism, the depth of the impression depending upon the number of the blows. When two or more phenomena occur in the environment invariably together, they are stamped to the same depth or to the same relief, and indissolubly connected ...[31]

Although critics have claimed that Woolf's scientific language is 'cunningly chosen so as to have an air of scientific modernity, and, also, so as to seem intangible', her previously unacknowledged adaptation of Tyndall's language demonstrates a much more specific source of her ideas about modern authorship.[32] The 'stamping' – or in Woolf's terms

---

[27] Ibid.   [28] Woolf, 'Modern Fiction', p. 160, emphasis mine.   [29] Ibid.
[30] Woolf, 'Modern Novels', p. 33.   [31] Tyndall, *Address*, p. 51.
[32] Hermione Lee, *The Novels of Virginia Woolf*, new edn (Abingdon: Routledge, 2010), p. 15.

'engraving' – of impressions upon the human sensorium is, to quote a later passage in Tyndall's Address, 'wholly ultra-experiential'; which is to say that ancient atomists such as Lucretius did not require empirical proof to intuit the originary influence of matter on human thought and behaviour.[33] For Tyndall, as for Woolf, then, sensory impressions bear a direct relationship to atomic structure and molecular force: infinitesimal particles are not just 'constitutive of plant and animal life', as Tyndall puts it; they also represent the synthesis of spirit and matter. Molecules are the stuff from which consciousness proceeds.[34]

This is not the first time Woolf's engagement with Tyndall has been noted. Gillian Beer proposes that his writing on wave-forms inspired both the structure and characterisation of Woolf's seventh novel *The Waves* (1931) and points out that he is named as an early influence on Clarissa's education in *Mrs Dalloway* (1925).[35] As Beer elaborates, the Tyndalls were friends of the Stephens and, by imbedding his influence on her own early education in her later novels, Woolf proves that 'the Victorian reading bases of her imagination were not simply expunged, outdated by modernist writing and science'.[36] Yet, as the next section of this chapter makes clear, Woolf did not draw her ideas about climate and consciousness from scientific reading bases alone. Her engagement with the work of Brontë and Richardson teaches us that rather than simply drawing on climate as a metaphor for human consciousness, her writing continues a tradition of female authorship that represents ethereal women as spiritual subjects and artistic innovators.

Gender and the Aerial Climate in *Villette* and *Pilgrimage*

Published more than half a century apart, Charlotte Brontë's *Villette* and Dorothy Richardson's *Pilgrimage* each bears clear autobiographical connections to the life of its author, but they have much else in common. Comprising twelve 'chapter-volumes' put out by Duckworth and J. M. Dent between 1915 and 1938 (with the unfinished *March Moonlight* appearing posthumously in 1967), *Pilgrimage*, like *Villette*, is the story of a young middle-class woman thrust into the working world. In Brontë's novel, Lucy Snowe suffers a sudden and nearly complete loss of kin and seeks subsistence first as companion to the ailing Miss Marchmont, then as

---

[33] Tyndall, *Address*, p. 53.   [34] Ibid., p. 53.
[35] Gillian Beer, *Virginia Woolf: the Common Ground* (Edinburgh University Press, 1996), p. 89.
[36] Ibid., p. 108.

English teacher at Madame Beck's *pensionnat* in the fictional town of Villette (a stand-in for Brussels). Finally, she becomes head of her own school and author of her own life story. In the first chapter-volume of *Pilgrimage, Pointed Roofs*, family bankruptcy leaves Miriam Henderson suddenly emancipated. She seeks work as a pupil-teacher of English at a girl's school in Hanover and, over the course of the remaining twelve volumes, lives as a governess, a dental assistant in a London office, and finally, a writer.

Given these similarities and Richardson's references to *Villette* throughout *Pilgrimage*, it is not surprising that critics have tended to focus on the later author's intertextual engagement with Brontë's work. Hilary Newman, for instance, examines Richardson's reliance on *Villette* for basic aspects of plot, including the preponderance of storm scene and metaphor, while Horace Gregory claims that Richardson takes *Villette* as a 'model for action'.[37] Just as often, though, critics note Richardson's radical departure from Brontë's literary style and contextual concerns. Anita Levy asserts that Richardson negates 'an earlier realism that located gender in a set of female personality traits, labors and desires . . . If Miriam Henderson is not Jane Eyre, neither is she Lucy Snowe . . . whose fears and suspicions become laughable in Richardson's hands.'[38] But Levy's focus on the domestic qualities that 'materialize gender' overlooks Richardson's subtle and sustained engagement with the work of her predecessor – especially her debt to Brontë's ability to shift narrative focus away from Lucy's bodily materiality and external event and on to her subjective response to atmospheric states.[39]

In 1943, at the age of seventy, Richardson admits that the final volume of *Pilgrimage* 'has moved along . . . at the rate of something like three words per day', but '*Villette* I am always reading, for I know it almost by heart'.[40] In this letter, Richardson suggests that her decades-long experiment in representing female consciousness coincides with her 'reading' of *Villette*; Brontë's novel is therefore a constitutive element of the literary and personal consciousness – Richardson's and Miriam's – at the heart of *Pilgrimage*. This influence becomes even clearer when we examine the

---

[37] Hilary Newman, 'The Influence of *Villette* on Dorothy Richardson's *Pointed Roofs*', *Brontë Studies*, 42 (2017), 15–25; Horace Gregory, *Dorothy Richardson: an Adventure in Self-Discovery* (New York: Holt, Rinehart and Winston, 1967), pp. 23–5.

[38] Anita Levy, 'Gendered Labor, the Woman Writer and Dorothy Richardson', *Novel: a Forum on Fiction*, 25 (1991), 63–4.

[39] Ibid., 65.

[40] Dorothy Richardson, 'To Bernice Elliott' in *Windows on Modernism: Selected Letters of Dorothy Richardson*, ed. Gloria Fromm (Atlanta: University of Georgia Press, 1995), pp. 458–9.

ways in which both novels understand atmosphere as a source of creative endeavour.

At the end of the chapter titled 'The Long Vacation', the devoutly Protestant Lucy recounts the hurricane she encounters upon her return from a desperate confession at Villette's Catholic church. Scholars have traditionally read this episode as an expression of Lucy's nervous illness, a diagnosis offered by the protagonist herself when she claims: 'My nervous system could hardly support what it had for many days and nights to undergo' during the solitary vacation.[41] Yet, closer attention to the storm scene that concludes with Lucy swooning on the church steps reveals that the scene harks back to her earlier, invigorating responses to storm. Opening the window to sit on the ledge amidst a hurricane that rocks the terrified inhabitants of the *pensionnat* in their beds in the novel's twelfth chapter, Lucy experiences the wakening of the vibrant 'being' she is 'always lulling': 'I was roughly roused and obliged to live', she recalls.[42] This call to vitality re-emerges again in chapter 30 as the personified 'Creative Impulse' that at 'some long-trembling sob of the wind ... would wake unsolicited, would stir strangely alive'.[43] In each of these scenes, which punctuate the novel, dramatic event is supplanted by Lucy's impassioned response to climate: her engagement with atmosphere does not propel the plot so much as encourage the deeply sensory expressions of female consciousness, desire, and creativity that comprise the narrative.

In 'The Long Vacation', then, what we might mistake for hysteria is best understood as a dramatic liberation of sprit from the 'materialized gender' Levy associates with domestic fiction. Indeed, Lucy perpetually rejects homely comforts in pursuit of atmospheric communion: she leaves the empty schoolhouse not with the intent of reaching the Catholic church but rather to fulfil her 'wild longing to breathe this October wind': a desire that leads to the wish, just before she loses consciousness, that she 'could ascend the gale ... career in its course, sweep where it swept'.[44] More than mere nervous collapse, Lucy's speculation as to the state of her spirit during this loss of consciousness presages Woolf's description of the novelist's duty to convey 'uncircumscribed spirit': 'She may have gone upward', Lucy surmises, 'deeming that her painful union with matter was at last dissolved ...

---

[41] Brontë, *Villette*, 157. On Lucy and nervous illness, see Beth Torgerson, *Reading the Brontë Body: Disease, Desire, and the Constraints of Culture* (Basingstoke: Palgrave-Macmillan, 2005); Athena Vrettos, *Somatic Fictions: Imagining Illness in Victorian Culture* (Stanford University Press, 1995).
[42] Brontë, *Villette*, p. 109.   [43] Ibid., p. 356.   [44] Ibid., pp. 163–4.

I know she re-entered her prison with pain.'[45] We see a similar ability of 'spirit' to transcend 'substance' when, at the height of her affection for Dr John, Lucy condemns the 'dry, materialist views' underlying his critique of the actress Vashti.[46] Inviting all 'materialists' to 'draw nigh and look on', Lucy champions the disembodied spirit and climatic force behind the actress's performance: 'Scarcely a substance herself, she grapples to conflict with abstractions'; yet Dr John remains unmoved: 'for what belonged to storm, what was wild and intense . . . he had no sympathy'.[47]

In both of these scenes, Brontë employs climate as a natural element that instigates and provokes the inner 'being' Lucy admires in women like Vashti, yet usually strives to subdue. *Villette* thus expresses a shrewd awareness that women's artistic production necessitates a certain degree of separation from the material embodiment that threatens to overshadow or prevent its production. 'He judged her as a woman, not an artist: it was a branding judgement', Lucy pointedly concludes of Dr John's response to Vashti's wild performance.[48] Climatic event and metaphor are therefore powerful ways for Brontë, and her narrator Lucy, to conceive of the position of the female artist (the author who writes her life story). By moving the spirit outside the body, just as Woolf urges the writer of modern fiction to do, *Villette* demonstrates that what 'belong[s] to storm' opposes the materialist views of a medical man like Dr John – for his focus is the body, just as it is for the twentieth-century realists Galsworthy, Bennett, or Wells.

In *Revolving Lights* (1923), Miriam Henderson confronts the character Hypo Wilson – famously based on Wells – with a critique of masculinity that echoes Woolf's earlier critique of her male contemporaries: 'whereas a few men here and there are creators, originators, *artists*, women are this all the time', Miriam claims.[49] 'Women are emancipated . . . through their pre-eminence in an art. The art of making atmospheres . . . not one man in a million is aware of it. It's like air within the air.' For Miriam, a woman carries atmosphere with her, emitting a 'way of "being"' evident not only in the words she may write but also in 'the way she pours out tea'; for Miriam this extra-embodied quality is highly feminine and interpersonal: 'I feel the atmosphere created by the lady of the house as soon as I get on to the door-step.'[50] By contrast, as she explains to Hypo in an earlier

[45] Woolf, 'Modern Novels', p. 33; Brontë, *Villette*, p. 165.   [46] Brontë, *Villette*, pp. 165, 257.
[47] Ibid., p. 258.   [48] Ibid., p. 260.
[49] Dorothy Richardson, *Pilgrimage*, 4 vols. (London: Virago, 1979), vol. III, p. 256.
[50] Ibid., vol. III, p. 257.

conversation, 'men have no sense of atmosphere. They only see the appearances of things, understanding nothing of their relationships.'[51]

Importantly, the twentieth-century author John Cowper Powys applies this femininity of atmosphere to Richardson's own artistic practice:

> Perhaps no writer has ever devoted so much attention to the 'atmospheric' aspects of her backgrounds ... the way the greyness of a colourless sky impregnates the simplest things in a room ... the way the mystery of the rain is felt behind closed windows ... the way such rain in London is different from all other rain; all these things are part of the very essence of her revelation as to what women, in their subconscious nature, respond to day by day ...'[52]

Here, Powys fascinatingly reproduces Richardson's own gendering of climate in her fiction, simultaneously acknowledging the extent to which atmosphere occupies its female protagonist's attention and mediates her sensory experience. Yet the air that 'impregnates' the domestic scenes in *Pilgrimage* is anything but a 'background'. Prominent and expansive, aerial climates in the novel sequence are neither buried in the 'subconscious' nor fixed in the distance of discrete scenes, as Powys mistakenly suggests. For Miriam, climate is integrative: it connects thoughts and individuals in the flow of ideas and subjectivity we associate with stream of consciousness. The entirety of chapter 8 in *Interim* (1919) – published the same year as Woolf's 'Modern Novels' – follows the ebb and flow of Miriam's consciousness by narrating how she responds, first, to the heat of a summer day and then to the colour of twilight. Eschewing external event, the chapter follows Miriam's sensory perception of these climatic shifts (changes in temperature and colours of light) as a way of establishing temporal and spatial fluidity:

> Brilliant ... *brilliant*; and someone was seeing it. There was no thunderstorm, no clouds or pink edges on the brilliant copper grey ... There was no air, nothing to hold her body separate from the scene.
>
> ...
>
> In the twilit dining-room one's body was like a hot sun throbbing in cool dark air ... coolness poured out through the wide-open windows ... cool and cool until the throbbing ceased.
>
> ...
>
> The drawing-room was filled with saffron light filtering in through the curtains ... the elastic outer air was there and, away at the end of the street, a great gold-pink glow
>
> ...

[51] Ibid., vol. III, p. 100.
[52] John Cowper Powys, *Dorothy M. Richardson* (London: Joiner and Steele, 1931), pp. 12–13.

The rosy gold was deepening and spreading.

. . .

The rosy light shone into far-away scenes with distant friends. They came into her mind rapidly one by one, and stayed grouped in a radiance, sharper and clearer than in experience . . . Her friends drifted forward, coming too near, as if in competition for some central place. To every claim, she offered her evening sky as a full answer.[53]

Here, the shifting sensations of heat and illumination mediate between the immediate passing of time and Miriam's memory. Climate loosens the boundaries between body and air: there is 'nothing to hold her body separate from the scene'. At the same time, Miriam's sensations are realised not through an immediate awareness of her gendered embodiment but rather by analogy to atmospheric states: 'one's body was like a hot sun throbbing in cool dark air'. In this already ethereal state, consciousness becomes increasingly fluid: present atmospheres allow Miriam to move further into the past and away from the claims of an immediately palpable present. The 'character space' and 'character system' Woloch describes similarly collapse as this cast of minor, unnamed characters become part of the ebb and flow of Miriam's atmospherically mediated thought and perception.

If, in this scene, climate directs Miriam's and the reader's attention away from the external surface of the body and on to the 'semi-transparent envelope, or luminous halo', that surrounds it, the novel's focus on science urges us to confront Miriam's distaste for bodily materialism more directly. When her employer takes her to a lecture at the Royal Society, for instance, Miriam anticipates hearing 'the very best science there was . . . the idea of the breaking up of air and water and rays of light'.[54] Yet her interest in the lecture is diminished by the realisation that her companion has been bored to sleep. Recalling Lucy and Dr John's trip to the theatre in *Villette*, this scene opposes 'the life and air and fresh breath coming up from the platform' with the materialism that Miriam, like Lucy, associates with masculinity and medicine: 'Did he want science', Miriam wonders of Mr Hancock, 'or would he really rather be in a drawing-room with "pretty ladies" . . . ?'[55]

Later, Miriam contemplates this tension between gender and science at greater length:

[53] Richardson, *Pilgrimage*, vol. II, pp. 402–6.   [54] Ibid., vol. II, pp. 100–1.
[55] Ibid., vol. II, pp. 105–6.

And the modern men were the worst . . . 'We can now, with all the facts in our hands, sit down and examine her at our leisure.' There was no getting away from the scientific facts . . . her development arrested in the interest of her special functions . . . women stopped being people and went off into hideous processes . . . The wonders of science for women are nothing but gynaecology – all those frightful operations in the *British Medical Journal*.[56]

At issue here, as in Woolf's essays and Brontë's Victorian novels, is the tension between a scientific view of climate that sees matter as disembodied – as belonging to wild storms and azure skies – on the one hand, and a medical view of the body that sees gendered materiality as a series of 'special functions', on the other. Because intellectual endeavour and artistic production promise to circumvent or at least ignore these functions, climate promises – for each of the ethereal women discussed here – a more transcendent form of 'life itself'.

There is nothing less modern (or more realist) about Brontë's hurricanes than Richardson's sunsets; both resist a materiality that would have the sexed body overshadow the mind, or the sanctity of the home dull the thrill of the storm. For Woolf, this ethereal modernity forms the basis of what we continue to think of as a predominantly twentieth-century appeal to fluid thought, or stream of consciousness, rather than the restrictive, gendered materialism of realist prose. Yet in her essay on '*Jane Eyre* and *Wuthering Heights*', which appeared alongside 'Modern Fiction' in the first volume of *The Common Reader*, Woolf notes that Charlotte's and Emily's 'storms, their moors, their lovely spaces of summer weather are not ornaments': they do more than exercise the pathetic fallacy; they 'carry on the emotion and light up the meaning of the book'.[57] Taken alongside the essay's consideration of the storm scenes in Charlotte's 'finest novel' *Villette*, Woolf's discussion of weather in the Brontës' fiction reaffirms the importance of climate in creating what she had termed 'the psychological sentence of the feminine gender' in her review of Richardson's *Revolving Lights* just two years earlier. Woolf's 1923 review of Richardson's work thus affords her no small praise (personal rivalries notwithstanding) for there Woolf returned to and consolidated the influence of femininity, psychology, and climate she had already articulated so powerfully in her treatise on the modern novel in 1919. Richardson's prose, she admits, is 'capable of stretching to the extreme, of suspending the frailest particles, of enveloping the vaguest shapes'.[58]

---

[56] Ibid, vol. II, pp. 219–20.
[57] Woolf, '*Jane Eyre* and *Wuthering Heights*', in *The Essays of Virginia Woolf*, vol. IV, p. 168.
[58] Woolf, 'Romance and the Heart', 229.

This argument for the continuity of climatic representations of female consciousness from Brontë to Richardson and Woolf matters not simply because it puts further stress on our already attenuated notions of a modernist break with realist form. Instead, their representations of ethereal femininity help to redirect our critical histories of the realist novel. 'If the self is a constant flux' in modern writing, Shlomith Rimmon-Kenan explains, 'the concept of character changes or disappears'.[59] Yet realising the ways in which Victorian authors embrace the physical and psychic fluidity of climate belies a narrative that would mistake this volatility as unique to twentieth-century prose, or overlook the significance of scientific views of climate and femininity in shaping character from the realist to the modernist novel. As D. H. Lawrence famously writes in his 1914 letter to Edward Garnett, the modern novelist wants nothing to do with 'the old stable ego of the character . . . what is interesting in the laugh of the woman is the same as the binding of the molecules of steel or their action in heat'.[60] Much like Woolf's assertion that the modern novelist should record 'the atoms as they fall upon the mind . . . however disconnected and incoherent', Lawrence shows us that femininity is synonymous with this seemingly new fluidity of self.[61] Yet this fluidity owes much to modern writers' sustained debt to ethereal femininity in nineteenth-century realism (it need not be said that Lawrence read Hardy attentively). And if Victorian science reaffirmed realism's narrative affinity between atmospheric matter and spirit, we may do well to remember, amidst our own anthropocenic crisis, that the voice of a highly literate minority may prove the most enduring refrain.

[59] Shlomith Rimmon-Kenan, *Narrative Fiction: Contemporary Poetics* (London: Routledge, 1996), p. 30.
[60] D. H. Lawrence, 'To Edward Garnett', in Lawrence, *The Letters of D. H. Lawrence, Volume 11: June 1913–October 1916*, ed. George J. Zytaruk and James T. Boulton (Cambridge University Press, 1979), p. 183.
[61] Woolf, 'Modern Novels', p. 33.

CHAPTER 12

Planetary Climates: Terraforming in Science Fiction

Chris Pak

Terraforming narratives are based on a recognition that control of a planet's climate is fundamental to its successful colonisation and habitation. Dealing with planetary-scale modifications to environments, such stories have encouraged scientific speculation about climate processes on other planets within our solar system, spurring thought about how the development of these extra-terrestrial systems provides models that help us to understand Earth's. Terraforming refers to planetary adaptation to enable their habitation by Earthbound life. In its guise as geo-engineering, or terraforming on Earth, this speculation extends to environmental issues related to our home planet. Indeed, the IPCC's 2014 report describes geo-engineering as a possible emergency solution to catastrophic climate change, particularly with regard to carbon management, carbon sequestration, and solar radiation management.[1] This chapter examines the evolution of terraforming in science fiction (sf) through three important contributions to the tradition: Arthur C. Clarke's *The Sands of Mars* (1951), Frank Herbert's *Dune* (1965), and Kim Stanley Robinson's 'Mars' trilogy, comprising *Red Mars* (1992), *Green Mars* (1993), and *Blue Mars* (1996).[2]

Fundamental to terraforming narratives is a totalising perspective informed by climate science, ideas of weather control, and sf speculation about scientific and technological mastery over nature. The representation of advanced technology creates narrative possibilities for controlling an entire planet's environmental parameters and invites a particular fantasy of systematic

---

[1] IPCC, *Mitigation of Climate Change: Working Group III Contribution to the Fifth Assessment Report of the Intergovernmental Panel on Climate Change*, ed. Ottomar Edenhofer, Ramón Pichs-Madruga, Youba Sokona *et al.* (Cambridge University Press, 2014).

[2] Arthur C. Clarke, *The Sands of Mars* (London: Sidgwick and Jackson, 1976); Frank Herbert, *Dune* (Sevenoaks, Kent: New English Library, 1965); Kim Stanley Robinson, *Red Mars* (London: Voyager, 1996); Robinson, *Green Mars* (London: Voyager, 1996); Robinson, *Blue Mars* (London: Voyager, 1996). All hereafter cited parenthetically in the text.

environmental control that draws from sf's relationship with ideas of space as a new field for expansion, conquest, and settlement. Paul N. Edwards argues that the history of climate science and modelling is based on a scientific project involving the construction of a global infrastructure of data capture enabling multiple parameters of Earth's environment to be monitored (such as the atmosphere's chemical composition, temperature, and circulation). This data is analysed and used to build simulations of the Earth, which in turn allow a greater degree of control over an imagined Earth: 'If you can simulate the climate, you can do experiments. God-like, you can move the continents, make the sun flare up or dim, add or subtract greenhouse gases, or fill the stratosphere with dust. You can cook the Earth, or freeze it, and nobody will even complain. Then you can watch and see what happens.'[3] Enhanced knowledge of Earth's processes implies that these processes can be manipulated and controlled. Exemplifying the prevalence of support for weather control during the Cold War, Edwards cites von Neumann's assertion that 'There is little doubt [that] one could intervene on any desired scale, and ultimately achieve rather fantastic effects.'[4] Terraforming narratives extend ideas of weather and climate control to dramatise this enhanced ability to manipulate nature in accordance with human desire.

Themes of control connect terraforming to colonial American frontier narratives, which have shaped sf's texture and its critical engagement with climate change. The two themes are related: the colonisation and terraforming of other planets strongly recalls pastoral myths of America as both a wilderness to be tamed and a landscape offering an unparalleled abundance to those determined to cultivate it. The fulcrum for control of nature in terraforming narratives, however, is mastery over the climate. Transplanted to space, such narratives scrutinise the technological mastery of the climate and its concordance with American pioneer narratives. Terraforming narratives represent an escalation of the imperialist colonial imagination to climatic scales, thus connecting the colonial myth not just to the ecological aspects of expansion and habitation, but also to their underlying climatological dimensions.

Jack Williamson coined the term 'terraforming' in his short story 'Collision Orbit'.[5] The term shaped a tradition of scientific speculation

---

[3] Paul N. Edwards, *A Vast Machine: Computer Models, Climate Data, and the Politics of Global Warming* (Cambridge, MA: MIT Press, 2010), p. 140.

[4] Ibid., p. 190.

[5] Jack Williamson, 'Collision Orbit', in Stephen Haffner and Richard A. Hauptmann (eds.), *Seventy-Five: the Diamond Anniversary of a Science Fiction Pioneer* (Royal Oak, MI: Haffner Press, 2004), pp. 216–77.

and research into the colonisation and adaptation of other planets. Against the background of contemporary climate change on Earth, renewed interest in space colonisation has led to public–private partnerships and corporations investing in infrastructures for the capitalist development of the solar system.[6] Terraforming represents an instance of the feedback between sf, science, politics, and economics and is thus a necessary literature of the Anthropocene. By examining how the terraforming tradition engages with themes of systematic environmental control and the persistence of the American colonial frontier narrative, this chapter highlights important critiques of power and mastery that are relevant to contemporary debates over the climate, particularly climate change and its mitigation.

Arthur C. Clarke's *The Sands of Mars*

The Sands of Mars is structured as a utopian tour of a burgeoning Martian colony as seen from the perspective of the sf writer Martin Gibson. Visiting Mars as a journalist to document his experience of the colony for an audience on Earth, Gibson participates in the Martian community's lifestyles and inspects the scientific and technical institutions terraforming the planet. Gibson must negotiate Earth's widespread scepticism of the project and the interests of Martian officials desirous of favourable reports that might help secure public support and continued funding for the project. Many on Earth see colonisation as a financial sinkhole, thus exacerbating tensions between the two planets. This scepticism is partly responsible for driving the forms of systematic climatic control on Mars, most notably the oxygenation of Mars' atmosphere, a form of climatic manipulation that is predicated on the ability to harness nature for human ends. Terraforming seductively promises the godlike power to reshape matter to provide ideal foundations for a new society.

American colonial narratives are an enduring structuring device that connects the colonising project to the colonists' relationship with the Martian landscape. The colony's Chief Executive regards Mars as an enemy to be fought, thus revisiting a long tradition whereby the American landscape was alternately portrayed as a land of ease and plenty or as a wasteland, an enemy to be resisted and subdued. These narratives, particularly those emphasising hardship and calling for strenuous work to meet the demands of habitation in new lands, are transplanted to the colonisation of Mars which, as an exceedingly hostile landscape,

---

[6] Deep Space Industries, Space-X, and Virgin Galactic are examples.

complements the emphasis placed on the brutality of living on another planet. Frontier narratives suggest appropriate orientations to Mars and imply a series of suitable actions and behaviours based on the model of those stories. Such myths offer a framework for translating novel experience into familiar terms and affords the colonists a sense of control over their lives.

Yi-Fu Tuan argues that the hardships nature presents encourage a desire to escape from that nature, instilling a Promethean fear that incentivises technological development, urbanism, and the formation of institutions that attempt to exert control over those forces.[7] Why embark on an interplanetary colonising process if the relative dangers far exceed those on Earth? The desire to surpass human limits by controlling and shaping nature can be seen as an expression of the desire to escape from the vicissitudes of nature and from the limits it imposes on humankind. This desire is emergent from the same impulses that drove the colonisation of America: a desire for self-determination was linked to an impulse to escape from the social control and infrastructures of the Old World to return to a simpler past where, it was imagined, people could shape their own lives. These impulses inform the desire to establish colonies on Mars. A pastoral desire for a return to a simpler time where fulfilment could be attained drives the frontier myth.

While *The Sands of Mars* revisits these frameworks, Clarke is aware of the tendency to relate frontier narratives to sf and has his narrator remark on the dangers of structuring the experience of Mars accordingly. Gibson learns that while these narratives have some explanatory potential, 'the analogy cannot be pressed too far' (90). Narratives of Mars colonisation represent an escalation of historical expansionist tendencies and construct Mars as more hostile and thus a prominent target for climatic control. The irony with which these patterns are treated in *The Sands of Mars* establishes a critical distance while the points of correspondence between the two models of experience draw them closer together. The differences, however, call upon the colonists to apply sophisticated technology and a plan for systematised control to meet the demands of habitation.

Every aspect of the colony, from its town planning, research and development, and its social dimension, is systematised according to scientific principles geared towards creating subjects suitably adapted for life on Mars. Although this top-down approach to systematised town planning provides a framework for order and control, Mars' Warden notes how,

[7] Yi-Fu Tuan, *Escapism* (Baltimore: Johns Hopkins University Press, 1998), p. 10.

unofficially, a different system for naming parts of the colony arises, based on cultural familiarity rather than scientific planning. These unofficial naming practices align the colony closely to examples of colonisation on Earth and draw the frontier narrative closer to narratives of Mars colonisation. This form of systematisation relies not on scientific planning but on a cultural mapping of one experience on to another.

The genetic modification of a native Martian airweed is essential to the terraforming project. The cultivation of this plant, which is expected to accelerate the oxygenation of the Martian atmosphere, involves an infrastructure of scientific research, experiments in adaptation, and a systematised cataloguing of and expansion across Mars. Terraforming projects based on this 'ecopoietic' model resemble representations of the agricultural pastoral experience of American colonisation, but connect this theme directly to that of climatological mastery.[8] Especially troubling is the surprise discovery of native Martian fauna: a herbivorous and docile species that the colonists believe is following the airweed into decline. A curious young representative of this new species follows Gibson back to the colony, where it is discovered that it is amenable to training to facilitate the spread of the modified airweed across the Martian landscape.

These creatures exemplify how all aspects of nature are incorporated into the colonising process. The colonists see themselves as stewards who hold Mars in trust for the Martians while they restore the planet to a state suitable for the flourishing of native life-forms. However, the shadow of the frontier myth raises the spectre of slavery, where the ease of living in the new American continent sublimates the slave labour that makes such habitation possible. These scenes associate terraforming with ecological imperialism, itself a systematising project of control over nature that enables human habitation of new lands and the displacement of indigenous peoples, flora, and fauna.[9] In *The Sands of Mars*, indigenous life-forms are instrumentalised, modified, and incorporated into the systematising project according to the administrator's plan.

Another component of the terraforming project extends the colonists' incorporation of nature to greater scales and emphasises how sophisticated

---

[8] Coined by the scientist Robert H. Haynes, ecopoiesis refers to 'The creation of a self-sustaining ecosystem, or biosphere, on a lifeless planet . . . a new word which means "the making of an abode for life"'; see Haynes, 'How Might Mars Become a Home for Humans?' (1993), *The Terraforming Information Pages* users.globalnet.co.uk/~mfogg/haynes.htm. Accessed 13 March 2018. The term combines *eco*, derived from the Greek oikos (οἶκος) for home, house, household, or family, with the Greek *poiesis* (ποίησις), for fabrication, creation, or production.

[9] Alfred W. Crosby, *Ecological Imperialism: the Biological Expansion of Europe, 900–1900*, 2nd edn (Cambridge University Press, 2004).

technologies lead to enhanced powers of control over the climate. The clandestine Project Dawn involves the transformation of Phobos, one of Mars' moons, into a new sun. This intervention into cosmological nature provides a new source of energy that would increase Mars' energy budget and accelerate the expansion of the airweeds across Mars. Because a planet's climate is shaped by its position in relation to nearby stars, mastery over the creation of these fundamental sources of energy represents the ultimate form of climatic colonisation. Symbolically, the creation of a new sun is synonymous with the creation of new life and the birth of the colony. The ability to control matter at such scales positions humankind as new gods, a common theme for terraforming narratives, focused as they are on the creation of new societies, new cultures, new life, and new worlds. Terraforming is thus a colonial narrative of climatological control at ever-increasing scales.

Science and technology enable humankind to assume the mantle of gods by mastering the climate and systematically incorporating nature into its designs. Project Dawn helps the colony to achieve a level of self-sufficiency that allows the colonists to divest themselves of a reliance on Earth and enables them to thrive. It also helps to overturn Earth's scepticism towards the project since this demonstration of technological capability far exceeds that of Earth's scientists. Colonising Mars enables humankind to exceed its limits and escape from its reliance on nature, with all the unpredictability and vulnerability that entails. The godlike power of control is thus a retreat from the uncertainties of nature. While a fear of nature might lead us to infer that interplanetary colonisation would be avoided, the promise of becoming masters over the climate encourages the attempt to overcome nature and render it manageable. Crucially, an anachronistic convergence of scientific planning, infrastructure management, and an integrated work-force living according to principles of American pastoralism makes these transformations possible.

Frank Herbert's *Dune*

Dune begins with the arrival of the ducal family Atreides to Arrakis, Duke Leto having accepted a contract for the management of spice production from the development corporation Combine Honnete Ober Advancer Mercantiles (CHOAM). Spice extends life, grants prescience, and enables the Guild navigators to plot courses for spaceships travelling throughout the interplanetary empire. As such, spice holds the galactic empire together and is critical to its feudal power structures. Should spice production fail, the contract will be revoked and the Atreides will be barred from a seat on the CHOAM board of directors. The Atreides' mortal enemies, the House Harkonnen – with covert support from the Emperor – lead a surprise assault and kill Duke Leto, spurring an escape into the desert for Leto's concubine Jessica and his son Paul. Thus begins Paul's trial to marshal the native Fremen to oust the Harkonnen and assume control of the galactic empire.

Power is *Dune*'s central theme and is connected to the landscape, Arrakis' climate and ecology, and to the Fremen societies who have adapted to the planet. The planet's arid climate shapes the possibilities for social development and political self-determination throughout the novel. Herbert's inspiration for the Fremen comes in part from his early fascination with an idea of Native American cultures as representing ideal adaptations to their climates and as practising ecologically sound and low-impact lifestyles. Spice and water scarcity on the desert planet function as metaphors for oil or any number of scarce resources for which a struggle for control and management occurs.

Herbert's engagement with power and politics draws much from twentieth-century capitalist expansionism and the incorporation and control of natural resources. *Dune* references the systems of global exchange that supported American colonisation but overlays this with a contemporary critique of oil politics and American expansion in the Middle East and Latin America, thus drawing parallels between the colonisation of America and economic colonisation in the twentieth century. CHOAM is modelled on OPEC and thus *Dune*'s politics is rooted in an organisation that was constituted in response to Eisenhower's import quotas on oil in the 1960s and, ironically, organised in imitation of collective bargaining strategies between states in America.[10]

Control of spice is the ultimate aim of the economic and political infrastructures of *Dune*, and for Leto scientific planning is the key to achieving control. In one scene Leto and Paul witness a sandworm consuming a spice harvester. Without Leto's quick action in response to the failure of the precautionary measures designed to prevent the loss of life and property, the workforce would have died. Leto decries the lack of efficiency and the sloppiness of the operation and makes clear that his mission is to introduce a system of control that would replace the power derived through oppression, brutality, and violence that the Harkonnen

---

[10] Timothy Mitchell, *Carbon Democracy: Political Power in the Age of Oil* (London: Verso, 2013), p. 167.

employed during their tenure as governors of the Arrakeen colony. Leto thus offers a vision of control over the planet based on industrial models for efficient resource extraction that is akin to the industrial terraforming models that Robinson would later critique in the Mars trilogy. The planet, however, resists Leto's attempts to impose a foreign order upon its landscapes and its inhabitants.

The other major organisations and houses of the empire rely on scientific planning as a means of control. The Bene Gesserit, an all-female society trained in the arts of psychological manipulation and body and mind control, have long been engaged in a breeding programme designed to produce an ideal male subject, the Kwisatz Haderach, an *übermensch* whose visions are untethered to space and time and who is thus able to see the past, future, and, crucially, the present. This generations-long breeding programme fails when Jessica rejects her selected partner in favour of Leto; her son, Paul, an unplanned factor in the Bene Gesserit scheme, is a living testament to the fantasy of the Bene Gesserit's overarching plans for control.

The myth of the Kwisatz Haderach dovetails with the Fremen myth of 'The Shortening of the Way', the compression of the Fremen terraforming project from generational to individual timescales. Pardot Kynes, the father of the incumbent Imperial Planetologist Liet-Kynes, initiates this long-term project and marshals the Fremen to transform Arrakis' climate into a verdant, water-rich system. The complementarity of the two myths is no accident, but a consequence of Bene Gesserit efforts to seed myths into colonial societies to enable future control and manipulation of the population – a scheme that Jessica capitalises on during her and Paul's flight into the desert. The Fremen terraforming project as seeded by Pardot Kynes thus is not only rooted in an enhanced form of colonial mastery, but is later appropriated by Paul to establish his own imperial authority.

Terraforming in *Dune* is informed by Norbert Wiener's theorisation of cybernetics and its utility for understanding feedback mechanisms in climatological and ecological systems. Communication and control are central concepts for establishing these feedback systems and became popular ideas in ecological discourse in the 1960s. Cybernetics shares with sf an interest in technical speculation on closed systems. Wiener posits societies as elements within a system that is able to exert pressure to shift those systems from one state of equilibrium to another and to maintain them in the desired state.[11] In *Dune*, this understanding of systems becomes the

---

[11] Norbert Wiener, *The Human Use of Human Beings: Cybernetics and Society* (New York: Da Capo, 1988).

lynchpin for controlling societies by transforming the climate. When the Harkonnen successfully oust the Atreides, they leave Liet to die of exposure in Arrakis' deep desert. Liet hallucinates his father's early lectures, which employ the discourse of cybernetics to understand how the Fremen might alter Arrakis' climate by functioning as 'an ecological and geological force of almost unlimited potential' (467).

Terraforming encompasses temporal and physical dimensions that play on compression and control, the failure of which illustrates the fragility of such plans when confronted with the unexpected and with competing interests. Paul's prescient visions function as a critique of control: his ability to see the past, future, and the present as it unfolds is a metaphor for climatological modelling systems. Edwards recounts the history of climate modelling that emerged from research into weather prediction and weather control.[12] Ecological principles fundamental to climate modelling, such as sensitive dependence on initial conditions, feedback systems, and cascading effects, are omnipresent in *Dune*, while Paul's prescience is described as being subject to the same limiting factors as climatological models. Paul's ability to foresee the future implies a capacity to shape that future. However, his visions are not inevitable and are dependent on the actions of other entities, which may reveal new configurations of the future previously inaccessible to his foresight. The Bene Gesserit goal of creating the ultimate predictive modelling system – a human computer – would allow them to future-proof their society and to achieve an unheard of level of control. Paul's actual experience of prescience and his failure to foresee all facets of the future and, more troubling still, his inability to intervene to avoid the jihad that promises to sweep the empire once he assumes authority at the narrative's end show how power and its use must constantly negotiate limitations. Control over a planet and its population is at best fraught and at worst a fantasy.

Kim Stanley Robinson's Mars Trilogy

Robinson's groundbreaking Mars trilogy reflects on and connects different modes of terraforming to climate change and geo-engineering on Earth. The trilogy juxtaposes two trajectories for the adaptation of a planet's climate: industrial models that focus on the extraction of key resources for consumption on Earth, and ecopoietic and 'eco-economic' models that take seriously the destructive potential of climatological mastery and

---

[12] Edwards, *Vast Machine*.

attempt to mitigate climatological and ecological collapse. Like *Dune*, the Mars trilogy emphasises an unpredictability that deflates fantasies of total systematic control. It rejects top-down forms of authority in favour of a distributed power that Colin Milburn connects to the figure of nano-technology but which, in line with terraforming themes, can be repre-sented by the bacterium and ecopoiesis, itself a metonymy for ecological and social networks.[13] The trilogy documents the formation of a Martian society from a small research community of one hundred scientists, its expansion and revolution against Earth's metanationals, right through to the creation of an independent Martian government. Recalling *The Sands of Mars*, this transformation of political self-determination is compared to the colonisation of America. The dangers of using such analogies are raised even as capitalism and terraforming are aligned to the exploitation of peoples and their land. The interlacing of environmental ethics, the social and ecological impact of climate change, and the relationship of science to society and politics are core themes of the trilogy's investment in terraforming.

The ideological opposition between terraforming Mars and leaving it untouched is dramatically presented as an opposition between Sax Russell and Anne Clayborne. Clayborne attempts but fails to explode fantasies of control to reveal how politics and economics shape history. Metanationals begin transforming Mars into an annexe of Earth in *Red Mars*, seeing it as a mine for supplying scarce resources that is overseen by their own security forces. These plans are incommensurate with those who left Earth to escape its bureaucratisation and its looming environmental and social crises. Loss of control is a prevalent theme that is exacerbated by the increasing complexity of the diversifying communities on Mars. John Boone laments the loss of control, explicitly challenging the scepticism with which scien-tific planning is met: 'societies without a plan, that was history so far' (*Red Mars*, 336). Boone grasps for a plan that would give him a sense of control over unfolding events, treating with ambivalence the diversity of interests that lead to outcomes unaccounted for in his vision of a Martian society. The systematising project he envisions exemplifies the struggle to create a utopia on Mars, 'a scientific system designed for Mars, designed to their specifications, fair and just and rational and all those good things' (*Red Mars*, 335). The scientifically planned utopia confronts the realities of

---

[13] Colin Milburn, 'Greener on the Other Side: Science Fiction and the Problem of Green Nanotechnology', *Configurations*, 20 (2012), 53–87.

terraforming and settlement and becomes both a struggle and a compromise over ideal modes of existence.

Boone speculates on a scientific utopia based on rationalism and liberalism, attempting to work through a new approach to a problem undermined by the history of applied science. Arkady Bogdanov's corrective – that scientists working to create a pocket utopia that excludes the wider population represents a failure of utopianism – is taken up by other members of the First Hundred scientists on Mars and later by the Martian underground, culminating in the formation of a Martian government based on a distributed political power. Russell, the core architect of the terraforming project, establishes several plans for planetary adaptation that exclude other voices from decisions over ideal approaches to transforming the land. He initiates schemes that contravene ethical and practical prohibitions on terraforming, such as the unauthorised seeding of modified lichens across the planet. Russell sees Mars as a lab, a testing ground for approaches to transforming the planet. This is more than an analogy, but a statement of the degree to which systematic climatological control undergirds the terraforming project. If the planet is a lab, how far do the colonists' competing interventions into Mars' climate afford experimental controls? The illusion of control harks back to colonial narratives and Russell begins to reflect on the intersection between science, society, and politics in *Green Mars* and *Blue Mars*. His change of outlook is tied to a new orientation to his ideological difference regarding terraforming with Clayborne, who resists the project as an imperial subjugation of nature to Earth's destructive consumption of matter.

Revolution is asymptomatic of the desire to cut ties with Earth and to free Mars' future from a systematising economic plan. Instead of overarching control, the colonists seek a distributed agency guided by agreement to principles set out in the Dorsa Brevia agreement of *Green Mars*. The terraforming plan is also subject to revision following expressions of alternative visions for Mars' future. Terraforming becomes a chance to remake history to avoid the mistakes of the past. Frontier narratives provide thematic and formal elements that inform representations of interplanetary colonisation but are also the subject of the trilogy's reflection on history. Terraforming is a form of systematic colonial mastery that ties climatological change to society and politics, with history as one dimension of the system that sits as a shadow to contemporary events. Climatological control, control of the future of the planet, and political and social control converge at the end of *Green Mars* through a revolution that exemplifies the diffusion of power among the populace, leaving the

First Hundred as powerless as anyone. Recalling the jihad of *Dune,* Toitovna acknowledges their lack of control and accepts that they 'could only ride the tiger' (*Green Mars,* 681).

There is a naivety and hubris involved in thinking that the new Martian society can be imposed from above, a view that resonates with the social control envisioned in *Dune.* The models that inform policy on Mars and guide the scientific programme are undermined throughout the trilogy, notably because the system's social and political levels cannot be modelled. Following Bogdanov, many colonists take control of their fate to break out of a 'fantasy of the past' (*Red Mars,* 410). Habitation provides a different perspective on appropriate relationships to the land. Underscoring the pervasiveness of Earth's social systems in influencing the development of terraforming and colonisation, Bogdanov diagnoses the problem thus: 'To be twenty-first century scientists on Mars, in fact, but at the same time living within nineteenth century social systems, based on seventeenth century ideologies' (*Red Mars,* 113). The colonists' early refusal to assess the systems within which they are embedded bespeaks their preference for a fantasy of control that dominates the colonising process as the systems Bogdanov speaks against are instantiated on Mars.

In *Red Mars,* the colonists celebrate a milestone in the terraformation project: an ice comet is directed on a collision course to Mars, bringing with it water while raising the atmosphere's temperature. Boone delivers a speech at a festival in which he offers a vision of syncretism that uses the figure of the splice to characterise the process of societal construction on Mars. Boone raises the analogy between Mars colonisation and the colonisation of North America even as he acknowledges the differences between the two, calling for 'a new Martian way, a new Martian philosophy, economics, religion!' (*Red Mars,* 410). This is not a call for systematic environmental control so much as a call for engagement, experimentation, and invention. After the invention of a life-extending treatment on Mars, Frank Chalmers reflects on America and Russia's attempt to withhold the treatment on Earth to mitigate the climate crisis through strict population controls. The colonists later learn that the life-extending treatment 'was being used as an instrument of control back on Earth' (*Green Mars,* 601). These responses to climate change function as an alibi for authoritarian control.

Boone reacts to the economic plan that is enacted on Mars when arguing with Phyllis Boyle about her brand of venture capitalism. She accepts as an article of faith the idea that 'Everyone on Mars will profit from it, that's [capitalism's] nature', to which Boone replies that 'the colonial era is over'

(*Red Mars*, 364). Ironically, when Russell takes Boyle on a tour of Mars' landscape, he tries, as Clayborne once tried with him, to show her the Martian landscape from a different perspective, one not tied to the interests of the metanationals she represents. Boyle fails to recognise the beauty and wonder that Russell sees and asks who was responsible for designing the lichens they walk amongst. He replies, 'Could be no one. Quite a few of the species out here weren't designed' (*Green Mars*, 235), and later reflects on the ecopoietic model of terraforming as 'fundamentally intriguing. The birth of a world. Out of their control' (*Blue Mars*, 450). Russell's approach to terraforming from *Green Mars* onward eschews total control for a responsive engagement with nature, an outlook that would go on to shape the developing Martian community.

Nevertheless, as Michel Duval points out, this incessant search for answers can be seen as a desire to escape from fear by establishing a measure of control over nature through the accumulation of knowledge. Russell describes science as 'a system for generating answers', yet fails to explain the purpose for these answers (*Green Mars*, 502). Russell begins to reflect on the relationship between history and natural history, both of which resist experimentation: 'Values drove history, which was whole, nonrepeatable, and contingent. It might be characterized as Lamarckian, or as a chaotic system, but even those were guesses, because what factors were they talking about, what aspects might be acquired by learning and passed on, or cycling in some nonrepetitive but patterned way?' (*Green Mars*, 280). By introducing human history to Mars, control of the land becomes a way to control the development of human communities within those environments. Russell recalls Chalmers's claim that 'colonialism had never died . . . it just changed names and hired local cops. We're all colonies of the transnats' (*Green Mars*, 283). Industrial terraforming models of the type Boyle endorses thus reveal themselves to be an enhanced form of colonial mastery. The history of capitalism explains their current status as subjects of corporate control – a control that extends its systematising and incorporating influence to Mars.

Arthur Randolph explains that the new communities arriving on Mars 'had been trying specifically to get away from dominant powers – transnational, the West, America, capitalism – all the totalizing systems of power. A central system was just what they had gone to great lengths to get away from' (*Green Mars*, 422). Nadia Cherneshevsky points out that 'America also stands for the melting pot. The idea of the melting pot. It was the place where people could come from anywhere and be a part of it. Such was the theory. There are lessons there for us' (*Green Mars*, 422). The myth of

America is contradictory and combines residual associations that still have power and utility for thinking about the formation of new cultures. These reflections inform the Martians' approach to building an independent government.

Randolph's view of the tension between global and local interests emphasises a contradiction at the heart of Martian values: 'We truly want some global control, and yet we want freedom for the tents as well' (*Blue Mars*, 135). Despite the model of the Swiss canton Graubunden, 'the truth was, they were in a new situation. There was no historical analogy that would be much help to them now' (*Blue Mars*, 136). The complexly interpenetrated economies of Mars present challenges that cannot be translated by models on Earth. When several members of the Martian government visit the budding colonies on Saturn in an attempt to build an interplanetary alliance, one Saturnian accuses the Martian delegation of hypocrisy and of attempting to exert control from above. Mars' environmental policy attempts to maintain environmental equilibrium, but in doing so autonomy is threatened at the local level. Russell's reflections on scientists and technicians as apolitical leads him to think of politics as a form of science. He concludes that the distributed power of a polyarchy would theoretically lead to 'the greatest amount of individual freedom and collective good, by maximising the amount of control that an individual had over his or her life'. In *Green Mars*, Russell attempts to explain to Clayborne his goals for the terraforming project: 'It's hard to express. Something like a net gain in information. A net gain in order' (*Green Mars*, 186). This is a functional description of life itself for Russell, an anti-entropic increase in complexity, rather than a form of systematic, totalising control. These two visions of order come into conflict as control inhibits Russell's quest for a net gain in complexity.

Vlad Taneev and Marina Tokareva argue that 'Economics serves to justify the current power structure' (*Red Mars*, 352) and that the arbitrariness of the assigned values to specific resources elides the realities of humankind's exploitation of the planetary environment and its inhabitants. They propose an economic system that attempts to address the totalising incorporation of nature by entailing a return to the land. The Mars trilogy argues that humankind must embrace their powers for control in the service of nature and human communities. Remarking on the power that nanotechnology promises for the construction of a space elevator that would connect Earth and Mars, Boone links humankind's technological capacity to issues of claim-making, ownership, sovereignty, and conflict: 'People squabbling like those old gods on Olympus, because nowadays we're just as powerful as they were' – or more, chimes Nadia (*Red Mars*, 381). Technology provides an unmediated power which gives an illusion of systematic control. This power invites political and economic disputes that challenge how that power is wielded. Eco-economics emerges as an alternative distinctive for its determination of value based on ecological principles and not capital. Eco-economics is enshrined in the Dorsa Brevia agreement alongside a principle that situates Mars as a model for further expansion into space: 'What we do here will set precedents for further human habitation of the solar system, and will suggest models for the human relationship to Earth's environment as well' (*Green Mars*, 489). This chapter highlights a cusp beyond which multiple histories might develop along two broad lines: greater or less totalising control through the reshaping of the climate to satisfy human desire. These choices are encapsulated in the opposition between industrial and ecopoietic models that respectively position humankind as masters of or participants in shaping the climate.

Terraforming has become an increasingly important subgenre of sf in relation to climate and climate change, having developed into a mode of literature that critically engages with the fantasies of control that advanced technology seems to offer for mastering nature. Terraforming invites speculation regarding the nature of power and control over space and time, particularly with regard to the climate. It highlights the pitfalls attendant on the recycling of historical orientations towards nature and society, primarily in its engagement with colonisation, empire, and economic expansion. By mapping how the past reasserts itself in new forms, it draws attention to the persistence of cultural memory and to the difficulties of adapting to new contexts. Such works also seek to preserve the utopian potential embedded in these sequences of interaction and mythmaking. *The Sands of Mars* and the Mars trilogy point to the utopian potential offered by the idea of terraforming and inhabiting other worlds – of building new societies that might escape the mistakes of the past. By the time Robinson's Mars trilogy was published, utopia and the patterning of frontier narratives on sf literature was recognised as far more problematic than in Clarke's context, yet both writers were concerned with identifying and stripping away the fantasies that accompany ideas of systematic control over nature and the habitation of new lands as recapitulating American colonial frontier narratives. Herbert's *Dune*, by contrast, attempted to deflate myths of power and control and was critical in reshaping notions of the sf hero as a flawed character unable to escape the implications of such mythmaking.

These narratives trace a movement in sf that is both iterative and reflective. Terraforming narratives build models, not only for thinking about the future, but for thinking about the impact of the past and present on the trajectory of that future. They enact a practice of speculation, critical thinking, and testing with regard to the key themes of systematic climate control, community, and the modes appropriate to engagement with non-human nature. These models are not primarily intended to shape specific practices (although specific examples of sf make the attempt), but rather construct imaginative landscapes where the influence of history on society can be posited, critiqued, and debated. As Robinson's Mars trilogy exemplifies, sf engages with other works in the tradition as well as with developments in the sciences and humanities to revise the assumptions of earlier narratives while offering new ways of conceptualising social, political, and economic relationships that might offer productive approaches to understanding and inhabiting a world subject to climate change.

CHAPTER 13

The Mountains and Death: Revelations of Climate and Land in Nordic Noir

Andrew Nestingen

Jag såg mot himlen och mot marken och rakt fram
och skriver sen dess ett långt brev till de döda
på en maskin som inte har färgband bara en horisontstrimma
så orden bultar förgäves och ingenting fastnar.

(I looked up to the sky and to the ground and straight ahead
and since then have been writing a long letter to the dead
on a typewriter that has no ribbon, just a thread of horizon
so the words knock in vain and nothing sticks.)

Tomas Tranströmer, *Östersjöar* (*Baltics*)[1]

Climate, the land, and place are central in a definitive scene of Nordic noir,[2] near the beginning of Henning Mankell's *Sidetracked*.[3] Inspector Kurt Wallander is summoned to a farmstead at Marsvinsholm, which lies in the jurisdiction of Ystad, Sweden. A farmer has called to report a young woman loitering in his canola (rapeseed) field. Wallander agrees to respond, because other officers are occupied. 'A few minutes later, Wallander drove off from the station. He turned left at the roundabout and took the road toward Malmö ... When he got out onto the E65, he rolled down the window. The yellow rape fields stretched out on both sides. He couldn't remember the last time he felt as good as he felt now.'[4] At first glance, the local roads and yellow fields are a picture of summery locality. Sweden's climate makes summer a manic season, as the locals try to squeeze maximum enjoyment from the long, but few, warm summer days. Summer is a time to be out of doors, from sunrise at three in the

---

[1] Tomas Tranströmer, *Bright Scythe: Selected Poems*, trans. Patricia Crane (Lexington, KY: Sarabande Books, 2015).

[2] I use the terms Scandinavian crime fiction and Nordic crime fiction interchangeably to designate the crime fiction of Denmark, Finland, Iceland, Norway, and Sweden.

[3] Henning Mankell, *Sidetracked*, trans. Steven T. Murray (New York: Vintage Crime, 2003).

[4] Ibid., p. 25.

morning to sunset in the wee hours. By contrast, the rainy, snowy, short, grey days of winter slow activity, requiring warm clothes, indoor activities, candlelight, a slow pace, and perhaps heliotherapy. As the cold, rainy, and dark setting of Sarah Lund's (Sofie Gråbol) Copenhagen shows in *The Killing*,[5] winter is a soggy, depressing time. Climate figures centrally in many novels and films that fall in the category of Nordic noir, from the Icelandic moors of Arnaldur Indriðason and Yrsa Sigurðardóttir to the urban, coniferous forests of Leena Lehtolainen's Espoo to the fields, forests, and lakes of Karin Fossum's southern Norway. The representation of climate helps constitute the reality of Nordic noir.

Close analysis of the novels and films of Nordic noir reveals that the representation of locality, involving place and climate, often constitutes an apparent reality through climatological and geographical specificity. Crime investigation in the context of these same climatological and geographical features reveals human powers at work, which are often made more evident by being represented as figures of land and climate. In this way, representations of climate, land, and locality serve a double purpose. They create a plausibly particular construction of reality, at the same time as such representations work figuratively, and anthropocentrically, to give aesthetic expression to the human dramas being narrated in crime fiction.

Sidetracked is set in the summer months, and its narrative chronology builds on Nordic summer mania for its pacing, with chapters and sections titled by date and even time of day, with the football World Cup occurring at the same time, popping up here and there. The Nordic summer is woven into the narrative – not unlike the summer of Ingmar Bergman's *Summer with Monika*.[6] Other Wallander novels integrate season and climate as well, for instance, *One Step Behind*,[7] another summer novel, or the autumnal *Dogs of Riga*.[8] In Mankell's hands, and many others', nature and climate are figures in the service of melodramatic narration. They make evident the moral underpinnings of the world created by the story, making place legible as an expression of a human system of meaning. Implicit in this construction is a nature–culture dualism. Nature is a screen on to which human drama may be projected, as scholars of ecocriticism have documented.[9]

[5] Søren Sveistrup, *The Killing* (*Forbrydelsen*), DR, 2007–12.
[6] *Summer with Monika*, dir. Ingmar Bergman, Svensk filmindustri, 1953.
[7] Mankell, *One Step Behind*, trans. Ebbe Segerberg (New York: Vintage Crime, 2003).
[8] Mankell, *The Dogs of Riga*, trans. Laurie Thompson (New York: Vintage Crime, 2003).
[9] See, for example, Timothy Clark, 'Nature, Post-Nature', in Louise Westling (ed.), *The Cambridge Companion to Literature and the Environment* (Cambridge University Press, 2014), pp. 76–7.

Scholars of Nordic culture and literature have shown the extent to which such representations use the representation of locality to serve the touristic gaze, as an economic resource. Anne Marit Waade points out in her study *Wallanderland* that the yellow canola fields serve as a backdrop to an image of Kenneth Branagh playing Kurt Wallander, which has figured prominently in the marketing of the BBC drama series; Swedish summer light and the yellow fields became the iconic image of the BBC TV adaptations.[10] The Swedish scholar Olof Hedling has observed that the foregrounding of such images was also part of a broader, regional economic development strategy, in which film images also were harnessed to campaigns marketing the region as a tourist destination.[11] Crime-fiction scholar Kerstin Bergman's book *Deckarnas svenska landskap: Från Skåne till Lappland* (Crime Fiction's Swedish Landscape: From Scania to Lappland) shows the extent to which local officials have built tourism campaigns throughout Sweden around the representation of distinct localities in crime fiction.[12] Nationally and internationally, the touristic gaze is embedded in Scandinavian crime fiction.

Yet it is possible to see another dimension to the representation of place, when we broaden it to concern the representation of the non-human world. Key Nordic crime novels seem to seek to represent the natural world as what the political theorist Jane Bennett would call an 'actant', or an 'operator', that is, non-human agencies and orchestrating forces, which bring about key effects in the world.[13] Some of those effects impact human cultural perception and practice. In some cases, crime fiction emphasises the cultural expressions they cause, as the literary scholar Linda Rugg suggests happens in what she calls 'ecocrime fiction'.[14] Yet other such representations use the crime novel to reveal an underlying reality of climate and land that are post-Romantic representations of nature, which do not concern the mystification of the natural world, but depict it as a force that traumatises and destroys, and to which fiction fails to attribute

[10] Anne Marit Waade, *Wallanderland. Medieturisme og skandinavisk TV-krimi*. Studier i krimi og kriminaljournalstik (Aalborg: Aalborg Universitetsforlag, 2013).
[11] Olof Hedling,' Murder, Mystery and Megabucks? Films and Filmmaking as Regional and Local Place Promotion in Southern Sweden', in Erik Hedling, Olof Hedling, and Mats Jönsson (eds.), *Regional Aesthetics: Locating Swedish Media* (Stockholm: National Library of Sweden), pp. 263–90.
[12] Kerstin Bergman, ed., *Deckarnas svenska landskap: Från Skåne till Lappland* (Gothenburg: Makadam förlag), 2014.
[13] Jane Bennett, *Vibrant Matter: a Political Ecology of Things* (Durham, NC: Duke University Press, 2010), p. 9.
[14] Linda Rugg, 'Displacing Crimes against Nature: Scandinavian Ecocrime Fiction', *Scandinavian Studies*, 89 (2017), 597–615.

meaning. Indeed this is a larger theme in Nordic literature, as, for example, one can see in the epigraph taken from Tomas Tranströmer's magisterial poem *Baltics* (*Östersjöar*), which is a meditation on the aporias of artistic representations of the natural world, such as the Baltic sea and its features.[15] This chapter traces similar aporias and contrasts in the representation of climate and land in Nordic crime fiction, including figurative locality, ecocrime fiction, and post-Romantic nature.

Climate, Location, Genre

The setting of the crime novel is a fundamental generic element. Subgenres of crime fiction can be determined by their setting: the isolated country house of the whodunit, the big-city streets of the hardboiled, the police station of the procedural, the intelligence offices of the spy novel. These locations are semantically rich. The setting often gives expression to texts' notions of the source of crime – the traumatic family home, the dangerous city streets. So, too, in Scandinavian crime fiction, modifying setting and the representation of locality has been a means of identifying and differentiating national and regional texts, at the same time as their particularity locates them in a globalised popular culture.

The typical way of reading the representation of climate in Scandinavian crime fiction is to view it as a construction of locality, which makes sense in the context of genre. Slavoj Žižek has argued that Mankell's representation of climate, as we see in the example above, can be understood as the way in which Mankell transforms the Swedish crime novel into globalised detective fiction. Žižek writes that Mankell's novels are 'staged in the bleak Scandinavian countryside, with its grey oppressive clouds and dark winter days'.[16] For Žižek, Mankell foregrounds the representation of locality as a means of generic differentiation and identification. To put it another way, Žižek argues that Mankell revises the semantics of the crime novel. Semantics of genre is part of terminology popularised by film theorist Rick Altman. By semantics of genre, he means the 'common traits, attitudes, characters, shots, locations, sets, and the like', the units of meaning which in combination some theorists have argued define genres.[17] The premise of Žižek's point is that the semantics of the crime novel have been defined by the representation of setting and locality:

---

[15] I am thankful to Norman Hirsh for our discussion of Tranströmmer's 'Baltics'.
[16] Slavoj Žižek, 'Parallax', *London Review of Books*, 25.22 (November 2003), 24.
[17] Rick Altman, *Film/Genre* (London: British Film Institute, 1999), p. 10.

> The main effect of globalisation on detective fiction is discernible in its dialectical counterpart: the specific locale, a particular provincial environment as the story's setting … the eccentric locale, is the rule. The global stance of 20th-century Modernism asserted itself in the guise of cosmopolitanism or membership of a global Americanised culture; this is no longer the case. A truly global citizen today is one who discovers or returns to (identifies with) particular roots, who displays a specific communal identity. The 'global order' is in the end only the frame and container of this shifting multitude of particular identities.[18]

Žižek implies that the 'truly global' crime novel finds its identity in differentiating itself from the ersatz semantics of the 'Americanised' crime novel. The implication of Žižek's emphasis on climate and land in Mankell's novels is that they are important to defining specificity, a means of marrying the familiar with the exotic.

Here it is worth remembering how locality and criminality are often tied together. Criminologists write:

> Crime is not randomly distributed across a city or community, or the globe, but is, instead, highly concentrated at certain places known as crime 'hot spots.' For example, it is estimated that across the United States, 10 percent of the places are sites for around 60 percent of the crimes. In the same way that individuals can have criminal careers, there are criminal careers for places.[19]

Such patterns have led to crime-prevention strategies that seek to target such hotspots with big data and algorithmic analysis. Elected officials increasingly believe in predictive policing, in which 'police-car laptops … display maps showing locations where crime is likely to occur, based on data-crunching algorithms developed by scientists'.[20] It is important to note that crime hotspots may also be luxurious homes or apartments, which serve as a meeting place for organised-crime actors; they may be urban homes or street-corner payphones, where crimes are arranged; or they may be locations far from cities or towns, as Kerstin Bergman's book on the landscape of Swedish crime fiction convincingly shows.[21] In the USA, suburban crime rates have risen since 2010:

---

[18] Žižek, 'Parallax', 24.
[19] Brandon C. Welsh and David P. Farrington, 'Crime Prevention and Public Policy', in Welsh and Farrington (eds.), *Oxford Handbook of Crime Prevention* (Oxford University Press, 2012), 10.1093/oxfordhb/9780195398823.013.000.
[20] Mara Hvistendahl, 'Can "Predictive Policing" Prevent Crime before it Happens?' *Science* (28 September 2016), 10.1126/science.aah7353.
[21] Bergman, *Deckarnas svenska landskap*.

'Criminologists and public officials cite weaker and more resource-strapped law enforcement in some suburbs for the increase, among other factors. That, in turn, attracts criminals who focus on suburbs, because they are looking for easier places than relatively well-policed cities to commit crimes.'[22]

The geographic and geopolitical redistribution of crime is at the heart of Mankell's novels. He frequently asserts that crime has become ubiquitous beyond stereotypical hotspots; all of his novels place their crimes in surprising locales, in which crime is not supposed to happen, just as Nesbø, Larsson, Marklund, Lehtolainen, and others also do. Season 3 of *The Killing* offers yet another such example, located as it is in the homes and offices of Denmark's national elite. Critics writing outside Scandinavia may overlook the semantics of setting, but they frequently make the point that Scandinavia on the whole is not supposed to be a site of criminality. One writes:

> Scandi noir enthralled people because it fashioned a competing narrative to our conventional view of Scandinavia. We'd learnt that these people were liberal, egalitarian, wealthy, balanced and beautiful, and yet here was a whole genre built around airing their darkest and most squalid secrets. Reading is a kind of tourism, and these novels, television series and films promised us a series of unsettlingly revealing insights into life amid the glaciers and mountains, fjords and lakes.[23]

It is interesting to note that the critics use evidence in a way that recalls Žižek's: climatological features, 'glaciers and mountains', become metonymy for a claim that seeks to contrast the apparent peaceful reality of Scandinavia with a fictional criminal depiction that undermines the apparent reality.

Such critics suggest that the contrast between apparent social realities created by representations of locality ('egalitarian, wealthy, balanced and beautiful', 'glaciers and mountains')[24] and underlying 'more real' realities (dark and squalid secrets) is a definitive feature of Nordic noir. Indeed, this notion is part of a much broader argument made by the sociologist Luc Boltanski in his book on crime fiction, *Mysteries and Conspiracies*. Boltanski writes that crime fiction always concerns two representational levels of reality: 'social reality as initially perceived by a naïve observer (or

---

[22] Cameron McWhirter and Gary Fields, 'Crime Migrates to Suburbs: As Homicides Fall Sharply in Cities, They Are Rising in Surrounding Communities', *Wall Street Journal* (8 December 2012).

[23] Alex Preston, 'Michael Fassbender on Murder, Misogyny and the Making of Jo Nesbø's The Snowman', *Telegraph* (27 September 2017).

[24] Ibid.

reader), with its order, its hierarchies and its principles of causality, reverses itself and unveils its fictional nature, revealing another much more real reality, that it had been concealing ... powers whose existence, indeed, whose very possibility, had not been suspected by anyone'.[25] The investigation story in any crime novel concerns uncovering, and usually seeking understanding and mastery over, a reality that had not been perceived, the reality that is the source of the crime investigated. The 'glaciers and mountains' hide 'squalid secrets', the underlying reality of the Scandinavian societies, if we view matters from Boltanski's perspective. Locality, in which climatic conditions play a part, thus functions to establish a social reality to be unmasked by the investigator.

Climate and Human Drama

In comparison to Mankell's representation of Wallander's drive to Marsvinsholm in *Sidetracked*, the internationally produced television serial *Occupied*,[26] set in an imagined future Norway, raises a set of compelling questions about the representation of locality and climate as they are inflected by genre in Scandinavian crime fiction and Nordic noir.[27]

Let us consider the credit sequence of *Occupied*. It is a montage of the fictional Hurricane Maria and its environmental and political consequences. In this future of climate change, the European Union has become increasingly dependent on Norwegian oil for energy, because of political changes in the Middle East and the United States. At the same time, climate change is unleashing hurricanes even in the European North Atlantic. Maria devastates the Norwegian coast, contributing to the election of an activist climate party, the Norwegian Greens led by Jesper Berg (Henrik Mestad). Berg decides to cease Norway's oil production, and transition to use of 100 per cent renewable energy sources, including increased use of a newly discovered, clean fuel. In response, the European Union covertly cooperates with Russia to force Norway to recommence oil production. Russia begins a covert occupation,

[25] Luc Boltanski, *Mysteries and Conspiracies: Detective Stories, Spy Novels and the Making of Modern Society*, trans. Catherine Porter (Cambridge: Polity Press, 2014), 13–14.

[26] *Occupied (Okkupert)*, created by Karianne Lund, Erik Skjoldbærg, and Jo Nesbø, Norway TV2, Via Play, Yellow Bird, 2015–.

[27] I am treating *Occupied* as Nordic noir, because of its creators' identity (one of the writers is crime writer Jo Nesbø), but more importantly because of the centrality of the investigation narrative in the series, following Todorov's definition of crime fiction. Two principal characters in the series are professional investigators, the security officer Hans Martin Djupvik (Eldar Skar) and the journalist Thomas Eriksen (Vegar Hoel), and their investigations are a key narrative structure in the series.

transforming the Norwegian government into its puppet and dictating Norwegian energy and security policy.

Here again, the depiction of locality and climate furnishes the image on which the series builds a credible world. The credit sequence depicts locality, altered by climate change, implying that the changes are the cause of governmental and broader political crisis. Time-lapse photography of glaciers breaking up segues into a rapid montage of crashing waves, overwhelmed seawalls, rescues, helicopters, and flooded streets. These transition into political posters and images of Prime Minister Berg at work. Other central characters are introduced, and we see oil platforms, men in military gear, military equipment being prepared, police in action, images of Norwegian patriotic celebrations, and military activity and street protests by anti-occupation Norwegians, all of which end in tumultuous, dark ocean waves. The brown colour palette of the sequence makes the environmental crisis depicted more alien, with the palette highlighting the pollution. It's a drama of the late Anthropocene, if you will. At the same time, it is evident that climate change will be depicted through the actions of individual human agents, the dramatis personae of *Occupied*.

The last aspect is given emphasis by the montage's time-lapse images and strong percussive, minor-key musical theme, which directly call to mind the credit sequence of the Netflix series *House of Cards*.[28] That show's credit sequence is built around time-lapse images of Washington, DC and a percussive opening in a minor key. It also includes images of the Potomac river's polluted shore. The *House of Cards* opening sequence figuratively suggests that the American capital is poisoned and befouled, combining as it does images of historical landmarks and wealth with images of pollution and poverty. In contrast, by putting images of the polluted and disturbed environment first in the opening sequence of *Occupied*, the film makes the environment and the climate catastrophe depicted the cause of the politics, not a figurative reflection of human activity, as in *House of Cards*. Yet in both cases, it is individual humans who will transact the political drama. In *House of Cards* that drama is a figuration of 'Inside-the-Beltway' corruption. In *Occupied* it is the damaged Earth's climate that is the ultimate source of the drama, which is then played out as politics and indeed war by humans.

Like Mankell's novels, *Occupied* is concerned with representing locality and climate in ways that exoticise the Nordic setting – a powerful hurricane

---

[28] *House of Cards*, created by Beau Willimon, Media Rights Capital, Panic Pictures, Trigger Street Productions, 2013–.

near Arctic waters creates curiosity. Yet *Occupied* involves a different response to the question 'What is the source of crime?' In Mankell and other Nordic noir writers' work, the disconnect between crimes and their location suggests a new ubiquity of crime. Crime has penetrated places where it previously was not found. Images of society, the land, and climate are thus figurations of human dramas, pressed into extremity by changing human relationships under late capitalism. In *Occupied*, images of climate and locality are not figurative of human drama, but the cause of the drama. Altered by climate change, nature has become the source of crime. Yet, the nature–culture dualism remains, for the solution to the environmental and political problems depicted is implied to be a more rational, cooperative, and peaceful politics, which can be delivered by well-meaning pursuit of the truth through reasonable means. As a result, environmental politics are represented 'as a kind of corrective, striving to address cultural forces that are seen as distorting a more natural or lost relation of humanity to its environment'.[29]

Ecocrime Fiction

The reason for drawing this contrast is to consider how *Occupied* can be understood as what the literary scholar and Scandinavianist Linda Rugg has analysed as the ecocrime fiction tradition in Nordic noir. In an important article,[30] Rugg argues for connections between *Occupied* and what she argues are signal Scandinavian ecocrime novels, Peter Høeg's *Smilla's Sense of Snow*[31] and Kerstin Ekman's *Blackwater*.[32] What unites these texts, writes Rugg, is narratives in which crimes against nature are displaced on to crimes against human victims, thus deferring the investigation and effort to comprehend crimes against nature, as the investigation into crimes committed by and against humans becomes the focus. As crimes against nature are displaced into anthropocentric interactions, the attempt to understand human crimes against nature is deferred.

A key part of Rugg's argument is that the generic form of crime fiction is entangled in this dynamic of displacement and deferral. Displacement and deferral are mediated by the relationship between the story of investigation and the story of crime, definitive features of crime fiction, as Tzvetan Todorov argues in his crucial statement, 'Typology of Detective

---

[29] Clark, 'Nature, Post-Nature', pp. 78–9.   [30] Rugg, 'Displacing Crimes against Nature'.
[31] Peter Høeg, *Smilla's Sense of Snow*, trans. Tiina Nunnally (New York: Farrar, Straus and Giroux, 1993).
[32] Kerstin Ekman, *Blackwater*, trans. Joan Tate (New York: St Martin's Press, 1996).

Fiction'.³³ Todorov maintains that crime fiction always includes two
stories: 'the story of the crime and the story of the investigation'.³⁴
The story of the crime precedes the story of investigation, making crime
fiction some kind of recounting of the investigation into the story of the
crime. In this sense, crime fiction, according to Todorov, is always
a narrative of investigation. The crime novel or story concludes when the
story of the investigation can retrospectively tell the story of the crime.

   A tension arises in the ecocrime story, argues Rugg, for the story of
investigation and the story of the crime necessarily include human characters – a victim, a perpetrator, an investigator – as they are necessary
semantic categories of the genre. Yet, as Rugg shows, when the story of the
crime concerns acts against nature and the Earth, the semantics of the
crime story become insufficient. How can a victim be defined as nature, for
example? How can individual human characters resolve criminal matters
involving what Rugg calls 'actants', following Jane Bennett (and Bruno
Latour) – that is, non-human sources of agency such as climate, geology,
and disease, among others?³⁵ The mismatch of anthropocentric perspectives and non-human actants is unresolvable, which is why Rugg argues
that the combination of human and environmental actants in the ecocrime
story leads to displacement. Human characters may perpetrate crimes and
investigate them, suffer from them, but they operate on a different temporal and spatial scale to the non-human actants. A story of ecocrime
becomes a story of human crime and investigation, deferring the inquiry
into the non-human, which is at the heart of the story in the first place,
whether entangled in victimhood or the sources of crime. Human culp-
ability absorbs the guilt, as the crime story's semantics require.

   Rugg's analysis of *Occupied* suggests that while the premise of the drama
is the consequences of environmental catastrophe in a future of changed
climate, 'nature as victim moves ... smoothly to Norway as victim, and
then individual Norwegians as victims'.³⁶ Rugg's argument shows that
what *Occupied* is primarily about – the human drama, the actions of
individuals, and even its representation of politics – is reduced to this
schematic individualized depiction, which flattens the institutional actions
and state relationships into matters of individual character. While such
a dynamic contrasts with the way climate and nature become a figuration
of human drama in Mankell and a good deal of other Nordic noir, in

³³ Tzvetan Todorov, *The Poetics of Prose*, trans. Richard Howard (Ithaca, NY: Cornell University Press, 1981).
³⁴ Ibid., p. 44.   ³⁵ Bennett, *Vibrant Matter*.   ³⁶ Rugg, 'Displacing Crimes', 609.

ecocrime fiction, as Rugg argues, the non-human is held as distinct and separate from the human, but then displaced on to the human, while investigation of crimes against nature is put aside.

Erlendur on the Mountain

In addition to the representational relationships outlined so far, there is also at least a third tradition in Nordic noir, in which climate and the land are actants. Two prominent writers in this connection are Norwegian Karin Fossum and the Icelander Arnaldur Indriðason. In Fossum's novels, crime tends to be situational, occurring in places of isolation, in which fantasies of human mastery collapse, as climate and nature exert force. So, too, in Arnaldur Indriðason's novels, anthropocentric notions of mastery over climate and land are undermined. To recall Boltanski's argument, Arnaldur Indriðason's novels reveal that the reality and powers underlying social reality are forces of nature, the land, and climate, forces beyond human control and mastery.

Such uses of the crime novel contradict a typical argument about it. The predominant view is that crime fiction is a conservative genre. Its primary concern is to assert rational mastery over human affairs by narrating how those affairs are disrupted by crime, only for order to be reinstated through rational investigation. In the novels of Fossum and Arnaldur Indriðason, however, climate and land resist the logic of investigation and reinstatement, and the mastery and reassurance that are part of the genre are questioned. They are post-Romantic, in the sense that they are shorn of idealising constructions. The dualism that we have traced in other examples is diminished, or absent. Climate and nature are actants, which engender effects. Arnaldur Indriðason's novels are the key example.

The most prominent narrative structure in Arnaldur Indriðason's novels is a parallelism that subtly yet recurrently positions the victims of crimes investigated by the protagonist Inspector Erlendur as an analogue to the inspector himself. His investigations reveal that victims' traumas share similarities with his own traumatic past.

For Erlendur, the original trauma is the disappearance and presumed death of his brother Bergur in a blizzard on the high Icelandic moors of Mount Harðskafi when Bergur was eight and Erlendur ten. Rounding up sheep before a threatening blizzard, the threesome are caught on the slopes when the snow begins to fall. Soon they cannot see at all. Erlendur's father vanishes. Erlendur loses his brother in the whiteout conditions: 'I was holding Beggi's hand . . . I held on to it as long as I could, then suddenly he wasn't there anymore. I was alone. I don't know what happened.'[37] A search party is mustered and dispatched. They find Erlendur, but not Bergur. Erlendur awakens in his home at Eskifjördur, having almost died of hypothermia himself, his memory of the event shrouded in darkness. Erlendur blames himself for his brother's death, because his words had prodded his brother to join his father and himself on the trip during which his brother lost his life. At home again, Erlendur learns that his father had searched for his brother until he had to crawl to safety, badly frostbitten. 'I couldn't help it . . . I couldn't help it' he mutters, when Erlendur first encounters him after the event. His brother's body is never recovered. The traumatic childhood event haunts Erlendur throughout the eleven novels of the series, gradually increasing in intensity in each one.

Early in the series, there are traces of the trauma made evident. In the early novel *Jar City*, the narrator tells of Erlendur's leisure reading: 'Eventually he picked up the book he was reading . . . It was from one of his favorite series, describing ordeals and fatalities in the wilderness. He continued reading where he'd left off in the story called "Lives Lost on Mosfellsheidi" and was soon in a relentless blizzard that froze young men to death.'[38] Erlendur's investigations always seem to come back to experiences related to missing persons. 'People go missing all the time', says Erlendur.[39] In other novels, Erlendur is sometimes nostalgic for his home, and expresses an idealised view of the land and its place in the national past. The contrast of traumatic memory and nostalgia makes Erlendur's character ambivalent.

The critic Katrín Jakobsdóttir writes that such ambivalence is key to Arnaldur Indriðason's novels. She points out that this ambivalence is heightened through conflicts between characters. Sometimes Erlendur expresses a view or opinion that is later questioned or undermined by another character's more convincing ideas or arguments. 'Criticism of society is very conspicuous . . . and encompasses criticism of various standard Icelandic notions of nationality', she writes.[40]

In the last novel of the Erlendur series, a missing person, and the trauma associated with the disappearance, are again the source of the parallelism.

---

[37] Arnaldur Indriðason, *Strange Shores*, trans. Victoria Cribb (New York: Picador, 2012), p. 29.
[38] Arnaldur Indriðason, *Jar City*, trans. Bernard Scudder (New York: Picador, 2004), p. 17.
[39] Arnaldur Indriðason, *Strange Shores*, p. 164.
[40] Katrín Jakobsdóttir, 'Meaningless Icelanders: Icelandic Crime Fiction and Nationality', in Andrew Nestingen and Paula Arvas (eds.), *Scandinavian Crime Fiction* (Cardiff: University of Wales Press, 2011), p. 52.

Just as Bergur disappeared in a blizzard near Eskifjördur, a young woman named Matthildur also disappeared in a storm in the same area, while walking over a pass to another village some years before the disappearance of Bergur. In fact, a group of British soldiers had also been lost in a storm crossing the same pass during the Second World War: 'Their route over the pass had turned out to be too dangerous due to icy conditions, but instead of going back the way they came they had headed further inland.'[41] Most were rescued by the locals, but a number died. Erlendur looks into the case of Matthildur while on leave from work, but it is also a pretext to search for some clue to the remains of his lost brother. His investigation leads to the discovery that Matthildur's estranged, abusive husband had asserted that she had set off to cross the pass in bad weather, but he had instead killed her and secretly buried her in the village cemetery, avenging an affair Matthildur was having with another local man. Erlendur's reconstruction of the crime stirs up old cruelties and painful memories, and it offers ambivalent closure to Matthildur's lover, who is still alive. Yet the investigation also acquaints Erlendur with locals who recall Bergur's disappearance, and the consequential dissolution of his parents' marriage and their departure for Reykjavik. Ultimately, it also leads to a discovery that shakes Erlendur.

Erlendur hears of a local commercial hunter, Daníel Kristmundsson, an expert on the land and its animals, including its foxes. Erlendur visits Daníel's home, but discovers he has died. Daníel's son invites him to look at Daníel's junk collection, an archive of things and objects collected over the years. Rummaging through the garage with Daníel, Erlendur discovers an envelope labelled 'Harðskafi, North flank?'. Erlendur opens the envelope:

> He saw immediately that the small bones it contained were human. He had after all once dug up the remains of a four-year-old girl. A shiver ran like cold water down his spine.
> 'What have you got there?' . . .
> 'Did your father ever mention someone going missing on the moors around here?' asked Erlendur . . .
> 'Missing? No.'
> 'A child from Eskifjördur, lost on the moors forty years ago?'
> 'No, he never mentioned it' . . .
> Erlendur stared at the question mark on the lid. Old Daníel hadn't known what it was that he had found on the northern slopes of Mount

[41] Arnaldur Indriðason, *Strange Shores*, p. 16.

Harðskafi, but he had shoved the bones in his pocket anyway because of his collecting mania . . .

There were two bones. He didn't dare touch them, but was convinced he was right. One part was a chinbone, the other a cheekbone.

They were not fully grown.

They belonged to a child.[42]

Strange Shores makes Erlendur's putative discovery of Bergur's remains the culmination of Erlendur's recollection of the blizzard, his attempt to settle Matthildur's missing-person story, and his attempt to revisit the trauma he experienced on the slopes of Mount Harðskafi. His nostalgic return home is also a confrontation with his traumatic past.

The novel's conclusion also shows the extent to which the nature–culture dualism evident elsewhere is diminished in *Strange Shores*. Mount Harðskafi, Bergur's remains, the trauma are connected in an unidealised way. Discoveries of underlying, hidden realities are typically the object of investigation narratives in crime fiction. Boltanski writes that crime fiction seeks to reveal a reality beneath 'reality', a feature of crime fiction's nineteenth-century lineage; crime fiction is a kind of sociology, argues Boltanski, seeking to divulge underlying truths about social function. Such a notion underlies Erlendur's ongoing investigation of missing persons. Yet Erlendur's final investigation reveals that the perpetrator of his trauma was blizzard, winter, climate. They divulge no meaning. Erlendur solves the Matthildur case, but his investigation of his brother's death offers no mastery, even if it provides some closure. At the end of the novel, Erlendur sets off into falling snow on the north flank of Harðskafi, and the novel ends with him in an apparent fugue state, reunited with Bergur.

While land and climate have run throughout the argument so far, the focus has fallen on Erlendur's subjective working through of his trauma, which is of course an anthropocentric view of the world. What is the connection to what Rugg calls ecocrime fiction, and earlier discussed figurative representations of climate and land?

Erlendur's trauma is a consequence of land and climate's 'crime' against his brother, if such an anthropocentric term really fits. Without the blizzard, Bergur would not have died. Without the foxes, his remains might have been recovered. The climate of the Icelandic mountains, the north flank of Mount Harðskafi, and the fauna that thrive there bring about Bergur's death, and are the conditions that Erlendur must encounter in approaching the trauma. It is the occurrence of and traumatic after-

---

[42] Arnaldur Indriðason, *Strange Shores*, pp. 266–7.

effect of Bergur's death that tie together the eleven Inspector Erlendur
novels. 'When a loved one went missing, time changed nothing', Erlendur
thinks.[43] The novels' investigations repeat the attempt to find out what
happened, how the missing loved one disappeared, but in every case they
reveal the terrifying reality, that the murderer was hiding in plain sight.
The world itself, the climate, Mount Harðskafi, took Bergur's life. Climate
and land are the source of the 'crime' and the trauma that Erlendur
investigates through analogies and effigies of the lost Bergur in every
novel in the series. His investigations over the course of the novels align
many missing persons and trauma stories with his own, and in doing so
allow him to pull away the illusion. The body is found, the murder is
revealed, but the revelation provides no relief to Erlendur. Rather it gives
him a view of the mountain and the land as a world that took Bergur, and
his family, and a world that will take him too. The novel's elegiac tone
shows that crime fiction, too, can explore the limits of writing's, and art's,
capacity to represent the natural world, as such writers as Tomas
Tranströmer also show.

   While the predominant mode of depicting locality in Nordic noir
represents nature figuratively, in relation to human dramas, the tradition
of ecocrime fiction and the post-Romantic dimensions of Arnaldur
Indriðason's, and also Fossum's, novels show a variety of representations
of climate and land in Nordic noir. If, as Boltanski argues, crime fiction
seeks to confront, and ultimately control, a disturbing reality beneath
quotidian social reality, ecocrime fiction and its post-Romantic depictions
of nature and climate usher readers towards urgent topical questions, such
as climate change, but also towards the distinctive features of life in places
in which human actors' lives and societies are ambivalently embedded in
nature in ways that remain traumatically alive in memory and experience.
For Arnaldur Indriðason at least, recognising Iceland and its climate and
nature in that way is an encounter with death, a theme that runs throughout his novels, and to which he puts the generic and ideological features of
crime fiction to distinct use.

---

[43] Arnaldur Indriðason, *Strange Shores*, p. 280.

PART III

Application

CHAPTER 14

The Rise of the Climate Change Novel

Axel Goodbody and Adeline Johns-Putra

One of the readiest pieces of evidence of a new climate imaginary in the Anthropocene is climate change fiction or climate fiction. In this chapter, we consider the parameters of the phenomenon, outlining its emergence and summarising the key means and modes with which fiction has so far represented climate change. While climate fiction started by approaching the issue within the framework of existing popular genres such as science fiction, the thriller, and the disaster novel, authors have broadened the range of approaches in the past ten years, blending these and other genres. We pay particular attention to the extent to which climate fiction has worked within the established conventions of literary realism.[1] In order to capture the complexity of the challenges that climate change poses to individuals and societies, climate change novels must meet the many representational challenges mounted by climate change, confronting not just the invisibility of climate as opposed to weather, but also the gulfs between the standard, quantitative discourses of climate and the imaginative language of literature, as well as between the unprecedented scale of climate change effects and the human dimensions of fiction. We therefore discuss examples of literary realism, and consider their ability to render the abstract and intangible phenomenon of climate change visible, and relate it to readers' lives. However, we argue that there is also a significant body of writing on the subject which turns to alternative forms and narrative strategies in the effort to represent climate change, and manages to overcome some of the limitations of realism. In other words, where climate fiction meets the challenges of representing climate change, it has the potential to provide a space in which to address the Anthropocene's emotional, ethical, and practical concerns.[2]

[1] For a more extensive exploration of the relationship amongst climate, time and literary realism, see Chapter 15 by Adeline Johns-Putra in this volume.
[2] For a critique of climate fiction's ability to meet the ethical demands of the Anthropocene, see Chapter 16 by Claire Colebrook in this volume.

Emergence

The emergence of climate fiction was widely reported in several newspapers in mid-2013 – probably the first time the birth of a literary genre actually made the news.[3] The story, which made considerable footfall in print and digital media, originated in a US National Public Radio broadcast,[4] as did the word that was used to describe it, 'cli-fi'.[5] Since then, the term (a neologism apparently coined by journalist Dan Bloom in 2007), along with the idea of a new literary category, has gained traction, not least because of Bloom's dedicated online campaigning on its behalf.[6] Bloom was not alone in noticing the emergence of climate change as subject matter in fiction. For example, in 2009, an interdisciplinary group of academics set out to examine and compare imaginings of climate change, including literary ones.[7] The team found that what had originally appeared as a paucity of fictive responses to climate change was a rapidly growing literary trend.[8] The precise number of works, always a moving target, was estimated at 150 (the figure that one of the project's literary researchers, Adam Trexler, would go on to use in *Anthropocene Fictions*, the first book-length study of climate fiction).[9] Literary engagements with climate change have – in the second decade of this century – become even more marked, encompassing drama and poetry as well as fiction, and, as this chapter hopes to show, emerging as an international phenomenon beyond the confines of the Anglophone world.[10]

---

[3] See, for example, Rodge Glass, 'Global Warming: the Rise of Cli-fi', *The Guardian* (31 May 2013).

[4] Angela Evancie, 'So Hot Right Now: Has Climate Change Created a New Literary Genre?', *NPR* (20 April 2013).

[5] Dan Bloom, 'Thanks to TeleRead and NPR, Cli-fi is now an Official Literary Term', *Tele-Read* (28 May 2013).

[6] As Bloom has stated, 'I never give up. This is my life's work now and has been since I first read that IPCC report. It's all I do, and it's all I think about . . . I see myself as a cli-fi missionary, a cheerleader for novelists and screenwriters, a PR guy with media contacts, a literary theorist, and an advisor to novelists seeking publication advice and direction', Amy Brady, 'The Man Who Coined "Cli-Fi" Has Some Reading Suggestions for You', *Chicago Review of Books* (8 February 2017).

[7] Combined Universities in Cornwall, *Review 2011*, Redruth, 2012, p. 25, available at cuc.ac.uk/assets/uploads/ar2011.pdf.

[8] Adam Trexler and Adeline Johns-Putra, 'Climate Change in Literature and Literary Criticism', *WIREs Climate Change*, 2 (2011), 185–200. The rise of climate fiction is also demonstrated by the popularity of internet blogging about it, making climate novels and films a prime focus for discussion of the social function of literature, film and popular culture.

[9] Trexler, *Anthropocene Fictions: the Novel in a Time of Climate Change* (Charlottesville: University of Virginia Press, 2015), p. 7.

[10] See Axel Goodbody, 'Telling the Story of Climate Change: the German Novel in the Anthropocene', in Caroline Schaumann and Heather I. Sullivan (eds.), *German Ecocriticism in the Anthropocene* (New York: Palgrave-Macmillan, 2017), pp. 293–314; Goodbody, 'Frame Analysis and the Literature of Climate Change', in Timo Müller and Michael Sauter (eds.), *Literature, Ecology, Ethics: Recent Trends in Ecocriticism* (Heidelberg: Universitätsverlag Winter, 2012), pp. 15–33.

Discussions of the volume and impact of climate fiction invariably raise the issue of generic boundaries and definitions. The obvious definition of climate fiction is in terms of its thematic focus. Yet this turns out not to be straightforward, because although almost all climate fiction published since the 1970s is concerned with the contemporary discursive object known as climate change, holding too fast to this definition excludes novels that do not explicitly name climate change but might be read as addressing it. Most obvious in this regard is Cormac McCarthy's *The Road*, which never refers to global warming but has been hailed by some as an expression of and for 'the globally warmed generation'.[11] But climate change has also become part of the standard repertoire of ways in which human actions have irreparably damaged the global natural environment in the future storyworlds of a range of Anglophone, French, German, Spanish, Dutch, and Icelandic novels, even though it does not always carry a thematic focus or play a significant role in the plot.[12]

Moreover, a simple thematic focus on the relatively recent environmental phenomenon of anthropogenic climate change potentially disregards novels and short stories about climatic change in general. Although it is useful to identify the advent of public concern over global warming as a turning point in environmental fiction, one should not be too quick to discount the many earlier – and, one might say, prescient – representations of disastrous human interventions into global climatic conditions. Such early examples of science fiction as Jules Verne's novel *The Purchase of the North Pole* (1889) and Alexander Döblin's sprawling *Mountains Oceans Giants* (1924) imagine botched attempts to reconfigure the global climate in a bid to free natural resources.[13] In the 1950s and 1960s, a new wave of what Jim Clarke has called 'proto-climate-change' fiction emerged; this includes not just the dystopian

---

[11] Cormac McCarthy, *The Road* (London: Picador, 2006).

[12] For example, Margaret Atwood, *Oryx and Crake* (London: Bloomsbury, 2003), *The Year of the Flood* (London: Bloomsbury, 2009), *Maddaddam* (London: Bloomsbury, 2013); Sarah Hall, *The Carhullan Army* (London: Faber, 2007); Michel Houellebecq, *La possibilité d'une île* (Paris: Fayard, 2005), translated as *The Possibility of an Island*, trans. Gavin Bowd (London: Weidenfeld and Nicholson, 2005); Dirk Fleck, *GO! Die Ökodiktatur* (Hamburg: Rasch und Röhring, 2004); Rosa Montero, *El peso del corazón* (Madrid: Planeta, 2015), translated as *Weight of the Heart*, trans. Lilit Žekulin Thwaites (Seattle: AmazonCrossing, 2016); Peter Verhelst, *TongKat* (Amsterdam: Prometheus, 1999), translated as *Tonguecat*, trans. Sherry Marx (New York: Farrar, Straus and Giroux, 2003); Yrsa Sigurðardóttir, *Auðnin* (Reykjavik: Verröld, 2008), translated as *The Day is Dark*, trans. Philip Roughton (London: Hodder and Stoughton, 2011).

[13] Jules Verne, *The Purchase of the North Pole* (London: Sampson Low, 1890); Alexander Döblin, *Berge Meere und Giganten* (Berlin: S. Fischer, 1924). See also Chris Godwin's translation of an excerpt, Alexander Döblin, 'Mountains Oceans Giants', trans. Chris Godwin, *The Brooklyn Rail* (December 2016), available at http://intranslation.brooklynrail.org/german/mountains-oceans-giants.

novels of J. G. Ballard, which Clarke discusses, but the first full-length Japanese science fiction novel, Kōbō Abe's *Dai-Yon Kampyōki* (or *Inter Ice Age 4*), first serialised in 1958–9 and set in a near-future Japan threatened by melting polar ice caps.[14] Many of these early depictions of climatic change portray either deliberate (if misguided) efforts to change the climate for the better, or non-anthropogenic climate deterioration, and thus constitute what Trexler calls a 'considerable archive of climate change fiction', offering models for the depiction of climatic crisis.[15]

Yet, while it is useful to acknowledge this literary prehistory, a consideration of climate fiction in terms of the phenomenon we now think of as anthropogenic climate change helpfully narrows the subject down to fictional engagement with the discursive history of this phenomenon in particular. Among the earliest novels to take cognisance of the emerging phenomenon of global warming as a result of the increase in the carbon dioxide level in the atmosphere were Ursula LeGuin's short sci-fi novel, *The Lathe of Heaven* (1971), which is set in the climate-changed world of 2002 and explores the question of our responsibility as humans to fix the damage we have done to the planet, and Arthur Herzog's thriller, *Heat* (1977), which follows a heroic group of scientists as they battle the possibility of so-called 'runaway greenhouse'.[16] It was a decade before these were followed by the next significant work of climate fiction, *The Sea and Summer* (1987), written by the Australian critic and science fiction author George Turner, which presciently detailed the effects of the greenhouse effect, polar ice-melt, and rising sea levels in a near-future Melbourne.[17] Into the 1990s, climate fiction kept pace with developments in climate change awareness, namely, the growing scientific and public recognition of the phenomenon of global warming as the effect of greenhouse gases, through to increased political – particularly international – efforts to understand and address climate change, and on to the widespread collective anxiety around humanity's impact on its environment that marks the Anthropocene.[18] In the first decade of the twenty-first century, and in conjunction with high-profile efforts such as Al Gore's presidential campaign, defeat, and subsequent climate activism, the tension between

[14] Jim Clarke, 'Reading Climate Change in J. G. Ballard', *Critical Survey*, 25 (2013), 7–21; Kōbō Abe, *Inter Ice Age 4*, trans. E. Dale Saunders (New York: Perigee Trade, 1981).

[15] Trexler, *Anthropocene Fictions*, p. 8.

[16] Ursula K. LeGuin, *The Lathe of Heaven* (New York: Scribner, 2008, originally published in *Amazing Science Fiction Stories*, 44. 6–7, 1971); Arthur Herzog, *Heat* (New York: Simon and Schuster, 1977), p. 101.

[17] George Turner, *The Sea and Summer* (London: Faber, 1987).

[18] Trexler, *Anthropocene Fictions*, p. 9.

growing awareness about climate change and seeming inaction around it, occurring at the intersection of the realms of science, politics, and public perception, further invited imaginative narrative. In the light of the University of East Anglia Climatic Research Unit email controversy (dubbed 'Climategate' by journalists who believed they were exposing global warming as a conspiracy of climate scientists) and the failed Copenhagen conference in 2009, debates about our responsibility for maintaining an environment in which future generations can flourish have been conducted in a context of latent distrust of bodies such as the IPCC, disillusionment with international negotiations, and stubborn indifference to alarmist scenarios of the future and strident calls for tight state regulation of private consumption and the economy. Recent writing has thus tended to reflect a degree of detachment from catastrophist visions of the future, and to include characters and plots expressing both scepticism about the efficacy of well-meant, but naïve, direct-action eco-activism, and distrust of the political motives of proponents of radically progressive climate policies.

Representing Climate Change

Many novels about climate change frame it as a problem to be dealt with in some way (a motivator of plot or antagonist of character) or as a condition under which plot or character take shape (that is, as part of what we think of as setting). In terms of plot or character, for example, climate change occurs as, among other things, a complex political problem demanding just as complex solutions (Kim Stanley Robinson's 'Science in the Capital' trilogy (2004, 2005, 2007) or Matthew Glass's *Ultimatum* (2009)), a possibly insuperable challenge for a humanity hard-wired to pursue individual gain at the expense of others and the environment (Ian McEwan's *Solar* (2010)), or a cultural construct to be exploited for ulterior ends (Rock Brynner's *The Doomsday Report* (1998), Norman Spinrad's *Greenhouse Summer* (1999), or even Michael Crichton's *State of Fear* (2004)).[19] With regard to setting, climate change is often encountered – as we have already indicated – as one of a panoply of dystopian effects, as, for example, in

---

[19] Kim Stanley Robinson, *Forty Signs of Rain* (New York: Spectra, 2004), *Fifty Degrees Below* (New York: Spectra, 2005), *Sixty Days and Counting* (New York: Spectra, 2007); Matthew Glass, *Ultimatum* (London: Atlantic, 2009); Ian McEwan, *Solar* (London: Jonathan Cape, 2010); Rock Brynner, *The Doomsday Report: a Novel* (New York: William Morrow, 1998); Norman Spinrad, *Greenhouse Summer* (New York: St Martin's Press, 1999); Michael Crichton, *State of Fear* (New York: HarperCollins, 2004).

Margaret Atwood's Maddaddam novels (2003, 2009, 2013). Very broadly speaking, one could map these strategies of plot and character, on the one hand, and setting, on the other, on to two types of climate change novels: the first type tends to be set in a recognisable, realist present (or very near future) and the second in a futuristic climate-changed world, which one could characterise as apocalyptic, post-apocalyptic, or dystopian, depending on just how much this is premised on sudden disaster, its aftermath, or a prolonged state of decline. Sylvia Mayer makes a distinction along these lines between climate change novels that are set in the present and those set in the future, describing the former as 'anticipatory' and the latter as 'catastrophic'.[20] Moreover, as both Trexler and Astrid Bracke suggest, the settings of many futuristic climate change novels draw on existing generic traditions – not just apocalyptic ones, but flood stories, polar exploration narratives, and forms of pastoral and anti-pastoral, both rural and urban.[21]

Nonetheless, it is worth recognising an overlap between the realistic and the futuristic, for as many climate change novels (such as T. C. Boyle's *A Friend of the Earth* (2000), Jeanette Winterson's *The Stone Gods* (2007), and Nathaniel Rich's *Odds against Tomorrow* (2013)) show, quite often the intellectual or existential dimensions of climate change overlap with its futural, dystopian elements.[22] That is to say, what is crucial about both future worlds marked by climate catastrophe and everyday milieus touched by climate concerns is that they provide drama, and thereby engage readers' attention in a way which non-fiction cannot replicate without recourse to elements of fictionalisation and personification. Whether climate change is identifiable as a component of setting, plot, or character, it occurs in the climate change novel as something, whether individually or collectively, that affects psychological, emotional, physical, or political experience, and relates directly to readers' lives.

In representing climate change, however, fiction must grapple with the problem of the relative unrepresentability of the phenomenon. Climate change is, for want of a better word, invisible. It is, as Sheila Jasanoff notes,

---

[20] Sylvia Mayer, 'Explorations of the Controversially Real: Risk, the Climate Change Novel, and the Narrative of Anticipation', in Mayer and Alexa Weik von Mossner (eds.), *The Anticipation of Catastrophe: Environmental Risk in North American Literature and Culture* (Heidelberg: Universitätsverlag Winter, 2014), pp. 21–37.

[21] Trexler, *Anthropocene Fictions*, pp. 75–118; Astrid Bracke, *Climate Crisis and the Twenty-First-Century British Novel* (London: Bloomsbury, 2017), pp. 49–77, 105–31.

[22] T. C. Boyle, *A Friend of the Earth* (New York: Penguin, 2000); Jeanette Winterson, *The Stone Gods* (London: Hamish Hamilton, 2007); Nathaniel Rich, *Odds against Tomorrow* (New York: Farrar, Straus and Giroux, 2013).

'an impersonal, but naturalized, object of concern'.[23] Indeed, invisibility is the very condition of its existence as a 'scientific phenomenon', since, like climate itself, climate change has come about via 'techniques of aggregation and deletion, calculation and comparison that exhaust the capacities of even the most meticulously recorded communal memories'.[24] That is, while scientific discourse is the source of climate change knowledge, it is also an abstract way of 'knowing' about climate, the polar opposite of the experiential and personal mode of knowing that tends to be associated with literature. As Jasanoff puts it, quoting George Eliot, 'If the novelist's mission is to celebrate the specificity of "all ordinary human life", science's mission has been to transcend it.'[25] Herein, then, lies one of the key challenges to the climate change novelist – the existence of climate change outside immediate experience and its construction by the rational discourse of science. Put another way, climate change is always already mediated. It exists as an aggregate of scientific facts, garnered through a particular convention-laden process of observation, experimentation, statistical analysis, and peer review. And the scientific discourse thus shaped, which represents climate change in much day-to-day life, is often resistant to narrative drive and imaginative appeal.

Related to such difficulties in apprehending climate change is the question of its enormous scale, both spatial and temporal. After all, science tells us that climate change is not just a global environmental phenomenon but a global ecological one; that is, it is the effect of changes in the many components of a complexly, delicately interconnected and interactive climatic system. Moreover, its effects are of a temporal order of magnitude – extending over not just centuries but millennia – that lies much beyond even supposedly wide-angle human perspectives, such as the historical epoch or *longue durée*. Much recent philosophical attention has been paid to the challenge of scale to the representation of climate change, from Timothy Morton's assignment of climate change to the category of 'hyperobjects', or 'things that are massively distributed in time and space relative to humans', to Timothy Clark's diagnosis of 'Anthropocene disorder', a result of the 'demand to think of human life at much broader scales of space and time'.[26] The critical consensus has been that the extreme scale of climate change has all too often led writers and film-makers to opt

---

[23] Sheila Jasanoff, 'A New Climate for Society', *Theory Culture Society*, 27 (2010), 238.
[24] Ibid., 238.   [25] Ibid., 234.
[26] Timothy Morton, *Hyperobjects: Philosophy and Ecology after the End of the World* (Minneapolis: University of Minnesota Press, 2013), p. 1; Timothy Clark, *Ecocriticism on the Edge: the Anthropocene as a Threshold Concept* (London: Bloomsbury, 2015), pp. 139–55, 13.

for implausible tipping-point scenarios, engage in an almost comic tele-scoping of the time taken for climatic change to unfold, and construct plots in which the protagonists travel ceaselessly around the world, in an effort to relate the punctual and local experience of individuals to deep time and the global.

A third way in which climate change presents a profound challenge to the human dimensions of much art, particularly narrative art, is that it resists the sort of resolution which comes with normal plots and their expectation of closure. This brings into view a further trap into which the climate novelist can fall. The rendering of climate change as an object of experience rather than of science – that is, the transformation of the abstracted, longitudinal understanding of climate change into immediate and emotional response – might mean reinstating the anthropocentric arrogance that has caused climate crisis in the first place. This concern is at the heart of Clark's analysis. For Clark, the Anthropocene's scalar derangement means that we attempt to understand it by 'scale framing', that is, by reframing of the problem within a manageable scale.[27] Though scale framing is, to some extent, an unavoidable part of any human attempt to comprehend a complex problem, Clark argues that it leads, in the case of Anthropocene phenomena such as climate change, to a reductive percep-tion of it as a human problem, and thereby to a recommitment to ideas of human exceptionalism. For Clark, the novel and the kind of literary criticism it invites, with their investment in human-sized and human-shaped problems, are especially prone to this: 'the newly counter-intuitive demands on representation being made by issues such as climate change mean that . . . still-dominant conventions of plotting, characterization and setting in the novel need to be openly acknowledged as pervaded by anthropocentric delusion'.[28] In other words, the unrepresentability of climate change mounts not just a challenge for fiction but a dilemma. It would then be not just a question of how to represent climate change in experiential – that is, human – terms, as Jasanoff suggests, but a question of whether it is desirable to do so at all.

Literary Realism: Problems and Potential

Our discussion of the representation of climate change in fiction so far has suggested that there is little evidence of the challenge to anthropocentrism for which Clark calls. If we return to Mayer's categories of the anticipatory

---

[27] Clark, *Ecocriticism on the Edge*, pp. 71–96.   [28] Ibid., p. 187.

and catastrophic, we find that both depend on traditional, anthropocentric expectations. Climate fiction that invokes a recognisable present (or very near future), and explores the threat of climate change as an ethical, political, or economic dilemma for the individual, clearly depends on highly conventional and canonical novelistic techniques grounded in identification and empathy with characters. Meanwhile, futuristic settings, indebted as they are to the generic conventions of science fiction and its traditions of building alien, but nevertheless internally consistent, environments, invite readers to enter into new worlds and align themselves with the inhabitants.[29] Yet, rather than bemoaning the anthropocentricism of conventional realism, it is worth reflecting on the usefulness of such realist tendencies.

Climate thrillers, science fiction, disaster novels, crime and conspiracy novels, young adult novels of personal development, social satire, and even work in the genres of cyberpunk, horror, and fantasy, all embrace some elements of realism. But they tend to employ highly conventional literary strategies of world-building and character development, with one-dimensional characters (scientists, journalists, politicians, environmental activists), wooden dialogue, stock motifs, clichéd plotlines, and unquestioned gender stereotypes. As Trexler notes, Richard Kerridge has lamented the relative paucity of more ambitious realist writing on climate change, speculating that literary realism may be incapable of exploring the emotional complexity of our responses to the phenomenon because we are collectively avoiding its import.[30] Trexler himself has argued that realism cannot in any case imagine novel technological, organisational, and political approaches to climate change because of its commitment to the status quo.[31] Yet Trexler writes of a recent 'rise of realist fiction about the Anthropocene'.[32] He discusses three novels, by Jonathan Franzen, Barbara Kingsolver, and Robert Edric, as evidence of the emergence of a new body of realist fiction about the Anthropocene in the twenty-first century, suggesting that, in the hands of these authors at least, climate fiction can bring home to readers the reality of climate change. Relying on world-building, empathy, and identification, the climate change novel reflects a tension at the heart of the naming of the Anthropocene. After all, the great paradox of the Anthropocene is not simply that it exposes the

---

[29] See, for example, Darko Suvin, *Metamorphoses of Science Fiction: on the Poetics and History of a Literary Genre* (New Haven, CT: Yale University Press, 1979), p. 63; Tom Moylan, *Scraps of the Untainted Sky: Science Fiction, Utopia, Dystopia* (Boulder, CO: Westview, 2000), p. 7.

[30] Richard Kerridge, 'The Single Source', *Ecozon@*, 1 (2010), 159.

[31] Trexler, *Anthropocene Fictions*, pp. 224, 233, 236.   [32] Ibid., p. 233.

myth of human exceptionalism; it forces humans to consider how to transform that myth into some kind of ethical responsibility. In Trexler's words, the novel offers 'a medium to explain, predict, implore, and lament' the political tensions, ethical conundrums, and psychological dilemmas of climate change.[33]

Realist fiction possesses an authenticity and cogency deriving, on the one hand, from vivid observational detail and, on the other, from personalisation, dramatisation, and emotional focalisation. This enables it to contribute to climate discourse by exposing readers to the experiences of others, and distributing their empathy in ways which lead them to break down existing habits of thought and identify with new perspectives. In *Freedom* (2010), Franzen gives a nuanced portrait of the plight of American liberalism in the first decade of the twenty-first century, using the figure of the well-meaning but morose Walter Berglund as a way of exposing the personal motivations and latent misanthropic tendencies lurking behind the fixation on wilderness preservation in mainstream US environmentalism.[34] Against the background of a rich, detailed account of the political, economic, and social milieus of a range of characters, Berglund's attempts to address environmental issues are simultaneously justified and pathologised. Although the reader understands his desperate attempt to save a little-known bird (the cerulean warbler) from extinction, it is presented as an act of madness, doomed to failure.

Kingsolver's *Flight Behaviour* (2012) builds an equally complex portrait of contemporary America, again combining insights into society with acute observations on how individuals' situations dictate their feelings and worldviews.[35] Realist climate fiction is a medium through which the psychological mechanisms behind climate scepticism and inertia, seemingly irrational responses to climate change, can be better understood. In her study of climate change 'denial' in a small town in Norway, the social psychologist Kari Norgaard has shown that, while she encountered practically no outright disputation of global warming as a fact and general acceptance of scientific predictions of its long-term consequences, refusal to recognise any link with the subject's personal actions and any implications for their way of life was widespread.[36] She explains this 'denial' as a means of stabilising collective and individual identities in situations where they are threatened by climate change. *Flight Behaviour* offers valuable

[33] Ibid., p. 9.   [34] Jonathan Franzen, *Freedom* (New York: Farrar, Straus and Giroux, 2010).
[35] Barbara Kingsolver, *Flight Behaviour* (London: Faber, 2012).
[36] Kari Norgaard, *Living in Denial: Climate Change, Emotions, and Everyday Life* (Cambridge, MA: MIT Press, 2011).

insight into the reasons for the presence of climate scepticism in the United States, by showing how it has become part of the self-understanding and perception of many individuals in poor, marginalised rural communities in the southern states. Fiction that fosters understanding of such communities, without concealing the distortion in their perception of climate change as an obsession of the middle classes which threatens their freedom and prosperity, enables readers to see the world through the eyes of others and appreciate their situation. At the same time, it has the ability to school readers in recognition of common avoidance strategies, and model ways of dealing with them. As Trexler puts it, Kingsolver 'does the good work of literary realism, complicating the stereotypical certainty of scientists, and the ignorance of rural southerners', as well as the effectiveness of interventions by well-meaning activists. Such realism goes beyond the simple oppositional politics of earlier climate change novels, with their prophecies of doom, mediation of popular science, heroic rescue plotlines, calls for voluntarily reduced consumption, and advocacy of neoprimitivism. Trexler finishes his comments on the emergence of the realist climate novel with an account of Robert Edric's novel, *Salvage* (2010).[37] Reading this work as realist 'in its refusal of fanciful technologies or spectacular disaster', he argues that its plot successfully stages socioeconomic conflicts over climate change, showing through different characters how and why different groups interpret climate change in different ways, and thereby contributing to adaptation to it.[38]

Overall, Trexler proposes there has been a more general shift from novels portraying climate change as a final disaster which will either precipitate a collective human commitment to radical change or end in devastation, to realist writing, acknowledging that climate change has already been with us for some time, its effects are gradual and incremental, and they differ from one place to another.[39] He cites Robinson, Paolo Bacigalupi, and Saci Lloyd as further examples of authors describing a world characterised by 'new forms of political agency', in which 'insurance companies' join 'scientific organizations, government groups, international businesses, zoos, spiritual leaders, technology companies, refugees, homeless people, ... stay-at-home parents' and other social actors in realistic social panoramas.[40] Robinson, in particular, who continues to publish realist climate novels, tells the professional and personal stories of scientists and policy makers, and explores in meticulous detail the

[37] Robert Edric, *Salvage* (London: Doubleday, 2010).   [38] Trexler, *Anthropocene Fictions*, p. 229.
[39] Ibid., p. 233.   [40] Ibid., p. 236.

institutional and political processes that shape the pursuit of scientific knowledge.[41]

Recognising and addressing human responsibility for climate change does not automatically absolve climate change fiction from the charge of human exceptionalism, particularly if its moral and political insights, suggestions, and calls to action overestimate the reach of humans as moral agents or ignore the significance of the non-human as moral patients. As Trexler notes, while *Freedom* and *Flight Behaviour* make highly effective use of both social and psychological realism to demonstrate the many paradoxes of climate change and the complexity of the challenges it poses, they are less successful in acknowledging the agency of the non-human (and he argues that *Salvage,* with its combinations of human and non-human agency, does better in this respect).[42] We must turn to other novelists such as Winterson to find the potential realised not just to clarify human responsibility but to actively critique myths of human supremacy. *The Stone Gods* shows how human arrogance – expressed as techno-scientific over-reach – has destroyed not just one but several planetary biospheres. Yet, rather than advancing a solution based on mere human agency, the novel points to the need for an awareness of the contingency of human identity and the permeability of human–non-human boundaries.[43] Here, the use of familiar techniques of world-building and empathy does not necessarily translate into an affirmation of narrowly human experience. It is possible, in other words, for anthropocentric worlds and identities to be not just depicted and deployed in fiction, but deconstructed too.

Alternatives to Literary Realism

In his comprehensive study of the environment and American literature, *The Environmental Imagination*, Lawrence Buell states that realism relativises human control over nature by directing attention to the natural

---

[41] Most recently, Kim Stanley Robinson, *New York 2140* (New York: Orbit, 2017).

[42] Trexler, *Anthropocene Fictions*, pp. 224–33.

[43] Winterson, *The Stone Gods*; see also Nicole M. Merola, 'Materializing a Geotraumatic and Melancholy Anthropocene: Jeanette Winterson's *The Stone Gods*', *Minnesota Review*, 83 (2014), 122–32; Adeline Johns-Putra, 'The Unsustainable Aesthetics of Sustainability: the Sense of No Ending in Jeanette Winterson's *The Stone Gods*', in Johns-Putra, John Parham, and Louise Squire (eds.), *Literature and Sustainability: Text, Concept, and Culture* (Manchester University Press, 2017), pp. 177–94.

environment.[44] 'Disciplined extrospection', he writes, is 'an affirmation of environment over self, over appropriative homocentric desire'.[45] However, he does not claim that classical realism is superior to other modes of literary and artistic representation in this respect. Noting the greater capacity of the stylised image than the photograph in bird guides 'to put the reader or viewer in touch with the environment', he cautions that verbalisations 'are not replicas but equivalents of the world of objects', and pleads rather for a 'symbiosis of object responsiveness and imaginative shaping'.[46] Environmental representation has the 'power to invent, stylize, and dislocate while at the same time pursuing a decidedly referential project'.[47] Indeed, 'rendering the object world' is 'sometimes best achieved through what would seem to be outright fiction or distortion'.[48]

One form of literary stylisation which constitutes an alternative to mimetic realism in climate fiction is allegory. In McEwan's *Solar*, for instance, the protagonist, Michael Beard, serves as a modern everyman as well as a particular type of scientist and entrepreneur, and a transparently allegorical scene set in a boot room on a trip to the Arctic demonstrates the inability of the group to support each other and organise themselves harmoniously for the common goal of contributing to public awareness of the ecological crisis.[49] Symbolism is another such literary technique. In the post-apocalyptic future storyworld of Emmi Itäranta's *Memory of Water*, water has become a precious commodity which the military control access to and use to terrorise the population.[50] A young girl's spirited resistance as guardian of a secret spring becomes a tale of speaking truth to power, and a hymn to ritual, tradition, and writing as vehicles for the expression of ethical principles. Water is associated with life, ecological connectedness, sharing with others, and the memory of a truth which the authorities seek to suppress. At the same time, it symbolises the inevitability of the passing of time, change, and death. Comfort is found in the very impossibility of containing it, and the wider inability of humans to control nature: 'There are no man-made chains which will hold the water and the sky.'[51] One of many climate change novels depicting future water shortage and water wars (see, for instance, Jean-Marc Ligny's *Aqua^{TM}*, Lloyd's

[44] Lawrence Buell, *The Environmental Imagination: Thoreau, Nature Writing, and the Formation of American Culture* (Cambridge, MA: Harvard University Press, 1996), pp. 83–114.

[45] Ibid., p. 104.   [46] Ibid., pp. 97–8, 99.   [47] Ibid., p. 99.   [48] Ibid., p. 103.

[49] See Evi Zemanek, 'A Dirty Hero's Fight for Clean Energy: Satire, Allegory, and Risk Narrative in Ian McEwan's *Solar*', *Ecozon@*, 3 (2012), 51–60.

[50] Emmi Itäranta, *Memory of Water* (London: HarperVoyager, 2014).   [51] Ibid., p. 259.

Carbon Diaries 2015, and Bacigalupi's *Water Knife*[52]), this sci-fi teen novel is distinguished, on the one hand, by its sensuous evocation of the sight, sounds, smell, and taste of water, and, on the other, by its use of the element as a multidimensional symbol, enabling the issue of climate change to be overlaid with exploration of personal development and gender issues, and beyond these with reflection on the meaning of life and the ability of art to provide a permanence which human life does not afford.

In other novels, departures from the human focalisation and linear narrative structure traditionally associated with literary realism serve to undermine Cartesian exceptionalism, to expose what Clark refers to as 'the illusions of autonomous personhood', thus revealing 'the presence or intervention of the nonhuman in the human field of perception', and 'the finitude and thingness of the human itself'.[53] Some authors go beyond the traditional focus on human development and social questions by making nature itself the narrator. In Dale Pendell's novel *The Great Bay*, part of the action is narrated by the Californian landscape, a striking formal intervention, considering the relative rarity of prosopopeia (the representation of an abstract thing, or an absent or imagined person as speaking) in prose compared with poetry.[54] However, as Clark comments elsewhere, anthropomorphism 'can be a powerful tool for questioning the complacency of dominant human self-conceptions', and 'acquire provocative value as a way of doing justice to the agency of the non-human'.[55] Going further than the agential deconstructions of a novel such as Winterson's *The Stone Gods*, Ilija Trojanow's *EisTau* (2011), translated as *The Lamentations of Zeno* in 2016, makes use of anthropomorphism while calling explicitly for displacement of the human.[56] Castigating his contemporaries and lamenting their destruction of the natural environment, in particular through anthropogenic climate change, the geologist Zeno Hintermeier calls for humanity to be removed from its pedestal, to save both the planet and the human race. At the same time, he likens icebergs in the Antarctic and a glacier in the Alps (which he has played in as a child, and whose gradual melting he has spent his adult life studying) to vast

[52] Jean-Marc Ligny, *Aqua*^TM (Nantes: l'Atalante, 1993); Saci Lloyd, *Carbon Diaries 2015* (London: Hodder Children's Books, 2008); Paolo Bacigalupi, *The Water Knife* (London: Orbit, 2015).
[53] Clark, *Ecocriticism on the Edge*, p. 187.
[54] Dale Pendell, *The Great Bay: Chronicles of the Collapse* (Berkeley, CA: North Atlantic Books, 2010).
[55] Clark, *The Cambridge Introduction to Literature and the Environment* (Cambridge University Press, 2011), p. 192.
[56] Ilija Trojanow, *EisTau* (Munich: Deutscher Taschenbuch, 2011); Trojanow, *The Lamentations of Zeno*, trans. Philip Boehm (London Verso, 2016).

animals, portraying himself as the latter's lover.[57] The Indigenous Australian writer Alexis Wright portrays nature as animate, structuring her novel *The Swan Book* (2013) around myth, and cloaking her political messages about climate change and the treatment of her people in legend and dream symbols.[58] The novel, indeed, could be read as an application of 'magical realism' in critique of what Australian ecocritic Val Plumwood called the 'androcentric, eurocentric, and ethnocentric, as well as anthropocentric' tendencies of dominant Western cultures.[59]

In the conclusion of her study *Sense of Place, Sense of Planet*, Ursula Heise discusses further non-realist narrative structures as ways of representing climate change.[60] Displacing the dominant apocalyptic narrative by framing or satirising it, adopting the fragmented narrative techniques of high modernist fiction, and frustrating readers' expectations of unity and coherence of plot and character can all serve as formal correlatives to the limitations of human control over the natural environment. Pendell's *The Great Bay* and David Brin's *Earth* make use of such techniques.[61] Pendell juxtaposes poetic imagery with news-reporting-style writing, interviews with survivors, and maps documenting the geographic changes. The result is an assemblage of personal narratives, scientific and sociological reports, anthropological studies, folktales, and legends.[62] In *Earth*, Brin similarly develops a panoramic vision of world society in 2038 through a narrative montage that includes a large number of characters and episodes, and insets fragments of 'authentic' discourse (quotations from news announcements, letters, legal texts, books, and online newsgroup discussions) into the fictional story. But this is only one aspect of the

---

[57] See Goodbody, 'Melting Ice and the Paradoxes of Zeno: Didactic Impulses and Aesthetic Distanciation in German Climate Change Fiction', *Ecozon@*, 4 (2013), 92–102.

[58] Alexis Wright, *The Swan Book* (Artarmon, NSW, Australia: Giromondo, 2013).

[59] Val Plumwood, *Environmental Culture: the Ecological Crisis of Reason* (London: Routledge, 2002), p. 101; see also Adeline Johns-Putra, 'The Rest is Silence: Postmodern and Postcolonial Possibilities in Climate Change Fiction', *Studies in the Novel*, 50 (2018), 26–42.

[60] Ursula Heise, *Sense of Place and Sense of Planet: the Environmental Imagination of the Global* (Oxford University Press, 2008), pp. 205–10.

[61] David Brin, *Earth* (London: Orbit, 1990).

[62] Alexa Weik von Mossner sees this move as only partially successful in her discussion of the novel: 'Pendell responds to [the] representational challenge by compiling a wide variety of texts that zero in on individual humans at different points in the future rather than offering a continuous story or central character. In a way, that place is taken by the geographical region that is the focus of the narrative and gives the book its title. Timothy Morton has argued that because we live in the Anthropocene we can no longer understand history as exclusively human. Pendell's "Chronicle of the Collapse" suggests that the same is true for storytelling, offering readers the story of a nonhuman protagonist that changes slowly over time. The result is a highly fragmented narrative that is interesting for what it tries to achieve but at the same time remarkably unengaging'; see Alexa Weik von Mossner, 'Science Fiction and the Risks of the Anthropocene: Anticipated Transformations in Dale Pendell's *The Great Bay*', *Environmental Humanities*, 5 (2014), 203–16.

novel. As Heise explains, it possesses an unusually sophisticated architecture, in which the planet itself becomes the main character, as an electronic Gaia of sorts, created by a fusion of Earth with the internet: 'This allegorization of the planet as an epic persona contrasts with the high modernist fragmentation of the plot to create an image of a global environment that is both one and multiple, holistic and heterogenous.'[63]

One of the most radical alternatives to conventional narrative form and traditional realism is Max Frisch's *Man in the Holocene* (1980), which has recently attracted critical attention as a work of climate fiction.[64] (The novel pre-dates popular concern with climate change, but was informed by scientific research: Frisch refers to a recent 'retreat' of glaciers in the Alps and melting of polar ice caps, and imagines New York being flooded as a result of rising sea levels.) In this story of the last days of the 74-year-old Herr Geiser, who lives alone in a farmhouse in a remote valley in the Italian Swiss Alps, incessant rain and thunderstorms have caused a landslide, cutting the village off from the outside world. Geiser suffers from dementia, and his slide into memory loss and mental incoherence progresses alongside the erosion and seeming disintegration of the external world. There is in fact a three-way parallel between individual ageing and mental and corporeal vulnerability (Geiser also suffers a stroke), the economic decline of the village, which is becoming depopulated and is dependent on subsidies (serving as a symbol for a wider decline of civilisation), and natural decomposition and instability, which is further reflected in signs of the seasons being out of sync and the spread of chestnut tree cancer. What Geiser thinks, reads, and writes is reported through internal focalised narration. The notes and cuttings from reference works, with which he plasters the walls in an attempt to organise and record knowledge, form a collage of factual information interrupting the narrative. Reflections on the position of humanity in the context of geological time underline human marginality against the horizon of the Earth's history, and the emphasis on constant change suggests humankind will one day become extinct. Geiser's increasingly disjointed consciousness is conveyed through what can be thought of as a 'poetically' structured text, circling around key topics and returning to them periodically, while his

---

[63] Heise, *Sense of Place and Sense of Planet*, p. 83.

[64] Max Frisch, *Der Mensch erscheint im Holozän* (Berlin: Suhrkamp, 1979), translated as *Man in the Holocene*, trans. Geoffrey Skelton (San Diego: Harcourt Brace, 1980). See Gabriele Dürbeck, 'Climate Change Fiction and Ecothrillers in Contemporary German-Speaking Literature', in Dürbeck, Urte Stobbe, Hubert Zapf, and Evi Zemanek (eds.), *Ecological Thought in German Literature and Culture* (Lanham: Lexington, 2017), pp. 331–45; Bernard Malkmus, '"Man in the Anthropocene": Max Frisch's Environmental History', *PMLA*, 132 (2017), 71–85.

bodily and mental decline and the threat of physical isolation from the rest of humanity because of the weather serve as correlatives of the fate of humanity. As Gabriele Dürbeck points out, Frisch stops short of conceiving the mutual dependency of humans and nature implied by the conception of the Anthropocene.[65] However, there is an unmistakable ironic intention behind Frisch's juxtaposition, at the central point of the text, of an enyclopaedia entry confidently asserting the special status of humans with a passage explaining how human life could not have emerged without the propagating and fertilising properties of bird excrement, and surmising that we will be outlived as a species by birds and fish.

Climate fiction has become a significant literary phenomenon, addressing profound, complex issues, in a range of realist and non-realist forms, and going far beyond the genres of popular reading with which it started. It continues to evolve, with a small number of authors (Robinson and Bacigalupi, in particular) focusing their literary production on depicting climate change, and new titles coming out every year.[66] Literature's unique ability to capture complexity enables it to play a special role in the discursive construction of knowledge of climate, and its multiple interconnections with issues of class, race, and gender. As a medium for negotiating social values and a vehicle for reflection on how we want future society to be, climate fiction complements and informs political and scientific discourses. Reflecting on humankind's place in Earth history, the dilemmas of resource consumption and future conflicts over its distribution, population growth, and our responsibility for managing the planet, it contributes to the development of a new Anthropocene subjectivity, and makes a unique contribution to the evolving climate imaginary through its vividness, immediacy, and appeal to the emotions as well as the intellect, helping us to internalise what we merely know cognitively. Literary texts transport us to other worlds, giving readers access to unfamiliar environments, and they foster understanding of different experiences and imaginations by cueing us to inhabit new vantage points. Research at the interface of narratology and neurophysiology has shown that narratives have a greater impact than non-narrative modes of communication, because the experience which is simulated in reading them is a powerful means of forming attitudes. Climate fiction helps to define our perception of climate change, while drawing out its social and political, philosophical and ethical implications.

---

[65] Dürbeck, 'Climate Change Fiction', p. 335.
[66] Publications in 2017 included Maja Lunde, *The History of Bees* (London: Scribner, 2017); Robinson, *New York 2140*; Ashley Shelby, *South Pole Station* (London: Picador, 2017); David Williams, *When the English Fall* (Chapel Hill, NC: Algonquin, 2017).

CHAPTER 15

Climate and History in the Anthropocene: Realist Narrative and the Framing of Time

Adeline Johns-Putra

The context for this chapter is the demand from some for a new understanding of history, one fit for purpose in the age we now call the Anthropocene – specifically, one that responds to the identification of humans as geological agents capable of profound and long-term effects on the biosphere and on non-human species. I consider the effect on literature of a reframing of our temporal experience – as some historians and cultural theorists have recently asked us to – not according to the individual 'time frame of several years' or the historical 'time frame of perhaps a few decades', but at a scale on which 'a certain impersonal ecological dynamic start[s] to become visible'.[1] I speculate, in particular, on what a renovated sense of history might mean for literary realism, closely connected as it is to history and the depiction of the passing of time: what possibilities might a climatological understanding of time open up for realist narrative in the Anthropocene?

This chapter begins with an overview of recent historical and philosophical work into the need for a new understanding of history. Attending particularly to what Dipesh Chakrabarty has called 'species history', along with Chakrabarty's argument that the Anthropocene requires the imbrication of individual, epochal, and species histories, the chapter speculates on the multi-scalar logic – the need to 'zoom in' and 'zoom out' – that this would entail.[2] It then considers the implications of this scale-shifting for literary realism, adopting, via the work of Ian Baucom, Walter Benjamin's conceptualisation of history.[3] For Benjamin, history is more than the

---

[1] Timothy Clark, *Ecocriticism on the Edge: the Anthropocene as a Threshold Concept* (London: Bloomsbury, 2015), pp. 99–100.

[2] Dipesh Chakrabarty, 'The Climate of History: Four Theses', *Critical Inquiry*, 35.2 (2009), 212; Chakrabarty, 'Whose Anthropocene? A Response', *RCC Perspectives*, 2 (2016), 111.

[3] Ian Baucom, 'History 4°: Postcolonial Method and Anthropocene Time', *Cambridge Journal of Postcolonial Literary Inquiry*, 1 (2014), 123–42; Baucom, '"Moving Centers": Climate Change, Critical Method, and the Historical Novel', *Modern Language Quarterly*, 76 (2015), 137–57.

dialectical interplay between the universal and individual that historians assume it is; a true understanding of history demands an awareness that goes beyond a chronology of historical events, and beyond even an understanding of those events as a dialectic between the general and the particular. Benjamin argues for the recognition of the 'image' of history, a recognition occurring in a moment of 'arrest' in the flow of time and of thought.[4] The chapter thus ends by proposing a new Anthropocene realism operating on something like a Benjaminian principle of arrest.

Species: a New Sense of History

Chakrabarty's 2009 essay 'The Climate of History: Four Theses' quickly became an influential analysis of the need for the normally anthropocentric fields of knowledge designated as 'the humanities' to adopt a geologically and climatically attuned awareness of history.[5] Chakrabarty's proposals chime with those of scholars or writers of literature, such as Timothy Clark, Timothy Morton, and, most recently, novelist Amitav Ghosh.[6] The conventional subject of history, suggests Chakrabarty, is *human* history, as distinct from the scientific realm of natural – that is, non-human – history. This is most obvious in the idea of history as grand narrative, with freedom as its central preoccupation and the human as its subject (in so many senses of that word). However, even later modes of historicising – modes that offer a stratified, granular, uneven account of the human as labouring under the forces, pressures, and conflicts of imperialism, colonisation, capitalism, globalisation, and so on – repeat the error of insulating the human from non-human impacts. Chakrabarty finds even the post-colonial, subaltern view of history that he helped to establish to be wanting on this account. In place of – or, rather, in tandem with – all previous constructions of history as human, Chakrabarty ends his essay with a call for a new kind of historical thinking – a long view of humanity's effects on the meteorological and geological composition of the biosphere it inhabits. This is 'species thinking' or 'species history'.[7] Specifically, arguing for the 'cross-

---

[4] Walter Benjamin, 'Theses on the Philosophy of History', in Hannah Arendt (ed.), *Illuminations*, trans. Harry Zohn (New York: Schocken, 1969), pp. 255, 262.

[5] Chakrabarty, 'The Climate of History', 197–222.

[6] Clark, *Ecocriticism on the Edge*; Timothy Morton, *Hyperobjects: Philosophy and Ecology after the End of the World* (Minneapolis: University of Minnesota Press, 2013); Amitav Ghosh, *The Great Derangement: Climate Change and the Unthinkable* (University of Chicago Press, 2016).

[7] Chakrabarty, 'The Climate of History', 212–13.

hatching' of such an inter-species understanding of the human with the intra-species focus on the human that has hitherto characterised historical study, Chakrabarty asks that we 'mix together the immiscible chronologies of capital and species history'.[8]

Chakrabarty's proposal for a species history has generated much debate. One potent strand of criticism against Chakrabarty is the accusation that species history risks reinstating the essentialist narrative of humanity it seeks to displace. Andreas Malm and Alf Hornborg have warned that species thinking 'blatantly overlooks the realities of differentiated vulnerability on all scales of human society'.[9] Recently, several scholars, engaged in dialogue with Chakrabarty under the aegis of the Rachel Carson Center in Munich, have echoed Malm and Hornborg's critique.[10] Such concerns about the essentialist flavour of species thinking stem, I would argue, from a misapprehension of Chakrabarty's position. They are, however, useful for my purposes in this chapter because they have provoked Chakrabarty into clarifying just what species thinking might look like, a clarification directly pertinent to an understanding of historical representation and literary realism.

Scales: Zooming In and Out

It is important not to gloss over – although Malm and Hornborg do – Chakrabarty's emphasis on holding multiple, inter-, and intra-special conceptualisations of history together, that is, on mixing the seemingly immiscible. In his response to his Carson Center interlocutors and to Malm and Hornborg, Chakrabarty repeats his commitment to 'maintaining a postcolonial vigilance against "universals" that actually hide particular interests'.[11] In an important addition, he describes just what this act of simultaneous vision of the universal and particular means: it 'requires us to both zoom into the details of intra-human justice – otherwise we do not see the suffering of many humans – and to zoom out of that history, or else we do not see the suffering of other species and, in a manner of speaking, of the

---

[8] Ibid., 220.
[9] Andreas Malm and Alf Hornborg, 'The Geology of Mankind? A Critique of the Anthropocene Narrative', *Anthropocene Review*, 1 (2014), 66.
[10] Kathleen McAfee, 'The Politics of Nature in the Anthropocene', *RCC Perspectives*, 2 (2016), 67; Jessica Barnes, 'Rifts or Bridges? Ruptures and Continuities in Human–Environment Interactions', *RCC Perspectives*, 2 (2016), 43; Lisa Sideris, 'Anthropocene Convergences: a Report from the Field', *RCC Perspectives*, 2 (2016), 93.
[11] Chakrabarty, 'Whose Anthropocene?', 109; see also 'The Politics of Climate Change Is More Than the Politics of Capitalism', *Theory, Culture and Society*, 34 (2017), 25–37, based on this response.

planet'.[12] Where Chakrabarty's previous work tends to adopt the language of imbrication and blending, he here productively deploys the imagery of proportions and scales. This recalls, certainly, Morton's label of 'hyperobjects' – 'things that are massively distributed in time and space relative to humans' – for climate change and other symptoms of the Anthropocene.[13] It recalls even more readily Clark's analysis of the challenges facing the cultural and creative imagination in the Anthropocene. For Clark, the disparity between, on the one hand, the immediate and individualised concerns of the discourse of modern human life, including of conventional novelistic narrative, and, on the other hand, the extreme temporal and spatial dimensions of human impacts creates what he calls 'derangements of scale'.[14] This unsettling nature of the Anthropocene – so-called 'Anthropocene disorder' – is a result of 'scale effects'.[15] All this brings to mind, furthermore, Ghosh's diagnosis of the Anthropocene – inspired by Chakrabarty but also in language that is identical to Clark's – as an era 'that will come to be known as the time of the Great Derangement'.[16]

Perhaps most importantly, such scalar logic, explicitly describing the mixing of historical understandings as a zooming in and zooming out, gives to this new multi-conceptual view of history the suggestion of a method. Here, it is worth turning to Baucom's recent interventions into Chakrabarty's theses. Baucom rightly notes of Chakrabarty that his two modes of intra-special historical understanding – the universalist and the subaltern – 'are not fully incorporated within his new method' of species history.[17] Baucom purports to go further, not simply stating the importance of enfolding these three modes of historical thinking, but describing such enfolding as a matter of 'slip-knotting' these historical approaches 'into one more braided order of time'.[18] Thus, what Baucom, after Chakrabarty, labels History 1, History 2, and History 3, along with their respective constructs of the human, are held together in what Baucom proposes as 'History 4'.[19] These several understandings of history

---

[12] Chakrabarty, 'Whose Anthropocene?', 111; see also 'Politics of Climate Change', 33–4; 'The Human Significance of the Anthropocene', in Bruno Latour and Christophe Leclercq (eds.), *Reset Modernity!* (Cambridge: MIT Press, 2016), pp. 189–99.

[13] Morton, *Hyperobjects*, p. 1.

[14] Timothy Clark, 'Derangements of Scale', in Tom Cohen and Henry Sussman (eds.), *Telemorphosis: Essays in Critical Climate Change*, vol. 1 (Ann Arbor: Open Humanities Press, 2012), pp. 148–66.

[15] Clark, *Ecocriticism on the Edge*, pp. 139, 72.   [16] Ghosh, *The Great Derangement*, p. 11.

[17] Baucom, 'History 4°', 139.   [18] Ibid., 142.

[19] Baucom, 'Moving Centers', 141; see Chakrabarty, *Provincializing Europe: Postcolonial Thought and Historical Difference* (Princeton University Press, 2007), for identification of the first two as History 1 and History 2, p. 50.

'continue to relate nonsynchronously, undecidably, and supplementarily to one another', with History 4° naming 'a time of the human as coincidentally, contradictorially, and cosynchronously the bearer of Enlightenment rights, subaltern difference, and planetarily reshaping geophysicial force'.[20]

This in itself moves very little further from Chakrabarty's argument for mixing the immiscible. Baucom, building on Chakrabarty's image of 'zooming' between scales, explains the process by which History 4° holds Histories 1, 2, and 3 in tandem as one of movement between the general and the particular, between the collective and the individual. Specifically, according to Baucom, the method of understanding history that is History 4° is akin to Jean-Paul Sartre's conceptualisation of the human individual as a *'universal singular'*, that is, as defined simultaneously in universal terms by the epoch he inhabits and in singular terms by his own experiences: 'Summed up and for this reason universalized by his epoch, he in turn resumes it by reproducing himself in it as singularity ... he requires simultaneous examination from both ends.'[21] In the case of History 4°, it would seem that there occur multi-angled, rather than double-ended, shifts; it is, says Baucom, 'a relational totality', one that encapsulates 'the relation of times, scales, and ontologies to one another' in a 'correlational human and nonhuman totality'.[22]

Even more strikingly, for my purposes, Baucom notes that this conception of History 4° resembles, too, the argument made by Benjamin's 'Theses on the Philosophy of History' (1942), in Thesis XVII, in which Benjamin describes the historical materialist's thought process as a matter not merely of holding the scales of the individual or the epoch together but of a certain kind of recognition of the individual's place within the epoch and in history.[23] I would add to Baucom's analysis that, for Benjamin, the historical materialist does not simply seek to rationalise the 'crude and material things' of the past into a comprehensive, teleological lesson for the present (this being the domain of the mere historian, who mines the past for a 'universal history', or a heroic tale of human progress).[24] In Thesis XVII, Benjamin explains instead how the historical materialist

---

[20] Baucom, 'Moving Centers', 141.
[21] Jean-Paul Sartre, *The Family Idiot: Gustave Flaubert, 1821–1857*, trans. Carol Cosman, 5 vols. (University of Chicago Press, 1981–94), vol. 1, p. ix, original emphasis; see Baucom, 'Moving Centers', 142.
[22] Baucom, 'Moving Centers', 142–3.
[23] Benjamin, 'Theses', pp. 262–3; see Baucom, 'Moving Centers', 144.
[24] Benjamin, 'Theses', p. 262.

'recognizes ... a revolutionary chance in the fight for the oppressed past' and uses this to 'blast a specific era out of the homogenous course of history – blasting a specific life out of the era or a specific work out of the lifework'.[25] Here, according to Baucom, the 'crucial difference' between Sartre and Benjamin is that Benjamin's concept of history is capable of including species history, for Benjamin's final Thesis XVIII, in which he cites 'a modern biologist', reminds us that 'the paltry fifty millennia of *homo sapiens* constitute something like two seconds at the close of a twenty-four-hour day'.[26] For Baucom, this last thesis, with its recognition of human existence as 'a tiny margin' of 'organic life', and its realisation that 'organic life' in turn 'barely registers on the clock of the universe', renders Benjamin's philosophy of history an apt definition of History 4°, for it surely acknowledges the existence of species history.[27] I would add that the peculiar double-sidedness of its insights into humankind in the present is also of import: Benjamin considers that the present 'coincides exactly with the stature which the history of mankind has in the universe', but never clarifies whether he is belittling that stature or acknowledging its significance. What this implies is that, while humankind's status is a mere fraction of that of the universe, it is, nevertheless, the vantage point of humankind in the present that offers a view on history, whether that is human, species, or cosmological history.[28] Most of all, that vantage point reveals what Baucom, after Benjamin, calls the existence of 'messianic time, the theological margin of humanity's traffic with the nonhuman', which I would gloss as not the presumptuous totalising gesture of universal history but the ability to step outside the chronology of history itself, which is, crucially, different, and a point that will emerge later in this chapter.[29]

This emphasis on the moment of recognition is, I would argue, the most useful aspect of Benjamin's concept of history for a consideration of realism in the Anthropocene. For Benjamin, in the process of understanding history:

> Thinking involves not only the flow of thoughts, but their arrest [*Stillstellung*] as well. Where thinking suddenly stops in a configuration pregnant with tensions, it gives that configuration a shock, by which it crystallizes into a monad. A historical materialist approaches a historical

---

[25] Ibid., p. 263.   [26] Ibid., p. 264; see Baucom, 'Moving Centers', 144–5.
[27] Baucom, 'Moving Centers', 145.   [28] Benjamin, 'Theses', p. 264.
[29] Baucom, 'Moving Centers', 145.

ADELINE JOHNS-PUTRA

subject only where he encounters it as a monad. In this structure he
recognizes the sign of a Messianic cessation [*Stillstellung*] of happening . . .'[30]

Stillstellung, literally a position or posture of stillness, suggests the verb
stillstehen ('to come to a standstill') and thus connotes a pause or freeze in
a hitherto mechanical or taken-for-granted process.[31] That is, the switch
from one scale to another involves a moment of calm but also of tension
and suspense, since it is both temporary and precedes recognition. But why
might an arrest in thought be necessary to a conception of species history?
One might say that it is inevitable when there are such disparities in scale,
for one could also call it a derangement, born of an acute and dizzying
change in perspective, as do Clark and Ghosh.[32] Yet, what is more pertinent to the arrest of thought than simple disparities in scale (however
extreme they may be) is the profound epistemological difference between
those planes of what Benjamin calls life, era, and history. Baucom astutely
points out there is an important distinction between Histories 1 and 2, on
the one hand, and History 3, on the other, akin to the difference between
the individual and the epochal: 'although both History 1 and History 2 can
be experienced, the new geophysical form of "human collectivity" brought
about by the anthropocene [*sic*] escapes our capacity to "experience"'.[33]
What Baucom does not note, however, is that this produces shock. What
he calls History 4° is more than the 'slip-knotting' of previous versions of
history; it is what Benjamin would describe as a 'monad' of a larger whole,
and it is apprehended in a jolt of meta-experiential awareness.

The History of Realism/History and Realism

If, in the Anthropocene, our apprehension of history (like the insights that
come to Benjamin's historical materialist) happens in a moment of arrest,

---

[30] Benjamin, 'Theses', pp. 262–3.
[31] There has been some discussion amongst Benjamin scholars on the precise meaning of *Stillstellung*,
and debate about the accuracy of 'arrest' as a translation; Dennis Redmond, for example, has
suggested the phrase 'zero-hour' instead. See Walter Benjamin, *On the Concept of History*, trans.
Dennis Redmond (2001; Rome: Global Rights Books, 2016), n.p. Though the word is sometimes
considered to be a Benjaminian neologism, it is certainly in circulation amongst German speakers
today to suggest the removal of an individual, particularly in an emergency, to a position of quiet and
stillness. I thank Hannes Bergthaller for clarification on this point.
[32] Clark, 'Derangements of Scale', pp. 148–66; Ghosh, *The Great Derangement*, p. 11; see also Derek
Woods's suggestion that 'scale variance' means disavowing 'the nested dolls, Leibnizean ponds, and
worlds-in-a-grain-of-sand of Romantic scale aesthetics' and instead acknowledging 'disjunctures
and incommensurable differences among scales'; 'Scale Critique for the Anthropocene', *Minnesota
Review*, 83 (2014), 135.
[33] Baucom, 'History 4°', 139.

what kind of literary narrative could convey not just that history but that arrest? As I have already indicated, to some degree, literary realism is also historical realism. As Fredric Jameson reminds us, the great theorist of historical fiction, György Lukács, 'is not really interested in the historical novel at all, but rather in the novel as such, in realism and the realistic novel, which when it comes into its own will be profoundly historical'.[34] However, in an age of a meta-experiential awareness that is also, perforce, a meta-historical awareness, the realist novel becomes a very different thing from what it once was.

Jameson's history of the historical novel charts a series of shifts in which the genre is defined and inaugurated by a fascination with the relationship between the individual and epochal, before disintegrating, along with a concomitant disintegration of or disinvestment in epochal history, in favour of multiple, individualistic narratives; Jameson ends with a consideration of whether the realist novel might now be revived by an impulse back towards the collective. Jameson's analysis, in other words, maps surprisingly easily on to Chakrabarty's chronology of successive forms of historical consciousness from the totalising of the subject to its splintering and then to the need for a species history. Jameson begins with the historical novel as it is understood in Lukács's terms, as 'human-historical portrayal', that is, as the intertwining of the concerns, developments, and destinies of both a fictitious, complex individual and a historically accurate, social order.[35] As the historical novel evolves through the nineteenth century, it is sufficient that history is represented not by historically prominent individuals but by a pervading sense of society and its characters as shaping and shaped by history.[36] But what is also of interest here is that the essentialised historical subject that, for Lukács, is formulated by the historical novel pertains also to the view of history that Chakrabarty calls History 1. What is more, this recalls Sartre's definition of the subject as the universal singular – one who is simultaneously an individual possessed of consciousness and an index of his epoch (Sartre's universal singular is therefore not the radical model for History 4° that Baucom suggests it is, being as old as the historical novel as Lukács

---

[34] Fredric Jameson, *The Antinomies of Realism* (London: Verso, 2015), p. 264.

[35] Georg Lukács, *The Historical Novel*, trans. Hannah and Stanley Mitchell (London: Merlin Press, 1962), p. 53; for Lukács, of course, this finds its first and clearest expression in Walter Scott's Waverley novels, whose appeal rests on the 'interactions between individuals and the unity of social existence', p. 45; see also Jameson, *Antinomies*, pp. 263–72.

[36] The key figure in this turn is Honoré de Balzac, who, according to Lukács, 'passes from the portrayal of *past history* to the portrayal of the *present as history*', Lukács, *The Historical Novel*, p. 83, original emphasis; see Jameson, *Antinomies*, pp. 273–4.

described it). The perception of history as expressed by the individual in his epoch subsequently undergoes a 'process of critical reexamination, of historical intervention into the stereotypes of the past, of fresh historiographic revision', leading to the creation of multiple, individualised narratives that Jameson associates with the rise of modernism and postmodernism and that Chakrabarty perceives as the fracturing of subjecthood that inaugurates subaltern historiography.[37]

What, then, of the possibility of realism with the advent of the Anthropocene? In what is almost an aside, Jameson asserts that

> historicity today – an acute consciousness of what Heidegger would call the historicality of our historical situations – demands a temporal span far exceeding the biological limits of the individual human organism: so that the life of a single character . . . can scarcely accommodate it; nor even the meager variety of our own chronological experiences of a limited national time or place.[38]

This points, of course, to the new transformation to our historical consciousness that Chakrabarty argues is in order. What Jameson describes here is an immense leap of imagination beyond realist confines but also beyond mere modernist and postmodernist critiques of such. This requires not, *pace* Jameson, a Heideggerian historicality but a Benjaminian conceptualisation of history.

There is more to this than zooming into and out from, or even knotting together, the different scales of history. For one thing, it is worth recalling that shifts of scale are not new to the realist novel. The effect of realism in fiction is born of the difference between the immediate and the universal (that is, between the individual's consciousness, sensations, ideas, and experience, on the one hand, and a sense of larger – that is, national, historical, mythical – purpose, on the other), and has always depended on *movement* between the immediate and the universal. This, according to Jameson, is realism's antinomy of '*roman*' and '*récit*'.[39] *Roman* describes novelistic detail – not just the elements of scene or the sensations of characters, but the way these conjure up 'a present of consciousness and time' that is 'impersonal', 'eternal or existential'.[40] Meanwhile, récit, rather than the more usual term 'narrative', refers to the way in which the story is told, but evokes not merely plot but 'events completed, over and done with, events that have entered history once and for all'.[41] That the two exist in antinomy is because the effect of realism emerges – as usual with

[37] Jameson, *Antinomies*, p. 288.   [38] Ibid., pp. 301–2.   [39] Ibid., p. 16.   [40] Ibid., pp. 24–5.
[41] Ibid., p. 18.

a Jamesonian analysis – dialectically. The novel's capacity to express higher truths, its sense of deep social, political, or philosophical meaning, requires both the immediate sensations of character and setting, on the one hand, and an evocation of history, on the other.[42] Nonetheless, as I now argue, a literary realism that responds to species history – what one might call an Anthropocene realism – would not be simply antinomic in Jameson's sense.

Anthropocene Realism

Rather than emerging out of an interplay between two apparently contradictory scales, Anthropocene realism would produce a larger – perhaps only dimly perceived – awareness of that which exists beyond them. One could invoke the Hegelian dialectical process, with its suggestion of thesis, antithesis, and synthesis, to suggest that species realism requires metasynthesis. Yet, this too neatly connotes a supra-historical truth, which would in turn point to a hyper-essentialised subject position for the human as species. Similarly, Baucom's concern with a 'relational totality' risks emphasising the summation of these *as* totality. To do so is to fall foul of the kind of criticism levelled at Chakrabarty, that species history is essentialism at a further remove. Rightly speaking, the human as species is beyond essentialising because it is beyond envisioning and expressing. As Chakrabarty reminds us, species is a concept, and 'one never experiences being a concept'.[43] Rather than a totalising vision of humanity as species, Anthropocene realism instead would point to 'a figure of the universal that escapes our capacity to experience the world'.[44] In other words, it would afford what Benjamin calls an image.

Benjamin's concept of the image is of an awareness of the past that appears momentarily, lasting only as long as those in the present are able to grasp its meaning. As Benjamin states in Thesis V of the 'Theses on the Philosophy of History', 'The past can be seized only as an image which flashes up at the instant when it is recognized and is never seen again ... For every image of the past that is not recognized by the present as one of its own concerns threatens to disappear irretrievably'.[45] Hence, Chakrabarty's final suggestion

---

[42] The antinomic workings of the realist novel allow its readers to engage with a sense of climate (though not, it must be said, climate *change*). For useful discussions of the construction of climate via the dialectics of realism, see Jesse Oak Taylor, *The Sky of Our Manufacture: the London Fog in British Fiction from Dickens* (Charlottesville: University of Virginia Press, 2016); Jennifer Tanner, 'The Climate of Naturalism: Zola's Atmospheres', *L'esprit Créateur*, 57 (2017), 20–33, as well as Chapter 2 by Taylor and Chapter 11 by Justine Pizzo in this volume.
[43] Chakrabarty, 'The Climate of History', 220.   [44] Ibid., 222.   [45] Benjamin, 'Theses', p. 255.

in 'Four Theses' that species history is really 'a negative universal history' brings to mind the Benjaminian image, which, like a photographic negative, is recognisable by that which it is not.[46] But note too that Chakrabarty argues that the concept of species 'may indeed be the name of a placeholder for an emergent, new universal history of humans that flashes up in the moment of the danger that is climate change. But we can never understand this universal.'[47] Barbara Leckie elaborates, 'For Benjamin, as for Chakrabarty, this moment – whether it is captured as a flash, climate, or species – is a placeholder for what we cannot fully know. It gestures toward what cannot be realized in human expression.'[48] As an image, the concept of species acts in a placeholding capacity to a universalising truth about humanity because there can never be a straightforward expression of or synonym for such a truth; after all, for Benjamin, a 'universal history' – where this suggests a 'completed history' – is a chimera.[49]

While these insights emphasise the elusiveness and transience of species-historical awareness, what neither Chakrabarty nor Leckie unpack is the nature of this truth, especially its relationship to familiar sensations or ideas, and its effect on the reader or perceiver – that is, for my purposes, what Anthropocene realism might look like and how it might work. There are several important oppositions in Benjamin's view of history to consider here. Benjamin distinguishes the meta-historical, meta-experiential image from two further, different accounts of history, each as pernicious as the other. The one is a simple, workaday idea of history as chronological time; the other is an essentialising impulse, the need to reveal a triumphant, self-aggrandising history usually (though not always) designated as 'universal history'.[50] Notes Philippe Simay, 'the first, which is well known, postulates the existence of a historical evolution', while the second is 'a conception of time apparently close to Benjamin's – discontinuous, retrospective, entirely devoted to the present – which however swims the current, because it considers the past as a reserve of moments and things freely exploitable'.[51]

[46] Chakrabarty, 'The Climate of History', 222.
[47] Ibid., 221–2, evoking Benjamin's warning that 'To articulate the past historically . . . means to seize hold of a memory as it flashes up at a moment of danger', 'Theses', p. 255.
[48] Barbara Leckie, 'Sequence and Fragment, History and Thesis: Samuel Smiles's *Self-Help*, Social Change, and Climate Change', *Nineteenth-Century Contexts*, 38 (2016), 311.
[49] Benjamin, 'Theses', p. 262; see Dimitris Vardoulakis, 'The Subject of History: the Temporality of Parataxis in Benjamin's Historiography', in Andrew E. Benjamin (ed.), *Walter Benjamin and History* (London: Bloomsbury, 2005), p. 120.
[50] Benjamin, 'Theses', p. 262; see Vardoulakis, 'The Subject of History', pp. 119–21.
[51] Philippe Simay, 'Tradition as Injunction: Benjamin and the Critique of Historicisms', in Benjamin, *Walter Benjamin and History*, pp. 137–8.

Both these unsatisfactory forms of historicism depend on a principle of time as chronology. In contrast, as several Benjaminian commentators have shown, the event in which the image is recognised, described in Benjamin's unfinished *Arcades Project* (for which the 'Theses' served a notational function), is the same as that by which the 'configuration' of historical objects is crystallised into a greater truth in Thesis XVIII.[52] In the 'Theses', the image is apprehended in a moment of arrest, or more accurately, the stoppage of what had been taken for granted; in the *Arcades Project*, Benjamin describes the image as 'dialectics at a standstill'.[53] 'What these [other] different types of historicism have in common', notes Dimitris Vardoulakis, 'is a conception of time as continuous. Conversely, historical materialism has to blast apart the historical continuum. Time has to come to a standstill. The dialectical image activates the "emergency brakes" of history'.[54] The dialectic between universal and singular, the Lukácsian human-historical, which Jameson argues is conveyed in literary realism as the antinomy between récit and *roman*, is abruptly stalled.

There are two important corollaries of this for a consideration of Anthropocene realism. First, in order to produce the effect of shock as stoppage, such realism must nonetheless produce, beforehand, the traditional, familiar processes of what Baucom calls History 1 (or even 2), that is, the human-historical dimension of experience. Kate Marshall proposes something like this when she muses of the novel in the Anthropocene that it requires an internal critique of novelistic realism, which she calls, citing Ramón Saldívar, 'speculative realism'.[55] Marshall goes on to discuss novels that actively challenge realist norms, that 'enter the reflexive abyss of the Anthropocene' and that therefore 'can be understood as novels of a geological epoch that has become self-aware'.[56] It is the process of *becoming* that so matters here; going further than Marshall, I would suggest that the speculations of speculative realism arise not just from critiquing

---

[52] Vardoulakis, 'The Subject of History', p. 118; Simay, 'Tradition as Injunction', pp. 152–3.

[53] Walter Benjamin, 'Convolutes N [On the Theory of Knowledge, Theory of Progress]', in *The Arcades Project*, trans. Howard Eiland and Kevin McLaughlin (Cambridge, MA: Belknap Press, 1999), p. 463.

[54] Vardoulakis, 'The Subject of History', p. 123.

[55] Kate Marshall, 'What Are the Novels of the Anthropocene? American Fiction in Geological Time', *American Literary History*, 27.3 (2015), 530–1; Ramón Saldívar, 'The Second Elevation of the Novel: Race, Form, and the Postrace Aesthetic in Contemporary Narrative', *Narrative* 21.1 (2013), 3. The term deliberately recalls the speculative realism propounded by philosophers such as Ray Brassier, Graham Harman, and Quentin Meillassoux.

[56] Marshall, 'What Are the Novels of the Anthropocene?', 533–4.

realism but by being shocked – in the manner described by Benjamin – out of it. Realism, as Jameson suggests, engages the reader both in terms of affect (immersing her in mood or 'sense-data') and temporality (engrossing her in following a series of events).[57] One might think of this as an immersion in a fictional world, an investment in identifying and empathising with characters, or a desire to know what happens next; what is clear, in any case, is that the reader is engaged on a journey, a journey that might productively be brought to a grinding halt.

Simply disrupting the dialectical interplay of narrative chronology would be nothing new, however – there are plenty of examples of such interventions from the category of fiction we call postmodern. The second key to Anthropocene realism is the emergence of a new configuration from this arrest, one based on interpretation (though not the kind of egregious, totalising interpretation that for Benjamin would constitute universal history). Benjamin was insistent, even in the face of strong objections from Max Horkheimer, on the need for the historian (or, rightly, the historical materialist) to acknowledge the subjectivity of her position in the present, a point from which the historical object is blasted out of the course of history and a configuration of objects is thought into being as a monad.[58] For Benjamin's concept of history, unlike Heidegger's abstraction of history as historicity or historicality, acknowledges that the moment of meta-historical awareness is a particular interpretation at a particular time.[59] Where the Heideggerian phenomenologist unites past objects and present on the basis of their essences, the Benjaminian historian understands the object's historicised characteristics, what Benjamin calls its 'historical index', which situates it both in its moment in the past and in the moment in the present from which it is interpreted. In one of the 'convolutes' of the *Arcades Project*, in the passage in which he declares that 'image is dialectics at a standstill', Benjamin also writes:

> What distinguishes images from the 'essences' of phenomenology is their historical index. (Heidegger seeks in vain to rescue history for phenomenology abstractly through 'historicity'.) ... For the historical index of the

---

[57] Jameson introduces the Heideggerian term '*Stimmung*'; *Antinomies*, p. 38.
[58] Vardoulakis, 'The Subject of History', pp. 121–2; Howard Caygill, 'Walter Benjamin's Concept of Cultural History', in David S. Ferris (ed.), *The Cambridge Companion to Walter Benjamin* (Cambridge University Press, 2004), pp. 94–5.
[59] Simay, 'Tradition as Injunction', pp. 149–50; Werner Hamacher, '"Now": Walter Benjamin on Historical Time', in Benjamin, *Walter Benjamin and History*, pp. 57–8; David S. Ferris, 'Introduction: Aura, Resistance, and the Event of History', in Ferris (ed.), *Walter Benjamin: Theoretical Questions* (Stanford University Press, 1996), pp. 7–12.

images not only says that they belong to a particular time; it says above all that they attain to legibility only at a particular time . . . It is not that what is past casts its light on what is present, or what is present its light on what is past; rather, image is that wherein what has been comes together flash-like with the Now to form a constellation.[60]

The past has been made *legible* to the present – there occurs, writes Benjamin, an 'acceding "to legibility"'.[61] As Simay suggests, 'the fragments come into connection in order to form a constellation intelligible to the present, because no kind of continuity exists between them and it'.[62] Similarly, as Vardoulakis argues, Benjamin's concept of history presupposes not just 'interruption' but the existence of 'judgement'.[63]

What I am sketching here is the context for a literary realism that arrests the reader not just out of the flow of the Lukácsian human-historical but into an awareness of the myriad connections that constitute species history. This would require, too, that those connections speak to not merely intra-species relations but inter-species ones, situating the reader ecologically. Such realism thrusts its reader into an understanding of a connection with others in history, not with a sense of history as grand narrative (what Baucom calls Chakrabarty's History 1), nor with a keen eye for its sub-alterns (History 2). The first would be a gesture towards transcendence and the second would localise attention on to human relations, when what is being asked for is a glimpse of the evolutionary history that has led to the complex patterns of species co-habitation of the biosphere. In proposing such a formal intervention, my argument finds much sympathy with Leckie's proposal for a Benjaminian literary form: 'Importantly, like species, like climate, this flash cannot be represented in any way except through formal disjunctures. We cannot, in other words, "understand" it. Benjamin is concerned for us to . . . see a different history that only strikes unexpectedly and briefly, in sparks and flares and flashes.'[64] For Leckie, such a Benjaminian literary mode might be fragmentary; she describes being 'drawn to fragments for the way they make me think, the way two discordant ideas can collide and spark' and contemplates 'an espousal of formal fragmentation'.[65] Certainly, for Benjamin, montage constitutes a viable and important 'methodological procedure' rather than a mere 'stylistic device'.[66] Where I diverge from Leckie, however, is in reiterating Benjamin's insistence that the connections, collisions, and

---

[60] Benjamin, 'Convolutes N', pp. 462–3.   [61] Ibid., p. 462.

[62] Simay, 'Tradition as Injunction', p. 147.   [63] Vardoulakis, 'The Subject of History', pp. 132–4.

[64] Leckie, 'Sequence and Fragment', 311.   [65] Ibid., 312–13.

[66] Vardoulakis, 'The Subject of History', p. 123.

sparks of those fragments be made legible and intelligible, for the montage is also to be a monad.[67] That is to say, the arrest is not just an interruption, but a *critical* interruption, as the reader is called upon to see how certain events, figures, symbols, or even objects come together in a way that is both relevant to her Now and revelatory of something outside it.

A promising place to look for Anthropocene realism is David Mitchell's *Cloud Atlas* (2004), discussed by both Jameson and Baucom as a newly relevant form of historical novel. While a full summary and analysis of this novel are beyond the scope of this chapter, a few observations will point to its relevance. The novel contains six stories, each in a different temporal setting and told in a different genre, ranging from a mid-nineteenth-century journal set on a schooner in the South Pacific to twentieth-century tales of crime and comedy to futuristic dystopias. These read as separate vignettes, but are, upon closer inspection, connected. Formally, the narratives are nested within each other: they proceed chronologically, each ending mid-stream, and culminate in the sixth tale, after which the previous stories are resumed and resolved in reverse chronological order. Moreover, some narratives emerge, self-referentially, as cultural artefacts in others: for example, the first protagonist's journal, posthumously published, finds its way to a library where it is read by the second protagonist. Motifs recur, for a comet-shaped birthmark unites all the protagonists. Then, there are thematic resonances in the plots and their resolutions; these comprise a 'history of imprisonments', certainly, but, strikingly, one in which unlikely bonds of friendship emerge in struggles against entrenched power structures.[68] Finally, the whole narrative is glossed over with the sheen of transcendence, as the central narrative sees the protagonist of the narrative immediately preceding – an enslaved human clone named Sonmi-451 – emerge as a messianic figure with divine power; Sonmi's auguries allow the central narrative's protagonist, Zachry, to save himself and others from captivity.

For Baucom, the novel literally supplies Benjaminian images, focalised through characters at crucial moments; these images include the newly liberated Sonmi-451's sight of a petro-clouded sky and Zachry's vision of Sonmi in the clouds.[69] According to Baucom, Sonmi-451's vision registers all the Histories at once; she is read as 'inheriting an Enlightenment project of freedom and then refracting it through the biographical, the zoological, and the nomological orders and chronologies of her being'.[70] Meanwhile,

---

[67] Simay, 'Tradition as Injunction', 147.   [68] Jameson, *Antinomies*, p. 311.
[69] Baucom, 'Moving Centers', 148–52.   [70] Ibid., 149.

Zachry's vision unites these orders on a theological plane: he sees 'the plenitude, the possibility of a sacredly nonhuman order of actants, a distinctive, affective, vernacular way of being within the blasted totality of planetary catastrophe'.[71] But such a meta-historical and meta-experiential understanding – what Benjamin would have as a brief glimpse of that beyond conception – is here rendered suspiciously all-encompassing, essentialised, and, moreover, available to experience through the character of Sonmi-451/Sonmi. Indeed, she is, for Baucom, an advanced version of Lukács's historical protagonist, capturing the spirit of the age or, in this case, 'accumulating compound "historical" and "extrahistorical" spheres, layers, scales, ages, and forces'; in Baucom's reading, Sonmi simply repeats, rather than interrupts, the gestures of realism.[72]

For the moment of arrest and its image, then, one must look elsewhere. Jameson, I would argue, is closer to the mark when he suggests that *Cloud Atlas*'s claim to be 'a new form of historical novel' lies in its structure rather than its content, and that the thematic recurrences may well have been 'thrown out ... as a sop to the reader who still needs "meanings"'.[73] The text may be, as Jameson puts it, 'an elevator of a novel that stops briefly at a number of disparate floors on its way to the far distant future'; if so, the arrest in thought occurs not at the opening of the elevator doors on to each new vista, but with the realisation that one is in an elevator and, with it, the further realisation (as one rides between floors, as it were) of the impossibility of capturing all those views at once.[74] The keynote, then, is not the *Cloud Atlas Sextet* composed by one of the novel's protagonists, not just the title but the form of which is self-referential.[75] It is, instead, a passage buried in the novel as the thoughts of a minor character, who speculates on a '*model of time: an infinite matryoshka doll of painted moments, each "shell" (the present) encased inside a nest of "shells" (previous presents) I call the actual past but which we* perceive *as the virtual past. The doll of "now" likewise encases a nest of presents yet to be, which I call the actual future but which we* perceive *as the virtual future.*'[76] This realisation, almost straight from the pages of Benjamin, is of none other than the fallacy of mistaking actual pasts ('*previous presents*' impossible to recreate) for virtual pasts (events as they are narrated and exploited as universal history). This realisation is, in Benjamin's terms, an image of history.

---

[71] Ibid., 152.   [72] Ibid., 155.   [73] Jameson, *Antinomies*, pp. 305, 312.   [74] Ibid., p. 303.
[75] David Mitchell, *Cloud Atlas: a Novel* (New York: Random House, 2004), p. 445.
[76] Ibid., p. 393, original emphasis.

In constellation with the novel's form (its elevator ride), this flashes up for the reader the fallacy, in the Anthropocene, of making history via universal singulars.

The Anthropocene – specifically, its apprehension of the histories of human and non-human, inter- and intra-species dynamics at once – demands a different process of cognition from the dialectics of time and affect that have shaped realism till now. It asks that the train of history judder to a halt, that dialectics come to a standstill, that evocations of individuals in their epochs bear scrutiny. It invites a new realism that, first, would solicit the reader's attention, initially with conventional norms and practices, but eventually with a jolt out of convention and thus out of a unified sense of history; this new realism would, second, enable not just an awareness of other forms of history but a snapshot of the impossibly complex patterning of their co-existence.

CHAPTER 16

The Future in the Anthropocene: Extinction and the Imagination

Claire Colebrook

At first glance it would appear that two words that are much in critical vogue – 'extinction' and 'Anthropocene' – are both related to each other, with this interrelation having provided expansive challenges for the imagination. Something has happened to extinction as a concept as it enters the Anthropocene. No longer does the thought of ends generate a sense of what lies beyond the present. Apocalypse once swept away the contingency and meaninglessness of this world, for the sake of a higher end so brilliant and transcendent that its revelation could not be figured within the terms of this world. The timeline of extinction was also, even when twinned with Darwinian evolution, a way of thinking beyond the human world to a proliferation of lifeforms beyond the world as it is now. Darwin concludes *The Origin of Species* with extinction playing a role in a timeline of progressive grandeur; extinction is mentioned as part of a series of laws in which lesser makes way for greater:

> These laws, taken in the largest sense, being Growth with Reproduction; Inheritance which is almost implied by reproduction; Variability from the indirect and direct action of the external conditions of life, and from use and disuse; a Ratio of Increase so high as to lead to a Struggle for Life, and as a consequence to Natural Selection, entailing Divergence of Character and the Extinction of less-improved forms. Thus, from the war of nature, from famine and death, the most exalted object which we are capable of conceiving, namely, the production of the higher animals, directly follows. There is grandeur in this view of life, with its several powers, having been originally breathed by the Creator into a few forms or into one; and that, whilst this planet has gone cycling on according to the fixed law of gravity, from so simple a beginning endless forms most beautiful and most wonderful have been, and are being, evolved.[1]

---

[1] Charles Darwin, *On the Origin of Species: a Facsimile of the First Edition* (Cambridge, MA: Harvard University Press, 1964), p. 490.

263

Darwin does not specify that the 'higher animals' towards which extinction moves will be human. One possible implication of the Darwinian opening to geological time is that humans will be but one moment in a history of grandeur. The Anthropocene has, however, put paid to that notion of extinction as a means to 'exalted objects': the line and time of extinction is now a moment within the politics of human history. Certain types of humans (capitalist, imperialist, hyper-consuming, enslaving) will have altered the planet as a living system to the point that one can no longer imagine a procession of 'endless forms most beautiful and most wonderful'. Humans as a species have precipitated the extinctions of other species, accelerated the sixth mass extinction event, and started to imagine our own end *not* as a sweeping away of feeble humanity for the sake of a more wondrous world, but as the end of the only thing that we deem to be worthy of the notion of 'world': us. This is why today's 'end of the world' scenarios are post-apocalyptic; humans are pictured as living on after the end of Western liberal affluence. It is no wonder then that the West's preliminary mourning for its own end has been met with the charge that the 'end of the world' has already been imposed on those peoples the West harnessed, conquered, and erased for its own benefit.[2] The 'end of the world' has come to mean the end of 'our' way of life, while extinction has more often than not been figured as the loss of the forms of biodiversity that allowed us to survive. What has become unthinkable is a radical end that would not be an end for us, and that might generate another world. This contraction of the imaginative range of extinction has taken several forms over the past few centuries, but reaches fever pitch in the age of Anthropocene studies. We imagine the end of human existence as the end of the world rather than – as in traditional apocalyptic thought – a moment on its way to a transcendent and inhuman age of wonder. Even more myopically still, we imagine human existence as necessarily taking the forms of affluent urbanity that generated the changes to climate that eventually reached the level of geological transformation: the thought of humans as nomadic, as hunter-gatherers, as no longer attached to each other by way of global media has only expressed itself as a post-apocalyptic dystopia. Not only have Hollywood blockbusters conflated the end of major cities such as London and New York with the end of the world (*The Day After Tomorrow* (2004), *Cloverfield* (2008), *28 Days Later* (2002)) and not only have major cli-fi novelists repeated this tendency to see

[2] Déborah Danowski and Eduardo Viveiros de Castro, *The Ends of the World*, trans. Rodrigo Guimaraes Nunes (Cambridge: Polity Press, 2016).

New York (Kim Stanley Robinson) or London (Maggie Gee) as synec-
doches for humanity; when such 'worlds' end they depict a life without
urbanity, global media, and consumerism as the last of days.[3] This is given
its most extreme expression in Cormac McCarthy's *The Road* (2006),
where all wandering humans can hope to find in order to live on are the
past productions of modern capitalism (tins of food in abandoned houses)
or other humans.[4] In the world of *The Road* there are only humans; the
Earth offers no life. It is as though once the trappings of capitalist production have been erased there is no production at all. The end of capitalism is
the end of the world. One of the many ways to read *The Road* is not as
a prediction of the future, not as an admonitory dystopia, but as an allegory
of the present: without capitalist production there is no life at all. We are
already living as though the planet itself had no life, already able to make
our way in the world only by holding on to dreams of a lost world of care
and benevolence that has always been an alibi for the ways in which we
have looked on all life other than our own as the end of the world.

While there was something still apocalyptic in Darwin's notion that
extinction was an event in the process and progress of life's grandeur,
climate change discourse has identified the end of the human-friendly
world with the end of the world *per se*. Ends are no longer transcendent,
apocalyptic, or heroic: neither a divine pestilence nor an alien invasion will
place humanity in the position of triumphant survivors. The end is now of
our making, and its mode will be that of slow attrition. Far from imagining
how humanity might continue in other modes, the fear of planetary
destruction has generated a series of displacements. In Hollywood cinema
and novels, spectacular ends are given in the form of viral pandemics
(*World War Z* (2013), *Outbreak* (1995), *The Year of the Flood* (2009)),
nuclear catastrophes (*On the Beach* (1959), *Testament* (1983)), alien inva-
sions (*Oblivion* (2013)), species bifurcation (*Mad Max: Fury Road* (2015),
Elysium (2013)), zombie takeovers (*28 Days Later*), or acute climate events
(*The Day After Tomorrow*).[5] And what these disaster narratives yield is
rarely a thought of the end of *a world* – this particular world of capitalist
hyper-consumption – giving way to other viable forms. Rather, the end of

---

[3] *28 Days Later*, dir. Danny Boyle (Fox Searchlight, 2002); *The Day After Tomorrow*, dir. Roland
Emmerich (Twentieth Century Fox, 2004); *Cloverfield*, dir. Matt Reeves (Paramount, 2008).
[4] Cormac McCarthy, *The Road* (London: Picador, 2006).
[5] *World War Z*, dir. Marc Forster (Paramount, 2013); *Outbreak*, dir. Wolfgang Petersen (Warner Bros,
1995); Margaret Atwood, *The Year of the Flood* (London: Bloomsbury, 2009); *On the Beach*, dir.
Stanley Kramer (United Artists, 1959), *Testament*, dir. Lynne Littman (Paramount, 1983); *Oblivion*,
dir. Joseph Kosinski (Universal, 2013); *Mad Max: Fury Road*, dir. George Miller (Warner Bros., 2015);
Elysium, dir. Neill Blomkamp (TriStar, 2013).

Western urbanity reveals nothing other than the desire to save or mourn the very world of hyper-consumption that brought about its own end, and that of many others, precisely because no other form of existence counts as a world. The forms of life that capitalism, imperialism, colonisation, and slavery already extinguished – indigenous and nomadic – are the very forms that are deployed to depict the end of the world, but always in a perverse and fantasmatic form. I have already mentioned *The Road*, where being without the trappings of Western urbanity leaves one only with memories of a deluded past. Emily St John Mandel's novel *Station Eleven* (2014) depicts post-viral-apocalypse humans in a condition of wandering and gathering the last few items of capitalist mass production, all the while holding on to the ability to perform Shakespeare, as they journey to an abandoned airport that is now the museum of humanity.[6] In Hollywood blockbusters this motif of *the end of capitalism as the end of the world* is more insistent and more flagrant. The narrative force of climate disaster epics, such as *The Day After Tomorrow* or *Into the Storm* (2014), depicts 'us' against climate disaster.[7] There is no question that 'we' ought to survive. The same can be said for the combination 'end of world' of *Blade Runner 2049*, where runaway artificial intelligence and climate change enable the seizing of power by corporations, and where the miraculous figure of childbirth promises a humanity to come that will return us to the familial form destroyed by capitalism. The shape of the narrative of most post-apocalyptic cinema allows climate change to appear as an invasive foe, with 'we' the people emerging as triumphant. It is in this context that Naomi Klein will publish *This Changes Everything: Capitalism vs. the Climate*,[8] as though the destruction wrought on the planet could be set up as a war of good and evil, with humans ultimately winning by taking down corporations and once again distributing the spoils of the Earth fairly, and without destructive excess. By seeing climate change as a disaster that happens *to* us, by imagining the end of the world in heroic terms as a battle that we must win, it becomes impossible to think of extinction in anything but a narcissistic manner.

In this respect, the Anthropocene is the age of the post-apocalyptic: extinction cannot, must not, be a moment in which this mode of humanity gives way to what Darwin hinted at as a higher or exalted object. This humanity, so bound up with notions of higher forms and life as exaltation,

---

[6] Emily St John Mandel, *Station Eleven* (New York: Alfred A. Knopf, 2014).
[7] *Into the Storm*, dir. Steven Quale (Warner Bros, 2014).
[8] Naomi Klein, *This Changes Everything: Capitalism vs. the Climate* (New York: Simon and Schuster, 2014).

stops short of imagining its own end as apocalyptic. This humanity's end will not be apocalyptic; it will only yield images of what we must not become. The end of *this* humanity is deemed to be the end of the world. There is no conception of extinction as an inhuman event, either as a sense of the loss of life beyond what it means for humans and their recent attachment to biodiversity, or a sense of a certain mode of humanity reaching its end and giving way to other forms.

Reason and Anti-Apocalypse

By the time Darwin was writing *The Origin of Species* in 1876 there was already a liberal political tradition that was counselling against a 'superior tone', a mode of philosophising that Jacques Derrida identified as 'apocalyptic'.[9] Whereas philosophy once speculated (and often imagined itself speaking for) what lay beyond everyday knowledge and experience, philosophy from the Enlightenment onwards has been determined to purge thought of its spectres; all that we can know or speak about is what is given to us, as reasoning individuals. Modernity and liberalism have often been defined as modes of anti-foundational, constructivist, or post-metaphysical thought.[10] The exemplary figure here is Immanuel Kant, who will strive to eliminate any elevated reach of thought beyond this world, and any 'intimation' of the law beyond that of reason. Those later apocalyptic moments of Romanticism, where poets looked at this world but imagined a higher world of spirit, were at once violations of Kant's attempt to remove superior tonalities from philosophy at the same time as they continued the Kantian commitment to the world of what we know (such that an intimated beyond would from now on be contained within the human imagination):

> It is immediately apparent that intimation consists in a certain mysterious rhythm [*mystischer Takt*], a vaulting leap (*saito mortale*) beyond concepts into the unthinkable, a capacity to grasp what evades every concept, an expectation of secrets or, rather, a suspense-ridden tendering of secrets that is actually the mistuning of heads into exaltation [*Verstimmung der Köpfe zur Schwärmerei*]. For intimation is obscure preexpectation and contains the

---

[9] Jacques Derrida, 'Of an Apocalyptic Tone Recently Adopted in Philosophy', trans. John P. Leavey, in Peter Fenves (ed.), *Raising the Tone of Philosophy: Late Essays by Immanuel Kant, Transformative Critique by Jacques Derrida* (Baltimore: Johns Hopkins University Press, 1993), pp. 63–97.

[10] John Rawls, *A Theory of Justice*, rev. edn (Cambridge, MA: Harvard University Press, 1999); Jürgen Habermas, *Postmetaphysical Thinking: Philosophical Essays*, trans. William Mark Hohengarten (Cambridge, MA: MIT Press, 1994).

hope of a disclosure that is only possible in tasks of reason solved with concepts; if, therefore, those intimations are transcendent and can lead to no proper *cognition* of the object, they must necessarily promise a surrogate of cognition, supernatural communication (mystical illumination), which is then the death of all philosophy.[11]

This critique of thinking beyond this world as it is known was not simply (or even) secularism; it was, rather, a refusal to look to the end of this world, a refusal to set aside experience and humanity for the sake of what cannot yet be experienced. Kant, whose insistence on the transcendental nature of subjectivity will be crucial for liberalism, Romanticism, and twentieth-century theory, insisted that we cannot know any world other than that which is given through the temporal and spatial syntheses of the finite subject. It would follow, then, that without subjectivity there is no world. Any end to human reason would be the end of the world. Writing in this Kantian tradition, Derrida will contemplate what would happen were the entire archive to be erased in a nuclear war,[12] and later – in the same tradition – Bernard Stiegler will argue that it is only art and the archive that can grant us a future. The *only* plane of spirit is not an apocalyptic beyond, but a 'hypermatter': all the ways in which reading, hoping, and desiring give us a future.[13] For Kant, it is the height of philosophical irresponsibility to posit a world and truth beyond that of reason. Adopting a 'superior tone' – or judging this world from a higher world – can only occur if one makes an exception of oneself. The counter- or post-apocalyptic project of the Enlightenment requires that one assume every other human to be as rational as oneself, as a member of the 'kingdom of ends'.[14] There can be no radically different world; there is one world of human reason. In terms of ethics and politics, this would mean that any posited good or law could *not* appeal to a standard or truth beyond human reason: if a decision is lawful then it must be universalisable for any subject whatever. Nature and the world, too, must appear to us as in accord with our sense of causality, and with a sense of progress towards some form of rational cosmopolitanism. If something is true or legitimate, then it must be reasonable to assume that it would accord with any other reasoning subject. To adopt an apocalyptic

---

[11] Derrida, 'Of an Apocalyptic Tone', p. 61.

[12] Derrida, 'No Apocalypse, Not Now (Full Speed Ahead, Seven Missiles, Seven Missives)', trans. Catherine Porter and Philip Lewis, *Diacritics*, 14 (1984), 20–31.

[13] Bernard Stiegler, 'The Proletarianization of Sensibility', trans. Arne De Boever, *Boundary 2*, 44 (2017), 16.

[14] Immanuel Kant, *Groundwork of the Metaphysics of Morals*, trans. Mary J. Gregor and Jens Timmerman (Cambridge University Press, 2011).

tone or to appeal to a truth beyond this world betrays the dignity and purity of human reason. If there is to be an apocalypse it must, as M. H. Abrams once claimed with regard to revolution, shift from being a political event to an individual spiritual event.[15] One might think here of the way Giorgio Agamben (via Walter Benjamin and Ernst Bloch) recalls the notion that the world after redemption will be *this* exact world; what will have changed is that one no longer sees redemption as requiring another world:

> The Hassidim tell a story about the world to come that says everything there will be just as it is here. Just as our room is now, so it will be in the world to come; where our baby sleeps now, there too it will sleep in the other world. And the clothes we wear in this world, those too we will wear there. Everything will be as it is now, just a little different.[16]

Capitalism and the World without End: Counter-Apocalypse

Kant's definition of human reason as counter-apocalyptic is no minor philosophical event. It is made possible by a history of capital, empire, and increasingly private conditions of human existence, such that one can view the world as if it were a stability in accord with human reason, while viewing all other humans as similarly reasoning members of 'the kingdom of ends'. One can only imagine the world as in accord with human reason and the progress of globalism if what comes to be known as climate is rendered stable. The Western world increasingly experienced nature not as volatile and subject to change, but as harmonious and offering itself to appropriation. 'Nature' is effectively manufactured through art and agriculture as a balanced, cyclic, and expressive order in accord with a human history of increasing felicity and reason. Once the Enlightenment notion of rational cosmopolitanism becomes possible, and once humans become ends in themselves and not means, the threat to human existence (and apocalypse) becomes internalised: the only world is the human world, and the only apocalypse or end that we imagine is one in which we lose ourselves. Extinction and apocalypse become events of the subject. What we fear is not the catastrophic disturbance of the Earth as a living system, but losing ourselves: for Kant this would mean falling back into mysticism,

---

[15] M. H. Abrams, *Natural Supernaturalism: Tradition and Revolution in Romantic Literature* (New York: Norton, 1971).
[16] Giorgio Agamben, 'Halos', in *The Coming Community* (Minneapolis: University of Minnesota Press, 1993), p. 53.

while in the twenty-first century this self-extinction takes the form of us all living like slaves, the colonised, refugees, or indentured labourers (*Elysium, Oblivion*). It is not surprising that Kant and the writers of his time used the metaphor of slavery (and sometimes annihilation) to describe various forms of self-loss. William Blake's conception of 'mind-forg'd manacles', along with his apocalyptic demand for self-annihilation, was articulated in the urban milieu of late eighteenth-century abolitionist London. Just as the West was beginning to recognise the horrors of the slavery it had imposed on others, it began to internalise slavery and self-destruction as conditions of its own spiritual condition. Annihilation, slavery, and imprisonment were psychological, rather than global, predicaments. The greatest prison one can imagine is one's own self-restriction, and the only apocalypse worth the name is one of self-overcoming:

> I will go down to self annihilation and eternal death,
> Lest the Last Judgment come & find me unannihilate
> And I be siez'd & giv'n into the hands of my own Selfhood . . .
> I in my Selfhood am that Satan: I am that Evil One!
> He is my Spectre! in my obedience to loose him from my Hells
> To claim the Hells, my Furnaces, I go to Eternal Death.[17]

For Blake and the writers around him enslavement, apocalypse, and annihilation became ways of thinking about the self's failure to live up to its proper potentiality. In the twenty-first century, this motif of human self-annihilation becomes intertwined with planetary destruction. It is because we can so easily enslave and destroy ourselves that we have also failed to attend to the planet. 'We' are now at risk of becoming inhuman, and the end of the world becomes ever more frequently imagined as the end of the 'favorable conditions' that allowed us to be rational cosmopolitans. This tendency to imagine ourselves as reduced to the inhuman conditions that many in the world already experience is bound up with the increasingly intense sense of the alteration of the Earth as a living system. Philosophy, from Kant onwards, would warn against reason's capacity to fall back into animality; now that Earth's resources are dwindling, and climate change is threatening the Enlightenment image of harmonious nature, it seems that we may all be reduced to conditions that would preclude liberal modernity's assumptions regarding what counts as a normative human life and world. Despite the heroic and Manichaean nature of much cli-fi and post-apocalyptic fiction and cinema, climate change and the threat of extinction

---

[17] William Blake, *Milton: a Poem*, in *The Complete Poetry and Prose of William Blake*, ed. David V. Erdman (New York: Anchor, 1988), plate 14, ll. 24–6, 32–4.

are not events that are external or accidental to the history of reason. The very processes that enabled the subject capable of viewing the natural world as a reflection of his own interests are the same that have rendered the planet hostile to liberal individualism. The very form of the novel (of an individual who makes his way in the world, triumphing over adversity) was bound up with the spirit of capitalism, where the world is so much standing reserve and opportunity. It is that same ongoing spirit of individualism, progress, and fortune that expresses itself in much cli-fi and apocalyptic culture – the heroism of *Blade Runner 2049* in film, or the focus on intersecting individual projects and lives in Kim Stanley Robinson's *New York 2140* (2017).[18]

There have been many dates suggested for the starting point of the Anthropocene, ranging from the beginning of intensive agriculture to Hiroshima. What is worth noting in terms of the imagination is that these suggested thresholds mark the point at which the very industries and technologies that enable certain humans to flourish and conquer the planet are also world-destructive. From Romanticism's sense that nature is a kindred spirit, to ecopoetry's insistence that we are at one with this world, and on to the blockbuster imagination where 'we' save ourselves and the planet, there is an insistence on a proper humanity that will redeem all life. Yet the same literary and philosophical tradition is haunted by the possibility that humans will not save themselves and will be seduced and reified by the technologies that are also destroying the planet. Mary Shelley's *Frankenstein* (1818) is perhaps the clearest expression of the ways in which the wondrous enchantment with life ultimately generates its monstrous other.[19] For Kant, it is always possible that we do not act upon reason and imagine ourselves and others as mere parts of the world, as ends not as means. It is this notion of humans failing to be properly human that becomes intensified as humans become aware of their possible actual extinction. This is why perhaps the most important twenty-first-century novel about the end of human life as we know it, McCarthy's *The Road*, followed a series of novels by the same writer, all testifying to a sense of human existence as bound up with its own non-being.

Rather than see the literary and cinematic imagination as having been transformed by climate change to become post-apocalyptic – becoming aware that there is only this Earth and no 'planet B' – climate change has

---

[18] *Blade Runner 2049*, dir. Dennis Villeneuve (Sony, 2017); Kim Stanley Robinson, *New York 2140* (New York: Orbit, 2017).

[19] Mary Shelley, *Frankenstein, or The Modern Prometheus*, ed. M. K. Joseph (Oxford University Press, 2008).

become one more way to think about the ways in which human life has an essential relation to self-extinction. The mode of life that yields progress requires and intensifies a blindness to the very nature upon which it relies, and that progressive blindness ultimately deadens and destroys the subject. Cinematically, this dialectical destruction is dealt with by dividing human-ity in two: the plunderers versus those who will save the planet. *Interstellar* (2014) pits the frontier spirit of a retired astronaut against the corporate managerialism that would reduce the world to mere survival. In novels, climate change becomes an opportunity to intensify the gender or class dynamics that already divide the planet: one can think here of the sexual politics of Gee's *Ice People* (1998) or the Marxist finance analytics of Robinson's *New York 2140*.[20]

Climate Change as Symptom of Modern Self-Annihilation

In Mary Shelley's *Frankenstein*, Victor's captivation with the majesty and power of nature drives him to create the very life that he will then fear in its power to replicate, proliferate, and possibly overtake the very human species that was its masterful origin. One way to read *Frankenstein* is as a critical diagnosis of Romanticist and Enlightenment narcissism: our seduction with nature is always a love affair with *our* nature, and an inability to countenance any life other than our own as populating this planet. Nature has the power to inspire majesty and due reverence, but that very same affective force will also generate various forms of tyranny. This ongoing concern with self-annihilation is not simply a Romantic motif; it will continue into modernism and twentieth-century philosophy, and will be intensified with the growing awareness of anthropogenic climate change. The nature that we ought to view with reverence, allowing us to think of ourselves as similarly divine and blessed with spirit, can appear as an object world to be mastered – and that very drive for mastery will enslave us all. William Blake's apocalyptic prophecies view redemption *not* as the annihilation of this world for another supra-human realm of exis-tence, but as a renewed and non-fallen perception that will see this world in all its glory; and yet Blake will also see each apocalyptic renewal as tending towards repeated collapse. Blake's apocalyptic prophecies are exemplary in their description of a self at war with itself, a self struggling to give itself form, and yet at the same time becoming tyrannised by those portions of itself that have taken on form:

[20] Maggie Gee, *The Ice People* (1998; London: Telegram, 2008); Robinson, *New York 2140*.

... Silent Milton stood before
The darkend Urizen; as the sculptor silent stands before
His forming image; he walks round it patient labouring.
Thus Milton stood forming bright Urizen; while his Mortal part
Sat frozen in the rock of Horeb: and his Redeemed portion,
Thus form'd the Clay of Urizen; but within that portion
His real Human walkd above in power and majesty
Tho darkend; and the Seven Angels of the Presence attended him.[21]

The revolutionary forces that free us from tyranny are the same that will lure us again into self-enslavement. The canonised high modernists will use the image of hell to describe the life in the city that has lost all relation to spirit and nature. Texts such as T. S. Eliot's *The Waste Land* (1922), James Joyce's *Dubliners* (1914), and Ezra Pound's *Cantos* (1925) anticipate twenty-first-century post-apocalyptic narratives: humans become the walking dead in their own world, not because of any external accident but because the very relation to nature that generated wonder tipped over into blind mastery and reification. Theodor Adorno, whose aesthetic theory emerged from the modernist experience of alienation, saw the trajectory of Western art and reason as one in which the terrifying force of nature was increasingly subjected to the rigid order of reason, ultimately generating the damaged life that could only be expressed negatively in an art that would intimate the suffering of nature.[22]

Extinction and apocalypse were internalised in modernity, with the experience of climate change and other existential threats to the species repeatedly being narrated as just one of the ways in which the human relation to life is essentially destructive. If one rejects the higher world, and if there is nothing but this world given through human reason and imagination, then the corruption of the imagination will amount to the end of the world. Those very poets who saw nature itself as divine – from British Romanticism, to American transcendentalism and beyond – also recognised that human life could destroy itself by way of its complex relation to nature. Percy Bysshe Shelley's 'The Triumph of Life' (1822) watches a pageant of those whose intellects, spirits, and imaginations have been captivated by this world to the point that they become nothing more than the walking dead; the very life that might have allowed for imaginative expansion also has the power to seduce and captivate, allowing us to annihilate the very soul that makes us human. The capacity to master and enslave the world is bound up

---

[21] Blake, *Milton: a Poem*, plate 20, 8–16.
[22] Theodor W. Adorno, *Aesthetic Theory*, trans. Robert Hullot Kentnor (London: Athlone, 1997).

with the tendency towards self-enslavement – and both these tendencies are bound up with a blindness to nature:

> And weary with vain toil & faint for thirst
> Heard not the fountains whose melodious dew
>
> Out of their mossy cells forever burst
> Nor felt the breeze which from the forest told
> Of grassy paths, & wood lawns interspersed
>
> With overarching elms & caverns cold,
> And violet banks where sweet dreams brood, but they
> Pursued their serious folly as of old ...
>
> ... like clouds upon the thunder blast
>
> The million with fierce song and maniac dance
> Raging around; such seemed the jubilee
> As when to greet some conqueror's advance
>
> Imperial Rome poured forth her living sea
> From senatehouse & prison & theatre
> When Freedom left those who upon the free
>
> Had bound a yoke which soon they stooped to bear.[23]

Cli-fi and Human Self-Extinction

Post-apocalyptic literature, and cli-fi, should be read within this broader context of human self-annihilation. Climate change – in post-apocalyptic fiction and cinema – appears as yet one more example of the capacity for human existence to take the very means of progress and flourishing and allow that same force to become a path to annihilation. Today when various popular science theories explain why we have evolved not to take climate change seriously,[24] or when media theorists declare that twenty-first-century attention spans cannot assimilate the complexities of climate change,[25] they continue a tradition going back (at least) to Kant, where the human relation to existence is at once creative and destructive. We are, according to Stiegler, beings whose very capacity to become individuated is bound up with dis-individuation and

---

[23] Percy Bysshe Shelley, 'The Triumph of Life', in *Shelley's Poetry and Prose*, ed. Donald H. Reiman and Neil Fraistat, 2nd edn (New York: Norton, 2002), pp. 485–6.
[24] George Marshall, *Don't Even Think about It: Why Our Brains Are Wired to Ignore Climate Change* (London: Bloomsbury, 2014); Robert Gifford, '33 Reasons Why We Can't Think Clearly about Climate Change', *New Scientist* (8 July 2015).
[25] Robin Hicks, 'Why is the Media Under-reporting Climate Change?' *Eco-business* (7 March 2017).

the annihilation of the human future.[26] It is not simply climate change and resource depletion that threaten human existence, but social media, smart devices, Google, and the commodification of attention. These two types of threats (external and internal) are intertwined: it is the humanity of hyper-consumption, spectacle, and global reach who have altered the planet, and it is the culture of distraction and privacy that precludes any imaginary plane beyond that of this self-englobed species. It is for this reason that Stiegler sees the geological event of the Anthropocene, climate change, and extinction as a symptom of a much broader malaise: the human being's relation to life is 'pharmacological'. The very technologies that enable us to read, think, flourish, and desire also bear the capacity for destruction.[27]

While there is a growing body of climate change fiction, and a similarly rich and expansive tradition of ecopoetics, it is worth noting a less obvious expression of the increasing sense of human extinction in forms of fiction and poetry focused on self-annihilation through the combined damage done to the planet and to attention. Adrienne Rich's *An Atlas of the Difficult World* (1991) is, in part, a text about how one continues to read in a world that is unreadable, and how one witnesses damage in a milieu oriented towards distraction, evasion, and untranslatability. Rich's entire volume describes a world of waste and indifference, a wrecked landscape combined with an insistent not-knowing:

> Here is a map of our country:
> here is the Sea of Indifference, glazed with salt
> This is the haunted river flowing from brow to groin
> we dare not taste its water
> This is the desert where missiles are planted like corms
> This is the breadbasket of foreclosed farms
> This is the birthplace of the rockabilly boy
> This is the cemetery of the poor
> who died for democracy   This is a battlefield
> from a nineteenth-century war   the shrine is famous
> This is the sea-town of myth and story   when the fishing fleets
> went bankrupt   here is where the jobs were   on the pier
> processing frozen fishsticks   hourly wages and no shares
> These are other battlefields   Centralia   Detroit
> here are the forests primeval   the copper   the silver lodes
> These are the suburbs of acquiescence[28]

[26] Bernard Stiegler, 'Power, Powerlessness, Thinking, and Future', *Los Angeles Review of Books* (18 October 2015).

[27] Stiegler, *Neganthropocene*, trans. Daniel Ross (Ann Arbor, MI: Open Humanities Press, 2018).

[28] Adrienne Rich, *An Atlas of the Difficult World: Poems 1988–1991* (New York: Norton, 1991), p. 12.

Claudia Rankine's *Citizen: an American Lyric* (2014) is also not immediately concerned with the climate or humans as a species coming to an end, but it does have a counter-apocalyptic tone. This lyric is a narration of constant and irredeemable damage, of living a life that is undone *not* because of any predicament of 'the human' and not because of a general or universal dialectic between human power over nature and the reification of that power. Rather, the voice of *Citizen* is clear in its diagnosis that 'the world is wrong' and refuses the forms of nostalgia that would see the present state of depletion as a loss of what we properly (ideally) once were:

> The world is wrong. You can't put the past behind you. It's buried in you; it's turned your flesh into its own cupboard. Not everything remembered is useful but it all comes from the world to be stored in you. Who did what to whom on which day? Who said that? She said what? What did he just do? Did she really just say that? He said what? What did she do? Did I hear what I think I heard? Did that just come out of my mouth, his mouth, your mouth? Do you remember when you sighed?
> Memory is a tough place. You were there. If this is not the truth, it is also not a lie. There are benefits to being without nostalgia. Certainly nostalgia and being without nostalgia relieve the past. Sitting here, there are no memories to remember, just the ball going back and forth. Shored up by this external net, the problem is not one of a lack of memories; the problem is simply a lack, a lack before, during, and after.[29]

I draw attention to Rich and Rankine here precisely because they are poets of difficult, damaged, or 'wrong' worlds. One way to think about climate change and literature is to look at 'our' growing awareness of our increased fragility, and to see this expressed in cli-fi and in post-apocalyptic obsession with ends. 'We' are becoming aware of our possible extinction, concerned that there may be a world without us – which would amount to no world at all. Another way to think about this recent concern with ends is to look to literary experiences of what it is like to be already without a world, to have already experienced social death. This might take the form of Rich's *Atlas* where urban life is already a form of worldlessness, an inability to find connection or sense. More acutely, one might look to traditions of writing where non-being and the experience of possible annihilation are built into daily life. Rankine's 'wrong' world provides a way to think about the present beyond the post-apocalyptic imperative that this world is our only world and that it is because 'we' are threatened

[29] Claudia Rankine, *Citizen: an American Lyric* (Minneapolis: Graywolf, 2014), pp. 63–4.

that we must survive. Many peoples have lived with the experience of near-extinction well before the vogue of the post-apocalyptic, and many writers – from Frantz Fanon onwards – have realised that the 'end of the world' might offer them a chance for existence.[30]

One of the dominant features of post-apocalyptic writing, from Kant to the present, is to allow the figure of a soon-to-be-extinguished humanity to generate the imperative that 'we' ought to be saved. This can take a pop culture form: aliens threaten to annihilate the human species, and so a heroic battle must allow 'our' end to be averted. We must survive. It can also take more elevated philosophical and theoretical forms, where humanity is defined in a very narrow and normative sense as the man of reason, and what must be saved at all costs is *this* form of intelligence.[31] The twenty-first-century motif of the post-apocalyptic, where urban affluent humans face the conditions of exposure that many humans have experienced for centuries (often for the sake of that same civil and urbane polity) generates the illusion that there is such a thing as 'man': this being threatened here and now, who is unified and constituted by the threat of possible non-being. The post-apocalyptic imperative is: 'we are threatened with extinction, and therefore we *must be*'.

The apocalyptic visions of writers like William Blake and Mary Shelley, who imagined that a radical aesthetic might destroy the same dull round and generate a new Jerusalem, steadily gave way to ends being nothing more than reminders that we must survive. Far from climate change prompting writers to question whether the mode of human existence that altered the planet as a living system should be extinguished to make way for other forms of life, the threat to human existence and the witnessing of the sixth mass extinction event has enabled a contraction of the human imagination not merely to the human species, but to humanity in its urban, affluent, hyper-consuming, and globally subsuming form.

Consider the stark difference between the placelessness, abstraction, and existential violence of mythic apocalypse (in its Western and non-Western forms) where the end of the world prompts a thought of the inhuman and eternal, and the steady efflorescence of post-apocalyptic literature, where the end of the world (sometimes wrought by climate change) leaves humans mourning the recently lost affluence and urbanity of the modern Western city. If Mary Shelley could contemplate the last man, and a sense

[30] Frantz Fanon, *Black Skin, White Masks*, trans. Richard Philcox (New York: Grove Press, 2006), p. 76; Jared Sexton, 'Unbearable Blackness', *Cultural Critique*, 90 (2015), 159–78.

[31] Nick Bostrom, *Superintelligence: Paths, Dangers, Strategies* (Oxford University Press, 2014).

of the fragility of the species, and do so by looking towards the spirit of
nature, twenty-first-century post-apocalypse – even in the midst of the
sixth mass extinction – seems only to be able to imagine or desire Western
man's living on, survival at all costs. Shelley's *The Last Man* (1826) concludes, perhaps in the tradition of Milton's *Paradise Lost* (1667), with the
end of a world being a *felix culpa* – the sweeping away of empire in order to
see the world anew. Lionel may be the last *man*, but what he sees is not the
end of the world:

> I long to grapple with danger, to be excited by fear, to have some task,
> however slight or voluntary, for each day's fulfilment. I shall witness all the
> variety of appearance, that the elements can assume – I shall read fair augury
> in the rainbow – menace in the cloud – some lesson or record dear to my
> heart in everything. Thus around the shores of deserted earth, while the sun
> is high, and the moon waxes or wanes, angels, the spirits of the dead, and the
> ever-open eye of the Supreme, will behold the tiny bark, freighted with
> Verney – the LAST MAN.[32]

Such notions of endings generating new worlds became increasingly
incapable of imagining the end of man, and some other life beyond that
end. Instead what would occur would be the end of some humans' world
for the sake of others. Those who left empire and said goodbye to humanity
as it had been known 'found' a new world, but in doing so precipitated the
end or near-end of other humans and other worlds. The new world has
always been bound up with extinction and genocide. The mournful gaze of
the narrator of James Fenimore Cooper's 1826 novel, *The Last of the
Mohicans*, allows the narrative to conclude with the end of a people who
become almost gentlemanly in their resignation that their days are over:

> Chingachgook grasped the hand that, in the warmth of feeling, the scout
> had stretched across the fresh earth, and in an attitude of friendship these
> two sturdy and intrepid woodsmen bowed their heads together, while
> scalding tears fell to their feet, watering the grave of Uncas like drops of
> falling rain.
>   In the midst of the awful stillness with which such a burst of feeling,
> coming as it did, from the two most renowned warriors of that region, was
> received, Tamenund lifted his voice to disperse the multitude.
>   'It is enough,' he said. 'Go, children of the Lenape, the anger of the
> Manitou is not done. Why should Tamenund stay? The pale faces are
> masters of the earth, and the time of the red men has not yet come again.
> My day has been too long. In the morning I saw the sons of Unamis happy

[32] Mary Shelley, *The Last Man*, ed. Morton Paley (Oxford University Press, 1994), p. 470.

and strong; and yet, before the night has come, have I lived to see the last warrior of the wise race of the Mohicans.'[33]

Something has happened. Kant's warning against an apocalyptic tone has been heeded: there is no world other than the world *we* form for ourselves. Certain peoples can meet their end, but those extinctions are not the end of *the world*. On the contrary, the 'pale faces are masters of the earth', to the point where only *their* end will be the end of the world. Far more recent than Fenimore Cooper's historical novel is the late twentieth-century Australian documentary – similarly mourning the end of a people – *The Last Tasmanian* (1978), directed by Tom Haydon.[34] Despite the almost-guilty narration of a people's near-genocide, the use of the word 'last' in *The Last of the Mohicans* and *The Last Tasmanian* has a performative function. It ends the world of a people, and makes way for those who begin to imagine their world as *the world*.

Although I have drawn a contrast between an apocalyptic tradition capable of imagining the end of this world for the sake of an other barely imaginable world that is *not* our own, and a post-apocalyptic tradition that can imagine nothing other than its own survival and redemption as the only world worthy of the name, the two modes are intertwined. One could draw a stark contrast between biblical apocalypse and pre-modern plague narratives, where the end of this fragile and fleeting world is a haunting possibility that allows for the thought of a world beyond the mundane, and the current vogue for imagining the 'end of the world' as nothing more than the end of liberal and affluent capitalist urbanity. On the one hand, the thought of the end of the world is an opening to the infinite, while, on the other, the 'end of the world' is this world without the luxuries and favourable conditions that have elevated some humans to think of themselves as humanity in general. Yet while this contrast is important it is also impossible to maintain in any sort of purity. The apocalyptic tradition that chastens humanity and mundanity by imagining a transcendent divinity has often been intertwined with an attempt to find that divinity on *this* Earth, and will do so by finding a new world that will (in turn) amount to the end of the world for others. Those texts that celebrated the apocalyptic destruction of a reified, imperialist, and unjust humanity – such as Blake's *Jerusalem* (1804) or *Milton* (1804–10) – could sit alongside his shorter prophecy, *America* (1793), where the affirmation of apocalypse and finding a new Jerusalem does not consider the genocidal effects it will have on the

[33] James Fenimore Cooper, *The Last of the Mohicans* (New York: Random House, 2001), p. 342.
[34] *The Last Tasmanian*, dir. Tom Haydon (Australian Film Commission, 1978).

'new' world. The redemptive annihilation of the old world is often the
barbaric capture of a new world: the end of the world for some is the dawn
of the world for others. Apocalyptic thought, even as late as Blake, could
imagine the destruction of a world, to make way for another – as though
the cosmos were composed from multiple worlds. Yet Blake also imagined
the new world – sometimes as a transformed London, but sometimes as the
'new' world of America. Well before Blake, Milton could at once conclude
Paradise Lost with Adam and Eve having the world 'all before them', *and*
affirm the violent end of this world in *Samson Agonistes* (1671). By the time
Darwin posited the theory of evolution, where extinctions were part of
life's progressive grandeur, there was already a sense of coupled affirmation
and mourning tied to the endings of worlds that would nevertheless
enable – ultimately – *the world*.

What ties traditional, mythic, and pre-modern apocalyptic thought to
the Darwinian conception of extinction is a notion of ends as redemptive
and inhuman: life's grandeur makes its way through forms that are an
expression of a power for formation or creativity that is bound up with
destruction. The logic of apocalypse (as opposed to the post-apocalyptic
wave of the twenty-first century) ties extinction to redemption, tying ends
to the opening of a new world – whether that be an eternal realm beyond
the Earth or an Earth transformed. While apocalypse and the sense of
a radically other world 'to come' has perhaps always had some reference to
a transformation and redemption of this world, the twenty-first-century
imaginary, especially by way of the trope of the Anthropocene, has become
intensively counter-apocalyptic. If there is something like 'Anthropos'
unified by way of its capacity to generate planetary destruction, then it is
this world that becomes the only horizon and only end. There is no 'planet
B' and no other world. Climate change and the Anthropocene are bound
up with a transformed sense of extinction and ends: variability is no longer
figured as life's grandeur, and ends are no longer the sweeping away of
deadened worlds for the sake of a future.

CHAPTER 17

Climate Criticism and Nuclear Criticism

Daniel Cordle

In February 2018, in a widely reprinted article, *The Conversation* reported a study by scientists at the University of New South Wales and University College London of a spruce tree, growing on Campbell Island in the Pacific Ocean. More than 170 miles from any other tree and 400 miles south of New Zealand, it is reputedly the 'loneliest tree on the planet', yet its wood contains traces of the 'radiocarbon produced by above ground atomic bomb tests'. Peaking in 1965, these remnants of the early atomic age provide a 'potential marker for the start of the Anthropocene'.[1]

Whether 1965 is eventually adopted in this way, whether a different date is preferred, or something other than nuclear fallout is used to mark the Anthropocene's inception, the story illustrates the enmeshment of nuclear technologies and culture with matters of the climate.[2] Of course, even if nuclear fallout does become the primary signifier for this new geological epoch, it does not mean it is its main causal agent: it simply serves a practical function by providing a synchronous signal legible in the geological record far into the future. No doubt, though, part of the appeal of nuclear technologies in debates about the Anthropocene is their cultural potency, particularly as signifiers of the power of humans to wreak changes to the planet.

---

[1] Chris Turney, Jonathan Palmer, and Mark Maslin, 'Anthropocene Began in 1965, According to Signs Left in World's "Loneliest Tree"', *The Conversation* (19 February 2018). The article was widely reprinted and reported, for example, by the BBC and *Newsweek*: see Jonathan Amos, '"Loneliest Tree" Records Human Epoch', *BBC News* (19 February 2018) and Turney, Palmer, and Maslin, 'Anthropocene: How the Loneliest Tree in the World Recorded the Start of Our Global Domination', *Newsweek* (22 February 2018). For the scientific paper on which these news items were based, see Turney, Palmer, Maslin *et al.*, 'Global Peak in Atmospheric Radiocarbon Provides a Potential Definition for the Onset of the Anthropocene Epoch in 1965', *Scientific Reports*, 8 (2018), article no. 3293.

[2] It is also possible that the Anthropocene is not accepted as a geological epoch. Regardless, the term remains a powerful tool for thinking the long-term human impact (material and cultural) on the planet.

As this chapter shows in its first two sections, there is a longstanding preoccupation in nuclear texts with weather and climate. Representations of nuclear explosions, actual and fictitious, show them releasing energy and materials that create weather and even shape climate. Nuclear literature might usefully therefore be considered a special subcategory of climate fiction. Potent signifiers of modernity, nuclear technologies are a point where humans, their artefacts, and planetary ecosystems are imagined to meet.

There is too a relatively young – a quarter century or so – but thriving tradition of nuclear criticism and theory that the final section of this chapter discusses. Opening up three key problematics – nuclear geographies, nuclear temporalities, and nuclear subjectivities – nuclear criticism brings into focus the interdependence of global and local, the significance of deep time, and how humans are produced by their interactions with technology and nature. This critical tradition can feed usefully into the understanding of climate fiction.

Nuclear Weather: Sharp Dawns of Fire and Cloud

Without a sound, the sun was shining; or so it looked.

Otto Frisch

And so there was this sense of this ominous cloud hanging over us. It was so brilliant purple, with all the radioactive glowing. And it just seemed to hang there forever ... It was very terrifying.

Frank Oppenheimer[3]

The first atomic explosion, the Trinity Test of 16 July 1945 (another potential start date for the Anthropocene),[4] was experienced as a sharp, sudden dawn, a false and terrible second sun born in the New Mexico desert. According to one observer, the fireball was a 'half-risen sun but twice as large' that, in the words of another, 'enveloped [one] with a warm brilliant yellow white light – from darkness to brilliant sunshine in an instant'.[5] In the words of the great *New York Times* reporter, William L. Laurence, the only journalist present, it was 'a sunrise such as the world

---

[3] Otto Frisch, qtd. in Gerard DeGroot, *The Bomb: a History of Hell on Earth* (London: Pimlico, 2005), p. 61; Frank Oppenheimer, qtd. in Richard Rhodes, *The Making of the Atomic Bomb* (London: Penguin, 1988), p. 675. Frank Oppenheimer was the brother of Robert J. Oppenheimer, the scientific director of the Manhattan Project.
[4] Jan A. Zalaziewicz and Mark Williams, 'First Atomic Bomb Test May Mark the Beginning of the Anthropocene', *The Conversation* (30 January 2015).
[5] R. D. Inglis and Ernest Lawrence, qtd. in Rhodes, *The Making of the Atomic Bomb*, pp. 673, 672.

had never seen, a great green supersun climbing in a fraction of a second to a height of more than 8,000 feet, rising ever higher until it touched the clouds, lighting up earth and sky all around with a dazzling luminosity'.[6] And after the sun were the fire and the cloud.

Frisch, one of the physicists on the Manhattan Project, reaching for words to describe what had yet to be labelled a 'mushroom cloud', wrote of something that looked 'a bit like a strawberry' that 'was slowly rising into the sky from the ground, with which it remained connected by a lengthening stem of whirling dust ... It was an awesome spectacle.'[7] To Lawrence, the fireball was 'about a mile in diameter, changing colors as it kept shooting upward, from deep purple to orange, expanding, growing bigger, rising as it was expanding, an elemental force freed from its bonds after being chained for billions of years'.[8]

These twin motifs of sun and cloud recur repeatedly in nuclear culture, both in descriptions of actual nuclear explosions (as at Hiroshima, Nagasaki, and in bomb tests in the decades afterwards) and in nuclear fiction. As will be apparent from the descriptions above, a key frame in which such explanations operate is that of the sublime. The atomic sublime is a particular incarnation of the technological sublime produced by modernity, as Peter Hales has discussed in relation to American culture.[9]

These moments of sublimity are experienced as a breach of the division between the human and natural worlds, between engineered and natural forces, or, perhaps more accurately, these moments starkly reveal the illusory nature of the division between the human/technological and the natural. The nuclear flash seems to put the power of the sun, the primary driver of our climate, on Earth, revealing both the power that humans wield and its ability to exceed and overwhelm them. The physicist, Isidor Isaac Rabi, described the flash from the Trinity Test as 'the brightest light I have ever seen or that I think anyone has ever seen. It blasted; it pounced; it bored its way right through you. It was a vision that was seen with more than the eye.'[10] A local woman, Elizabeth Ingram, claims there was a flash so bright that her blind sister, with her in a car, said 'What happened?'[11]

---

[6] William L. Laurence, 26 September 1945, rpt. in Laurence, 'Eyewitness Account of Bomb Test', *New York Times* (16 July 1985).
[7] DeGroot, *The Bomb*, p. 61.   [8] Lawrence, 'Eyewitness Account'.
[9] Peter B. Hales, 'The Atomic Sublime', *American Studies*, 32.1 (1991), 5–31. See also Frances Ferguson, 'The Nuclear Sublime', *Diacritics*, 14.2 (1984), 4–10.
[10] DeGroot, *The Bomb*, p. 61.
[11] Interview in *The Day After Trinity*, dir. Jon H. Else (PBS, 1981). Available at www.youtube.com/watch?v=Vm5fCxXnK7Y.

Inevitably, these modes of experiencing the nuclear moment also permeate fictional treatments of the subject. In Leslie Marmon's Silko's novel,
Ceremony (1977), Tayo's grandmother relates an experience similar to that
of Elizabeth Ingram's sister, seeing a 'flash of light' through the kitchen
window, so bright 'even my old clouded-up eyes could see it ... I thought
I was seeing the sun rise again.'[12] This is associated with climatic and
environmental catastrophe, for it is part of a pattern of destruction that
finds expression elsewhere in the novel in a drought that ravages the land.

In Pearl Buck's novel *Command the Morning* (1959), the Trinity Test is
an encounter with the sublime. First the sky 'burst into blinding light' –
the nuclear moment experienced as rupture and rapture – and then
'Colour splashed over the landscape, yellow, purple, crimson, grey. Every
fold in the mountain sprang into bold lines, every valley was revealed, every
peak stood stark.'[13] The superfluity of adjectives suggests the impossibility
of capturing in words how the desert landscape is transformed by the light
boiling across the visible spectrum, revealing it in new and vivid ways.

Crucially, this power is also experienced as an unleashing of weather.
Burton Hall, the character through whom this experience is mediated,
hears someone crying 'Look – look – ' and turns to see:

> A cloud as vast as the desert itself was rising from the spot where the tower
> had stood, a rolling, boiling, surging, swelling cloud of many colours.
> It swallowed every other cloud and soared towards the zenith. In utter
> silence they stared at the monstrous moving shape they had unleashed.
> The [*sic*] stared and watched, speechless until the colours faded and the mass
> was grey. They watched while the winds tore and pulled it to pieces and
> scattered it around the globe.[14]

This human dawn overwhelms the ordinary New Mexico dawn (the
atomic cloud 'swallows' others; it is as broad as the desert). Again, the
abundance of words – the flow of verbs to describe the living, roiling
cloud – suggests an outstripping of the language by which we might know
it, as does the way in which the watchers are rendered 'speechless'. Finally,
the 'scattering' of the cloud around the globe indicates the way in which
this human weather enters planetary atmospheric systems.

These clouds erupting into the Earth's skies are manifestations of
a human-induced atomic weather. Indeed, one of the shocks, following
Trinity, was how far radioactive fallout spread. As the *New York Times*
reported, 'temporarily radioactive by-products of a single bomb spread in

[12] Leslie Marmon Silko, *Ceremony* (New York: Penguin, 1986), p. 245.
[13] Pearl S. Buck, *Command the Morning* (London: Pan, 1962), p. 174.   [14] Ibid., pp. 174–5.

the course of a few days over an area about the size of Australia' – a discovery prompted, as I've discussed elsewhere, when the camera film company, Eastman-Kodak, launched an investigation to discover the source of fogged film after receiving complaints from customers in the summer of 1945. It was eventually revealed that strawboard from the Midwest, used to pack the film, had been rendered radioactive by fallout from Trinity.[15] Such effects became more common with the nuclear testing of the early Cold War. In 1959 the *Saturday Evening Post* reported how an 'atomic weather report' was drawn up from strips of gummed film sent in daily from 169 cities around the world, revealing that the 'pervasive by-product of weapons testing now blankets the entire planet' and 'every living creature, man included, has in its body a few particles of radioactive strontium 90, some of which will remain for life'.[16]

The atomic cloud became a resonant image in nuclear literature. In Robert Swindells's young adult novel, *Brother in the Land* (1984), Danny realises war has broken out when he sees a 'cloud, perched like an obscene mushroom on its crooked stem'. Further away, beyond 'the near horizon lay a pulsating arc of orange light. It breathed in and out like a living thing, its glow reflected on the bellies of the clouds'.[17] Characteristically, this depiction invests the cloud with life: a beast, unleashed by human hands, it 'breathes' rather as the cloud in Buck's novel is a 'monstrous moving shape'.

The world becomes strange and terrifying in these depictions. In other texts the nuclear weather is less visually dramatic but more insidious. In Nevil Shute's classic and influential (if scientifically dubious) depiction in *On the Beach* (1957), life in Australia is shadowed by the advance of a radioactive cloud, a deadly, invisible weather front from war in the northern hemisphere that will extinguish all human life on Earth. The world, normal to the eye, is rendered strange by people's knowledge that it is gradually and invisibly being permeated by radioactivity. Ordinary life continues as if there is a future, but every thought and action is shadowed by impending death. Peter and Mary, for instance, make detailed plans for their garden even though they know everyone will be dead in six months.[18]

[15] Walter S. Sullivan, 'Film Spots Trace Vast A-Bomb Range: Radioactive Particles Spread over Australia-Sized Area, Eastman Studies Show', *New York Times* (23 May 1946), 1. I discuss this, and the incident's appearance in Dexter Masters's novel *The Accident* (1955), in Daniel Cordle, 'Science/Humans/Humanities: Dexter Masters' *The Accident* and Being in the Nuclear Age', *Journal of Literature and Science*, 10.2 (2017), 74–87.

[16] Steven M. Spencer, 'Fallout: the Silent Killer', *Saturday Evening Post* (29 August 1959); www .unz.com/print/SatEveningPost-1959aug29-00026/?View=Tree.

[17] Robert Swindells, *Brother in the Land* (London: Puffin, 2000), p. 8.

[18] Nevil Shute, *On the Beach* (Thirsk: House of Stratus, 2000), p. 107.

This disjunction between intellectual knowledge of what is going to happen and the inability emotionally to accept it is an incarnation of what the anthropologist, Joseph Masco, calls the 'nuclear uncanny'. This is a forerunner, in some ways, of the terrifying ordinariness of climate change: day-to-day the world seems the same, for individual weather events cannot be definitively connected to it, but cumulatively a building sense of something awry reveals a strangeness at the heart of the familiar.

There are several dimensions to Masco's nuclear uncanny, but a key one is the disruption of 'the ability of individuals to differentiate their bodies from the environment'.[19] The nuclear uncanny is a psychological response to *potential* physiological contamination. Hence, 'sensory experience becomes haunted and untrustworthy': the human senses through which we expect to know the world no longer properly reveal, or guard against, its dangers.[20] This is precisely the effect that seems to be experienced by the eponymous English protagonist of Maggie Gee's novel *Grace* (1988), who finds herself distrusting her home environment when she hears news of the nuclear accident at Chernobyl. 'It [the radioactivity] couldn't be seen or heard or tasted; the ordinary senses let one down', Grace muses. How could she know if it was 'really there then . . . in the ordinary green leaves and the ordinary milk of breakfast'.[21]

Like the more dramatic imagined scenario of *On the Beach*, the problem with which Grace contends is that there 'was nowhere, really, to hide' because 'air is everywhere and goes everywhere' and hence the air in her home might be the 'air from Russia'.[22] What she and the doomed inhabitants of Australia in Shute's novel are dealing with is something that begins to cross the boundary from nuclear weather to a nuclear climate. They are faced not only with a passing phenomenon (nuclear weather), but with longer-term systemic changes in the causal agents underpinning the weather: a world in which ordinary weather systems are inflected by radioactive agents produced by human activity.

Nuclear Climates

If depictions of individual nuclear explosions frequently construct them in terms of nuclear weather, increasingly as the nuclear age progressed the cumulative effects of numerous nuclear explosions came to be seen as

[19] Joseph Masco, *The Nuclear Borderlands: the Manhattan Project in Post-Cold War New Mexico* (Princeton University Press, 2006), p. 32.
[20] Ibid., p. 28.   [21] Maggie Gee, *Grace* (London: Abacus, 1989), p. 2.   [22] Ibid.

having the potential to produce a new nuclear climate. Most dramatically, this possibility was captured in nuclear winter theory, first proposed in 1983 in the famous 'TTAPS' paper for the journal *Science*, and subsequently hugely influential in the public imagination of nuclear war.[23] The theory proposed that the volume of debris thrown into the atmosphere by nuclear war would cause temperatures on Earth to plunge with catastrophic consequences for the ecosystem. This very quickly became part of the assumed experience of nuclear war and nuclear winter scenarios of varying severity appeared in novels in subsequent years, including Kim Stanley Robinson's *The Wild Shore* (1984), Whitley Strieber's *Wolf of Shadows* (1985), Louise Lawrence's *Children of the Dust* (1985), Phyllis Reynolds Naylor's *The Dark of the Tunnel* (1985), Pamela Service's *Winter of Magic's Return* (1985), Paul Cook's *Duende Meadow* (1985), Lynn Hall's *If Winter Comes* (1986), Robert McCammon's *Swan Song* (1987), and William Brinkley's *The Last Ship* (1988).[24] As Lawrence Badash points out, drawing on the work of historian of science Spencer Weart, nuclear winter theory was a contemporary incarnation of a longstanding mythological sense of human activity and the climate being connected: 'humans since prehistoric times have linked severe weather and climatic conditions to human transgressions, such as a violation or a taboo or a failed offering to the gods'.[25]

This was part of a more general sense, by the late Cold War, that nuclear war would constitute a potentially catastrophic human intervention in the world's ecosystems, a perspective that made the alliance between environmental and anti-nuclear campaigning a particularly potent one in the 1980s. Even before nuclear winter theory, Jonathan Schell's popular book

---

[23] R. P. Turco, O. B. Toon, T. P. Ackerman, J. B. Pollack, and Carl Sagan, 'Nuclear Winter: Global Consequences of Multiple Nuclear Explosions', *Science*, 222.4630 (1983), 1283–92. It was known as 'TTAPS' for the initial letters of its authors' surnames. That one of them was Carl Sagan, the famous astronomer, physicist, and populariser of science, helped the dissemination of the theory. For an extended discussion of the impact of nuclear winter theory and the public debate about it, see Lawrence Badash, *A Nuclear Winter's Tale: Science and Politics in the 1980s* (Cambridge, MA: MIT Press, 2009).

[24] Kim Stanley Robinson, *The Wild Shore: Three Californias* (1984; New York: Tor/Forge, 1995); Whitley Strieber, *Wolf of Shadows* (New York: Knopf, 1985); Louise Lawrence, *Children of the Dust* (New York: Harper and Row, 1985); Phyllis Reynolds Naylor, *The Dark of the Tunnel* (New York: Athenaeum, 1985); Pamela F. Service, *Winter of Magic's Return* (New York: Athenaeum, 1985); Paul Cook, *Duende Meadow* (New York: Bantam, 1985); Lynn Hall, *If Winter Comes* (New York: Scribner, 1986); Robert McCammon, *Swan Song* (New York: Pocket Books, 2009); William Brinkley, *The Last Ship* (New York: Viking, 1988). For discussion of the literary impact of nuclear winter theory and its place within 1980s environmentalism, see my chapter, 'Dust, Winter and Refuge: Environmentalism and Nuclear Literature', in Cordle, *Late Cold War Literature and Culture: the Nuclear 1980s* (London: Palgrave-Macmillan, 2017), pp. 113–40.

[25] Badash, *A Nuclear Winter's Tale*, p. 49.

on the impact of nuclear war, *The Fate of the Earth* (1982), initially serialised in *The New Yorker*, situated its depiction of nuclear futures in the new environmentalist paradigm of 'the earth as a single system, or organism, [that] has only recently proceeded from poetic metaphor to actual scientific investigation'.[26] Though rooted (somewhat controversially) in scientific modelling, Schell's nightmare vision is a powerful fiction of the future and became an influential text through which to imagine nuclear war and the future of the planet. Its depiction of ravaged ecosystems, of the collapse of crops and species vital to the food chain, of surviving insects and animals blinded by increased ultraviolet light because of a depleted ozone layer, provided a powerful depiction of humans' ability to wreak change upon the planet that would be more fully explored, two decades later, in debates about the Anthropocene. Chillingly, *The Fate of the Earth* argues that 'abrupt interventions can radically disrupt any particular evolutionary configuration and dispatch hundreds of thousands of species into extinction' and that a 'full-scale nuclear holocaust could lead to the extinction of mankind'.[27] The impact of Schell's book is nicely illustrated by Stephanie Tolan's wonderful young adult novel, *The Pride of the Peacock* (1986), which opens with its teenage protagonist, Whitney, traumatised by reading a much-thumbed (the 'spine and front cover were creased from handling, and along the creases the shiny color had cracked') copy of Schell's book. Shivering, unable to sleep, with her muscles perpetually clenched, and horrified that 'the fate of the earth would also be the fate of [her young brother] Jeremy Whitehurst', the novel illustrates how deeply and personally – how corporeally – fears of the Earth's demise can be experienced.[28]

Nuclear literature – by which I mean not only texts focused primarily on nuclear technology and its consequences, but also those many more texts in which a nuclear context is part of the assumed background to everyday life – might, therefore, usefully be seen as a special category of climate fiction. Its predominant (though not exclusive) interest in dramatic and sudden human interventions in the climate is, of course, different to the predominant (though not exclusive) interest of climate fiction in more drawn-out and gradual change, but it also means that it captures symbolically our capacity to drive (and crash) the climate.

Like the fears expressed in climate fiction, nuclear anxieties can also have the positive impact of prompting globalised thinking. Fictions depicting

[26] Jonathan Schell, *The Fate of the Earth* and *The Abolition* (Stanford University Press, 2000), p. 93.
[27] Ibid.
[28] Stephanie S. Tolan, *Pride of the Peacock* (New York: Charles Scribner's Sons, 1986), pp. 1–3.

nuclear disaster and climate change frequently map human activity into ecosystems that transcend local and national boundaries to reveal a shared planetary vulnerability. Hence, nuclear texts are not a historical curiosity of the Cold War. Literature from that period continues to speak to us, there is a great deal of new nuclear literature being written, and nuclear technologies are still with us and still need making sense of.

To this end, nuclear criticism, though originating in the late Cold War, remains relevant. Indeed, it thrives, offering foci and approaches that can also help to illuminate climate fiction.

Nuclear Criticism and Climate Criticism: the Politics of Vulnerability

As I have discussed elsewhere, there are three problematics opened up by the intersection between nuclear texts and nuclear criticism, a space we might call nuclear theory: nuclear geographies, nuclear temporalities, and nuclear subjectivities.[29] These constitute territories for thinking that take us beyond historically specific moments of nuclear anxiety into more profound existential issues. They are linked by both a softening, sometimes a transgression, of boundaries, literal and conceptual, and an interest in scaling that exposes the connection between the small and the large, and the movement from one to the other.

Nuclear geographies, like climate geographies, are complex systems that map local and global into dynamic relationships. The radioactive fallout from the Trinity Test over the United States and the planetary distribution of radionuclides from weapons testing during the 1950s and 1960s, discussed above, illustrate the movement from local to global. More dramatically, nuclear winter theory proposed that multiple local nuclear explosions could effect a change so dramatic that the global climatic system would be altered. While it is tempting to think of the redistribution of nuclear agents in terms simply of the physics of explosions, fallout, and weather, there are also industrial, infrastructural, economic, social, political, and cultural systems that move nuclear materials and discourse about them around the planet. The ecosystem is bound up with this web of complex human systems.

Like much climate fiction, the effect of representing these complex systems is frequently to produce a sense of a mobile and widely shared peril. Nuclear consequences, like climate changes, cannot be conveniently

[29] Daniel Cordle, 'The Futures of Nuclear Criticism', *Alluvium*, 5.3 (2016).

contained. Indeed, containment, a highly charged Cold War term (both for the US foreign policy of containment of communism around the globe and for the 'containment culture' discussed by critics like Elaine Tyler May and Alan Nadel), is very much the issue in both cases.[30] While 'containment' is most frequently used to discuss US policy and culture, containment and its failure is more broadly the subject of many nuclear narratives.

The Indian writer and activist Arundhati Roy has written persuasively and beautifully against nuclear nationalism in her own country in 'The End of Imagination' (1998), pointing out that the convergence of nuclear and climate effects means India and Pakistan (its most likely nuclear enemy) share vulnerability. 'Though we are separate countries', she writes, 'we share skies, we share winds, we share water. Where radioactive fallout will land on any given day depends on the direction of the wind and the rain . . . If we bomb Lahore, Punjab will burn . . . Any nuclear war with Pakistan will be a war against ourselves.'[31]

Such failures of containment recur frequently in nuclear texts. Nuclear technologies are mapped in the cultural imagination as breaking beyond the localities in which they originate (in some cases, detonate) to interact with, and enter into, larger systems. These need not be the dramatic explosions of nuclear war narratives. In Bobbie Ann Mason's novel, *An Atomic Romance* (2006), about safety scandals in the nuclear industry, 'legacy waste' seeps through the boundaries of a uranium-enrichment plant, compromising a wildlife refuge where the protagonist, Reed Futrell, likes to camp. When it is reported that potentially radioactive 'scrap metal from the plant was being recycled commercially and might end up in such items as barbecue grills and tooth fillings', the problem of containment becomes that not only of nuclear waste but also of discourse about it, because 'Rumors were flying around like lost neutrinos.'[32] Human society is part of the ecosystem here, for materials travel vectors of dissemination that are not only to do with (say) the movement of water through soil and rock, but also commercial and industrial. Neither materials (scrap metal), nor knowledge about them (rumours), can be effectively

[30] Containment culture is the domestic corollary of the foreign policy of containment, manifesting in anxieties about home and family. See Elaine Tyler May, *Homeward Bound: American Families in the Cold War Era*, 2nd edn (New York: Basic Books, 1999); Alan Nadel, *Containment Culture: American Narratives, Postmodernism and the Atomic Age* (Durham, NC: Duke University Press, 1995). Late Cold War culture can be understood as a post-containment culture, a continuation of, and reaction against, this containment culture, as I discuss in Cordle, *Late Cold War Literature and Culture*.

[31] Arundhati Roy, 'The End of Imagination', in Roy, *The Cost of Living: the Greater Common Good and* The End of Imagination (London: Flamingo, 1999), p. 144.

[32] Bobbie Ann Mason, *An Atomic Romance* (New York: Random House, 2006), p. 79.

contained. The local site is part of, and traversed by systems from, the world outside.

In Terry Tempest Williams's memoir, *Refuge* (1991), about the eruption of breast cancer in the bodies of several of her female relatives, larger human–animal–environmental ecosystems are invoked. She situates her family's story as part of the larger story of 'downwinders' from the Nevada nuclear test site, for Williams alleges that a likely cause of the cancers is radioactive exposure from the nuclear testing of decades before. These US contexts are mapped into a global environment through another dimension of the narrative, Williams's work at the Bear River Migratory Bird Refuge, one of a planetary-wide network of stopping-off points for migrating birds. The 'magic of birds', for Williams, is 'how they bridge cultures and continents with their wings' and this becomes a metaphor by which to understand human communication across geographical space, for a tender letter to an ill friend collapses distance just as flight does: 'Our correspondences have wings – paper birds that fly from my house to yours – flocks of ideas crisscrossing the country.'[33]

Interconnection is hence the source of both weakness (the travel of carcinogenic substances through the ecosystem) and strength (the mutual support of newly identified communities of the vulnerable; the resilience of networks of migratory bird refuges in the face of disasters that befall individual sites). Lawrence Buell has discussed *Refuge* alongside other texts as an example of 'toxic discourse', dealing with the 'fear of a poisoned world', and the term might usefully be brought to bear upon *An Atomic Romance* too.[34] In particular, both speak to an 'imbrication of outback with metropolis', an 'interdependence' between human and natural worlds that challenges our tendency to think of them as separate things.[35] In Mason's novel, an unfolding, beautiful landscape, as Reed drives out on his motorcycle to the wildlife refuge, turns out to be that of an industrial, not a pristine natural world, for the source of 'fantastical shapes of rising white clouds' is eventually revealed to be industrial.[36]

In both cases, military and civilian nuclear sites, part of a broader planetary network of the 'plutonium economy', might not exactly be shaping climate directly, but they suggest an enmeshment of human and natural worlds that is tied up, particularly in Williams's case, with

---

[33] Terry Tempest Williams, *Refuge: an Unnatural History of Family and Place* (New York: Vintage, 2001), pp. 18, 84.
[34] Lawrence Buell, 'Toxic Discourse', *Critical Inquiry*, 24.3 (1998), 639. [35] Ibid., 659.
[36] Mason, *Atomic Romance*, p. 4.

something going awry.[37] Yet the shared vulnerability to which they point also becomes a source of strength: with a threat to one place a threat to every other, it becomes clear that a shared human vulnerability raises the potential for shared human solutions, albeit that, as Rob Nixon has pointed out in *Slow Violence and the Environmentalism of the Poor*, global capitalism works systemically to disseminate its effects iniquitously upon the poor.[38]

A contemporary climate fiction that might usefully be placed alongside Williams's and Mason's texts for its apprehension of the complex connections between local and global is Barbara Kingsolver's *Flight Behaviour* (2012).[39] In particular, the centrality of the image of flight maps it into the same set of concerns that motivate Williams's text. In Kingsolver's novel, it is monarch butterflies, not birds, that are migrating and have arrived unexpectedly and off course, presumably as a result of climate changes, in a remote part of Tennessee, and that arrest a different kind of flight, that of Dellarobia, who comes across them on the way to a tryst with a potential lover. Like Williams's memoir, in which Mormon female experience, and networks of women, are set in contrast to masculine conceptions of place and land, the experience of women is central. Like *Refuge*, the novel builds a sense of precariousness around family and images of flooding. In *Refuge*, the flooding of the Great Salt Lake threatens both the migratory bird refuge and the sense of sanctuary Williams finds there in the face of her family's illness: 'I could not separate the Bird Refuge from my family. Devastation respects no boundaries . . . the two things I had always regarded as bedrock, were now subject to change. Quicksand.'[40] At the end of *Flight Behaviour*, Dellarobia too is caught in a flood, her life and the fate of the monarch butterflies uncertain as the human and natural worlds are poised, vulnerable, before a precarious future.

In all these cases there is a sense of precariousness in the balance between the environment, humans, and the non-human inhabitants of

[37] See Masco, *Nuclear Borderlands*, pp. 132–44, for a discussion of the consequences of the plutonium economy.
[38] '[T]hose people lacking resources . . . are the principal casualties of slow violence . . . Our media bias toward spectacular violence exacerbates the vulnerability of ecosystems treated as disposable by turbo-capitalism while simultaneously exacerbating the vulnerability of those whom Kevin Bale, in another context, has called "disposable people"', Rob Nixon, *Slow Violence and the Environmentalism of the Poor* (Cambridge, MA: Harvard University Press, 2011), p. 4.
[39] Barbara Kingsolver, *Flight Behaviour* (London: Faber, 2012). For an excellent discussion of the ecological sensibility underpinning the novel, see Kristin J. Jacobson, 'Radical Homemaking in Contemporary American Environmental Fiction', *C21 Literature: Journal of 21st-Century Writings*, 6.1 (2018).
[40] Williams, *Refuge*, p. 40.

the world. In all three texts, human activity, impacting the environment, is understood as the product of socio-economic and geopolitical organisation: Reed is a blue-collar worker in the uranium-enrichment plant, both financially dependent on and threatened by the nuclear and post-Cold War economy; Williams's family's health is devastated by the military-industrial complex and its failure to recognise that, though the desert where the bomb tests take place is 'virtually uninhabited', she is one of those 'virtual uninhabitants'; and Dellarobia is caught in a low-wage economy, which reveals her to be as much a victim of neoliberal capitalism as the environment is.[41] While only *Flight Behaviour* is overtly about climate change, the connections all three texts find between humans and their environment – their ecological sense of an uncontainable precariousness, shared across boundaries – paradoxically provides a source of hope and possibility. With our futures resting on finding a way to function within the constraints of planetary ecosystems, a politics of vulnerability at the heart of nuclear and climate fictions reveals the shared threats faced by humans.

If nuclear and climate geographies tend often to stretch the local out into the global, nuclear and climate temporalities often move beyond the present moment, beyond indeed the span of human lifetimes by which our narratives usually measure significance, into deep time. Most obviously, there are those nuclear and climate texts that posit life after a future catastrophe. In these instances, it is, perhaps, often less deep time and more a gentle pushing of human lives into futures a few or many generations hence, with the effect of revealing the present as terrifyingly (as the present must always be) ephemeral.

Jacques Derrida's discussion of the 'archive' in perhaps the most influential essay of nuclear criticism, 'No Apocalypse, Not Now' (1983), is useful here for thinking both nuclear and climate fiction. What is most significantly threatened by the prospect of global nuclear war, Derrida suggests, is less 'the destruction of humanity, of the human habitat', than 'an irreversible destruction, leaving no traces, of the juridico-literary archive'.[42] It is our culture that produces our sense of what it is to be human and it is precisely the loss of that culture, manifested in the written word, that is more conceptually significant than the deaths of individual humans. With the erasure of the archive comes the erasure of the human.

---

[41] Ibid., p. 287.
[42] Jacques Derrida, 'No Apocalypse, Not Now (Full Speed Ahead, Seven Missiles, Seven Missives)', trans. Catherine Porter and Philip Lewis, *Diacritics*, 14 (1984), 27, 26.

Of course, we cannot fully think this absence of the human because we can only imagine it from within a human perspective. So, in Ray Bradbury's short story 'There Will Come Soft Rains' (1950), about a futuristic house that keeps functioning after its human inhabitants have been incinerated by a nuclear attack, the pathos of a world devoid of humans is produced by the house reading out Sara Teasdale's poem 'There Will Come Soft Rains' to a woman whose only trace is the blast shadow her body cast on the house's outside wall.[43] Yet, of course, the whole point is that there is no one left to feel any pathos, or to grieve the loss of humankind – but we cannot imagine that absence of feeling. The text seeks to conjure that absence, but immediately fills it with the reader's human presence, filling in for the absent listener to the poem.

The urgency and the difficulty of thinking human absence, of understanding what it means, is shared by both nuclear and climate fictions. In some cases, texts find innovative ways to at least gesture towards the deep timescales that are the subject of discussions provoked by the Anthropocene. Alla Ivanchikova has provided an innovative reading of Margaret Atwood's *Stone Mattress* (2014) and A. S. Byatt's 'A Stone Woman' (2003) as short stories about geology and people which directly address the Anthropocene.[44] In both, geological timescales come into contact with the lifetimes of humans (a rock becomes an object through which violent revenge is enacted in Atwood's story; a woman turns to stone in Byatt's) and our sense of the primacy of human time frames collapses.

Rather like these short stories, Tim O'Brien's novel *The Nuclear Age* (1985) contains a moment of temporal vertigo rooted in a moment of understanding that the fate of the material of human bodies is eventually to enter the geological strata. Its abusive narrator-protagonist, William Cowling, has, in the midst of a breakdown that manifests as terror of nuclear war, begun to dig a hole in the backyard for a bomb shelter. Terrified by the possibility that his wife will leave him (the catalyst for the breakdown), he eventually contemplates an end that may be nuclear or may be produced by his own detonation of explosives with which he has wired the nascent shelter:

[43] Ray Bradbury, 'There Will Come Soft Rains', originally published in *Colliers* (6 May 1950), rpt. as 'August 2026: There Will Come Soft Rains', in Bradbury, *The Martian Chronicles* (1950; New York: Simon and Schuster, 2012), 220–8.
[44] Alla Ivanchikova, 'Geomediations in the Anthropocene: Fictions of the Geologic Turn', *c21 Literature: Journal of 21st-Century Writings*, 6.1 (2018); Margaret Atwood, *Stone Mattress* (New York: Nan A. Talese/Doubleday, 2014); A. S. Byatt, 'A Stone Woman', originally published in Byatt, *A Little Black Book of Stories* (London: Chatto, 2003), rpt. as *A Stone Woman* (London: Penguin, 2011).

I watch the night reorganize itself, the movements of stars and shadows. The patterns tend toward stasis.

God knows I don't want it this way

Folded in forever like fossils. I don't want it but I can see it, as always, the imprints in rock, the wall shadows at Hiroshima . . . Here, she can't leave me. The fossils don't move. Crack open a rock and she'll be curled around me. Her smile will be gold and granite. Immutable, metamorphic, welded forever by the stresses of our age. We will become the planet . . . We will lace through the mountains like seams of ore, married like the elements.[45]

In this disturbing, violent fantasy, in William's desire for that destruction he most fears, the presence of an Anthropocene sensibility is marked by signifiers of deep time and of a becoming-geological.

Just as nuclear and climate geographies and temporalities unsettle our sense of place and time, so nuclear and climate subjectivities unsettle our sense of the human. Nuclear fictions often posit literal post-humans. In future fictions, these may be radioactively mutated peoples, though not necessarily for the worse: unusually, in John Wyndham's *The Chrysalids* (1955) and Lawrence's *Children of the Dust* (1985), genetic mutations catalyse new, higher human development.[46] Yet there is a more quotidian being-nuclear, too. John Hersey's great work of feature journalism, 'Hiroshima' (1946; updated 1985), traces effects of radiation sickness amongst survivors of the bomb.[47] This experience is partly an uncanny one in which symptoms come and go and often cannot be pinned down definitively to atomic causes, but it is also psychological and social. The consequences of being a *hibakusha* (explosion-affected person) include marginalisation, difficulty getting and holding down employment, and trouble forming relationships because of suspicions about the effects of the bomb on reproductive health. Of course, the term *hibakusha* might be widened to embrace many groups around the world: former service personnel who are veterans of atomic testing; those displaced peoples in the South Pacific, the Australian outback, and elsewhere, whose lands were used for nuclear testing; and all those downwind of bomb tests. Indeed, if

[45] Tim O'Brien, *The Nuclear Age* (London: Flamingo, 1987), p. 302.
[46] John Wyndham, *The Chrysalids* (1955; London: Penguin, 2008); Lawrence, *Children of the Dust* (New York: Harper and Row, 1985).
[47] John Hersey, 'Hiroshima', *The New Yorker* (31 August 1946); Hersey, 'Hiroshima: the Aftermath', *The New Yorker* (15 July 1985).

the definition of a *hibakusha* is exposure to radionuclides, then the category may expand, at least during the Cold War, to embrace everyone.[48]

There is an uncanny sense of displacement and decentring of the human in many nuclear narratives. The idea of an authentic human self against which otherness might be measured is unsettled because the psychological effect of 'being' nuclear is often to make one's own body feel other. Such concerns chime with projections in climate fiction of post-human selves. For instance, the eponymous narrator of Paul McAuley's novel *Austral* (2017) gives us the post-human perspective of a 'husky', someone bio-engineered for the harsh climate of a melting Antarctic ice cap, but the subject of prejudice because of her otherness.[49] Imagining a world where dissident 'ecopoets' have tried to produce new ecosystems, *Austral* posits complex connections between people, technology, and climate that echo the radioactive futures of nuclear fictions.

More radical still is Jeff VanderMeer's novel *Borne* (2017). In an anarchic future city, terrorised by an enormous flying bear and populated by proliferating experiments from a collapsed biotech company, Rachel rescues Borne, an amorphous being that is variously described as a sea anemone, a plant, an animal, a machine, a boulder, a monster, and a weapon. Borne becomes variously Rachel's child, her pupil, her teacher, her confidant, her lover, and a murderer. Borne's radical mutability is bound up with a world that has no 'natural' space, separate from humans; its environments are entirely produced by and through them. Borne is sensitive to a pollution that is partly nuclear in origin. 'I see it', Borne says, 'I taste it. All the contamination. The low-level radiation, the storage sites, the runoff. Every place is sick – there's sick everywhere.'[50] Yet, in the absence of an authentic human (Rachel's memories are themselves revealed as being at least partially engineered) or natural space, the novel's characters have to find ways meaningfully to inhabit their post-human futures.

This is perhaps the point of convergence for nuclear and climate fictions, and nuclear and climate criticism. They expose the vulnerability

---

[48] This broadening of the term is seductive, speaking as it does to a profoundly shared contemporary sense of being nuclear, but it is problematic too because it runs a significant risk of hiding the distinct and life-changing experience of being nuclear of more traditionally defined *hibakusha* communities. Another dilemma is whether the descendants of, say, survivors of atomic bombing should automatically be considered *hibakusha* for the genetic, social, and cultural experience of being atomic they inherit from their parents.

[49] Paul McAuley, *Austral* (London: Gollancz, 2017).

[50] Jeff VanderMeer, *Borne* (London: HarperCollins, 2017), p. 145 [Kindle edition].

of all we want to experience as solid and fixed and lasting, revealing mutability at the heart of things. While they often deal in terrifying futures, the inhabitants of those futures also frequently find ways to negotiate them. For all that it is constrained, there is frequently a place for (post-)human agency. If our nuclear and our climate criticism can make our fictions speak meaningfully to us, it must surely be to provoke a positive sense of our capacity to exercise agency in the present: to accept both the enmeshment of humans, technology, and the planet, and to find a way ethically to act in the face of that enmeshment.

Bibliography

Abe, Kōbō. *Inter Ice Age 4*. Trans. E. Dale Saunders. New York: Perigee Trade, 1981.

Abrams, M. H. *Natural Supernaturalism: Tradition and Revolution in Romantic Literature*. New York: Norton, 1971.

Abrams, M. H. and Geoffrey Galt Harpham. *A Glossary of Literary Terms*. 9th edn. Boston: Wadsworth, 2008.

Adorno, Theodor W. *Aesthetic Theory*. Trans. Robert Hullot Kentnor. London: Athlone, 1997.

Agamben, Giorgio. 'Halos'. In *The Coming Community*. Minneapolis: University of Minnesota Press, 1993. 53–6.

Alaimo, Stacy. *Exposed: Environmental Politics and Pleasures in Posthuman Times*. Minneapolis: University of Minnesota Press, 2016.

Althochdeutsches Lesebuch. Ed. Wilhelm Braune and Ernst A. Ebbinghaus, 17th edn. Tübingen: Niemeyer, 1994.

Altman, Rick. *Film/Genre*. London: British Film Institute, 1999.

Amorosi, Thomas, Paul Buckland, Andrew Dugmore, John H. Ingimundarson, and Thomas H. McGovern. 'Raiding the Landscape: Human Impact in the Scandinavian North Atlantic', *Human Ecology*, 25 (1997), 491–518.

Amos, Jonathan. '"Loneliest Tree" Records Human Epoch'. *BBC News* (19 February 2018).

Angus, Ian. *Facing the Anthropocene: Fossil Capitalism and the Crisis of the Earth System*. New York: Monthly Review Press, 2016.

[Appletree, Thomas.] 1703 Weather Diary. Lancing College Archives. Lancing, West Sussex.

Aravamudan, Srinivas. 'The Catachronism of Climate Change', *Diacritics*, 41 (2013), 6–30.

Aristotle. *Meteorologica*. Trans. Henry D. P. Lee. 1952. Cambridge, MA: Harvard University Press, 1987.

Armstrong, Nancy. *Desire and Domestic Fiction: A Political History of the Novel*. Oxford University Press, 1987.

Arnaldur Indriðason. *Jar City*. Trans. Bernard Scudder. New York: Picador, 2004. *Strange Shores*. Trans. Victoria Cribb. New York: Picador, 2012.

[Assey, Charles.] 'Narrative of the Effects of the Eruption from the Tomboro Mountain, in the Island of Sumbawa, on the 11th and 12th of April 1815'. *Transactions of the Batavian Society, of Arts and Sciences*, 8 (1816), 3–4.

Atwood, Margaret. *Maddaddam*. London: Bloomsbury, 2013.
Oryx and Crake. London: Bloomsbury, 2003.
Stone Mattress. New York: Nan A. Talese/Doubleday, 2014.
The Year of the Flood. London: Bloomsbury, 2009.
Austen, Jane. *Persuasion*. Ed. James Kinsley and Deirdre Shauna Lynch. Oxford University Press, 2004.
Babbage, Charles. *The Ninth Bridgewater Treatise: a Fragment*. London: John Murray, 1837.
Bacigalupi, Paolo. *The Water Knife*. London: Orbit, 2015.
Badash, Lawrence. *A Nuclear Winter's Tale: Science and Politics in the 1980s*. Cambridge, MA: MIT Press, 2009.
Banks, Charles Edward. 'New Documents Relating to the Popham Expedition, 1607'. *Proceedings of the American Antiquarian Society*, 39 (1929), 307–34.
Barnes, Jessica. 'Rifts or Bridges? Ruptures and Continuities in Human–Environment Interactions'. *RCC Perspectives*, 2 (2016), 41–5.
Bashford, Alison. 'Anticolonial Climates: Physiology, Ecology, and Global Population, 1920s–1950s'. *Bulletin of the History of Medicine*, 86.4 (2012), 596–626.
Bashford, Alison and Sarah W. Tracy. 'Introduction: Modern Airs, Waters, and Places', *Bulletin of the History of Medicine*, 86.4 (2012), 495–514.
Bate, Jonathan. *The Song of the Earth*. London: Picador, 2000.
Baucom, Ian. 'History 4°: Postcolonial Method and Anthropocene Time'. *Cambridge Journal of Postcolonial Literary Inquiry*, 1 (2014), 123–42.
'"Moving Centers": Climate Change, Critical Method, and the Historical Novel'. *Modern Language Quarterly*, 76 (2015), 137–57.
Specters of the Atlantic: Finance Capital, Slavery, and the Philosophy of History. Durham, NC: Duke University Press, 2005.
Beatty, W. K. 'Some Medical Aspects of Rudyard Kipling'. *The Practitioner*, 215.1288 (1975), 532–42.
Beer, Gillian. *Virginia Woolf: the Common Ground*. Edinburgh University Press, 1996.
Bell, Martin and Michael J. C. Walker. *Late Quaternary Environmental Change: Physical and Human Perspectives*, 2nd edn. Harlow: Prentice Hall, 2005.
Benjamin, Walter. *The Arcades Project*. Trans. Howard Eiland and Kevin McLaughlin. Cambridge, MA: Belknap Press, 1999. 456–88.
On the Concept of History. Trans. Dennis Redmond. 2001; Rome: Global Rights Books, 2016.
'Theses on the Philosophy of History'. In Hannah Arendt (ed.), *Illuminations*. Trans. Harry Zohn. New York: Schocken, 1969. 253–64.
Bennett, Jane. *Vibrant Matter: a Political Ecology of Things*. Durham, NC: Duke University Press, 2010.
Berggren, J. Lennart and Alexander Jones. *Ptolemy's Geography: an Annotated Translation of the Theoretical Chapters*. Princeton University Press, 2000.
Bergman, Kerstin, ed. *Deckarnas svenska landskap: Från Skåne till Lappland*. Gothenburg: Makadam förlag, 2014.

Bewell, Alan. 'Jefferson's Thermometer: Colonial Biogeographical Constructions of the Climate of America'. In Noah Heringman (ed.), *Romantic Science: the Literary Forms of Natural History*. Albany: State University of New York Press, 2003. 111–38.

The Bible. Introd. Robert Carroll and Stephen Prickett. Oxford University Press, 1997. Authorised King James Version.

[Bisset, Charles.] *An Essay on the Medical Constitution of Great Britain*. London: A. Millar and D. Wilson, 1762.

Bisset, Charles. *Medical Essays and Observations*. Newcastle-upon-Tyne: I. Thompson, 1766.

Blade Runner 2049. Dir. Dennis Villeneuve. Sony, 2017.

Blake, William. *The Complete Poetry and Prose of William Blake*. Ed. David V. Erdman. New York: Anchor, 1988.

Blome, Richard. *A Description of the Island of Jamaica with the Other Isles and Territories in America, to Which the English are Related*. London, T. Milbourn, 1672.

Bloom, Dan. 'Thanks to TeleRead and NPR, Cli-fi is now an Official Literary Term'. *Tele-Read* (28 May 2013).

Bohun, Ralph. *A Discourse concerning the Origine and Properties of Wind*. Oxford: W. Hall, 1671.

Boia, Lucian. *The Weather in the Imagination*. London: Reaktion Books, 2005.

Boltanski, Luc. *Mysteries and Conspiracies: Detective Stories, Spy Novels and the Making of Modern Society*. Trans. Catherine Porter. Cambridge: Polity Press, 2014.

Boner, Patrick J. 'Kepler's Early Astrological Calendars: Matter, Methodology and Multidisciplinarity'. *Centaurus*, 50 (2008), 324–8.

Borgfirðinga sǫgur, ed. Sigurður Nordal and Guðni Jónsson. Íslenzk fornrit 3. Reykjavik: Hið íslenzka fornritafélag, 1916–18.

Bostrom, Nick. *Superintelligence: Paths, Dangers, Strategies*. Oxford University Press, 2014.

Boumelha, Penny. *Charlotte Brontë*. New York: Harvester Wheatsheaf, 1990.

Bowker, David. 'Meteorology and the Ancient Greeks', *Weather*, 66.9 (2011), 249–51.

Boyle, T. C. *A Friend of the Earth*. New York: Penguin, 2000.

Bracke, Astrid. *Climate Crisis and the Twenty-First-Century British Novel*. London: Bloomsbury, 2017.

Bradbury, Ray. *The Martian Chronicles*. 1950; New York: Simon and Schuster, 2012.

Bradstreet, Anne. *The Works of Anne Bradstreet*. Ed. Jeannine Hensley. Cambridge, MA: Belknap Press of Harvard University Press, 2010.

Brady, Amy. 'The Man Who Coined "Cli-Fi" Has Some Reading Suggestions for You'. *Chicago Review of Books* (8 February 2017).

Brennu-Njáls saga. Ed. Einar Ól. Sveinsson. Íslenzk fornrit 12. Reykjavik: Hið íslenzka fornritafélag, 1954.

Brin, David. *Earth*. London: Orbit, 1990.

Brinkley, William. *The Last Ship*. New York: Viking, 1988.

Brontë, Charlotte. *Jane Eyre.* Ed. Margaret Smith. Oxford University Press, 2008.

  Villette. Ed. Margaret Smith and Herbert Rosengarten. Oxford University Press, 2000.

Brontë, Emily. *Wuthering Heights.* Ed. Ian Jack. Oxford University Press, 2009.

Brynner, Rock. *The Doomsday Report: a Novel.* New York: William Morrow, 1998.

Buck, Pearl S. *Command the Morning.* London: Pan, 1962.

Buell, Lawrence. *The Environmental Imagination: Thoreau, Nature Writing, and the Formation of American Culture.* Cambridge, MA: Harvard University Press, 1996.

  'Toxic Discourse'. *Critical Inquiry,* 24.3 (1998), 639–65.

Buffon [Georges-Louis LeClerc] Comte de. *Natural History, General and Particular,* trans. William Smellie. 3rd edn, 9 vols. London: A. Strahan and T. Cadell, 1791.

  Natural History of Man, the Globe, and of Quadrupeds. New York: Leavitt and Allen, 1857.

Bump, Philip. 'This Has Been the Most Active Month for Hurricanes on Record'. *Washington Post* (27 September 2017).

Burns, William E. *The Age of Wonders: Prodigies, Politics and Providence in England, 1657–1727.* Manchester University Press, 2002.

Burton, Richard F. *Goa and the Blue Mountains.* London: Richard Bentley, 1851.

  Wanderings in West Africa. New York: Dover, 1991.

Byatt, A. S. *A Stone Woman.* London: Penguin, 2011.

Byrhtferth of Ramsey. *Byrhtferth's 'Enchiridion'.* Ed. Peter S. Baker and Michael Lapidge. Early English Text Society, s.s. 15. Oxford University Press, 1995.

Byron, Lord [George Gordon]. *The Complete Poetical Works,* ed. Jerome J. McGann. 7 vols. Oxford: Clarendon Press, 1980–93.

Campbell, John. *A Political Survey of Britain.* 2 vols. London: Richardson and Urquhart, 1774.

Campbell, John, ed. *Navigantium Atque Itinerantium Bibliotheca. Or, A Complete Collection of Voyages and Travels.* London, [1744–]1748.

Carr, Nicholas. *The Shallows: How the Internet Is Changing the Way We Read, Think and Remember.* London: Atlantic, 2010.

Carroll, Siobhan. 'Crusades against Frost: *Frankenstein,* Polar Ice, and Climate Change in 1818'. *European Romantic Review,* 24 (2013), 211–30.

  An Empire of Air and Water: Uncolonizable Space in the British Imagination, 1750–1850. Philadelphia: University of Pennsylvania Press, 2015.

Cave of Forgotten Dreams. Dir. Werner Herzog. IFC Films, 2010.

Caygill, Howard. 'Walter Benjamin's Concept of Cultural History'. In David S. Ferris (ed.), *The Cambridge Companion to Walter Benjamin.* Cambridge University Press, 2004. 73–96.

Chakrabarty, Dipesh. 'The Climate of History: Four Theses'. *Critical Inquiry,* 35.2 (2009), 197–222.

'The Human Significance of the Anthropocene'. In Bruno Latour and Christophe Leclercq (eds.), *Reset Modernity!* Cambridge, MA: MIT Press, 2016. 189–99.

'The Politics of Climate Change Is More Than the Politics of Capitalism'. *Theory, Culture and Society*, 34 (2017), 25–37.

'Postcolonial Studies and the Challenge of Climate Change'. *New Literary History*, 43 (2012), 1–18.

Provincializing Europe: Postcolonial Thought and Historical Difference. Princeton University Press, 2007.

'Whose Anthropocene? A Response'. *RCC Perspectives*, 2 (2016), 103–13.

Chambers, W. F. *The London Medical Gazette: Or, Journal of Practical Medicine*, 2 (1828).

Chaplin, Joyce E. 'Nature Philosophy and an Early Racial Idiom in North America: Comparing English and Indian Bodies'. *William and Mary Quarterly*, 54 (1997), 229–52.

Chapman, Alison A. 'The Politics of Time in Edmund Spenser's English Calendar'. *Studies in English Literature, 1500–1900*, 42 (2002), 1–24.

Clare, John. *The Shepherd's Calendar*. Ed. Eric Robinson, Geoffrey Summerfield, and David Powell. 2nd edn. Oxford University Press, 2014.

Clark, Timothy. *The Cambridge Introduction to Literature and the Environment*. Cambridge University Press, 2011.

'Derangements of Scale'. In Tom Cohen and Henry Sussman (eds.), *Telemorphosis: Essays in Critical Climate Change*, vol. 1. Ann Arbor: Open Humanities Press, 2012. 148–66.

Ecocriticism on the Edge: the Anthropocene as a Threshold Concept. London: Bloomsbury, 2015.

'Nature, Post-Nature'. In Louise Westling (ed.), *The Cambridge Companion to Literature and the Environment*. Cambridge University Press, 2014. 75–89.

Clarke, Arthur C. *The Sands of Mars*. London: Sidgwick and Jackson, 1976.

Clarke, Bruce. *Energy Forms: Allegory and Science in the Era of Classical Thermodynamics*. Ann Arbor: University of Michigan Press, 2001.

Clarke, Jim. 'Reading Climate Change in J. G. Ballard'. *Critical Survey*, 25 (2013), 7–21.

Cohen, Jeffrey Jerome. *Stone: an Ecology of the Inhuman*. Minneapolis: University of Minnesota Press, 2015.

Cohen, Jeffrey Jerome and Lowell Duckert. 'Introduction: Welcome to the Whirled'. In Cohen and Duckert (eds.), *Veer Ecology: a Companion for Environmental Thinking*. Minneapolis: University of Minnesota Press, 2017. 1–15.

Coleridge, Samuel Taylor. *The Major Works*. Ed. H. J. Jackson. 1985. Oxford University Press, 2008.

Collings, David. *Stolen Future, Broken Present: the Human Significance of Climate Change*. Ann Arbor, MI: Open Humanities Press, 2014.

Combined Universities in Cornwall. *Review 2011*. Redruth, 2012. cuc.ac.uk/assets/uploads/ar2011.pdf

Conrad, Joseph. *Heart of Darkness*. Ed. Robert Kimbrough. 3rd edn. New York: Norton, 1988.

Cook, Alan. *Edmond Halley: Charting the Heavens and the Seas*. Oxford University Press, 1998.

Cook, Paul. *Duende Meadow*. New York: Bantam, 1985.

Cooper, James Fenimore. *The Last of the Mohicans*. New York: Random House, 2001.

Cordle, Daniel. 'The Futures of Nuclear Criticism'. *Alluvium*, 5.3 (2016).

Late Cold War Literature and Culture: the Nuclear 1980s. London: Palgrave-Macmillan, 2017.

'Science/Humans/Humanities: Dexter Masters' The Accident and Being in the Nuclear Age'. *Journal of Literature and Science*, 10.2 (2017), 74–87.

Cowper, William. *The Letters and Prose Writings of William Cowper*. Ed. James King and Charles Ryskamp. 5 vols. Oxford: Clarendon Press, 1979–86.

The Poems of William Cowper. Ed. John D. Baird and Charles Ryskamp. 3 vols. Oxford: Clarendon Press, 1980–95.

Craik, Elizabeth M. *The 'Hippocratic' Corpus: Content and Context*. New York: Routledge, 2015.

Crichton, Michael. *State of Fear*. New York: HarperCollins, 2004.

Crosby, Alfred. *Ecological Imperialism: the Biological Expansion of Europe, 900–1900*. 2nd edn. Cambridge University Press, 2004.

Cross, J. E. 'Aspects of Microcosm and Macrocosm in Old English Literature'. In Stanley Greenfield (ed.), *Studies in Old English Literature in Honor of Arthur G. Brodeur*. Eugene: University of Oregon Books, 1963. 1–22.

Cui, Ying and Lee R. Kump. 'Global Warming and the End-Permian Extinction Event: Proxy and Modeling Perspectives'. *Earth-Science Reviews*, 149 (2014).

Currie, William. *An Historical Account of the Climates and Diseases of the United States of America*. Philadelphia: T. Dobson, 1792.

Cushman, Gregory. 'Humboldtian Science, Creole Meteorology, and the Discovery of Human-Caused Climate Change in South America'. *Osiris*, 26 (2011), 16–44.

Cyprian of Carthage. *A Démétrien*. Ed. and trans. Jean-Claude Fredouille. Sources Chrétiennes 467. Paris: Cerf, 2003.

Daniels, Stephen and Georgina Endfield. 'Narratives of Climate Change: Introduction'. *Journal of Historical Geography*, 35 (2009), 215–22.

Danowski, Déborah and Eduardo Viveiros de Castro. *The Ends of the World*. Trans. Rodrigo Guimaraes Nunes. Cambridge: Polity Press, 2016.

Dante Alighieri. *The Divine Comedy*. Trans. Henry Francis Cary. Ware, Hertfordshire: Wordsworth Editions, 2009.

Darby, Peter. *Bede and the End of Time*. Farnham: Ashgate, 2012.

Darwin, Charles. *On the Origin of Species: a Facsimile of the First Edition*. Cambridge, MA: Harvard University Press, 1964.

Daston, Lorraine and Peter Galison. *Objectivity*. New York: Zone Books, 2007.

The Day after Tomorrow. Dir. Roland Emmerich. Twentieth Century Fox, 2004.

The Day after Trinity. Dir. Jon H. Else. PBS, 1981.

[Defoe, Daniel.] *The Storm: Or, a Collection of the Most Remarkable Casualties and Disasters Which Happen'd in the Late Dreadful Tempest Both by Sea and Land.* London: G. Sawbridge, 1704.

Defoe, Daniel. *The Storm.* Ed. Richard Hamblyn. London: Penguin, 2003.

DeGroot, Gerard. *The Bomb: a History of Hell on Earth.* London: Pimlico, 2005.

Derham, William. 'A Letter . . . Containing his Observations concerning the Late Storm'. *Philosophical Transactions of the Royal Society*, 24.289 (1704–5), 1530–4.

Derrida, Jacques. 'No Apocalypse, Not Now (Full Speed Ahead, Seven Missiles, Seven Missives)'. Trans. Catherine Porter and Philip Lewis. *Diacritics*, 14 (1984), 20–31.

'Of an Apocalyptic Tone Recently Adopted in Philosophy'. Trans. John P. Leavey. In Peter Fenves (ed.), *Raising the Tone of Philosophy: Late Essays by Immanuel Kant, Transformative Critique by Jacques Derrida.* Baltimore: Johns Hopkins University Press, 1993. 63–97.

Diamond, Jared. *Collapse: How Societies Choose to Fail or Succeed.* London: Penguin, 2005.

Dickens, Charles. *Bleak House.* Ed. George Ford and Sylvère Monod. New York: Norton, 1977.

Diogenes Laertius. *Lives of the Eminent Philosophers.* Ed. and trans. Tiziano Dorandi. Cambridge University Press, 2013.

Dionne, Craig. *Posthuman Lear: Reading Shakespeare in the Anthropocene.* New York: Punctum, 2016.

Dionne, Craig and Lowell Duckert, eds. 'Shakespeare in the Anthropocene'. Special issue of *Early Modern Culture*, 18 (2018).

DiPietro, Cary and Hugh Grady, eds. *Shakespeare and the Urgency of Now: Criticism and Theory in the 21st Century.* New York: Palgrave-Macmillan, 2013.

Döblin, Alexander. *Berge Meere und Giganten.* Berlin: S. Fischer, 1924.

'Mountains Oceans Giants'. Trans. Chris Godwin. *The Brooklyn Rail* (December 2016). http://intranslation.brooklynrail.org/german/mountains-oceans-giants.

Dong, Xuhui, Helen Bennion, Richard W. Battarbee, and Carl D. Sayer. 'A Multiproxy Palaeolimnological Study of Climate and Nutrient Impacts on Esthwaite Water, England over the Past 1200 Years'. *The Holocene*, 22 (2011), 107–18.

Dryden, John. *Prologue to the King and Queen at the Opening of Their Theatre, Spoken by Mr Batterton.* London: Jacob Tonson, 1683.

Duckert, Lowell. *For All Waters: Finding Ourselves in Early Modern Wetscapes.* Minneapolis: University of Minnesota Press, 2017.

Dugatkin, Lee Alan. *Mr Jefferson and the Giant Moose: Natural History in Early America.* University of Chicago Press, 2009.

Dugmore, Andrew J., Thomas H. McGovern, Orri Vésteinsonn, Jette Arneborg, Richard Streeter, and Christian Keller. 'Cultural Adaptation, Compounding

Vulnerabilities and Conjunctures in Norse Greenland'. *PNAS*, 109.10 (2012), 3658–63.

Dürbeck, Gabriele. 'Climate Change Fiction and Ecothrillers in Contemporary German-Speaking Literature'. In Dürbeck, Urte Stobbe, Hubert Zapf and Evi Zemanek (eds.), *Ecological Thought in German Literature and Culture*. Lanham: Lexington, 2017. 331–45.

Edric, Robert. *Salvage*. London: Doubleday, 2010.

Edwards, Paul N. *A Vast Machine: Computer Models, Climate Data, and the Politics of Global Warming*. Cambridge, MA: MIT Press, 2010.

Egils Saga. Ed. Bjarni Einarsson. London: Viking Society for Northern Research, University College London, 2003.

Ekman, Kerstin. *Blackwater*. Trans. Joan Tate. New York: St Martin's Press, 1996.

Elbow, Gary S. 'Creating an Atmosphere: Depiction of Climate in the Works of Gabriel García Márquez'. In Janet Pérez and Wendell Aycock (eds.), *Climate and Literature: Reflections on Environment*. Lubbock: Texas Tech University, 1995. 73–81.

Elder, John and Glenn Adelson, 'Robert Frost's Ecosystem of Meanings in "Spring Pools"'. *ISLE: Interdisciplinary Studies in Literature and Environment*, 13.2 (2006), 1–17.

Elysium. Dir. Neill Blomkamp. TriStar, 2013.

Empson, William. *Seven Types of Ambiguity*. New York: New Directions, 1966.

Evancie, Angela. 'So Hot Right Now: Has Climate Change Created a New Literary Genre?' *NPR* (20 April 2013).

Eyrbyggja saga. Ed. Einar Ól. Sveinsson and Matthías Þórðarson. Íslenzk fornrit 4. Reykjavik: Hið íslenzka fornritafélag, 1935.

Fagan, Brian. *The Little Ice Age: How Climate Made History*. New York: Basic Books, 2000.

Falconer, William. *Remarks on the Influence of Climate . . . [on] Mankind*. London: C. Dilly, 1781.

Fan, Ka-wai. 'Climate Change and Chinese History: a Review of Trends, Topics, and Methods'. *WIREs Climate Change*, 6 (2015), 225–38.

Fang, J. Q. 'Establishment of a Data Bank from Records of Climatic Disasters and Anomalies in Ancient Chinese Documents'. *International Journal of Climatology* 12 (2006), 499–519.

Fanon, Frantz. *Black Skin, White Masks*. Trans. Richard Philcox. New York: Grove Press, 2006.

Feldman, Theodore S. 'Late Enlightenment Meteorology'. In Tore Frängsmyr, J. L. Heilbron, and Robin Rider (eds.), *The Quantifying Spirit in the Eighteenth Century*. Berkeley: University of California Press, 1990. 143–79.

Ferguson, Frances. 'The Nuclear Sublime'. *Diacritics*, 14.2 (1984), 4–10.

Ferris, David S. 'Introduction: Aura, Resistance, and the Event of History'. In Ferris (ed.), *Walter Benjamin: Theoretical Questions*. Stanford University Press, 1996. 1–26.

Fiskio, Janet. 'Apocalypse and Ecotopia: Narratives in Global Climate Change Discourse'. *Race, Gender and Class*, 19 (2012), 12–36.

Fleck, Dirk. *GO! Die Ökodiktatur*. Hamburg: Rasch und Röhring, 2004.
Fleming, James Rodger. 'Global Environmental Change and the History of Science'. In Mary Jo Nye (ed.), *The Cambridge History of Science, Volume v: The Modern Physical and Mathematical Sciences*. Cambridge University Press, 2002. 634–50.
  Historical Perspectives on Climate Change. Oxford University Press, 1998.
Fleming, James Rodger and Vladimir Janković. 'Revisiting Klima'. *Osiris*, 26 (2011), 1–15.
Ford, Thomas H. 'Punctuating History circa 1800: the Air of *Jane Eyre*'. In Tobias Menely and Jesse Oak Taylor (eds.), *Anthropocene Reading: Literary History in Geologic Times*. University Park: Pennsylvania State University Press, 2017. 78–95.
Fort, Tom. *Under the Weather: Us and the Elements*. London: Century, 2006.
Fothergill, John. *The Works of John Fothergill*. Ed. J. C. Lettsom. London: Charles Dilly, 1784.
Fourier, Jean-Baptiste Joseph. 'On the Temperatures of the Terrestrial Space and Interplanetary Space', trans. R. T. Pierrehumbert (2004). https://geosci.uchicago.edu/~rtp1/papers/Fourier1827Trans.pdf.
Franzen, Jonathan. *Freedom*. New York: Farrar, Straus and Giroux, 2010.
Freedgood, Elaine. *The Ideas in Things: Fugitive Meaning in the Victorian Novel*. University of Chicago Press, 2006.
Frei, Karin M., Ashley N. Coutu, Konrad Smiarowski *et al.* 'Was It for Walrus? Viking Age Settlement and Medieval Walrus Ivory Trade in Iceland and Greenland'. *World Archaeology*, 74 (2015), 439–66.
Frisch, Max. *Man in the Holocene*. Trans. Geoffrey Skelton. San Diego: Harcourt Brace, 1980.
  Der Mensch erscheint im Holozän. Berlin: Suhrkamp, 1979.
F[ulke], W[illiam]. *Meteors: Or a Plain Description of All Kinds of Meteors*. London: William Leake, 1670.
Gallagher, Catherine. 'The Rise of Fictionality'. In Franco Moretti (ed.), *The Novel, Volume 1: History, Geography and Culture*. Princeton University Press, 2006. 359–61.
Gee, Maggie. *Grace*. London: Abacus, 1989.
  The Ice People. 1998; London: Telegram, 2008.
Gerbi, Antonello. *The Dispute of the New World: the History of a Polemic*. Trans. Jeremy Moyle. University of Pittsburgh Press, 1973.
Ghosh, Amitav. *The Great Derangement: Climate Change and the Unthinkable*. University of Chicago Press, 2016.
Gidal, Eric. 'Civic Melancholy: English Gloom and French Enlightenment'. *Eighteenth-Century Studies*, 37 (2003), 23–45.
  '"O Happy Earth! Reality of Heaven!": Melancholy and Utopia in Romantic Climatology'. *Journal of Early Modern Cultural Studies*, 8 (2008), 74–101.
Gifford, Robert. '33 Reasons Why We Can't Think Clearly about Climate Change'. *New Scientist* (8 July 2015).
Gilroy, Paul. *The Black Atlantic: Modernity and Double Consciousness*. Cambridge, MA: Harvard University Press, 1995.

Glacken, Clarence J. *Traces on the Rhodian Shore: Nature and Culture in Western Thought from Ancient Times to the End of the Eighteenth Century*. Berkeley: University of California Press, 1967.

Glass, Matthew. *Ultimatum*. London: Atlantic, 2009.

Glass, Rodge. 'Global Warming: the Rise of Cli-fi'. *The Guardian* (31 May 2013).

Golinski, Jan. 'American Climate and the Civilization of Nature'. In James Delbourgo and Nicholas Dew (eds.), *Science and Empire in the Atlantic World*. New York: Routledge, 2008. 153–74.

British Weather and the Climate of Enlightenment. University of Chicago Press, 2007.

'"Exquisite Atmography": Theories of the World and Experiences of the Weather in a Diary of 1703'. *British Journal for the History of Science*, 34 (2001), 149–71.

Goodbody, Axel. 'Frame Analysis and the Literature of Climate Change'. In Timo Müller and Michael Sauter (eds.), *Literature, Ecology, Ethics: Recent Trends in Ecocriticism*. Heidelberg: Universitätsverlag Winter, 2012. 15–33.

'Melting Ice and the Paradoxes of Zeno: Didactic Impulses and Aesthetic Distanciation in German Climate Change Fiction'. *Ecozon@*, 4 (2013), 92–102.

'Telling the Story of Climate Change: the German Novel in the Anthropocene'. In Caroline Schaumann and Heather I. Sullivan (eds.), *German Ecocriticism in the Anthropocene*. New York: Palgrave-Macmillan, 2017. 293–314.

Gorges, Ferdinando. 'A Brief Narration of the Originall Undertakings of the Advancement of Plantations into the Parts of America'. In James Phinney Baxter (ed.), *Sir Ferdinando Gorges and His Province of Maine*. 20 vols. Boston: Prince Society, 1890. Vol. XIX, 1–82.

Gould, Stephen Jay. *Time's Arrow, Time's Cycle: Myth and Metaphor in the Discovery of Geological Time*. Cambridge, MA: Harvard University Press, 1987.

Graybill, Andrew R. 'Boundless Nature: Borders and the Environment in North America and Beyond'. In Andrew C. Isenberg (ed.), *The Oxford Handbook of Environmental History*. Oxford University Press, 2014. 578–94.

Gregory, Derek, Ron Johnston, Geraldine Pratt, Michael J. Watts, and Sarah Whatmore. *The Dictionary of Human Geography*. 5th edn. Malden, MA: Wiley-Blackwell, 2009.

Gregory, Horace. *Dorothy Richardson: an Adventure in Self-Discovery*. New York: Holt, Rinehart and Winston, 1967.

Grettis saga Ásmundarsonar, Bandamanna saga, Odds þáttr Ófeigssonar. Ed. Guðni Jónsson. Íslenzk fornrit 7. Reykjavik: Hið íslenzka fornritafélag, 1936.

Griffiths, Devin. 'Romantic Planet: Science and Literature within the Anthropocene'. *Literature Compass*, 14 (2017).

Groom, Nick. *The Seasons: an Elegy for the Passing of the Year*. London: Atlantic, 2013.

Grove, Richard. *Green Imperialism: Colonial Expansion, Tropical Island Edens, and the Origins of Environmentalism, 1600–1860*. Cambridge University Press, 1995.

Gumbrecht, Hans Ulrich. *Atmosphere, Mood, Stimmung: on a Hidden Potential of Literature*. Trans. Erik Butler. Stanford University Press, 2012.

Gunnar Karlsson. *Iceland's 1100 Years: History of a Marginal Society*. Reykjavik: Mál og menning, 2000.

Habermas, Jürgen. *Postmetaphysical Thinking: Philosophical Essays*. Trans. William Mark Hohengarten. Cambridge, MA: MIT Press, 1994.

Hales, Peter B. 'The Atomic Sublime'. *American Studies*, 32.1 (1991), 5–31.

Hall, Lynn. *If Winter Comes*. New York: Scribner, 1986.

Hall, Sarah. *The Carhullan Army*. London: Faber, 2007.

Halley, Edmond. 'Some Considerations about the Cause of the Universal Deluge, Laid before the Royal Society, on the 12th of December 1694'. *Philosophical Transactions of the Royal Society*, 33.383 (1724), 118–23.

Hamacher, Werner. '"Now": Walter Benjamin on Historical Time'. In Andrew E. Benjamin (ed.), *Walter Benjamin and History*. London: Bloomsbury, 2005. 38–68.

Hamilton, Jennifer Mae. *This Contentious Storm: an Ecocritical and Performance History of* King Lear. London: Bloomsbury, 2017.

Hannah, Robert. *Greek and Roman Calendars: Constructions of Time in the Classical World*. London: Duckworth, 2005.

Time in Antiquity. New York: Routledge, 2009.

Haraway, Donna. 'Anthropocene, Capitalocene, Plantationocene, Chthulucene: Making Kin'. *Environmental Humanities*, 6 (2015), 159–65.

Staying with the Trouble: Making Kin in the Chthulucene. Durham, NC: Duke University Press, 2016.

Hardy, Thomas. *The Return of the Native*. Ed. Simon Gatrell, Nancy Barrineau, and Margaret R. Higonnet. Oxford University Press, 2008.

Tess of the D'Urbervilles. Ed. Simon Gatrell and Juliet Grindle. Oxford University Press, 2005.

Hare, F. Kenneth. 'The Concept of Climate'. *Geography*, 51 (1966), 99–110.

Hariot, Thomas. *A Briefe and True Report of the New Found Land of Virginia . . . .* London, 1588.

Harper, Kristine C. *Weather by the Numbers: the Genesis of Modern Meteorology*. Cambridge, MA: MIT Press, 2008.

Harris, Alexandra. *Weatherland: Writers and Artists under English Skies*. London: Thames and Hudson, 2015.

Harrison, Mark. *Climates and Constitutions: Health, Race, Environment and British Imperialism in India, 1600–1850*. Oxford University Press, 1999.

'Differences of Degree: Representations of India in British Medical Topography, 1820–c.1870'. In Nicolaas A. Rupke (ed.), *Medical Geography in Historical Perspective*. Volume xx of *Medical History*. London: Wellcome Trust Centre for the History of Medicine, 2000.

Haynes, Robert H. 'How Might Mars Become a Home for Humans?'. 1993. *The Terraforming Information Pages*. users.globalnet.co.uk/~mfogg/haynes.htm.

Hearne, Samuel. *A Journey from Prince of Wales's Fort in Hudson's Bay to the Northern Ocean, 1769, 1770, 1771, 1772*, ed. Richard Glover. Toronto: Macmillan, 1958.

Hedling, Olof. 'Murder, Mystery and Megabucks? Films and Filmmaking as Regional and Local Place Promotion in Southern Sweden'. In Erik

Hedling, Olof Hedling, and Mats Jönsson (eds.), *Regional Aesthetics: Locating Swedish Media*. Stockholm: National Library of Sweden. 263–90.

Heise, Ursula K. *Sense of Place and Sense of Planet: the Environmental Imagination of the Global*. Oxford University Press, 2008.

Heliand und Genesis. Ed. Otto Behaghel and Burkhard Taeger. 10th edn. Tübingen: Niemeyer, 1996.

Heninger, S.K. *A Handbook of Renaissance Meteorology*. New York: Greenwood Press, 1968.

Herbert, Frank. *Dune*. Sevenoaks, Kent: New English Library, 1965.

Hersey, John. 'Hiroshima'. *The New Yorker* (31 August 1946).

'Hiroshima: the Aftermath'. *The New Yorker* (15 July 1985).

Herzog, Arthur. *Heat*. New York: Simon and Schuster, 1977.

Hesiod, *Works and Days*. In *Theogony. Works and Days. Testimonia*. Ed. and trans. Glenn W. Most. Loeb Classical Library 57. Cambridge, MA: Harvard University Press, 2007. 86–153.

Heywood, John. *The Playe of the Weather*. London: Ihon Awdeley, 1573.

Hicks, Robin. 'Why is the Media Under-reporting Climate Change?' *Eco-business* (7 March 2017).

Higgins, David. *British Romanticism, Climate Change, and the Anthropocene: Writing Tambora*. London: Palgrave-Macmillan, 2017.

Romantic Englishness: Local, National, and Global Selves, 1780–1850. Basingstoke: Palgrave-Macmillan, 2014.

Hillary, William. *Observations on the Changes of the Air and the Concomitant Epidemic Diseases in the Island of Barbados*, 2nd edn. London: L. Hawes et al., 1766.

Hiltner, Ken. 'Reading the Present in our Environmental Past'. In Jennifer Munroe, Edward J. Geisweidt, and Lynne Bruckner (eds.), *Ecological Approaches to Early Modern English Texts: a Field Guide to Reading and Teaching*. Farnham: Ashgate, 2015. 29–36.

Hippocrates. *On Airs, Waters and Places*. London: Wyman and Sons, 1881.

Høeg, Peter. *Smilla's Sense of Snow*. Trans. Tiina Nunnally. New York: Farrar, Straus and Giroux, 1993.

Hooke, Robert. 'Method for Making a History of the Weather'. In Thomas Sprat, *The History of the Royal Society of London*. London: J. Martyn, 1667. 173–9.

Houellebecq, Michel. *La possibilité d'une île*. Paris: Fayard, 2005.

The Possibility of an Island. Trans. Gavin Bowd. London: Weidenfeld and Nicholson, 2005.

House of Cards. Created by Beau Willimon. Media Rights Capital, Panic Pictures, Trigger Street Productions, 2013–.

Howell, Jessica. *Exploring Victorian Travel Literature: Disease, Race and Climate*. Edinburgh University Press, 2014.

Malaria and Victorian Fictions of Empire. Cambridge University Press, 2018.

Hugenholtz, F. W. N. '*Les terreurs de l'an mil*: Enkele hypothesen'. In A. de Buck (ed.), *Varia historica: Aangeboden aan Professor Doctor A. W. Byvanck*. Assen: Van Gorcum, 1954. 110–23.

Hulme, Mike. 'Climate'. In Bruce R. Smith (ed.). *The Cambridge Guide to the Worlds of Shakespeare*. 2 vols. Cambridge University Press, 2015. Vol. 1, 30–1.
  Weathered: Cultures of Climate. London: Sage, 2017.
  Why We Disagree about Climate Change. Cambridge University Press, 2009.
Hume, David. 'Of National Characters'. In Hume, *Essays: Moral, Political Literary*, ed. Eugene F. Miller. Indianapolis: Liberty Classics, 1987.
Hutchings, Kevin. 'Writing Commerce and Cultural Progress in Samuel Hearne's *A Journey . . . to the Northern Ocean*'. *ARIEL: a Review of International English Literature*, 28 (1997), 49–78.
Hutton, James. *Theory of the Earth, with Proofs and Illustrations*. 2nd edn, 2 vols. Edinburgh, 1795.
Hvistendahl, Mara. 'Can "Predictive Policing" Prevent Crime Before It Happens?' *Science* (28 September 2016).
Ingold, Tim. 'Landscape or Weather-World?'. In Ingold, *Being Alive: Essays on Movement, Knowledge, and Description*. New York: Routledge, 2011. 126–35.
Into the Storm. Dir. Steven Quale. Warner Bros., 2014.
Iovino, Serenella and Serpil Oppermann, eds. *Material Ecocriticism*. Bloomington: Indiana University Press, 2014.
IPCC. *Mitigation of Climate Change: Working Group III Contribution to the Fifth Assessment Report of the Intergovernmental Panel on Climate Change*. Ed. Ottomar Edenhofer, Ramón Pichs-Madruga, Youba Sokona *et al.* Cambridge University Press, 2014.
Íslendingabók, Landnámabók. Ed. Jakob Benediktsson. Íslenzk fornrit 1. Reykjavik: Hið íslenzka fornritafélag, 1986.
Itäranta, Emmi. *Memory of Water*. London: HarperVoyager, 2014.
Ivanchikova, Alla. 'Geomediations in the Anthropocene: Fictions of the Geologic Turn'. *C21 Literature: Journal of 21st-Century Writings*, 6.1 (2018).
Jacobson, Kristin J. 'Radical Homemaking in Contemporary American Environmental Fiction'. *C21 Literature: Journal of 21st-Century Writings*, 6.1 (2018).
James, Erin. *The Storyworld Accord: Econarratology and Postcolonial Narratives*. Lincoln: University of Nebraska Press, 2015.
Jameson, Fredric. *The Antinomies of Realism*. London: Verso, 2015.
Janković, Vladimir. *Reading the Skies: a Cultural History of English Weather, 1650–1820*. Manchester University Press, 2000.
Jasanoff, Sheila. 'A New Climate for Society'. *Theory Culture Society*, 27 (2010), 233–53.
Jefferson, Thomas. *Notes on the State of Virginia* [1787]. In Jefferson, *The Portable Thomas Jefferson*, ed. Merrill D. Peterson. New York: Viking Press, 1975. 23–232.
Jeske, Hans. 'Zur Etymologie des Wortes *muspilli*'. *Zeitschrift für deutsches Altertum und deutsche Literatur*, 135.4 (2006), 425–34.
Johns-Putra, Adeline. 'Ecocriticism, Genre, and Climate Change: Reading the Utopian Vision of Kim Stanley Robinson's Science in the Capital Trilogy'. *English Studies*, 91 (2010), 744–60.

'Historicizing the Networks of Ecology and Culture: Eleanor Anne Porden and Nineteenth-Century Climate Change'. *ISLE: Interdisciplinary Studies in Literature and Environment*, 22 (2015), 27–46.

'The Rest Is Silence: Postmodern and Postcolonial Possibilities in Climate Change Fiction'. *Studies in the Novel*, 50 (2018), 26–42.

'The Unsustainable Aesthetics of Sustainability: the Sense of No Ending in Jeanette Winterson's *The Stone Gods*'. In Johns-Putra, John Parham, and Louise Squire (eds.), *Literature and Sustainability: Text, Concept, and Culture*. Manchester University Press, 2017. 177–94.

Johnson, James. *The British and Foreign Medico-Chirurgical Review, or, Quarterly Journal of Practical Medicine and Surgery*, 51 (1848).

Johnson, Samuel. *The Lives of the Poets*. Ed. John H. Middendorf. Vol. XIII of *The Yale Edition of the Works of Samuel Johnson*. Gen. ed. Robert DeMaria, Jr. New Haven, CT: Yale University Press, 2010.

Johnson, Susannah Willard. *A Narrative of the Captivity of Mrs Johnson. Containing an Account of Her Sufferings, During Four Years with the Indians and the French*. Walpole, NH: David Carlisle, 1796.

Jones, Gwilym. *Shakespeare's Storms*. Manchester University Press, 2015.

Jones, Philip D. and Michael E. Mann. 'Climate over Past Millennia'. *Reviews of Geophysics*, 42nd ser., RG2002 (2004), 1–42.

Jónsbók: Kong Magnus Hakonssons Lovbog for Island. Ed. Ólafur Halldórsson. Copenhagen: Møller, 1904.

Jordan, James W. 'Arctic Climate and Landscape ca. AD 800–1400'. In Herbert Maschner, Owen Mason, and Robert McGhee (eds.), *The Northern World AD 900–1400*. Salt Lake City: University of Utah Press, 2009. 7–29.

Jouanna, Jacques. *Greek Medicine from Hippocrates to Galen*. Boston: Brill, 2012. *Hippocrate*. Paris: Fayard, 1992.

Kalidasa. 'Rtusamhāram (The Gathering of the Seasons)'. *The Loom of Time*. Trans. Chandra Rajan. New Delhi: Penguin, 1999. 103–35.

Kalm, Pehr. *Peter Kalm's Travels in North America*. Ed. Adolph B. Benson. 2 vols. New York: Wilson-Erikson, 1937.

Kandlbauer, J., P. O. Hopcroft, P. J. Valdes, and R. S. J. Sparks, 'Climate and Carbon Cycle Responses to the 1815 Tambora Volcanic Eruption'. *Journal of Geophysical Research: Atmospheres*, 118 (2013), 12497–12507.

Kant, Immanuel. *Groundwork of the Metaphysics of Morals*. Trans. Mary J. Gregor and Jens Timmerman. Cambridge University Press, 2011.

Katrín Jakobsdóttir. 'Meaningless Icelanders: Icelandic Crime Fiction and Nationality'. In Andrew Nestingen and Paula Arvas (eds.), *Scandinavian Crime Fiction*. Cardiff: University of Wales Press, 2011. 46–61.

Keats, John. *The Major Works*, Ed. Elizabeth Cook. 1990; Oxford University Press, 2008.

Kennedy, Dane. *Island of White: Settler Society and Culture in Kenya and Southern Rhodesia, 1890–1939*. Durham, NC: Duke University Press, 1987.

Kermode, Frank. *The Sense of an Ending: Studies in the Theory of Fiction*. 1967; Oxford University Press, 2000.

Kerridge, Richard. 'The Single Source'. *Ecozon@*, 1 (2010), 155–60.

Kilgore, De Witt Douglas. 'Making Huckleberries: Reforming Science and Whiteness in Science in the Capital'. *Configurations*, 20 (2012), 89–108.

The Killing (Forbrydelsen). Created by Søren Sveistrup. DR, 2007–12.

Kingsolver, Barbara. *Flight Behaviour*. London: Faber, 2012.

Kington, John, ed. *The Weather Journals of a Rutland Squire: Thomas Barker of Lyndon Hall*. Oakham: Rutland Record Society, 1988.

Kintisch, Eli. 'The Lost Norse'. *Science*, 354.6313 (2016), 696–701.

Kipling, Rudyard. *The City of Dreadful Night and Other Places*. Allahabad: A. H. Wheeler and Company, 1891.

'De Profundis (A Study in a Sick Room)'. *Civil and Military Gazette* (7 August 1885). Rpt. in *Kipling's India: Uncollected Sketches 1884–1888*, ed. Thomas Pinney. New York: Schocken, 1986. 120.

Klein, Naomi. *This Changes Everything: Capitalism vs. the Climate*. New York: Simon and Schuster, 2014.

Knight, Sarah Kemble. *The Journal of Madam Knight*. Ed. George Parker Winship. Boston: Small, Maynard and Company, 1920.

Kupperman, Karen Ordahl. 'Fears of Hot Climates in the Anglo-American Colonial Experience'. *William and Mary Quarterly*, 41 (1984), 213–40.

'The Puzzle of the American Climate in the Early Colonial Period'. *American Historical Review*, 87 (1982), 1262–89.

Landes, Richard, Andrew Gow, and David C. Van Meter, eds. *The Apocalyptic Year 1000: Religious Expectation and Social Change, 950–1050*. Oxford University Press, 2003.

'Landzleigu bolkr'. In Rudolph Keyser and Peter Andreas Munch (eds.), *Norges gamle love indtil 1387*. Christiania, Oslo: Grøndahl, 1846–95. Vol. ii, pp. 104–49.

Langeslag, P. S. *Seasons in the Literatures of the Medieval North*. Cambridge: D. S. Brewer, 2015.

The Last Tasmanian. Dir. Tom Haydon. Australian Film Commission, 1978.

Latour, Bruno. 'Agency at the Time of the Anthropocene'. *New Literary History*, 45 (2014), 1–18.

Facing Gaia: Eight Lectures on the New Climatic Regime. Trans. Catherine Porter. Cambridge: Polity Press, 2017.

Laurence, William L. 'Eyewitness Account of Bomb Test'. *New York Times* (16 July 1985).

Lawrence, D. H. *The Letters of D. H. Lawrence, Volume ii: June 1913–October 1916*. Ed. George J. Zytaruk and James T. Boulton. Cambridge University Press, 1979.

Lawrence, Louise. *Children of the Dust*. New York: Harper and Row, 1985.

Leapor, Mary. *Poems upon Several Occasions*. London: J. Roberts, 1748.

Leckie, Barbara. 'Sequence and Fragment, History and Thesis: Samuel Smiles's *Self-Help*, Social Change, and Climate Change'. *Nineteenth-Century Contexts*, 38 (2016), 305–17.

Lee, Hermione. *The Novels of Virginia Woolf.* New edn. Abingdon: Routledge, 2010.

LeGuin, Ursula K. *The Lathe of Heaven.* New York: Scribner, 2008.

Lehoux, Daryn. *Astronomy, Weather, and Calendars in the Ancient World: Parapegmata and Related Texts in Classical and Near-Eastern Societies.* Cambridge University Press, 2007.

'Impersonal and Intransitive ἐπισημαίνει'. *Classical Philology*, 99 (2004), 78–85.

LeMenager, Stephanie. 'Climate Change and the Struggle for Genre'. In Tobias Menely and Jesse Oak Taylor (eds.), *Anthropocene Reading: Literary History in Geologic Times.* University Park: Pennsylvania State University Press, 2017. 220–38.

Lenton, Tim. *Earth System Science: a Very Short Introduction.* Oxford University Press, 2016.

Levy, Anita. 'Gendered Labor, the Woman Writer and Dorothy Richardson', *Novel: a Forum on Fiction*, 25 (1991), 50–70.

Lewis, Jayne Elizabeth. *Air's Appearance: Literary Atmosphere in British Fiction, 1660–1794.* University of Chicago Press, 2012.

Lewis, Simon L. and Mark A. Maslin, 'Defining the Anthropocene'. *Nature*, 519 (March 2015), 171–80.

Die Lieder des Codex Regius nebst verwandten Denkmälern. Ed. Gustav Neckel and Hans Kuhn. 5th edn, rev. edn. Heidelberg: Winter, 1983.

Ligny, Jean-Marc. *Aqua^{TM}.* Nantes: l'Atalante, 1993.

Lining, John. 'Extracts of Two Letters from Dr John Lining, Physician at Charles-Town in South Carolina, to James Jurin, MDFRS.' *Philosophical Transactions of the Royal Society*, 42.462–471 (1742), 491–509.

Livingstone, David N. 'Changing Climate, Human Evolution, and the Revival of Environmental Determinism'. *Bulletin of the History of Medicine*, 86 (2012), 564–95.

Lloyd, Saci. *Carbon Diaries 2015.* London: Hodder, 2008.

Lorris, Guillaume de and Jean de Meun. *The Romance of the Rose.* Trans. Charles Dahlberg. 1971; Hanover, NH: University Press of New England, 1986.

Lovell, Mary. *A Rage to Live: a Biography of Richard and Isabel Burton.* New York: Norton, 2000.

Luciano, Dana. 'Romancing the Trace: Edward Hitchcock's Speculative Ichnology'. In Tobias Menely and Jesse Oak Taylor (eds.), *Anthropocene Reading: Literary History in Geologic Times.* University Park: Pennsylvania State University Press, 2017. 96–116.

Luckhurst, Roger. 'The Politics of the Network: the Science in the Capital Trilogy'. In William J. Burling (ed.), *Kim Stanley Robinson Maps the Unimaginable.* Jefferson, NC: MacFarland, 2009. 170–80.

Lukács, Georg. *The Historical Novel.* Trans. Hannah and Stanley Mitchell. London: Merlin Press, 1962.

Lunde, Maja. *The History of Bees.* London: Scribner, 2017.

Lupton, Julia Reinhard. *Thinking with Shakespeare: Essays on Politics and Life.* University of Chicago Press, 2011.

Lynch, Deidre Shauna. *The Economy of Character: Novels, Market Culture, and the Business of Inner Meaning*. University of Chicago Press, 1998.

McAfee, Kathleen. 'The Politics of Nature in the Anthropocene', *RCC Perspectives*, 2 (2016), 65–72.

Macaulay, Thomas Babington. *The History of England from the Accession of James II*, vol. v, 1st edn. London: Longman, Brown, Green and Longmans, 1861.

McAuley, Paul. *Austral*. London: Gollancz, 2017.

McCammon, Robert. *Swan Song*. New York: Pocket Books, 2009.

McCarthy, Cormac. *The Road*. London: Picador, 2006.

McEwan, Ian. *Solar*. London: Jonathan Cape, 2010.

Macfarlane, Robert. *Original Copy*. Oxford University Press, 2007.

MacFaul, Tom. *Shakespeare and the Natural World*. Cambridge University Press, 2015.

Mad Max: Fury Road. Dir. George Miller. Warner Bros., 2015.

Malkmus, Bernard. '"Man in the Anthropocene": Max Frisch's Environmental History'. *PMLA*, 132 (2017), 71–85.

Malm, Andreas. *Fossil Capital: the Rise of Steam Power and the Roots of Global Warming*. London: Verso, 2016.

Malm, Andreas and Alf Hornborg. 'The Geology of Mankind? A Critique of the Anthropocene Narrative'. *Anthropocene Review*, 1 (2014), 62–9.

McMurray, George R. 'The Role of Climate in Twentieth-Century Spanish American Fiction'. In Janet Pérez and Wendell Aycock (eds.), *Climate and Literature: Reflections of Environment*. Lubbock: Texas Tech University Press, 1995. 55–65.

McWhirter, Cameron and Gary Fields. 'Crime Migrates to Suburbs: As Homicides Fall Sharply in Cities, They Are Rising in Surrounding Communities'. *Wall Street Journal* (8 December 2012).

Mandel, Emily St John. *Station Eleven*. New York: Alfred A. Knopf, 2014.

Mankell, Henning. *The Dogs of Riga*. Trans. Laurie Thompson. New York: Vintage Crime, 2003.

   One Step Behind. Trans. Ebbe Segerberg. New York: Vintage Crime, 2003.

   Sidetracked. Trans. Steven T. Murray. New York: Vintage Crime, 2003.

Mann, Michael E., Zhihua Zhang, Malcolm K. Hughes *et al*. 'Proxy-Based Reconstructions of Hemispheric and Global Surface Temperature Variations over the Past Two Millennia'. *PNAS*, 105.36 (2008), 13252–7.

Markley, Robert. 'A Brief History of Chronological Time'. *Danish Yearbook of Philosophy*, 44 (2009), 59–75.

   '"Casualties and Disasters": Defoe and the Interpretation of Climactic Instability'. *Journal of Early Modern Cultural Studies*, 8 (2008), 102–24.

   '"How to Go Forward": Catastrophe and Comedy in Kim Stanley Robinson's Science in the Capital Trilogy'. *Configurations*, 20 (2012), 7–27.

   'Summer's Lease: Shakespeare in the Little Ice Age'. In Thomas Hallock, Ivo Kamps, and Karen L. Raber (eds.), *Early Modern Ecostudies: From the Florentine Codex to Shakespeare*. New York: Palgrave-Macmillan, 2008. 131–42.

'Time, History, and Sustainability'. In Tom Cohen and Henry Sussman (eds.), *Telemorphosis: Essays in Critical Climate Change*, vol. 1. Ann Arbor: Open Humanities Press, 2012. 43–64.

Marshall, George. *Don't Even Think about It: Why Our Brains Are Wired to Ignore Climate Change*. London: Bloomsbury, 2014.

Marshall, Kate. 'What Are the Novels of the Anthropocene? American Fiction in Geological Time'. *American Literary History*, 27 (2015), 523–38.

Martin, Craig. *Renaissance Meteorology: Pomponazzi to Descartes*. Baltimore: Johns Hopkins University Press, 2011.

Masco, Joseph. *The Nuclear Borderlands: the Manhattan Project in Post-Cold War New Mexico*. Princeton University Press, 2006.

Maslin, Mark. *Climate: a Very Short Introduction*. Oxford University Press, 2013.

Mason, Bobbie Ann. *An Atomic Romance*. New York: Random House, 2006.

Mather, Cotton. *Things for a Distress'd People to Think upon Offered in the Sermon to the General Assembly of the Province of the Massachusetts Bay*. Boston: Duncan Campbel, 1696.

Maxwell, James Clerk. 'Molecules'. In Noel George Coley and Vance M. D. Hall (eds.), *Darwin to Einstein: Primary Sources on Science and Belief*. New York: Longman, 1980. 96.

May, Elaine Tyler. *Homeward Bound: American Families in the Cold War Era*. 2nd edn. New York: Basic Books, 1999.

Mayer, Sylvia. 'Explorations of the Controversially Real: Risk, the Climate Change Novel, and the Narrative of Anticipation'. In Mayer and Alexa Weik von Mossner (eds.), *The Anticipation of Catastrophe: Environmental Risk in North American Literature and Culture*. Heidelberg: Universitätsverlag Winter, 2014. 21–37.

Menely, Tobias. '"The Present Obfuscation": Cowper's *Task* and the Time of Climate Change'. *PMLA*, 127 (2012), 477–92.

'Traveling in Place: Gilbert White's Cosmopolitan Parochialism', *Eighteenth-Century Life*, 28 (2004), 46–65.

Menely, Tobias and Jesse Oak Taylor. 'Introduction'. In Menely and Taylor (eds.), *Anthropocene Reading: Literary History in Geologic Times*. University Park: Pennsylvania State University Press, 2017. 1–24.

Mentz, Steve. 'Enter Anthropocene, circa 1610'. In Tobias Menely and Jesse Oak Taylor (eds.), *Anthropocene Reading: Literary History in Geologic Times*. University Park: Pennsylvania State University Press, 2017. 43–58.

'Strange Weather in *King Lear*'. *Shakespeare*, 6 (2010), 139–52.

Merchants of Doubt. Dir. Robert Kenner. Sony, 2014.

Merola, Nicole M. 'Materializing a Geotraumatic and Melancholy Anthropocene: Jeanette Winterson's *The Stone Gods*'. *Minnesota Review*, 83 (2014), 122–32.

Meyer, William B. *Americans and Their Weather*. New York: Oxford University Press, 2000.

Mitchell, David. *Cloud Atlas: a Novel*. New York: Random House, 2004.

Mitchell, John. *The Present State of Great Britain and North America* . . . *Impartially Considered.* London: T. Becket and P. A. de Hondt, 1767.

Mitchell, Timothy. *Carbon Democracy: Political Power in the Age of Oil.* London: Verso, 2013.

Milburn, Colin. 'Greener on the Other Side: Science Fiction and the Problem of Green Nanotechnology'. *Configurations,* 20 (2012), 53–87.

Milton, John. *Paradise Lost.* Ed. Alastair Fowler. 2nd edn. London: Longman, 1998.

   Paradise Lost. Ed. Barbara K. Lewalski. Oxford: Blackwell, 2009.

Montero, Rosa. *El peso del corazón.* Madrid: Planeta, 2015.

   Weight of the Heart. Trans. Lilit Žekulin Thwaites. Seattle: AmazonCrossing, 2016.

Moore, Jason W. *Capitalism in the Web of Life: Ecology and the Accumulation of Capital.* London: Verso, 2015.

Morris, Pam. *Realism.* London: Routledge, 2003.

Morton, Thomas. *New English Canaan, or New Canaan containing an abstract of New England, composed in three bookes* . . . . Amsterdam: Jacob Frederick Stan, 1637.

Morton, Timothy. *Dark Ecology: for a Logic of Future Coexistence.* New York: Columbia University Press, 2016.

   Hyperobjects: Philosophy and Ecology after the End of the World. Minneapolis: University of Minnesota Press, 2013.

A Most True and Lamentable Report, of a Great Tempest of Haile. London: J. Wolfe, 1590.

Moylan, Tom. *Scraps of the Untainted Sky: Science Fiction, Utopia, Dystopia.* Boulder, CO: Westview, 2000.

Mukerjee, Radhakamal. *Migrant Asia: a Problem in World Population.* Rome: I. Failli, 1936.

   The Political Economy of Population. London: Longmans, Green, 1942.

Nadel, Alan. *Containment Culture: American Narratives, Postmodernism and the Atomic Age.* Durham, NC: Duke University Press, 1995.

Naylor, Phyllis Reynolds. *The Dark of the Tunnel.* New York: Athenaeum, 1985.

Neugebauer, Otto. *The History of Ancient Mathematical Astronomy.* New York: Springer-Verlag, 1975.

Newman, Hilary. 'The Influence of *Villette* on Dorothy Richardson's *Pointed Roofs*'. *Brontë Studies,* 42 (2017), 15–25.

Nixon, Rob. *Slow Violence and the Environmentalism of the Poor.* Cambridge, MA: Harvard University Press, 2011.

Norgaard, Kari. *Living in Denial: Climate Change, Emotions, and Everyday Life.* Cambridge, MA: MIT Press, 2011.

Numbers, Ronald. *Creation by Natural Law: Laplace's Nebular Hypothesis in American Thought.* Seattle: University of Washington Press, 1977.

Nutton, Vivian. *Ancient Medicine.* New York: Routledge, 2004.

Oblivion. Dir. Joseph Kosinski. Universal, 2013.

O'Brien, Chris. 'Rethinking Seasons: Changing Climate, Changing Time'. In Tom Bristow and Thomas H. Ford (eds.), *A Cultural History of Climate Change*. Abingdon: Routledge, 2016. 38–54.

O'Brien, Tim. *The Nuclear Age*. London: Flamingo, 1987.

Occupied (Okkupert). Created by Karianne Lund, Erik Skjoldbærg, and Jo Nesbø. Norway TV2, Via Play, Yellow Bird, 2015–.

O'Connor, Ralph. *The Earth on Show: Fossils and the Poetics of Popular Science, 1802–1856*. University of Chicago Press, 2007.

OED Online. Oxford University Press, January 2018.

Ólsen, Björn Magnússon. 'Landnáma og Hœnsa-Þóris saga'. *Aarbøger for nordisk oldkyndighed og historie*, 2nd ser., 20 (1905), 63–80.

On the Beach. Dir. Stanley Kramer. United Artists, 1959.

Opera didascalica II: De temporum ratione liber. Ed. Charles W. Jones. Corpus Christianorum Series Latina 123B: Bedae venerabilis opera 6. Turnhout: Brepols, 1977.

Oppenheimer, Clive. *Eruptions that Shook the World*. Cambridge University Press, 2011.

Outbreak. Dir. Wolfgang Petersen. Warner Bros., 1995.

Ovid. *Metamorphoses, Volume 1: Books 1–8*. Trans. Frank Justus Miller and ed. G. P. Goold. Loeb Classical Library 42. Cambridge, MA: Harvard University Press, 1916.

Parenti, Christian. 'Environment-Making in the Capitalocene: Political Ecology of the State'. In Jason W. Moore (ed.), *Anthropocene or Capitalocene? Nature, History, and the Crisis of Capitalism*. Oakland, CA: PM Press, 2016. 166–84.

Parrish, Susan Scott. *American Curiosity: Cultures of Natural History in the Colonial British Atlantic World*. Chapel Hill, NC: University of North Carolina Press, 2006.

Paster, Gail Kern. *Humoring the Body: Emotions and the Shakespearean Stage*. University of Chicago Press, 2004.

Paul, Henry N. *The Royal Play of Macbeth: When, Why, and How It Was Written by Shakespeare*. New York: Macmillan, 1950.

Pendell, Dale. *The Great Bay: Chronicles of the Collapse*. Berkeley, CA: North Atlantic Books, 2010.

Peterfreund, Stuart. '"Great Frosts and . . . Some Very Hot Summers": Strange Weather, the Last Letters, and the Last Days in Gilbert White's *The Natural History of Selborne*'. In Noah Heringman (ed.), *Romantic Science: the Literary Forms of Natural History*. Albany: State University of New York Press, 2003. 85–108.

Petersen, Sierra V., Andrea Dutton, and Kyger C. Lohmann. 'End-Cretaceous Extinction in Antarctica Linked to Both Deccan Volcanism and Meteorite Impact via Climate Change'. *Nature Communications*, 7.12079 (2016).

Pizzo, Justine. 'Charlotte Brontë's Weather Wisdom: Atmospheric Exceptionalism in *Jane Eyre*'. *PMLA*, 131 (2016), 84–100.

'Esther's Ether: Atmospheric Character in Charles Dickens's *Bleak House*'. *Victorian Literature and Culture*, 42 (2014), 81–98.

Plumwood, Val. *Environmental Culture: the Ecological Crisis of Reason*. London: Routledge, 2002.

Pointer, John. *A Rational Account of the Weather*. Oxford: S. Wilmot, 1723.

Porden, [Eleanor Anne]. *The Arctic Expeditions: a Poem*. London: John Murray, 1818.

Post, John D. *The Last Great Subsistence Crisis in the Western World*. Baltimore: Johns Hopkins University Press, 1977.

Powys, John Cowper. *Dorothy M. Richardson*. London: Joiner and Steele, 1931.

A Practical Discourse on the Late Earthquakes. London: J. Dunton, 1692.

Pratt, Mary Louise. *Imperial Eyes: Travel Writing and Transculturation*, 2nd edn. New York: Routledge, 2008.

Preston, Alex. 'Michael Fassbender on Murder, Misogyny and the Making of Jo Nesbø's The Snowman'. *Daily Telegraph* (27 September 2017).

Prettyman, Gib. 'Living Thought: Genes, Genres and Utopia in the Science in the Capital Trilogy'. In William J. Burling (ed.), *Kim Stanley Robinson Maps the Unimaginable*. Jefferson, NC: MacFarland, 2009. 181–203.

Pykett, Lyn. *Engendering Fictions: the English Novel in the Early Twentieth Century*. London: Edward Arnold, 1995.

Raffles, Thomas Stamford. *The History of Java*. 2 vols. 1817; Oxford University Press, 1965.

Rankine, Claudia. *Citizen: an American Lyric*. Minneapolis: Graywolf, 2014.

Rannveig Sigurdardóttir, Bernard Scudder, Jónas Thórdarson, Lilja Alfredsdóttir, and Helga Gudmundsdottir. *The Economy of Iceland*. Reykjavik: Sedlabanki, 2007.

Rawls, John. *A Theory of Justice*. Rev. edn. Cambridge, MA: Harvard University Press, 1999.

Redford, Catherine. '"No Love Was Left": the Failure of Christianity in Byron's "Darkness"'. *Byron Journal*, 43 (2015), 131–40.

Rhodes, Richard. *The Making of the Atomic Bomb*. London: Penguin, 1988.

Rich, Adrienne. *An Atlas of the Difficult World: Poems 1988–1991*. New York: Norton, 1991.

Rich, Nathaniel. *Odds against Tomorrow*. New York: Farrar, Straus and Giroux, 2013.

Richardson, Dorothy. *Pilgrimage*. 4 vols. London: Virago, 1979.

    Windows on Modernism: Selected Letters of Dorothy Richardson. Ed. Gloria Fromm. Atlanta: University of Georgia Press, 1995.

Ricœur, Paul. *Time and Narrative*, trans. Kathleen McLaughlin and David Pellauer. 3 vols. University of Chicago Press, 1984–8.

Rimmon-Kenan, Shlomith. *Narrative Fiction: Contemporary Poetics*. London: Routledge, 1996.

Robinson, Kim Stanley. *Blue Mars* London: Voyager, 1996.

    Fifty Degrees Below. New York: Spectra, 2005.

    Forty Signs of Rain. New York: Spectra, 2004.

    Green Earth. New York: Del Rey Books, 2015.

    Green Mars. London: Voyager, 1996.

    New York 2140. New York: Orbit, 2017.

    Red Mars. London: Voyager, 1996.

    Shaman. New York: Orbit, 2013.

Sixty Days and Counting. New York: Spectra, 2007.

The Wild Shore: Three Californias. 1984; New York: Tor/Forge, 1995.

Robinson, Thomas. *New Observations on the Natural History of this World of Matter.* London: John Newton, 1696.

Robertson, William. *History of America.* 2 vols. London: W. Strahan, 1777.

Roosth, Sophia. *Synthetic: How Life Got Made.* University of Chicago Press, 2017.

Roy, Arundhati. *The Cost of Living:* The Greater Common Good *and* The End of Imagination. London: Flamingo, 1999.

Rudwick, Martin J. S. *Bursting the Limits of Time: the Reconstruction of Geohistory in the Age of Revolution.* University of Chicago Press, 2005. 349–415.

Worlds before Adam: the Reconstruction of Geohistory in the Age of Reform. University of Chicago Press, 2008.

Rugg, Linda. 'Displacing Crimes against Nature: Scandinavian Ecocrime Fiction'. *Scandinavian Studies*, 89 (2017), 597–615.

Rusnock, Andrea. 'Hippocrates, Bacon, and Medical Meteorology at the Royal Society, 1700–1750'. In David Cantor (ed.), *Reinventing Hippocrates.* Aldershot: Ashgate, 2002. 136–53.

Rutty, John. *A Chronological History of the Weather and Seasons and of the Prevailing Diseases in Dublin.* London: Robinson and Roberts, 1770.

An Essay towards a Natural History of the County of Dublin. 2 vols. Dublin: W. Sleater, 1772.

A Spiritual Diary and Soliloquies, 2 vols. London: James Phillips, 1776.

Saldívar, Ramón. 'The Second Elevation of the Novel: Race, Form, and the Postrace Aesthetic in Contemporary Narrative'. *Narrative*, 21.1 (2013), 1–18.

Sartre, Jean-Paul. *The Family Idiot: Gustave Flaubert, 1821–1857.* Trans. Carol Cosman. 5 vols. University of Chicago Press, 1981–94.

Schell, Jonathan. *The Fate of the Earth* and *The Abolition.* Stanford University Press, 2000.

Scott, Charlotte. *Shakespeare's Nature: From Cultivation to Culture.* Oxford University Press, 2014.

Serres, Michel and Bruno Latour. *Conversations on Science, Culture, and Time.* Trans. Roxanne Lapidus. Ann Arbor: University of Michigan Press, 1995.

Service, Pamela F. *Winter of Magic's Return.* New York: Athenaeum, 1985.

Sexton, Jared. 'Unbearable Blackness'. *Cultural Critique*, 90 (2015), 159–78.

Shakespeare, William. *The Complete Works of William Shakespeare.* Ed. Peter Alexander. 2006; London: Collins, 2010.

The Norton Shakespeare. Ed. Stephen Greenblatt, Walter Cohen, Jean E. Howard, and Katharine Eisaman Maus. New York: Norton, 1997.

The Norton Shakespeare. Ed. Stephen Greenblatt, Walter Cohen, Jean E. Howard, Katharine Eisaman Maus, Gordon McMullan, and Suzanne Gossett. 3rd edn. New York: Norton, 2016.

Shaviro, Steven. *Doom Patrols.* London: Serpent's Tail Press, 1997.

Shelby, Ashley. *South Pole Station.* London: Picador, 2017.

Shelley, Mary. *Frankenstein, or The Modern Prometheus.* Ed. M. K. Joseph. Oxford University Press, 2008.

The Last Man. Ed. Morton Paley. Oxford University Press, 1994.

Shelley, Percy Bysshe. *Shelley's Poetry and Prose*. 2nd edn. Ed. Donald H. Reiman and Neil Fraistat. New York: Norton, 2002.

Shepard, Jim. 'The Netherlands Lives with Water'. In John Joseph Adams (ed.), *Loosed upon the World: the Saga Anthology of Climate Fiction*. New York: Saga, 2015. 143–70.

Shirane, Haruo. *Japan and the Culture of the Four Seasons: Nature, Literature, and the Arts*. New York: Columbia University Press, 2012.

Shute, Nevil. *On the Beach*. Thirsk: House of Stratus, 2000.

Sideris, Lisa. 'Anthropocene Convergences: a Report from the Field'. *RCC Perspectives*, 2 (2016), 89–96.

Sigurdur Thorarinsson [Sigurður Þórarinsson]. 'Population Changes in Iceland'. *Geographical Review*, 51.4 (1961), 519–33.

Silko, Leslie Marmon. *Ceremony*. New York: Penguin, 1986.

Simay, Philippe. 'Tradition as Injunction: Benjamin and the Critique of Historicisms'. In Andrew E. Benjamin (ed.), *Walter Benjamin and History*. London: Bloomsbury, 2005. 137–55.

Sinclair, May. 'The Novels of Dorothy Richardson'. *The Egoist*, 4 (1918), 57–9.

Sivaramakrishnan, Murali. 'Ecopoetics and the Literature of Ancient India'. In John Parham and Louise Westling (eds.), *A Global History of Literature and Environment*. Cambridge University Press, 2017. 65–79.

Smith, John. *The Generall History of Virginia, New England, and the Summer Isles with the Names of the Adventurers, Planters, and Governours from their First Beginning*. London: Michael Sparkes, 1624.

Snorri Sturluson. *Edda*. Ed. Anthony Faulkes. 4 vols. London: Viking Society for Northern Research, University College London, 1988–99.

Song, Haijun and Paul B. Wignall. 'Two Pulses of Extinction during the Permian–Triassic Crisis'. *Nature Geoscience*, 6 (2013), 52–6.

Soothill, William Edward. *The Hall of Light: a Study of Early Chinese Kingship*. 1951; Cambridge: James Clarke and Company, 2002.

Southey, Robert. *The Collected Letters of Robert Southey: a Romantic Circles Electronic Edition: Part Five: 1816–1818*, ed. Tim Fulford, Ian Packer, and Lynda Pratt. *Romantic Circles*, https://www.rc.umd.edu/editions/southey_letters/Part_Five/HTML/letterEEd.26.3083.html#back14.

Spark, Muriel, ed. *The Brontë Letters*. London: Peter Nevill, 1954.

Speed, John. *An Epitome of Mr John Speed's Theatre of the Empire of Great Britain and His Prospect of the Most Famous Parts of the World*. London: Thomas Basset, 1676.

Spencer, Steven M. 'Fallout: the Silent Killer'. *Saturday Evening Post* (29 August 1959). www.unz.com/print/SatEveningPost-1959aug29-00026/?View=Tree.

Spenser, Edmund. *The Shorter Poems*. Ed. Richard A. McCabe. London: Penguin, 1999.

Spinrad, Norman. *Greenhouse Summer*. New York: St Martin's Press, 1999.

Stiegler, Bernard. *Neganthropocene*. Trans. Daniel Ross. Ann Arbor, MI: Open Humanities Press, 2018.

'Power, Powerlessness, Thinking, and Future'. *Los Angeles Review of Books* (18 October 2015).

'The Proletarianization of Sensibility'. Trans. Arne De Boever. *Boundary 2*, 44 (2017), 5–18.

Stiles, Anne. 'Introduction'. In Stiles (ed.), *Neurology and Literature, 1860–1920*. Basingstoke: Palgrave-Macmillan, 2007. 1–23.

Strauss, Sarah and Benjamin S. Orlove (eds.), *Weather, Climate, Culture*. Oxford: Berg, 2003.

Strieber, Whitley. *Wolf of Shadows*. New York: Knopf, 1985.

Sullivan, Walter S. 'Film Spots Trace Vast A-Bomb Range: Radioactive Particles Spread over Australia-Sized Area, Eastman Studies Show'. *New York Times* (23 May 1946).

Summer with Monika. Dir. Ingmar Bergman. Svensk filmindustri, 1953.

Suvin, Darko. *Metamorphoses of Science Fiction: on the Poetics and History of a Literary Genre*. New Haven, CT: Yale University Press, 1979.

Swindells, Robert. *Brother in the Land*. London: Puffin, 2000.

Tanner, Jennifer. 'The Climate of Naturalism: Zola's Atmospheres'. *L'esprit créateur*, 57 (2017), 20–33.

Taub, Liba. *Ancient Meteorology*. London: Routledge, 2003.

Taylor, Jesse Oak. *The Sky of our Manufacture: the London Fog in British Fiction from Dickens to Woolf*. Charlottesville: University of Virginia Press, 2016.

The Terrible Stormy Wind and Tempest. London: W. Freeman, 1705.

Testament. Dir. Lynne Littman. Paramount, 1983.

Thomas, Sidney. 'The Bad Weather in a Midsummer-Night's Dream'. *Modern Language Notes*, 64.5 (1949), 319–22.

Thomson, James. *The Seasons*. Ed. James Sambrook. Oxford: Clarendon Press, 1981.

Thornes, John E. 'Cultural Climatology and the Representation of Sky, Atmosphere, Weather, and Climate in Selected Art Works of Constable, Monet, and Eliasson'. *Geoforum*, 39 (2008), 570–80.

Todorov, Tzvetan. *The Poetics of Prose*. Trans. Richard Howard. Ithaca, NY: Cornell University Press, 1981.

Tolan, Stephanie S. *Pride of the Peacock*. New York: Charles Scribner's Sons, 1986.

Torgerson, Beth. *Reading the Brontë Body: Disease, Desire, and the Constraints of Culture*. Basingstoke: Palgrave-Macmillan, 2005.

Totaro, Rebecca. *Meteorology and Physiology in Early Modern Culture: Earthquakes, Human Identity, and Textual Representation*. New York: Routledge, 2018.

Tranströmer, Tomas. *Bright Scythe: Selected Poems*. Trans. Patricia Crane. Lexington, KY: Sarabande Books, 2015.

Trexler, Adam. *Anthropocene Fictions: the Novel in a Time of Climate Change*. Charlottesville: University of Virginia Press, 2015.

Trexler, Adam and Adeline Johns-Putra. 'Climate Change in Literature and Literary Criticism'. *WIREs Climate Change*, 2 (2011), 185–200.

Trojanow, Ilija. *EisTau*. Munich: Deutscher Taschenbuch, 2011.

The Lamentations of Zeno. Trans. Philip Boehm. London Verso, 2016.

A True and Particular Account of a Storm of Thunder and Lightning. London: John Morphew, 1711.

Tuan, Yi-Fu. *Escapism.* Baltimore: Johns Hopkins University Press, 1998.

Turco, R. P., O. B. Toon, T. P. Ackerman, J. B. Pollack, and Carl Sagan. 'Nuclear Winter: Global Consequences of Multiple Nuclear Explosions'. *Science*, 222.4630 (1983), 1283–92.

Turner, George. *The Sea and Summer.* London: Faber, 1987.

Turner, Henry S. *Shakespeare's Double Helix.* London: Continuum, 2007.

Turney, Chris, Jonathan Palmer, and Mark Maslin. 'Anthropocene Began in 1965, According to Signs Left in World's "Loneliest Tree"'. *The Conversation* (19 February 2018).

'Anthropocene: How the Loneliest Tree in the World Recorded the Start of Our Global Domination'. *Newsweek* (22 February 2018).

Turney, Chris S. M., Jonathan Palmer, Mark A. Maslin *et al.*, 'Global Peak in Atmospheric Radiocarbon Provides a Potential Definition for the Onset of the Anthropocene Epoch in 1965'. *Scientific Reports*, 8 (2018), article no. 3293.

Tuve, Rosemond. *Seasons and Months: Studies in a Tradition of Middle English Poetry.* Cambridge: D. S. Brewer, 1933.

28 Days Later. Dir. Danny Boyle. Fox Searchlight, 2002.

Tyndall, John. *Address Delivered Before the British Association Assembled at Belfast with Additions.* London: Longmans, Green and Company, 1874.

Tyndall, John. *Fragments of Science for Unscientific People.* New York: D. Appleton and Company, 1971.

Tyrrell, Ian. *True Gardens of the Gods: Californian-Australian Environmental Reform, 1860–1930.* Berkeley: University of California Press, 1999.

Valenčius, Conevery Bolton. *The Health of the Country: How American Settlers Understood Themselves and Their Land.* New York: Basic Books, 2002.

VanderMeer, Jeff. *Borne.* London: HarperCollins, 2017.

Van Leeuwenhoek, Anton. 'Part of a Letter . . . Giving his Observations on the Late Storm'. *Philosophical Transactions of the Royal Society*, 24.289 (1704–5), 1537.

Vardoulakis, Dimitris. 'The Subject of History: the Temporality of Parataxis in Benjamin's Historiography'. In Andrew E. Benjamin (ed.), *Walter Benjamin and History.* London: Bloomsbury, 2005. 118–36.

Varnado, Christine. 'Queer Nature, or the Weather in *Macbeth*'. In Goran Stanivukovic (ed.), *Queer Shakespeare: Desire and Sexuality.* London: Bloomsbury, 2017. 177–96.

Veale, Lucy and Georgina H. Endfield. 'Situating 1816, the "Year without Summer", in the UK'. *Geographical Journal*, 182 (2016), 318–30.

Verhelst, Peter. *TongKat.* Amsterdam: Prometheus, 1999.

Tonguecat. Trans. Sherry Marx. New York: Farrar, Straus and Giroux, 2003.

Verne, Jules. *The Purchase of the North Pole.* London: Sampson Low, 1890.

Viswanathan, S. 'Milton and the Seasons' Difference'. *Studies in English Literature, 1500–1900*, 13 (1973), 127–33.

Vogel, Brant. 'The Letter from Dublin: Climate Change, Colonialism, and the Royal Society in the Seventeenth Century'. *Osiris*, 26 (2011), 111–28.

von Humboldt, Alexander and Aimé Bonpland. *Essay on the Geography of Plants.* Ed. Stephen Jackson and trans. Sylvie Romanowski. University of Chicago Press, 2009.

von Sneidern, Maja-Lisa. '*Wuthering Heights* and the Liverpool Slave Trade'. *ELH*, 62.1 (1995), 171–196.

Vrettos, Athena. *Somatic Fictions: Imagining Illness in Victorian Culture.* Stanford University Press, 1995.

Waade, Anne Marit. *Wallanderland. Medieturisme og skandinavisk TV-krimi.* Studier i krimi og kriminaljournalstik. Aalborg: Aalborg Universitetsforlag, 2013.

Wahrman, Dror. *The Making of the Modern Self: Identity and Culture in Eighteenth-Century England.* New Haven, CT: Yale University Press, 2004.

Walpole, Horace. *Horace Walpole's Correspondence with the Countess of Upper Ossory.* Ed. W. S. Lewis, Joseph W. Reed, and Edwine M. Martz. Oxford University Press, 1965.

Warren, Louis. 'Owning Nature: Towards an Environmental History of Private Property'. In Andrew C. Isenberg (ed.), *Oxford Handbook of Environmental History.* Oxford University Press, 2014. 398–425.

Watson, Robert N. 'The Ecology of Self in *Midsummer Night's Dream*'. In Lynne Bruckner and Dan Brayton (eds.), *Ecocritical Shakespeare.* Farnham: Ashgate, 2011. 33–56.

'Tell Inconvenient Truths, But Tell Them Slant'. In Jennifer Munroe, Edward J. Geisweidt, and Lynne Bruckner (eds.), *Ecological Approaches to Early Modern English Texts: a Field Guide to Reading and Teaching.* Farnham: Ashgate, 2015. 17–28.

Watt, Ian. *Conrad in the Nineteenth Century.* Berkeley: University of California Press, 1981.

Weart, Spencer R. *The Discovery of Global Warming.* 2nd edn. Cambridge, MA: Harvard University Press, 2008.

Weik von Mossner, Alexa. 'Science Fiction and the Risks of the Anthropocene: Anticipated Transformations in Dale Pendell's *The Great Bay*'. *Environmental Humanities*, 5 (2014), 203–16.

Wells, H. G. *The War of the Worlds.* Ed. David Y. Hughes and Harry M. Geduld. Bloomington: Indiana University Press, 1993.

Welsh, Brandon C. and David P. Farrington. 'Crime Prevention and Public Policy'. In Welsh and Farrington (eds.), *Oxford Handbook of Crime Prevention.* Oxford University Press, 2012. 10.1093/oxfordhb/9780195398823.013.000

Wenskus, Otta. *Astronomische Zeitangaben von Homer bis Theophrast.* Stuttgart: Franz Steiner, 1990.

Wheeler, Roxann. *The Complexion of Race: Categories of Difference in Eighteenth-Century British Culture.* Philadelphia: University of Pennsylvania Press, 2000.

White, Andrea. *Joseph Conrad and the Adventure Tradition: Constructing and Deconstructing the Imperial Subject.* Cambridge University Press, 1993.

White, Gilbert. *The Journals of Gilbert White: 1774–1783*. Ed. Francesca Greenoak. Vol. 11 of *The Journals of Gilbert White*. Gen. ed. Richard Mabey. London: Century, 1988.

The Natural History of Selborne. Ed. Richard Mabey. London: Penguin, 1987.

White, R. J. *Waterloo to Peterloo*. Harmondsworth: Penguin, 1957.

White, Richard. 'The Nationalization of Nature'. *Journal of American History*, 86.3 (1999), 976–89.

White, Sam. *A Cold Welcome: the Little Ice Age and Europe's Encounter with North America*. Cambridge, MA: Harvard University Press, 2016.

'Unpuzzling American Climate: New World Experience and the Foundations of a New Science'. *Isis*, 106 (2015), 544–66.

Whitington, Jerome. 'The Terrestrial Envelope: Joseph Fourier's Geological Speculation'. In Tom Bristow and Thomas H. Ford (eds.), *A Cultural History of Climate Change*. London: Routledge, 2016. 55–71.

Wiener, Norbert. *The Human Use of Human Beings: Cybernetics and Society*. New York: Da Capo, 1988.

Williams, David. *When the English Fall*. Chapel Hill, NC: Algonquin, 2017.

Williams, John. *The Climate of Great Britain; or, Remarks on the Change It Has Undergone, Particularly within the Last Fifty Years*. London: C. and R. Baldwin, 1806.

Williams, Linda. 'The Anthropocene and the Long Seventeenth Century'. In Tom Bristow and Thomas H. Ford (eds.), *A Cultural History of Climate Change*. London: Routledge, 2016. 87–107.

Williams, Terry Tempest. *Refuge: an Unnatural History of Family and Place*. New York: Vintage, 2001.

Williamson, Hugh. 'An Attempt to Account for the Change of Climate Which Has Been Observed in the Middle Colonies in North-America'. *Transactions of the American Philosophical Society*, 1 (1769–71), 272–80.

Williamson, Jack. 'Collision Orbit'. In Stephen Haffner and Richard A. Hauptmann (eds.), *Seventy-Five: the Diamond Anniversary of a Science Fiction Pioneer*. Royal Oak, MI: Haffner Press, 2004. 216–77.

Wilson, Alexander. *Some Observations Relative to the Influence of Climate on Vegetable and Animal Bodies*. London: T. Cadell, 1780.

Winterson, Jeanette. *The Stone Gods*. London: Hamish Hamilton, 2007.

Witze, Alexandra and Jeff Kanipe. *Island on Fire: the Extraordinary Story of a Forgotten Volcano that Changed the World*. London: Profile, 2014.

Woloch, Alex. *The One vs. the Many: Minor Characters and the Space of the Protagonist in the Novel*. Princeton University Press, 2003.

Wood, Gillen D'Arcy. *Tambora: the Eruption that Changed the World*. Princeton University Press, 2014.

Woods, Derek. 'Scale Critique for the Anthropocene'. *Minnesota Review*, 83 (2014), 135.

Woolf, Virginia. *The Essays of Virginia Woolf*. Ed. Andrew McNeillie. New edn. 6 vols. London: Hogarth Press, 1995.

'Romance and the Heart'. *The Nation and the Athenaeum*, 33 (1923), 229.

A Writer's Diary. New York: Harcourt Brace Jovanovich, 1973.

Wordsworth, William. *The Major Works.* Ed. Stephen Gill. 1984; Oxford University Press, 2008.

World War Z. Dir. Marc Forster. Paramount, 2013.

Wright, Alexis. *The Swan Book.* Artarmon, NSW: Giromondo, 2013.

Wulf, Andrea. *The Invention of Nature: Alexander von Humboldt's New World.* London: John Murray, 2015.

Wulfstan. *The Homilies of Wulfstan.* Ed. Dorothy Bethurum. Oxford: Clarendon, 1957.

Wyndham, John. *The Chrysalids.* 1955; London: Penguin, 2008.

Yrsa Sigurðardóttir. *Auðnin.* Reykjavik: Verröld, 2008.

    The Day is Dark. Trans. Philip Roughton. London: Hodder and Stoughton, 2011.

Zalaziewicz, Jan A. and Mark Williams. 'First Atomic Bomb Test May Mark the Beginning of the Anthropocene'. The Conversation (30 January 2015).

Zemanek, Evi. 'A Dirty Hero's Fight for Clean Energy: Satire, Allegory, and Risk Narrative in Ian McEwan's *Solar*'. *Ecozon@*, 3 (2012), 51–60.

Zhu Kezhen. 'A Preliminary Study on the Climatic Fluctuation during the Last 5000 Years in China'. *Scientia Sinica*, 16 (1973), 226–56.

Zilberstein, Anya. *A Temperate Empire: Making Climate Change in Early America.* Oxford University Press, 2016.

Žižek, Slavoj. 'Parallax'. *London Review of Books*, 25.22 (November 2003), 24.

Index

Index